KANT

Claudia Rajlich

Fundamental Painting (1975):

Lessons in Minimalist Painting

CONTENT

Acknowledgements . . . 7

INTRODUCTION . . . 11

1 THE BIRTH OF FUNDAMENTAL PAINTING . . . 15

1.1 Fundamental Painting at the Stedelijk Museum Amsterdam . . 16

1.1.1 "New Painting" in Europe . . . 22

1.1.2 Public acceptance of Fundamental Painting . . . 28

1.1.3 Evidence of Fundamental Painting . . . 34

1.2 The coining of "Fundamental Painting" . . . 35

1.2.1 The definition of Fundamental Painting . . . 39

1.2.2 Elements of Fundamental Painting . . . 40

1.2.3 Fundamental Painting does not equal Analytical Abstraction . . . 43

2 THE IDENTITY OF FUNDAMENTAL PAINTING . . . 49

2.1 Elements and tools of Fundamental Painting . . . 51

2.1.1 Format . . . 53

2.1.2 Size and scale . . . 59

2.1.3 Color . . . 62

2.1.4 Line . . . 71

2.1.5 Texture and facture . . . 77

2.1.6 Tools and materials . . . 81

2.1.7 Process . . . 84

2.1.8 Composition . . . 89

2.1.9 The viewer . . . 94

2.2 The Fundamental mentality . . . 97

2.2.1 The range in Fundamental mentality . . . 105

2.2.2 The Fundamental mentality at large . . . 110

3 THE ORIGINS OF FUNDAMENTAL PAINTING. 115
3.1 The early beginnings 117
3.1.1 The non-objective and the "end" of painting 124
3.1.2 Art Concret 129
3.2 Painting as Painting 133
3.2.1 Objecthood 138
3.2.2 Postwar art in Europe 144
3.2.3 Minimal Art. 151
3.3 The Fundamental era. 159
3.3.1 The path to Fundamental Painting 161
3.3.2 The Fundamental character 163
3.3.3 The influence of WWII 166
3.3.4 Postwar Europe in view of Fundamental Painting 168
3.3.5 Important factors for Fundamental Painting. 176
3.3.6 The future of Fundamental Painting. 180
Excursus: Fundamental Painting and the Czech Republic 181

4 THE SIGNIFICANCE OF FUNDAMENTAL PAINTING 185
4.1 The meaning of Fundamental Painting. 186
4.1.1 Fundamental Painting and the viewer 187
4.1.2 Painting on painting. 189
4.2 The metaphysical in Fundamental Painting 192
4.2.1 The traditional role of Fundamental Painting 192
4.2.2 Fundamental Painting as revelation 193

CONCLUSION 205
Postscript 217
BIBLIOGRAPHY. 239

Acknowledgements

First and foremost, I would like to thank the late Professor Vojtech Lahoda for his initial spark to, guidance on and encouragement throughout this project. I would also like to thank the rest of the faculty and staff of the Institute of Art History at Charles University in Prague, in particular Professor Petr Wittlich and Ms. Romana Jensenová, for their kind support on this thesis process; and last but not least, Jiří Valoch for his expert opinion.

My late professors Francesca Weinmann and Filiz Burhan of the American University in Paris were inspirational for my understanding of 20th century art and the Philosophy of Aesthetics. Serge Lemoine, who supervised my Master's degree at the Sorbonne-Paris IV, put me on the path towards researching Fundamental Painting.

I am especially grateful for the support of the late Rini Dippel and a number of *Fundamental Painting* participants who provided invaluable assistance with the historical details of this study, granting me interviews and in many cases conversations and letters of clarification. Also several critics active in the field of Analytical Abstraction have shared their knowledge and recollections with me. A special mention goes to Alan Charlton, Marco Meneguzzo, Edda Renouf, Stephan Rosenthal and Jerry Zeniuk; and, of course, I have enjoyed many discussions on painting with my father, Tomas Rajlich, over the years.

I would like to thank Michiel Nijhoff and Willem van Beek as well as the staff at the archives of the Stedelijk Museum Amsterdam for their wonderful collaboration – with special thanks for the photographs to Hetty Wessels. Also various other museum librarians and the staff of the RKD Netherlands Institute for Art History, in particular Dirk Torenvlied, were helpful in many ways, as were numerous representing galleries.

This book, from its inception as a PhD thesis in Czech to its present form, would have been impossible without the help of my friend and art historian Deborah Jenner, and my editor Roy Bicknell. My parents, family and friends – you supported me greatly and were always willing to help.

The central conceit of the artist that the work shall outlast his own death, the existential truth that great literature, painting, architecture, music have survived their creators, are not accidental or self-regarding. It is the lucid intensity of its meeting with death that generates in aesthetic forms that statement of vitality, of life-presence, which distinguishes serious thought and feeling from the trivial and the opportunistic.

Georges Steiner, *Real Presences,* University of Chicago Press, 1989 (141)

INTRODUCTION

"Fundamental Painting … a reflection on the foundations of painting" (FP 1)

Edy de Wilde, 1975

In 1975, the Stedelijk Museum in Amsterdam staged an exhibition entitled *Fundamental Painting*. It wished to give a clear, if not comprehensive, view of this "new life of painting" as the particular artform had been declared dead so many times before. The show was built around four American Minimalist painters. Altogether it featured eighteen artists of various nationalities, who had been working in this vein "since about 1972" (FP 12). The aim of this study is to explore this new kind of painting which had sprung up in the US in the late 1960s and in Europe in the early 1970s. As chief curator Rini Dippel (1931–2021) wrote in the exhibition catalogue, "it [was] in the air but [did] not fall from the sky" (FP 11). What exactly is Fundamental Painting? Where did it come from? Where did it go? Did it actually exist?

In line with the Stedelijk's exhibition's considerations, this research is limited to the artists who were among the very first to start working in this vein. The focus is on the Europeans, in contrast to the American painters of Minimal Art who have already had innumerable texts written about their work. Our focus will also be on these artists who were not only amongst the first to opt for this direction but also consistently stuck with it – a necessary criterion in order to "belong." The evolution of the artist's works will be taken into consideration in determining the range and outreach of Fundamental Painting. At the same time, this study is largely geared towards the defining years, i.e. the mid-1970s around the show *Fundamental Painting*. It is based on historical evidence; the critical analysis of theoretical texts, artists' writings, and interviews; and, above all, on the body of works themselves, which in itself constitutes a form of documentation. Finally, it must be noted that this study does not aim to be all-inclusive. It merely strives, following in the footsteps of the exhibition curators, to form a framework for a current that was under the radar in contemporary painting, and which at the time of this publication – almost half a century later – is still evolving.

Looking at key 20th century events and what led up to Fundamental Painting allows us to pinpoint and confirm its first appearance on the scene, how its name was coined, and its range of characteristics. In order to establish the background, we will need to go back to early 20th century art which was marked by a groundbreaking revolution called abstraction, leading to completely non-objective painting. Following the curators' lead, this study will center around a few painters from several generations of artists who had been developing a new consciousness of their medium and of the spirituality in abstract painting.

We will see how this quest for the absolute germinated in various places around Europe, how World War II (WWII) provoked both the end and a new beginning for painting, and how by the 1950s New York had taken center stage. Artists such as those of the New York School together with new immigrant artists from Europe would focus on the direct effect of the artwork on the spectator. This led to an unprecedented reductivism in the 1950s and increasingly involved research into the building blocks of a painting, the painterly elements, and the artist's intervention on them. This evolution would eventually culminate in Minimalist painting.

Meanwhile, in a state of creative crisis, certain European artists turned their attention to this new Americanized mode of painting. Thus, in the 1970s, European painting slowly reemerged as a new analytic current, soon resettling into a specifically European tradition. The ultimate aim of this study is to define and analyze the European analytic vein in painting referred to as Fundamental Painting, including its American counterpart (Minimal Art), as well as its overall significance within the history of art.

It will become evident that, for example, the way the canvas announces its impact depends on its size and shape, while color and structure give the canvas its personal characteristics and determine the perceived scale. Then again, line and evidence of the material will be seen to establish whether the observer sees the painting as a window onto the world or as an independent entity. These elements distinctly reflect the roots of Fundamental Painting and the influence of several key artists.

Moreover, it will become evident how the complex effects that painting has on the viewer (which here is proven to be largely determined by the heritage of Western art) are imperative for Fundamental Painting. For example, the everyday reality of the contemporary European viewers is still dominated by notions of Renaissance perspective. Therefore, they tend to search for representation, 3-D space, and visual logic in any image. On the other hand, the Philosophy of Aesthetics from Plato onwards – notably early abstract ideologies – have taught them to value an artwork more for its metaphysical components. It will become apparent how such various points of reference in the viewing of a Fundamental Painting give us the opportunity to revise our personal understanding of the history of art, by simultaneously comparing it to that of the artist.

This study outlines how the concepts of Fundamental Painting found their appeal thanks to their borrowing from various traditions of painting and their continuing with aesthetic notions. In the 1970s, Fundamental painters consciously went back to their roots to set themselves apart from the other new approaches to art of the time. Happenings promoted points of view proclaiming the end of art. This only strengthened the belief in painting of most Fundamental painters and pushed them to prove the existential necessity of the medium itself.

A large part of this study is dedicated to gaining an understanding of the work of long-time Fundamental painters. Notably, it shows the different ways the creative aim of Fundamental painting can be interpreted and the part national heritage plays in this. Some artists primarily explore the difference between an artwork and an object, the way using a material determines the object's classification as art, or the choice made by the artist during the production process. Most focus on the inherent elements of painting that touch upon composition: shape, color, line and structure. Others, then again, are more interested in the effect that the resulting artwork has on its viewer, basing their approach on vision and experience of space. All redefine the meaning of how painting materials are handled and how a painting is created. This study highlights how 20th century national currents connect to the development of Fundamental Painting and the artists' individual approaches.

Finally, the fundamental factor in Fundamental Painting is identified. This identification process is based on a consideration of the goals that the artists have formulated and the impact that their works generate. The ultimate *raison d'être* of a Fundamental Painting is conjectured, proposed and reiterated. In the process, the importance of Fundamental Painting in its time, as well as in the history of art, becomes clear. In conclusion, an objective assessment of the actual existence and significance of Fundamental Painting is at hand.

The reason for this study is that while Fundamental Painting follows a longstanding tradition in Western Painting, which needs to be brought to light and up to date, no extensive overview of this current in Europe has been given; even though since the early 1970s it is far more widespread than American Minimalist painting which has been largely researched. The only events documenting its existence have been a few sporadic exhibitions, starting with *Fundamental Painting* at the Stedelijk Museum Amsterdam in 1975. Most shows have featured random selections, like the itinerant *Concerning Painting....* of 1975[1] or *Von der Ungleichheit des Ähnlichen in der Kunst* of 1983[2]. Even more frequently, Fundamental Painting has been a category of works which were included yet ignored in those exhibitions touching upon a larger painterly theme, as, for example, *Colours in Painting: A European Situation* (Rome, 1976)[3] and *Abstrakt* (Dresden, 1993)[4]. A recent nonacademic and thus unsubstantiated attempt in the form of a group show entitled *Pittura 70* in Northern Italy has been the only undertaking to clear up the numerous misunderstandings surrounding European Fundamental Painting (or rather a wider current of Analytical Painting).

Printed information about and knowledge of Fundamental Painting is virtually non-existent. With this in mind, this study aims to restore it to its place in the story of painting by identifying its characteristics and background, thereby providing for a first professional overview. Part 1 establishes that Fundamental Painting is a separate something, based on the curators of the Fundamental Painting show and other shows, critics and others, with an aim to eliminate any confusion there might be. This includes separating it from Analytical Abstraction. Part 2 views the Fundamental Painting works, supported by artists' explanations about what Fundamental painters do. It becomes clear that they all agree how each formal element should or should not function. Part 3 links the influences as named by the curators of the show to Fundamental Painting and explains the similarities or differences, while sticking to the formal elements which seem to have been the basis for these suggestions. This does confirm some kind of continuity as well as the historical position of Fundamental Painting which is valid in and of itself. Part 3 concludes that Fundamental Painting is a continuity of other 20th century art. Part 4 concludes on what has been revealed, namely that Fundamental Painting is a separate current, which is in part due to the fact that the formal elements always work in certain ways. It shows how the metaphysical dimension underlines this. In the end, by following what Fundamental painters (and their works) do instead of just what others say, this study positions Fundamental Painting – including its metaphysical element – firmly in the history of art and aesthetics.

1 THE BIRTH OF FUNDAMENTAL PAINTING

In 1975 Rini Dippel, curator at the Stedelijk Museum Amsterdam, talked about a "current situation" concerning a number of "alternative" artists whom she and museum director Edy de Wilde had wished to present (FP 10). The result was a show with eighteen painters entitled *Fundamental Painting*, with the four painters of Minimal Art – Robert Mangold, Brice Marden, Agnes Martin, and especially Robert Ryman – playing a central role. As Dippel wrote in her letter to Naomi Spector: "This exhibition can be regarded as a sequel to Bob's [Robert Ryman's] exhibition. The idea is to show the important 'trend-setting' artists Ryman, Marden, Mangold, and Agnes Martin." Director De Wilde, in turn, wrote on the scope of the exhibition: "It appears that the younger artists have breathed new life into painting – which has been pronounced dead so many times this century. These painters are not carrying on with the results of a painterly tradition, they are looking for a new foundation on which to base painting" (FP 1).

Thus, De Wilde considered the show to be a demarcation of a new, separate tendency which – as he likewise noted – had already been around for several years. However, he was quick to add that it was in no way to be considered as the introduction of a new movement. The works on display were created over the previous five to eight years, while Dippel claimed in her catalogue text "Fundamental Painting: Some Aspects of Recent Developments in Abstract Painting" that this Fundamental tendency went back as far as ten or fifteen years. The selection was not meant to be exclusive. The artists shown, she further explained in the exhibition catalogue, were in no way a defined group but were bound together by their common artistic quest. She considered Fundamental Painting to be more of a "mentality," mainly framed in a common painterly focus on the painting process and its inherent elements (FP 10).

The words of Edward Strickland in his book *Minimalism: Origins* summarize the validity of such a categorization very well: "[V]irtually every painter associated with Minimalism, even those who arose in its heyday in the latter half of the sixties, has been explained as not really Minimalist on some grounds or other (… Martin's personal touch, Ryman's painterliness, Marden's intuitive process…)." He continues, explaining: "The canon is itself thus reduced to minimal form, if not erased, by a rigor of categories that exceeds the technical rigor of the art. Yet the radically reductive tendency … is an undeniable fact, and … clearly has more in common formally and stylistically than the work of, say, fellow 'Impressionists' Manet and Monet or 'Abstract Expressionists' Gorky and Kline" (8).

Above all, the 1975 show at the Stedelijk Museum Amsterdam marked the first occasion that Fundamental Painting had been defined. In the following chapters, we will see how the current was coined, and according to which criteria the selection of artists was made. The importance of the exhibition will become better understood, through documenting the existence of Fundamental Painting according to various curators, the public, the media, and the usage of the term (especially in the Netherlands). At the same time, it will become clear exactly what the term Fundamental Painting stands for, and what the defining characteristics of this kind of painting are (and are not).

1.1 *Fundamental Painting* at the Stedelijk Museum Amsterdam

The exhibition *Fundamental Painting/Fundamentele Schilderkunst*, which ran from 25 April through 22 June 1975 at the Stedelijk Museum Amsterdam, made an attempt which aimed at demarcating the one kind of "new" painting of that decade. The museum's archives have an undated meeting note, which is clearly an early one, entitled "Over de opzet tent. 'grenzen van de schilderkunst'" ("About the intention of the exh. 'limits of painting'") – later to become *Fundamental Painting*. It refers to a discussion between curators Rini Dippel, Geert van Beijeren, Frits Keers, and Piet van der Have. From this note, we learn that the basic idea for the show was to ask about ten to twelve artists to present their work in order to consider it for inclusion in the exhibition. The criterion for such an invitation was that "paint (paint treatment, brushstroke, support)" had to play a "central role" (my translation).[5]

In a letter dated 3 December 1974, museum director Edy de Wilde asked collector Count Panza di Biumo to loan a work for the show, summarizing the concept behind it as follows:

> It is an exhibition devoted to the theme Painting, to its essence, basis and limits. In the first instance [sic] we are thinking of the important "trend-setting" artists like Robert Ryman, Brice Marden, Agnes Martin, and Robert Mangold. This implies that we shall try to show two [sic] sides of the new forms of painting: on the one hand the painters who are exploring the material [itself], the paint, [and] the way of applying this paint (of whom Ryman is the most impressive representative), and on the other hand the painters who strongly emphasize the shape of the painting (notably Mangold).

More specifically, in the above meeting note, the preliminary list of potential participants is mentioned: Robert Ryman, Brice Marden, Richard Jackson, Jake Berthot, Rainer (sic) Girke, Rob van Koningsbruggen, Jaap Berghuis, John Walker, Carmengloria Morales, Icke Winzer, Kees Smits, and Jerry Zeniuk. This meeting note also mentions that these artists were to be "contrasted with the category 'form/sign' (Agnes Martin, Edda Renouf, Stephen Rosenthal, Tomas Rajlich, Bob [Robert] Mangold, Alan Charlton etc.), the category 'about painting' (Daniel Buren, Niele Toroni, Olivier Mosset, and the late group Supports/Surface), as well as possibly the category 'paint/light/color' (Antonio Calderara, Claudio Olivieri, Gotthard Graubner,

Piet Teraa, Jeff Verheyen and others)." The note furthermore indicates that the historical context needed to be highlighted with "some works by Gerhard Richter," as well as some earlier art.[6] (See Fig. 1)

A report on Rini Dippel's visit to New York City from 10 to 19 December 1974 gives more detailed insight into what work the curators had in mind at the time. It also gives us an insight into which artists American gallery owners suggested they should include in the show. Dippel visited art dealer Robert Elkon to get the contact details of persons in Europe for loans of Agnes Martin's works. She invited Brice Marden, Robert Mangold, and Stephen Rosenthal to participate in the show; and through Naomi Spector (then director of John Weber Gallery), she notified Robert Ryman who was ill at the time. Furthermore, she visited the artist's studios of Jerry Zeniuk, Jake Berthot, Ralph Humphrey, Jo Baer, and Andy Gerndt, as well as a number of galleries. Art dealer John Weber suggested artist Lucio Pozzi. Klaus Kertess of Bykert Gallery showed her works by Garry Stephan, Gordon Hart, Paul Mogensen, Kent Floeter, and David Novros; and Xavier Fourcade took some work by James Bishop out of storage for viewing. Michael Sonnabend, then again, suggested artists Marcia Hafif, Bruce Boice, and Robert Petersen, while Cuningham gallery wanted to see that John Walker, Alan Cote, David Diao, and Harvey Quaytman were included.

Dippel discussed her findings with Kynaston McShine and Jenny Licht of the Museum of Modern Art as well as with Linda Shearer and Linda Konheim of the Solomon R. Guggenheim Museum New York, as she likewise noted. Further exhibition planning documentation shows that only the pre-selected artists, some of whom Dippel contacted in New York, reappeared in *Fundamental Painting* in the end. So although they discussed their findings with the curators of other museums and used galleries as a source for ideas, the Stedelijk Museum's curatorial team would not be influenced much, especially not by any commercial sources.

A further undated note, "Grenzen van de schilderkunst (1e opzet)." ("Limits of painting [preliminary concept]"), initialed by Frits Keers and Geert van Beijeren, reveals that:

> Due to the absence of the previous proposal, the subject was briefly discussed anew. The same names (approximately) were named. There are nevertheless a few changes in the concept:
>
> 1. There is a tendency to revise the previous concept (few people with relatively a lot of works) to include a few more persons (without this necessarily implying fewer works) and to possibly divide these into a sort of core group (Marden, Ryman, Van Koningsbruggen, Berghuis, Girke, Berthot) along with a few tangent figures (Twombly, Hofschen, Jackson, Richter, Walker).
> 2. Either documented in the exhibition in images, a slide show, and/or in the catalogue, this group would be defined in relation to painterly categories:

a. Martin, Renouf, Rosenthal, Rajlich
b. Mangold, Charlton
c. Buren, Toroni, Mosset (etc.)
3. Clarifying the historical context? This could be seen in the mid-20th century with Rauschenberg, Johns – in the early 20th century with Malevich.
Kees Smits[7]

We see here the idea emerge of a central group, surrounded by a few contingent artists and supplemented by a few more painterly groups. Note that the various meeting notes to the exhibition almost make it seem as if there is an essentially "fundamental" kind of painting, purely focusing on the limits of the painting medium, and a few adjacent categories that explore these limits in a more painterly way. It defines the Fundamental current as something specific and crucial yet flexible – which recalls curator Rini Dippel's mention of a mentality in painting.

As we can conclude from a handwritten table in the museum's exhibition archives, the division had been thought out as follows:

- "+/- monochroom" ("more or less monochrome"): Berghuis, Girke, Smits, Richter, and Ryman
- "vlak" ("plane"): Zeniuk and Marden
- "vorm" ("shape"): Charlton and Mangold
- "raster" ("grid"): Rajlich, Renouf, Rosenthal, and Martin.

Cane is listed in a separate category entitled "doek" ("canvas"). Jackson and Van Koningsbruggen are categorized under the word "kleur" ("color"). Marthe Wéry and Jake Berthot are not included in the above division, while names like Ulrich Erben (listed under *monochrome*), Alan Green, John Walker, M. Lancaster, Vincent Bioulès (listed under *color*), Blinky Palermo (listed under *shape*), Giorgio Griffa (listed under *grid*), Noël Dolla, and Diego & Gaetano Esposito (listed under *canvas*) are included but such decisions are marked as not yet definite. (See Fig. 1)

Comparing and contrasting the above meeting notes with the above table, we can conclude that the curators identified two main poles in Fundamental Painting: the "truly" fundamental one called the core group and the more painterly one designated as "form/sign." These two groups were further divided into the subgroups of *monochrome*, *plane*, and *color* and the subgroups *shape* and *grid*, respectively. The group listed as "paint/light/color" would soon disappear completely from the curators' notes, while the group entitled "about painting" (also designated as *canvas*) was reduced to one sole artist from the group Supports/Surfaces. Lastly, there was the category that allowed for context, meaning both the early 20th century and the work of Gerhard Richter (who was newly included here in the so-called core group of Fundamental Painting).

A letter from Dippel to De Wilde, dated 10 January 1975, gave the rough draft of the final division of the exhibition, based on the above notwithstanding a few questions. The letter mentions that the curators of *Fundamental Painting* were planning to have a look at works from the exhibition *Nouvelle peinture en France* (New Painting in France), which were stored at the time in Aachen's customs offices. The exhibition focused on the French group Supports/Surfaces. In retrospect, we know that no works by artists from this exhibition would be included in the *Fundamental Painting* show. The only (former) group member that it did feature was Louis Cane who, even so, did not participate in the *Nouvelle peinture en France* exhibition.

At the same time, the curators were discussing whether or not to include Gerhard Richter in the *Fundamental Painting* exhibition. Gallery owner Konrad Fischer felt strongly that they should, Dippel wrote in her letter. This was yet one more indication of their strong resentment of any commercial influence, although they would agree on this suggestion in the end. Also, Dippel continued her comments with the statement: "After a visit to Art & Project I am positive about Rajlich.... I find him ... working on it much longer; especially as figure amidst artists like Martin and the real painters."[8] The importance of a conscious common Fundamental mentality and its continuity shines through in this sentence.

By the time of Dippel's letter to Edy de Wilde dated 10 January 1975, the exhibition circuit had been divided as follows: The exhibition would open with an educative room followed by a room with Ryman's works. The third room would display works by Girke and Zeniuk and connect with a room for Marden's. These were to be followed by separate spaces showing works by Rajlich and Smits, Richter and Berghuis (plus Bioulès) respectively. (Note how the artists grouped around Ryman and Marden were loosely dispersed around their vicinity. The groups concerning the monochrome and the plane were put together, while the works by Rajlich – which Dippel characterized as in between Ryman's and Martin's – were shifted into rooms connecting the groups around the latter two painters.) The exhibition was meant to continue with works by Jackson and Van Koningsbruggen, show Charlton's (and Baer's) next to Mangold's, and finish with those by Rosenthal, Wéry, Renouf, and Martin. Obviously, Walker, Morales, Winzer, Buren, Toroni, Mosset, Calderara, Olivieri, Graubner, Teraa, and Verheyen had been eliminated in the meantime. Although the number of artists in the show would be limited to eighteen in all, two of those mentioned here by Dippel were not exactly the same ones presented in the final group. (In the end Berthot and Cane replaced Bioulès and Baer.)

The reasoning behind the selection and categorization process is explained in detail in Dippel's undated note entitled "Gereduceerde schilderkunst" (Reduced Painting):

1) Agnes Martin is the oldest participant in the exhibition in terms of age. Lines in horizontals and verticals dominate her painting. Stephan [sic] Rosenthal does not work with a grid but solely with subtle horizontal lines – and since recently, with

diagonal lines. Thomas [sic] Rajlich, paints over (a more or less) regular grid-pattern and therefore is to be positioned between Ryman and Martin.
The French-American Edda Renouf works with a grid made from the woven canvas through pulling out several threads from the warp or weft to create structure and texture.

2) Out of all participants, Robert Ryman, by limiting himself mainly to white paint, has most researched the possibilities of the paint, the surface, the base, the techniques, and the media.
Raymund [sic] Girke, not quite correctly often compared to Ryman, works much less structurally and above all optically.
Jaap Berghuis's work, in which color – even if very subdued – plays a role, shows some similarity.
Brice Marden's apparently cool reductivism consists of painted panels with an extremely smooth surface (paint applied with the palette knife) joined into polyptychs or triptychs.
Jerry Zeniuk likewise works with "encaustic" (wax and coloring) in gray and dark-brown to black monochromes that show an opaque surface (although the underlining weave of the canvas remains visible through 25 layers of wax).
The greenish monochromes of Jake Berthot, who especially considers the edge of the painting – its closure – as a challenge, are remotely related.

3) Robert Mangold: no color range, no research on the carrier, but pure concentration on the shape of the canvas and the figure on the canvas; basic metric forms – the square and the circle and parts of these – and their possibilities within a chosen framework of the canvas shape, [are] often [explored] in series, like Ryman's.
Alan Charlton's paintings function as reliefs in which it is essential to determine formats and ratios. Gray monochromes, painted totally smoothly….
All mentioned artists do use color, but often in a "hidden" manner. (Brice Marden is planning on working with bright red and yellow; Zeniuk uses colors like red and blue but processes them into grays; Ryman uses colors underneath his white paint; Mangold's colors are unusual yet specific.)

5) But, none of them uses colors in such an extrovert way as Richard Jackson does….
His painted canvas – meticulously planned – creates a painting in its turn: Art creates art. The only artist in the exhibition, who creates a kind of environment.
Rob van Koningsbruggen does not work in color, but in whites and blacks (mainly). Here too, we find a focus on the essence of a painting, basic forms, [and] texture – but above all on research on the positive and negative form, [through] displacement of the canvas; the painting prints itself or creates its counter-form. (1-2)[9]

The meeting note "Werkbespreking *Grenzen*" ("Working meeting *Limits* [of Painting]") made by Dorine Mignot and dated 16 January 1975, and which belongs to the same documentation pool, shows once more that the curators were considering other works. They planned a viewing of works from the *Nouvelle peinture en France* exhibition and thought about French artists at large as well as British painters Peter Joseph and Bob Law. At the same time, they would politely inform the respective galleries that Ulrich Erben and Icke Winzer would not be included in the show. Berthot remained questionable, while Girke had definitively made it into the selection.

The final exhibition concept loosely grouped the new current, Fundamental Painting, into four categories based on the four American Minimalists: Robert Mangold, Brice Marden, Agnes Martin, and Robert Ryman. The other thirteen, mainly European painters, were the Germans Raimund Girke, Gerhard Richter, and Jerry Zeniuk (living in New York), Frenchman Louis Cane, the Belgian Marthe Wéry, and the Briton Alan Charlton, as well as the Americans Edda Renouf (living in France), Jake Berthot, Richard Jackson, and Stephen Rosenthal. The hosting country, the Netherlands, was represented by Jaap Berghuis, Kees Smits, and Tomas Rajlich (a Czech native) – and the Dutchman Rob van Koningsbruggen who was included for other reasons than for his Fundamental mentality (see Chapter 2.2).

The floor plan of the exhibition distributed at the door (Fig. 2), indicates that *Fundamental Painting* started with an education room and that its final layout was as follows: Ryman (Fig. 3 and 4) followed by Richter (Fig. 5) and Van Koningsbruggen (Fig. 6), Marden (Fig. 7) followed by Girke (Fig. 8). Zeniuk (Fig. 9), Berthot (Fig. 10), Berghuis and Smits (Fig. 11) shown together in one room, and Rajlich (Fig. 12) with Jackson (Fig. 13) in the following room. Cane's work (Fig. 14) was housed with that of Charlton (Fig. 15) in a room giving access to another with works by Mangold (Fig. 16). After an opportunity to watch a slide presentation (preserved only as audio) on the art of the Fundamental painters in the show, the exhibition was rounded off with Rosenthal (Fig. 17), Wéry (Fig. 18), Renouf (Fig. 19) and Martin (Fig. 20 and 21). Although this division was also partially due to spatial restrictions, we may notice the interchangeability of the Marden/Ryman groupings and, not in the least, the inclusion of Rajlich amongst these two. (In later years, Rajlich's works would indeed witness a shift of focus, moving from grid structures more towards questions of paint application and the monochromatic. This places them in line with Ryman more than with anyone else.)

During the exhibition *Fundamental Painting*, a number of works from the permanent collection of the Stedelijk Museum Amsterdam by the artists featured in the educative space of this exhibition are hung in adjacent rooms (Fig. 22).[10] These artists are Jasper Johns, Piero Manzoni, Yves Klein, Kazimir Malevich, Theo van Doesburg, Barnett Newman, Ellsworth Kelly, and Frank Stella. Their works can be viewed on the same floor as the show, across the main stairway that contains works by Ad Reinhardt and Carl André. The explanatory text distributed to the visitors of *Fundamental Painting* gives a clearer insight into the exhibition's theme and association with works from the collection. It reads:

> The end of painting has been heralded many times in this century. Time after time "limits" were reached, only to be transgressed later on. In the 1960s, painting seemed to have been eclipsed by many new expressions in art, including Minimal Art and Concept Art [sic]. Yet, these ended up inspiring painting anew.
>
> In the past few years, many painters engaged in new forms of abstract painting. Besides fundamental painting, there has also been discussion around silent, new, essential, planned, or analytic painting.
>
> The 18 painters in this theme show do not form a group. They have been brought together based on a similarly directed interest in the formal and fundamental principles of abstract painting. They are concerned with painting as painting, painting as surface, and not as a "hole in the wall." No longer is painting the means but the subject.
>
> In turn, the visual means are again scrutinized: format, dimensions, color, form, line, texture, material (different kinds of paint and support, and the different means of applying it). These means are used "economically." There is a visible preference for sober colors, like white and gray, and for the square plane. Compositional elements are often abandoned. Color ranges and lines are distributed evenly across the canvas. The way of working is often a long-term process, in which sometimes many layers of paint are painted on top of one another. A few artists strongly accentuate the thought process that precedes painting, while not excluding their intuition.
>
> There are many parallels as well as differences between earlier abstract painters and these contemporary painters. (1)[11]

What the curators conclude in their attempt to highlight the singular, specific, new mentality in painting of the 1970s is that these eighteen artists limit their work strictly to the inherent elements of painting – its essence. Materials and tools are the key. Different elements or issues might hold their particular interest, approaching either the purported core or the more painterly end of the range. The works as well as the words of the artists provide a retrospective view which allows us to see that the curators' final choice was a correct one. Above all, this study will shed more and more light on the interconnection of (and differences among) the artists of the one kind of "new" painting of the 1970s, which is self-reflective yet international and where paint plays a central role, as represented by the painters in *Fundamental Painting* and their predecessors.

1.1.1 "New Painting" in Europe

According to Rini Dippel's catalogue text, Edy de Wilde mentioned the necessity of organizing a show like *Fundamental Painting* as early as 1973 and "independently thereof, ideas in this direction existed amongst members of the painting and sculpture department of the museum" (FP 10). Please note the pivotal word *independently,* which signifies that a number of persons working in the art-historical or curatorial field sensed the same advent of a new direction in painting – and the Stedelijk Museum was not alone. In several European countries, a common need for identification and categorization of a new kind of painting in the "fundamental" sense appeared on the art scene that year – according to the *Fundamental Painting* 1975 exhibition catalogue.

The newsletter "Art Aktuell: Confidential Information about the International Art Scene" published by Dr. W. Bongard, dated January 1975, confirms this. It reads:

> I am to-day [sic] pointing out to you emphatically a development in the field of new painting; it is done mainly because all the signs, that something is about to "happen," are there. I am always presuming of course, that important – even great – art is that which is being taken for such by the appropriate instances [sic] and institutions and for this reason I am harboring the "suspicion," that a very specific kind of "new painting" will come through strongly – [by] being exhibited, by means of publication, by being bought by museums and (possibly) in the market itself....
>
> The newer works of these artists (and a few others) have been christened "Analytical painting" which means painting concerning itself with its own hypothesis, condition and mode of action....
>
> [T]here will be, in the near future exhibitions in the Netherlands and Belgium, which will place additional emphasis into [sic] this type of painting. There are also preparations going on for an Italian publication (published: Daniela Pallazoli [sic]) dealing generally with "new painting" – this in co-operation [sic] with [Klaus] Honnef. In other words, there is something brewing.

At the same time, Bongard points out the crucial importance of the show *Fundamental Painting* in this development when writing: "In connection to 'new painting' I must mention a 'trendsetting' forthcoming exhibition at the Amsterdam Stedelijk Museum, which is scheduled for April/June." How important on an international level the show *Fundamental Painting* would be is also indicated by a letter from the Kunsthalle Bern to the Stedelijk Museum Amsterdam, dated 6 February 1975. In this letter, director Johannes Gachnang asked for postponement of the show's opening in Amsterdam, which fell on the same day as the Carl André retrospective in Bern, as "such a [sic] overlap of two so important exhibitions" was not a good idea in his opinion.

Thus, *Fundamental Painting* at the Stedelijk Museum Amsterdam appears crucial for the European curatorial history of the mid-1970s, which shows public signs of a renewed interest in painting in general and of the non-objective kind in particular. A first exhibition around this theme was put on by Germano Celant and Cornelio Brandini at the Centro Comunitario di Brera in Milan. It was entitled *Arte come Arte* (Art as

Art) and opened its doors in April 1973. The show included the American Minimalist painters – Robert Ryman, Robert Mangold, Agnes Martin, and Brice Marden –, as well as it exhibited works by predecessors and contemporaries Ralph Humphrey, Jo Baer, Barnett Newman, Frank Stella, Richard Tuttle, Dorothea Rockburne, Ad Reinhardt, David Novros, and Ellsworth Kelly. The show was accompanied by an eponymous catalogue that included Douglas Crimp's text "Opaque Surfaces," which two years later would form the basis for *Fundamental Painting*.

That same year Michel Claura and René Denizot curated *Une exposition de peinture réunissant certains peintres qui mettraient la peinture en question* (An Exhibition of Works by a Number of Painters Who Seem to Question Painting) that opened in Paris in May. The show traveled to the ICC in Antwerp and Museum Abteiberg in Mönchengladbach. It included three of the American Minimalist painters: Brice Marden, Agnes Martin, and Robert Ryman; and it featured the following European artists: BMPT's Daniel Buren and Niele Toroni from France, the Italian Giorgio Griffa, the German Blinky Palermo, British painter Alan Charlton, and Bernd Lohaus from Belgium. It was the first show linking Europe's new kind of painting to American Minimal Art, whose four painters would be proposed as the founding fathers of the Fundamental Painting current in the eponymous show. (Besides the Americans, only Alan Charlton would reappear in the Amsterdam exhibition, although several of the participants of the 1973 one were considered in detail, as its curators reveal in their notes kept in the archive of the Stedelijk Museum Amsterdam at the City Archives.)

These first exhibitions were followed by a number of shows on contemporary abstract painting of Italian making: *Glossario, Qui Arte Contemporanea* (Glossary – Here's Contemporary Art) at the Galleria Editalia in Rome, June through July 1973, curated by Marisa Volpi Orlandini;[12] the traveling exhibition *Un Futuro Possibile – Nuova Pittura* (A Possible Future – New Painting) curated by Giorgio Cortenova, opening at the Palazzo dei Diamanti in Ferrara in September 1973 and continuing to Rocca Sforzesca, Imola (BO), then on to Galleria La Piramide in Florence;[13] and the show *La riflessione sulla pittura* (Reflections on Painting) at the Palazzo Comunale in Acireale (CT), 29 September through 15 October 1973, curated by Filiberto Menna, Italo Mussa, and Tommaso Trini.[14] Only the latter two shows included a European painter who would be back in *Fundamental Painting*: Raimund Girke and Louis Cane, respectively. The section "Analitica/Analytic" of the show *Contemporanea* (Contemporary things) at the Villa Borghese in Rome that same year included Louis Cane as well as American painters Mangold, Marden, Martin, and Ryman;[15] Gerhard Richter was included in the section entitled "Linea Sintetica/Synthetic" of the same show. Thus, although all included Robert Ryman and possibly another painter of Minimal Art, the above exhibitions virtually did not include any European artists that would figure in *Fundamental Painting* two years later.[16]

Simultaneously in Germany, in the fall of 1973, Evelyn Weiss, Konrad Fischer, Jürgen Harten, and Hans Strelow curated a pioneering exhibition focusing on the theme of painting that included both figurative and abstract works and which featured a large number of names, both European and American – a few of which would later be known as Fundamental painters. It was called *Prospect 73 – Maler/Painters/Peintres*, and took place from 28 September through 7 October at the Kunsthalle Düsseldorf. It included *Fundamental Painting* participants Jaap Berghuis, Louis Cane, Alan Charlton, Raimund Girke, Edda Renouf, Gerhard Richter, and Jerry Zeniuk, as well as Robert Mangold, Brice Marden, and Robert Ryman, amongst others.[17]

Meanwhile there also were signs in France of a new wind in painting with the show entitled *Nouvelle peinture en France* (New Painting in France), which opened at the Musée d'Art et d'Industrie in Saint-Étienne in the summer of 1974 and traveled to the Neue Galerie-Sammlung Ludwig in Aachen, amongst others. It was, however, focused solely on the French group Supports/Surfaces but it did exclude one member: Louis Cane, the only future *Fundamental Painting* inclusion. The previously mentioned *Fundamental Painting* curators' notes show that the artists in this show were considered but obviously not included in the *Fundamental Painting* one, organized at a time when the French group had already dissolved. So, it can be said that, nearing the mid-1970s, curators in the major European countries started turning towards an interest in contemporary painting. In trying to group and define its novelties, they would consistently include the Fundamental vein albeit sporadically.

The most extensive overview on contemporary painting currents in both the USA and Europe until the defining 1975 Amsterdam exhibition was *Geplante Malerei* (Planned Painting) at the Westfälischer Kunstverein in Münster from 30 March through 28 April 1974, curated by Klaus Honnef. Some of the participating artists would be included in the show *Fundamental Painting* the following year. *Geplante Malerei* once again exhibited American Minimalist painters Brice Marden and Robert Ryman as well as a large number of European artists – notably Jake Berthot, Raimund Girke, Edda Renouf, and Jerry Zeniuk.[18] A modified version of this exhibition was shown from 19 November 1974 through 8 January 1975 at the commercial Galleria del Milione in Milan. This time, it included Brice Marden and Robert Ryman as well as Robert Mangold and Agnes Martin, heralding *Fundamental Painting* as never before.[19] (A further modified version entitled *Analytische Malerei* [Analytical Painting] followed at the commercial gallery La Bertesca in Düsseldorf, almost simultaneously to *Fundamental Painting* in June 1975, excluding the American Minimalists again – as well as Berthot and Renouf.[20]) Honnef wrote in the introduction to the exhibition catalogue of Geplante Malerei: "Even though the individual artistic concepts of analytical painting may vary, there are fundamental common bonds of artistic attitude. These fully justify talking about a new development in the history of painting."

Thus, a number of shows from 1973 up to 1975 foresaw the arrival of a new kind of painting (or even Fundamental Painting itself) on the European scene in 1975, apparently all searching in the direction of the painting considerations proposed by Minimal Art. Then came *Fundamental Painting* in 1975 at the Stedelijk Museum Amsterdam. which on a national level was supported by the show entitled *Elementary Forms of Contemporary Painting and Drawing in the Netherlands*. The latter was curated by Gijs van Tuyl and accompanied by a text by Hans Sizoo, and opened in May 1975 at the Visual Arts Office for Abroad in the Dutch Capital. It exhibited works by artists Ben Akkerman, Jaap Berghuis, Kees Buurman, Edgar Fernhout, J.C.J. van der Heyden, Jan Hoving, Rob van Koningsbruggen, Tomas Rajlich, Martin Rous, Jan Schoonhoven, Toon Verhoef, Carel Visser, and Rudi van de Wint. It was an accumulation of all kinds of minimalist expressions, including the novel Fundamental one.

The interest in new currents – or *the* new current – in painting gained momentum. On 29 November 1975, Museum Van Bommel-Van Dam in Venlo opened the show *Betreffende het schilderen.../Concerning Painting...*, which traveled to the Stedelijk Museum in Schiedam and the Museum for Contemporary Art in Utrecht.[21] It is interesting to note that this exhibition was divided into five categories indicating the basic concerns of painters, namely: content, material, objecthood, subject, and substance. These seem to be a reference to the categories proposed by *Fundamental Painting* a few months earlier and to the Fundamental mentality in general. The show heralded a period of exhibitions subdivided into similar, more or less random but subdivisions which were perceived to be significant. (For example, the show *Progressiva - La gestione del colore* [Progressiveness – Managing color] at the Galleria Arco d'Alberti in Rome the following spring featured the categories "Il bianco e il nero" ["Black and White"], "Il grigio" ["Gray"], and "La grammatica del colore" ["The Grammar of Color"]. [Bonomi 24])

Then again, in Italy, a further number of exhibitions on painting popped up, characterized by a steady over-exposure of Italian artists. We can wonder if this indicated a nationalist tendency of the curators or an exceptionally large interest in non-objective (or even "new" kind of) painting by the artists. The traveling exhibition *Empirica* (Empirical) shown at the Galleria Civica, Rimini, and the Museo Castelvecchio in Verona, curated by Giorgio Cortenova, is an example.[22] The exhibition *Cronaca: Percorso didattico attraverso la pittura Americana degli anni 60 e la pittura Europea degli anni 70* (Chronicles: A Didactical Tour through American Painting of the Sixties and European Painting of the Seventies) at the Galleria Civica of Modena, 18 March through 2 May 1976, more specifically attempted to explore the link between the American forerunners and the European contemporary non-objective painters. It included Josef Albers who, coming from the Bauhaus and teaching art at Black Mountain College and later Yale University, had a major impact on the postwar generation of American painters. It likewise included Abstract Expressionists Mark

Rothko, Ad Reinhardt, and Frank Stella, and Color Field Painters Al Held, Ellsworth Kelly, Morris Louis, Kenneth Noland, Jules Olitsky, and Larry Poons. (Note that these are almost the same as the artists presented in the permanent collection of the Stedelijk Museum Amsterdam as part of the educative context during the exhibition *Fundamental Painting*.) Their works were linked to those of a number of Italians as well as those of other Western European contemporary painters – notably Jaap Berghuis, Louis Cane, Alan Charlton, Raimund Girke, and Gerhard Richter.[23] In summer 1976, *I colori della pittura: Una situazione Europea* (The Colors of Painting, a European situation), curated by Italo Mussa, took place at the Istituto Latino-Americano in Rome (8 July through 10 September 1976). It also included a number of Fundamental painters: Jaap Berghuis, Louis Cane, Raimund Girke, Tomas Rajlich, and Jerry Zeniuk.[24] It is noteworthy for its title that recalls Rini Dippel's use of the words "a situation" (FP 10).

The following year, the painting section at the *Documenta 6* in Kassel featured a few painters from *Fundamental Painting*, namely Raimund Girke, Jerry Zeniuk, and Louis Cane, while all the painters in this section produced abstract, mainly non-objective works.[25] And, opening on 8 December 1977 at the Rheinisches Landesmuseum in Bonn, *Bilder ohne Bilder* (Paintings without Images) made a clear statement as to its particular interest in non-objective painting by way of its title. It ran through 8 January 1978 and was curated by Klaus Honnef. Thirty-three European as well as American artists were included, with notably a majority of the Fundamental painters: Jaap Berghuis, Louis Cane, Raimund Girke, Tomas Rajlich, Stephen Rosenthal, and Jerry Zeniuk, as well as the American "founders," Minimalists Robert Mangold, Brice Marden, and Robert Ryman.[26]

The following summer, 19 June through 18 September 1978, the ARC – Musée d'art contemporain de la ville de Paris held the exhibition *Abstraction Analytique: Fractures du monochrome aujourd'hui* (Analytical Abstraction: Fractures of the Monochrome Today), curated by Bernard Lamarche-Vadel and Susanne Pagé. This was one more key step in the re-installment of non-objective painting on the European scene, as well as on the international one. The show included three Fundamental painters: Alan Charlton, Tomas Rajlich, and Jerry Zeniuk.[27]

In 1978, the prestigious *Biennale di Venezia*, curated by Jean-Christophe Amman, Achille Bonito Oliva, Antonio del Guercio, and Filiberto Mena that year, also boasted the title "Grande astrazione. Grande realismo." ("Great Abstraction. Great Realism.") for one of its sections. Unfortunately, the selection was rather restricted and Mediterranean[28] – which left only Louis Cane calling Fundamental Painting to mind. Nevertheless, it was surely a statement to the world that non-objective painting was an important phenomenon on the art scene at the time. (The fact that a number of commercial art galleries then "hopped on the bandwagon" confirms this.[29]) The mid-

1970s in Western Europe undeniably showed that Fundamental Painting (and other new analytical currents) were a major concern of the art scene, be it among painters or curators. The show *Fundamental Painting* was "simply" the crystallization of this shared idea which was very much "in the air" at the time.

In contrast to the above attempts to define an overall kind of painting, the Stedelijk's *Fundamental Painting* show of 1975 was restrictive. Only afterwards did curators start attempting to distinguish specific currents within 1970s European non-objective painting. The show's indication of a new category and all other events relative to the exhibition signify that Fundamental Painting is, indeed, something specific, something in existence, concerning a well-defined group of artists. This not only underlines that Fundamental Painting does exist as a distinct approach but also shows its significance in the history of late 20th century art.

1.1.2 Public acceptance of Fundamental Painting

Another indication that Fundamental Painting had already been "in the air" by the time the eponymous show was organized was the positive response from the public at the exhibition. Although museum director Edy de Wilde wrote in his preface to the catalogue that it was not a radically new beginning for art but a new step in painting, the exhibition's organizers expected the show to be difficult for the public to comprehend. A case in point is the introductory paragraph from a report of the inquiry made amongst visitors during the show which reads:

> During the preparation of *Fundamental Painting* basically everyone agreed that it would be a difficult exhibition for the general public. Therefore, after some discussion, two forms of support were chosen: A slide show that was to be mainly about the exhibition itself and an information room with textboards which would touch upon a number of common points among these painters and their differences from other earlier and contemporary abstract painters. (2)[30]

Judging from the informational letter to security and staff ("Algemene informatie voor het bewakingspersoneel over de tent. 'Fundamentele schilderkunst'") the curators even seemed to be prepared for the worst:

> Possibly many visitors will react negatively, because this exhibition will not be understandable to everyone. The usual remarks of: "What is this supposed to be?" or "Must this be hung in a museum?" are to be expected. This is all right; everyone may have their own opinion, but our scientific staff wants you to know that, in their opinion, the artists in this exhibition have indeed worked in a serious manner.

> The exhibited works are particularly delicate; most do not have a protective frame; the paint used is often mixed with wax, so that even a slight fingerprint remains visible and can never be removed. The large blank zones as well as the grid structures of many paintings may incite in some viewers the urge to draw on or paint over them.[31]

A detailed, multiple-choice questionnaire for the visitors of *Fundamental Painting*, which was set up by Drs. Steen, scientific researcher at the Pedagogisch Didactisch Instituut of the University of Amsterdam, shows however that the viewers were positive about the show. Of the estimated 1650 viewers who saw *Fundamental Painting*, 1495 filled out forms, 722 of whom were in Dutch and 773 in English, accounting for an estimated 90% of the total visitors (3). They indicated that 28% of the total number of visitors and 38% of the Dutch visitors had even specifically come to the museum to see *Fundamental Painting*. Moreover, 42.4% found the exhibition to be "comprehensible," 18.8% "difficult," and only 18.3% "non-comprehensible." The Dutch public seemed to have fewer issues with it than the English-speaking public. Nevertheless, 66.9% of all visitors (foreigners more often than the Dutch) found the show interesting (4-5).

About a third of all visitors discovered a preference for a certain artist. Interestingly enough, Louis Cane, Richard Jackson, and Rob van Koningsbruggen stole the show. The Minimalists followed: first Robert Ryman, then Robert Mangold, Agnes Martin, and (after Tomas Rajlich) Brice Marden. Even when we factor in the negative feedback, Cane and Van Koningsbruggen still led, closely followed by Robert Mangold and Tomas Rajlich, then Ryman, Martin and Marden (6). All the others had significantly less resonance.

As will be discovered later on, the above three preferred artists are not Fundamental painters, while the four Americans and Rajlich on the contrary are Fundamental painters *par excellence*. One might therefore suspect that this is not a coincidence. Possibly Fundamental Painting was "in the air" and thus preferred by a large audience, while at the same time a good part of the audience, who had not warmed up to the novel kind of painting, still nurtured a preference for more elaborate painting. All in all, the show of *Fundamental Painting* was a success.

On 1 July 1975 museum director Edy de Wilde wrote in a letter to one of the lenders, Count Panza di Biumo: "The show … attracted many visitors and got a great deal of attention in the press." The press response to the *Fundamental Painting* exhibition was abundant and international. This would indicate that the current was indeed "in the air" and that an exhibition like *Fundamental Painting* would presumably have taken place around 1975. Curator Rini Dippel's article – similar to her introductory text for the exhibition catalogue – appeared, translated into French, in the publication *Peinture, cahier théoriques*; and a participant in *Fundamental Painting*, Louis Cane, wrote a theoretical discourse entitled "Peinture fondamentale" as a train-of-thought piece for *Art Press*.

Independent art critics and magazines also reported on the show. Notably, Antje von Graevenitz wrote a number of articles for the Dutch and the German press. She wrote “Neuer Trend im Kunstinteresse?” (“A New Trend in the Interest of Art?”) for the *Süddeutsche Zeitung* and “Verf is verf” (“Paint Is Paint”) for *Vrij Nederland*, which was reprinted in a German version under the title “Malerei als Faktum oder ‘Das Einfache ist kein Pappenstiel’” (“Painting as a Fact or ‘Simplicity Is Not Child’s Play’”) in her column “Brief aus Amsterdam” (“Letter from Amsterdam”) in *Kunstforum International*. It is a lengthy text that tries to approach the exhibition objectively, but shows Von Graevenitz’s disagreement with its set-up. She regretted that the show only went back about fifteen years and felt the need to defend the European artists that had been grouped around four Americans. Thus, she made the link to predecessors and devoted as much detail as possible in just a few pages to a number of artists in the show. This shows her understanding of Fundamental Painting as that which focuses on the elements of painting by definition and her favorable stance to Fundamental Painting as such. In particular, in her article she defends the European current as something important in and of itself and not as a pale imitation of the American one. Her overall opinion, voiced in both *Vrij Nederland* and *Kunstforum International,* confirms the result of the public visitors’ poll, namely that “the exhibited simplicity does not seem hard at all to understand, as the painterly propositions are known to us” (31 and 196).[32]

The like-minded newspaper *De Groene Amsterdammer* published “Hoe fundamenteel is fundamentele schilderkunst?” (“How Fundamental Is Fundamental Painting?”) by Cor Blok, who also covered his entire two-page column on Holland in the English-language art magazine *Studio International* with an overview of the show. Like Von Graevenitz, Blok briefly discussed the show as well as a number of artists in detail. His words “The work presents itself in a single view and you can immerse yourself in the details,” show his understanding of the workings of Fundamental Painting. However, his conviction was that these artists had “remained virtually unknown in the Netherlands until now, except for a circle of insiders” (*Groene Amsterdammer*).[33] (It can, thus, be deduced that in other countries and among a certain group of people, it was already known.)

Blok criticized the museum’s meager, preliminary education and explanation about the show. He seemed to question how far this history of painting can go, and if the “common” viewer would continue to be able to follow, or if art and society will eventually grow apart. On a similar note, J.C. van der Waals in his article for the art review of the Dutch business newspaper *Het Financieel Dagblad* strongly recommended that the visitor remain open to the experience yet educate himself prior to visiting the show in order to make sure he will see the aesthetic quality of this seemingly “anti-aesthetic” painting. Still, in his opening paragraph he mentioned that, if for many people the previous two exhibitions had “little to do with art as known to them, this time is different.”[34] Thus, again, Van der Waals acknowledged that Fundamental Painting was not unknown.

Therefore, the exhibition curators' initial fears that the public might not understand the show seemed to live on amongst the press, while both parties seemed to agree that Fundamental Painting was not something entirely "coming out of the blue." Günther Engelhart in his article "Calvinisten der Leinwand" ("Calvinists of the Canvas") in the *Deutsche Zeitung* immediately threw in the towel and plainly regretted that this art might only resonate with a limited public of connoisseurs. He tried to help by promoting the show through a lot of international activity. Besides his regular column as mentioned above, he wrote "Malerei heute" ("Painting Today") for the Swiss weekly magazine *Die Weltwoche*. What's more, he incorporated the subject in his radio reports for the Norddeutscher Rundfunk, Westdeutscher Rundfunk and Hessicher Rundfunk in Germany, which covered almost all of what was then West Germany.

Betty van Garrel, on the contrary, was confident that with means like the educative information accompanying the *Fundamental Painting* show, the general public might find themselves liking this kind of painting, which – as she mentioned at the beginning of her article – was nothing new to her. Her article "Nulkunst in de nadagen" ("Zero-Art in Its Latter Years") in *NRC Handelsblad* (one of the most important newspapers in the Netherlands and a liberal newspaper which was well-known for its comprehensive section on art) concludes with "to make art with so little, one must be a genius."[35] Thus, we can say that critics like Blok, Van der Waals, Engelhart, and Van Garrel supported Fundamental Painting. They saw it as something that the public should know about, to keep up with the latest in art history.

Then again, Ton Frenken in his "Grondlagen van het schilderij" ("Painting Basics") written for the regional newspaper *Eindhoven's Dagblad* felt a need to correct the curators – not for their choice but for their explanations. Their saying that the artists limited themselves soberly to the basics of painting, "in his opinion, [was] already saying too much." He claimed that they "limit themselves to the basics of painting as a material fact, where they do not yet go as far as to differentiate the pictorial elements." He found it to be a reduction and a contrast to the much richer visual propositions of Abstract Expressionism, notably Barnett Newman's.[36] Again, this writer seems to have grasped the nature of Fundamental Painting quite well and does not dispute Dippel's catalogue introduction stating that Fundamental Painting had already been around for over a decade.

Jan Juffermans in "Schilderijen zonder poespas" ("Paintings without a Fuss") in the local newspaper *De nieuwe linie* analyzed and only partially dismissed the curators' choice. In his "Schilderen om het schilderen" ("Painting for Painting's Sake") for the newspaper *Algemeen Dagblad* (the second biggest newspaper in the Netherlands) which strives to remain neutral, Juffermans surprisingly gave a judgment when writing that "most of the artists have such different starting points and apply such different processes that it is impossible to ever consider them as a group."[37] (In retrospect, this statement would turn out to be partially right.) At the same time, Juffermans was positive that it showed a wide range of approaches within a direction focused on the same subject. Critic Jan de Carpenter, who dedicated his column "Kijk eens Kunst" ("Look at Art for once") in the local newspaper *Dagblad voor de Zaanstreek* to the exhibition, is the only one who came to the unconditional conclusion that "as a representation of a current, *Fundamental Painting* ha[d] become an excellent piece of documentation."[38] Implicitly, both seemed to accept the fact that the show was an overview of an existing artistic current.

The same goes for Georges Roque who wrote for the French language magazine *Clés*, featuring the article "Nihilisme et affirmation de la peinture" ("Nihilism and the Assertion of Painting"). He had a hunch which was similar to Juffermans'. Namely, he mused in his in-depth article on Fundamental Painting that it seemed to have two opposing currents: One moving toward the end of painting and the other resurrecting it. Similarly, Frits Bless in his "Fundamentele schilderkunst – een nieuw begin? Terug naar de basis" ("Fundamental Painting – a New Beginning? Back to Basics."), written for the newspaper *De Gelderlander*, asked himself if Fundamental Painting might lead to a new beginning in the history of painting, whose demise had been announced so many times previously. He was also not convinced that the selection of the curators was the best to favor a clarification of the situation. This duality between the end and new beginnings in non-objective painting of the 20th century will reappear in the discussion on predecessors to and influences on Fundamental Painting.

Despite public disagreement as to the selection and presentation of the show by its curators, the Fundamental Painting current does not seem to have been as drastically new to both public and press nor as impossible to understand as was specifically stated by a number of critics. Most of the press and public were satisfied with the experience. As both the poll and the articles show, there seemed to be a basic understanding of painting that allowed for positive acceptance of the Fundamental current. The poll even confirms that about two-thirds of the visitors were of the opinion that it was in step with the contemporary societal mentality. It seems to have truly been "in the air" by the mid-1970s, as Dippel claimed.

Only a few critics were not so visionary and positive about the *Fundamental Painting* show. For example, Fanny Kelk wrote an article entitled "Saaie tentoonstelling" ("Boring Show") in *Het Parool*, which was overtly left-wing due to its origins as a social-democrat newspaper founded during the Second World War. Although the Left tends to be seen as a supporter of the arts, the title of Kelk's article was one of few giving an overtly negative message. She seemed to have been convinced that "[the] research into method and technique that this fundamental painting is based on, ha[d] been proposed numerous times in the past already."[39]

Lambert Tegenbosch in his "Kunst als Ambacht" ("Art as Craft") published in the newspaper *Volkskrant*, which since the 1960s has set itself the task to address "readers with higher education" who are mainly left-wing and progressive, gave a similarly excruciating judgment. He found it unbelievable that this kind of painting would be new after its being declared dead only six years earlier by another show at the same museum (*Op losse schroeven* [Called into Question], 1969, featuring Conceptual Art). According to him, the exhibition was a show of processes, about as new as discovering that arts and crafts exist. He only spoke positively of the paintings by Tomas Rajlich, which he saw as "fascinating and unforgettable."[40] Nevertheless, this is still a positive call in terms of Fundamental Painting, even though a very limited one.

Kelk and Tegenbosch were seconded by Ron Kaal. According to his article "Oude koek in een nieuw trommeltje" ("Just the Same Old Thing") in the *Haagsche Courant*, it seems that he simply did not understand a show of this kind and was accordingly not impressed. At the same time, his comments again underline the fact that this kind of painting was nothing new but rather a continuation. Armine Haase was equally unimpressed. In her "Ein Kunsttrend aus der Retorte?" ("A Synthetic Art Trend") in *Rheinische Post*, she called Fundamental Painting "an artificially created trend,"[41] in which the only new thing was the fact that the curators finally grouped this kind of painting together into one show. At the end of the day, such a statement might even be considered as positive.

All in all, even from the negative press, an indisputable conclusion is that Fundamental Painting was "in the air" in 1975 – not only in the Netherlands, but also throughout Europe. This does not only become obvious from the previous chapter on related shows. Besides the large number of exceptionally elaborate articles that appeared in the international press, the exhibition was also covered from a more objective perspective in the Dutch magazines *Kunst Echo's*, *Avenue*, and *Uitkrant*, the Belgian *Kunst & Cultuur*, as well as in Massimo Minini's column "Girando per l'Europa" ("Big Tour Across Europe") in *Brescia Oggi*, a Northern Italian newspaper. The response to the exhibition can be considered significant and mostly positive, both among the press and the visitors. Curators and professionals were not the only ones of the art world to have spotted something new in painting from the 1970s. All this indicates a certain logic and acceptance of Fundamental Painting at the time.

Even if the opinions were divided on whom to include or reject in the Fundamental current, the resonance of the show in the public media seems to have spurred a new interest in painting at large. In the thank-you letters to lenders and artists, director Edy de Wilde wrote: "The exhibition attracted a big crowd, and caused many discussions and polemics. Which is something one can expect from that kind of exhibition, of course" (Letter to Jackson). And, more in detail: "In our view it has really contributed to the discussion round the theme 'painting,' particularly with regard to the question how 'fundamentally' one wishes to conceive 'fundamental.' This naturally has lead [sic] to much diversity of opinion" (Letter to Panza 1975). Hopefully, the present study may provide a definitive definition of Fundamental Painting.

1.1.3 Evidence of Fundamental Painting

In retrospect, there were already indications that Fundamental Painting has not been forgotten nor denied. Especially in Italy, since the turn of the 21st century critics and curators have been showing a renewed interest in the "new" mentality in painting of the 1970s including Fundamental artists.[42] Art critic Marco Meneguzzo has even ventured to write a book on the subject of Analytical Painting in Italy. In 2001, the Galleria comunale d'arte contemporanea Ai Molini in Portogruaro in cooperation with the Fondaco delle Biade in Feltre organized a show entitled *Suoni della superficie* (Sounds of the Surface).[43] And in 2004, from 27 March through 2 May and 10 October through 7 November, the Fondazione Zappettini in Chiavari and the Civica Galleria d'Arte Moderna di Gallarate together staged the show *Pittura70: Pittura Pittura e Astrazione Analitica* (Painting 70: Painting Painting and Analytical Abstraction), curated by Giorgio Bonomi. It included works by Alan Charlton, Raimund Girke, Tomas Rajlich, and Jerry Zeniuk, showing the artists' works from the 1970s in combination with their more recent ones. In 2009, the Museo d'Arte Contemporanea di Villa Croce in Genoa showed *Pensare Pittura: Una linea internazionale di ricerca negli anni settanta* (Thinking Painting: An International Field of Research in the Seventies), from 17 April through 11 October, curated by Franco Sborgi and Sandra Solimano. It showed a number of predecessors from all kinds of non-objective strands as well as contemporary artists (once again, mainly Italian) including works by half of the exhibiting artists of *Fundamental Painting*: Jaap Berghuis, Louis Cane, Alan Charlton, Raimund Girke, Tomas Rajlich, and Jerry Zeniuk, as well as Robert Mangold and Robert Ryman. These recent series of exhibitions on Italian Analytical Painting make a convincing case for the reinstatement of Fundamental Painting as part of a larger whole on an international level.

In Germany, the interest has grown as well. For example, in 1983 the Städtisches Museum, Gelsenkirchen, the Städtische Galerie, Lüdenscheid, and the Kunstverein Unna organized *Von der Ungleichheit des Ähnlichen in der Kunst* (About the Differences of the Similar in Art), including works on paper by Raimund Girke, Tomas Rajlich and Jerry Zeniuk.[44] In 1988, the then Kunstverein in Arnsberg even ventured to put on a show boldly entitled *Fundamentale Malerei* (Fundamental Painting), which presented works by artists from six countries,[45] while the major international overview of abstract art in the 20th century at the Albertinum in Dresden, organized by Der Deutsche Kunstlerbund in 1993 and simply named *Abstrakt*, included artists from Fundamental Painting.[46] The Städtische Galerie in Lüdenscheid did not neglect Fundamental Painting either in its 1996 show *Aspekte Niederländischer Kunst heute* (Aspects of Dutch Art Today), even though this was geographically limited to the Netherlands (and the movement represented by Tomas Rajlich solely).

As far as publications are concerned, Fundamental Painting is often specifically acknowledged in texts related to all above-mentioned exhibitions. However, a number of stand-alone publications on art of the 20th century picked up on the current of Fundamental Painting. On an international level these were the following publications. Catherine Millet's book *La grande histoire de la peinture moderne. Tendances d'aujourd'hui: 1960-1980*, published in 1982, includes a chapter entitled "Peinture fondamentale" (51-62). In 1989, Marcia Hafif discussed Fundamental Painting in "True Colors" in *Art in America* (138-139), while three years later Thomas McEvilley mentioned Fundamental Painting, and a few other names were given, in "Absence Made Visible" in *Artforum* (93-94). Also Daniel Buren in *The Ineffable - About Ryman's Work* of 1999 referred to "fundamental" artists at large, indicating a mentality similar to Ryman's. And, Jan Skřivánek classified Tomas Rajlich under Fundamental Painting in his article on the artist's retrospective show at the National Gallery in Prague in 2008 (15).

In the Netherlands, Fundamental Painting has clearly been acknowledged as forming a current in the history of art. The widely used and regularly reprinted referential art history book entitled *De Nederlandse Identiteit in de Kunst na 1945* (The Dutch Identity in Art after 1945), edited by Geurt Imanse, clearly incorporates a chapter on Fundamental Painting entitled "Schilderen als schilderen. Naar aanleiding van de tentoonstelling '*Fundamentele schilderkunst*.' 1975." ("Painting as Painting. In Reference to the Exhibition '*Fundamental Painting*,' 1975.") (Ch. 9, 174-198). Also the book *Nederlandse Schilderkunst: Tussen Detail en Grandeur* (Dutch Painting: Between Detail and Grandeur) written by Ad van der Blom, Ernest Kurpershoek, and Claudia Theunissen in 1997 incorporates a chapter on this theme. It is entitled "De terugkeer van het schilderij. Fundamentele kunst, nieuwe expressie, postmodernisme." ("The Return of the Painting. Fundamental Art, New Expression, Postmodernism.") (Ch. 18, 269-285). The series *Nederlandse schilderkunst* (Dutch Painting) of the national educational channel TELEAC – published likewise in book form, edited by Cor Blok – dedicates a section to this phenomenon in its volume on Dutch painting since 1900. In fact, Fundamental Painting takes up the entire part entitled "Schilderkunst" ("Painting") of the chapter on the years 1969 through 1979 (185-187). Thus, judging by both the exhibitions and the publications in the years following the Amsterdam show, Fundamental Painting does seem to have a specific place as such in the history of contemporary art.

1.2 The coining of "Fundamental Painting"

The term Fundamental Painting was coined by the organizers of the eponymous exhibition, which opened its doors on 25 April 1975 at the Stedelijk Museum Amsterdam (FP 2). In a later text on this subject, Rini Dippel stated that the title of the exhibition had been proposed by director Edy de Wilde (Imanse 183). She explained in an interview with the author on 25 August 2011 that she did not like the choice, as it recalled the fundamental Protestant communities in the Netherlands at the time, giving it a religious connotation which was often perceived negatively by the general public. Geert van Beijeren also opposed the term, but De Wilde insisted on it. As preparatory notes, letters to the artists and lenders, and other materials show, the title *Fundamental Painting* was given to the exhibition only around mid-March 1975, a few weeks before its opening. Throughout the preparatory stage the working title was simply *Schilderkunst* (Painting), then, from about December 1974, *Grenzen van de Schilderkunst* (Limits of Painting), while in Dippel's undated note this was changed to the title *Gereduceerde Schilderkunst* (Reductive Painting). From a purely linguistic point of view, in retrospect Dippel agreed – in the aforementioned interview with the author – that it was more accurate to refer to the fundaments instead of the limits.

There is an undated, handwritten note by one of the organizers in the archives of the Stedelijk Museum Amsterdam, referring to the exhibition *Schilderkunst* of 1975 – later to become *Fundamental Painting* – with a heading in Dutch "Schilderkunst. Noemers tot nu toe gebruikt" that translates into "terms used until now."[47] It reads as follows:

- nouvelle peinture (Millet, '74-'75)
- peinture-peinture
- réflexion sur la peinture (*La riflessione sulla pittura*, Menna, '73)
- essential painting (Spector, Mangold '74)
- Geplante Malerei (Honnef, Münster '74)
- anatomie van de schilderkunst (R. v. Koningsbruggen)
- neue konkrete Kunst (v. Berswordt, Bochum)
- Peindre (*Rencontres*, Paris 1974)
- Arte come Arte (Milan, '73)
- Fare pittura (Bassano, '73)
- Nuova Pittura (Ferrara, '73)•Modus operandi (Gaul, '74)
- Lavoro + modi di produzione (T. Trini)
- oppervlak – kleur – vorm[48]

In the 1975 catalogue text, chief curator Dippel explained that up to that point a common denominator for this new kind of painting had not yet been defined, although several terms referring to various Fundamental artists had been proposed. Notably, in 1967, Lucy Lippard had designated the work of a number of painters as "The Silent Art." She was referring to Minimalists Robert Mangold, Brice Marden, and Robert Ryman, listing Color Field artists Barnett Newman, Ad Reinhardt, and Mark Rothko as their precedents. She also mentioned Ralph Humphrey and Yves Klein, amongst others, in her article. (Later on, she would reserve the term for Robert

Mangold only.) Furthermore, Dippel indicated that Klaus Honnef used the term "analytische Malerei" (Analytical Painting) in the catalogue of the Italian version of *Geplante Malerei* (Planned Painting) in 1973, in relation to Winfred Gaul and Gianfranco Zappettini – both consciously not included in *Fundamental Painting* –, to link the American and European contemporaries.[49] That same year, Douglas Crimp proposed the term "Opaque painting," mainly referring to Brice Marden and Robert Ryman, while a year later Naomi Spector characterized Mangold's work as "essential painting." As Dippel wrote to Crimp, on 2 July 1975, she "refer[ed] several times to [his] article in [her] preface" to the *Fundamental Painting* catalogue, and, above all, she "notably followed [him] in the clear division of the various aspects of painting," in the eponymous show. In the catalogue text, Dippel explained that Ryman was a pioneer of this current, both American and European (11-12).

Dippel herself designated Fundamental Painting as "post-Conceptual" and "post-Minimal," a term allegedly coined by Nicolas Logsdail in the context of an exhibition on *British Painting* in Edinburgh in Fall 1974, in her catalogue text (10 and 12). (Also in her travel report, she used the term "post-Minimal" for works of artists presented to her by various galleries as potential inclusions in the Fundamental Painting show.) At the same time, she informed the reader that any terms expressing the "reducedness" of this kind of art are wrong, as it does not reduce a complicated composition to a limited structure. Anything in the direction of "elementary" would be acceptable, but would automatically bring to mind Theo Van Doesburg's Elementarism (a predecessor to his Art Concret). Possibly, the term "New Concrete Art" would not be too far off either but there are two major differences, according to Dippel: "'1. Art is universal'" and "'6. Search for absolute lucidity'." In the catalogue, the discussion about coining the term is headed "Fundamental-Elementary-Concrete" (12).

We note that this catalogue explanation refers to a number of terms which are not only included in but also added to the original list. More importantly, some of terms on the list are no longer mentioned, and a few formerly included terms have now been specifically excluded. Dippel wrote on this subject that:

> The Stedelijk Museum has now added yet another title to this often confusing list: "Fundamental Painting." It is not difficult to come up with something more imaginative – like "Painting – a Closer Look" or "The Limits of Painting." With the title "Fundamental Painting," however, the Stedelijk Museum means that it is presenting those artists of the "new painting" movement who are involved first and foremost with the basic principle of painting. That is to say, those who restrict themselves in the most self-critical manner to anti-illusionist painting, in which moreover all compositional elements are absent. (12)

Notably, Dippel made a point of stating that neither "nuova pittura" nor "Nouvelle Peinture," which indicate "totally different" directions in art, is to be confused with Fundamental Painting (11).

In coining this new category, the Stedelijk Museum in Amsterdam wished to designate a certain kind of new approach to the painting of the time. In his introductory speech to the exhibition – a draft of which is filed in the archives of the Stedelijk Museum Amsterdam –, as well as in the preface of the exhibition catalogue, Edy de Wilde wrote:

> The Amsterdam Stedelijk Museum has devoted several exhibitions to new tendencies in art albeit irregularly.... "*Fundamental Painting*," the exhibition that we are now, six years later, presenting, seems to be the opposite: .... It appears that the younger artists have breathed life into painting – which has been pronounced dead so many times this century....
>
> This exhibition does not claim to introduce a new current in art. We have in the past already drawn attention to several important figures in [F]undamental [P]ainting, as is shown by both our purchases and exhibitions. However, we hope – now that the contrasts are beginning to manifest themselves – to give a comprehensive although necessarily incomplete overview of the situation. (1)

Hence, there was the need to distill Fundamental Painting from the wide range of painting in previous shows, referred to in the listings above, and find a proper name for it. Fundamental Painting was parallel to American "Silent Art", "Essential Painting", and "Opaque Painting" – terms that never caught on but whose representative artists were included in the show –, and it was sometimes designated by Dippel as Post-Minimal or Post-Conceptual painting, both terms of American making.[50] Furthermore, she assigned to Fundamental Painting the typically Dutch or Western-European title of Concrete and Elementary. Obviously, the French "nouvelle peinture" and Italian "nuova pittura" were not acceptable to the organizers as terms for this new painting of the Fundamental kind, due to their difference in artistic foundation and results. Also, Klaus Honnef's exhibitions on *Geplante Malerei* (Planned Painting) and *Analytische Malerei* (Analytical Painting), which included a number of painters from Mediterranean countries, did not represent the same kind of painting as Fundamental Painting. Therefore, Fundamental Painting, as coined by Stedelijk Museum director Edy de Wilde, is a specific (rather North Atlantic) kind of new painting in the 1970s.

So, it can be concluded that the term *fundamental* was chosen with care, corresponding to the scope of the exhibition, which was to delineate the particular new current in painting. It was meant to mark a step forward. At the same time, it indicated a connection with American developments (at this point, already at the center of contemporary art) – as opposed to associating with Europe's stagnation, since Paris had long since lost its privileged position of capital of the arts. As Dippel confirmed in an interview with the author in August 2011, today she believes that the term *fundamental* was well thought out. It relates directly to the essence of these painters' work and to what makes it unique, without being reductive in underlining their rigorous concepts.

1.2.1 The definition of Fundamental Painting

This brings us to the question of what Fundamental Painting is and what it is not. It soon becomes clear from reading the texts by Italian authors that the confusion between Fundamental Painting and any kind of Italian "new" painting, which Dippel warned about, is widespread. In his catalogue text for *Pittura70: Pittura Pittura e Astrazione Analitica* (Painting 70: Painting Painting and Analytical Abstraction), Giorgio Bonomi mentioned that the kind of painting as presented in the exhibition has been given various names at various times – the first three being the most often used: "pittura pittura" ("painting as painting"), "nuova pittura" ("new painting") and "pittura analitica" (Analytical Painting). Following the same logic, he continues by listing terms like "fare pittura" ("painting painting"), "pittura progettata" (Planned Painting), "astrazione analitica" (Analytical Abstraction), "pittura riflessiva" ("reflective painting"), "pura pittura" ("pure painting"), "pittura radicale" (Radical Painting), "pittura di superficie" ("surface painting"), and – last but not least – "pittura fondamentale" (Fundamental Painting) (15). He therefore seems to consider all of these one and the same. On the other hand, Bonomi curiously does make a distinction between at least two kinds of painting of the 1970s in the title of the exhibition.

Clearly, Bonomi has opted for the Italian terms coined for the new kind of painting in the 1970s,[51] while Dippel in the *Fundamental Painting* catalogue focused on the precedents in the US – not surprisingly, as the show was built around four American Minimalist painters. She even made a point of saying that Italian artists were excluded from the exhibition, because their kind of "new" painting was not the same as Fundamental Painting. According to the organizers of the 1975 show in Amsterdam, a great number of (notably Italian) contemporary non-objective painters did not qualify as Fundamental due to their poetic nature, amongst other things (FP 13). In 2003, Italian art critic Marco Meneguzzo, who had been studying Italian Analytical Abstraction in the years just preceding, only confirmed her suspicion about their stark differences in proclaiming that German, Dutch, and English Analytical artists were at the opposite extreme of most of their Italian, and of almost all of their French, colleagues in the catalogue's text for *Pittura Analytica*. The exhibition (which preceded the 2008 monograph *Analytica* by the same author) only contained works by a number of Italian painters, while its catalogue included *Fundamental Painting* participants Raimund Girke and Tomas Rajlich. If Fundamental Painting is therefore part of Analytical Painting, it is a specific subcategory found in Northern Europe – England, the Benelux, and Germany – that strongly connects with New York Minimalism, which is at the opposite extreme of the analytical currents of other – especially Southern – European countries. (An interesting fact that we will see again and again, and a comparison which will be discussed at a later point.)

1.2.2 Elements of Fundamental Painting

Let us now take a closer look at this "new" and "fundamental" painting in the 1970s. The exhibition history mentioned in chapters 1.1.1, 1.2 and 1.2.1. indicates a wide and diverse range of painters and, one might say, it also indicates that curators were seeking a sensed novelty in painting at the time. Dippel noted in this context:

> The number of painters who concern themselves to a greater or lesser degree with various aspects of abstract painting has grown considerably over the past few years, both in America and in Europe.... Among the younger painters, there is a group which noticeably "follows" Newman. There are also several who are inspired by the informal art of the fifties, sometimes even with Neo-Abstract-Expressionist leanings. Both the cool as well as the emotional approach to painting are on the increase again. (FP 11)

An undated text entitled "Gereduceerde Schilderkunst" (Reductive Painting), contained in the *Fundamental Painting* exhibition archives of the Stedelijk Museum Amsterdam and paraphed by Rini Dippel, begins with the following comments:

> The painters participating in this exhibition are very different from each other. The reason that they are brought together is justified nonetheless by the fact that they all take painting very seriously, as a profession and as art, and focus on the basic inherent characteristics of painting. What is normally considered as simply the starting point or a means, in their work, becomes the aim. Viewed from the conventional way of thinking, this is a paradoxical situation.
>
> These painters very consciously reduce and rationally limit themselves to a certain number of essential matters in painting. This does not mean that no intuition is involved, nor that, as a result of this purely material approach, there would be no more "content." In the case of a few artists, one could even speak of a new, cool romanticism.... (1)[52]

As both Rini Dippel in 1975 and Giorgio Bonomi in 2004 mentioned, artists had been working in the non-objective vein since before 1972 – even going back well into the 1960s. Both curators also agreed that it is not a movement. Dippel called Fundamental Painting something of a mentality, and Bonomi seemed to agree in writing that Analytical Abstraction was not a formally defined group (FP 10 and Bonomi 17).[53] It should be remembered at this point that Italian curatorial and critical efforts continuously promoted Analytic painting, of which Fundamental Painting had often been considered a part. Yet, its specific delimitation from the larger whole has remained unclear until today. The organizers of Fundamental Painting had consciously and specifically excluded a large number of non-objective painters – especially the Italians and the French – in order to define and separate Fundamental Painting from other, non-objective currents around Europe in the 1970s.

In the catalogue text of *Fundamental Painting*, this approach is specified in detail. By explaining what Fundamental Painting is not, it manages to indicate what it is. The Italians and the French, who might have even been included in a number of other shows on the theme of 1970s non-objective painting, were excluded from the 1975 *Fundamental Painting* show for the following reasons: Italy occupied a special place, as commercial galleries were heavily promoting their artists by also including them in whatever current. Also, Italian artists occupied a special place, because they produced a "contained, pure painting in which white played a leading role" (apparently that of capturing the light) (11).

In the Italian works, color and light in combination with minimal shapes evoke a spatial illusion, which is often poetic. France, on the other hand, produced the only real group amongst the "new" painters, Supports/Surfaces, which had already disbanded by the time of the 1975 exhibition in Amsterdam. It included Vincent Bioulès, Daniel Dezeuze, Patrick Saytour, André Valensi, Claude Viallat, and Marc Devade. Their group magazine *Peinture, Cahiers Théoriques*, founded in 1971, examined painting from an ideological point of view under the direction of Louis Cane and Marc Devade. Fundamental Painting, as defined by the curatorial team of the Stedelijk Museum Amsterdam, is neither spatial and poetic nor based on an ideology. They also avoided all influence from commercial galleries. In the words of museum director Edy de Wilde:

> *Fundamental Painting* … seems to be the opposite [of the many breakthroughs and the expanding horizon of the art during the sixties]: a reflection on the foundations of painting…. These painters are not carrying on the results of a painterly tradition; they are looking for a new foundation on which to base painting. They employ the painterly means with the utmost sobriety, and attach an absolute importance to their points of departure. Relativity and humor are absent. (FP 1)

That was the new kind of painting that the 1975 exhibition was trying to describe. Further on in the catalogue, curator Rini Dippel specified that the new kind of painting entitled Fundamental Painting designates artists "who are involved first and foremost with the basic principles of painting. That is to say, those who restrict themselves in the most self-critical manner to the anti-illusionist painting, in which moreover all compositional elements are absent" (12).

Consequently, Fundamental Painting is, as summarized in Dippel's one-liner definition in the catalogue text, "involved first and foremost with the basic principles of painting" (12). Exhibiting artists were chosen as a representative selection of the "alternative" painters of the time who focused on the inherent elements of painting (10). As stated in her catalogue text to the 1975 *Fundamental Painting* exhibition, the common characteristics of the resulting artwork are as follows:

- The artist's choice of a neutral format, meaning a square or near square
- A good middle size that can be viewed easily over
- A human scale/relationship
- The choice of color, although important, shows a clear preference for neutral, sober colors, often limited to just one hue or layered so as to appear as one hue
- A non-indicative use of line, created by either a thin, linear gap formed by a real cleavage, a drawn line referring to the painting's edge, or even a grid pattern
- Consideration of form as figure
- Importance of texture, meaning a focus on the characteristics of the painterly materials used, in particular the paint or the woven support
- Consideration of the materials, painterly tools, and their effects
- The existence of a predefined, underlying process of creation, modified by intuition, which plays an equally important role

Visually the result is, as Dippel described it, "abstract, predominantly monochrome, mostly sober and muted paintings." Dippel continued to point out that these artists are interested in painting which is:

- "painting in a strict sense"
- "a flat plane"
- "without representation and without image" (10)

This entails an utmost limitation to non-objective, anti-illusionistic painting, without any compositional elements. Yet, this kind of painting is by no means simple. (Remember Dippel's specific statement for this kind of painting on the exclusion of terms indicating that which is reductive.) Its focus of interest is therefore on the traditional painterly materials and inherent elements of painting, which “are open to question once more” in every detail (FP 10). At the same time, the conceptual part and the process of painting have gained in importance. (Please note that Fundamental Painting in this respect indeed follows Douglas Crimp’s description of the work by the American Minimalist painters, around whom the exhibition was built, as Dippel wrote him in her letter of 2 July 1975; more about this in detail later.) Last but not least, this leads to the effect that Fundamental Painting solicits the regard of the beholders, even demands their attention much more than any realistic style of painting would.

In short, we can say that Fundamental painters are a group that shares not an ideology but a mentality. The latter did make Fundamental Painting a specific and clearly defined current in the painting of the 1970s. Its early works are often almost monochrome and sober in coloring. They are willingly anti-illusionist and non-objective without the slightest hint of compositional elements. They do not wish to be poetic but do have an interest in the absolute. They respect their two-dimensional surface and thus convey a concern for the foundations, or the formal aspects of painting and the painterly means. Accordingly, concept and process gain in importance.

As will become clear, Fundamental Painting concentrates strictly on typically painterly means and the pure essence of a painting. Elements like form, shape, structure, color, line, as well as materials and tools are all utilized towards this goal. The approach of Fundamental painters is a research into the inherent elements of painting unaltered by any rational composition or emotional expressiveness yet guided by intuition. Fundamental Painting demands the attentiveness of its beholder. What this concretely means in terms of painting will be revealed in further chapters through both visual and (sporadic) verbal statements from the artists.

1.2.3 Fundamental Painting does not equal Analytical Abstraction

At this point, for the sake of clarity, we should have a brief look at what Fundamental Painting is *not*. From an Italian perspective, Fundamental Painting seems to be interchangeable with “pittura pittura” (“painting as painting”) and Analytical Abstraction. From Rini Dippel’s framework, following the logical conclusion as understood by those who coined it, a description of Fundamental Painting excludes the creation of spatial illusions, poetics, as well as any ideological point of view (FP 11). Therefore – as announced by the exhibition catalogue and confirmed by later texts on the subject –, it excludes, in particular, all French and Italian non-objective painting of the same generation.

As mentioned already in the chapters on defining Fundamental Painting’s characteristics and upon coining the term, Italian curators and art critics seemed to consider this mentality as part of a larger whole. The definition of this whole is seemingly quite expansive, as is its name – notably summed up by the two terms "pittura pittura" ("painting as painting") and "astrazione analitica" (Analytical Abstraction). Giorgio Bonomi, curator of the show *Pittura70: Pittura Pittura e Astrazione Analitica* staged in Chiavari in 2004, defined it as follows: "'To re-found' or rather 'to redo' or, even better, only 'to make painting by painting': This is a common assumption of all the artists we examined, who find themselves … trying to start at point zero….". And, he continued: "Painting identifies itself with its own doing. The analysis on which all [works] are based … starts at the very moment at which the painting is formed." And, he finished by saying: "Still, and in sum, all the artists painters in the 1970s worked on the structures, the founding as well as fundamental elements of painting: Color, light, surface, sign, canvas, frame, entity, gesture, brushstroke, and the like."[54] An idea common to Fundamental Painting can be sensed. Yet, crucially, he also continued mentioning the fact that a dose of romanticism, lyricism, and "emotional tremor" is part and parcel of this kind of painting (18). This is in congruence with Dippel's mentioned difference, and it restricts Fundamental Painting once more to a very specific category within the whole of contemporary, non-objective, painterly expressions.

More specifically, in the catalogue of the above-mentioned Italian exhibition, art historian Bruno Corà listed the following characteristics for non-objective painting at large in the 1970s:

- A concern with process, in order to grasp the essence of painting in the interrelation of elements
- The active inherent antithesis of painting, creating contrasting phenomena, that is to say immateriality and spatiality, a color game that prevents accurate observation of the artist's brushstrokes (12)

In this context, let us remember the main points of the definition of Fundamental Painting that Rini Dippel gave in the catalogue text of the 1975 exhibition:

- Fundamental Paintings are often almost monochrome and sober in coloring, excluding the possibility of creating spatial illusions
- They are non-objective and non-poetic, existing on a flat plane
- Their raison d'être is the analysis of painting's formal basics by painterly means.
- They are absolute, excluding any compositional elements
- This kind of painting assigns relatively large importance to concept and process, modified by intuition, which plays an equally important role

The above five points highlighted by Dippel are almost the exact opposite of the two points highlighted by Corà, in terms of similar painterly characteristics.

Thus, while Dippel defined in detail the specific use of every element as a characteristic, Corà merely stated that the interrelation of painterly elements (which seems to relate to composition) is important to the Analytical painters. Both listed a heightened importance of process, while Dippel mentioned the importance of intuition in it. Therefore, Corà seems more lenient as to the former point, while Dippel seems so as to the latter. However, it is about the creation of what we can call atmosphere that Fundamental Painting and Analytical Abstraction basically differ: Corà's point on immateriality and spatiality (as well as Bonomi's allusions to painting's poetics) is directly opposed to Dippel's definition of Fundamental Painting. Once again, it has confirmed her impression of Italian artists' lyrical touch and spatiality, which the exhibition Fundamental Painting expressly excluded. It was even mentioned in the *Fundamental Painting* catalogue text as being specifically avoided – exactly because of this. (Also, Dippel cited Van Doesburg in relation to Fundamental Painting, who specified that a painting should be easy to reconstruct visually. This is an about-face from Corà's description of Analytical Painting.)

The term Analytical Painting has become a concept in Italy subsequent to Klaus Honnef's show *Geplante Malerei* (Planned Painting) of 1974 which included Fundamental artists Brice Marden, Robert Ryman, Raimund Girke, and Edda Renouf, as well as Jake Berthot and Jerry Zeniuk. A modified version of the exhibition – this time including Agnes Martin and Robert Mangold – entitled *Pittura Analitica* (Analytical Painting) was shown at Galleria del Milione in Milan around the end of 1974 and embedded the term into Italian art-historical vocabulary. Like Dippel, Klaus Honnef, at the point of writing the text for the catalogue *Analytische Malerei* (Analytical Painting) for the eponymous Italian show of 1974, saw and specifically pointed out a difference in Analytical Painting as executed by artists in Italy, France, Germany, Netherlands, and the USA.

He claimed that the autonomous painting is "the theoretical as well as practical investigation of the function of the character of art," which could apply to painting as painting but does not necessarily comprise only two-dimensional forms. Yet, he also defined it as a kind of painting "directed inwards." (Possibly, what he meant is that it is painting about painting with nothing from the outside world.) He considered Minimalist painters like Ryman and Marden to be the founding fathers of this kind of painting, which is "an elementary analysis by demonstrating painterly means (as independent carriers of expressions)." Honnef furthermore wrote in *Analytische Malerei*:

> The analytic painters investigate the verbal structures of paintings in the medium of art, and the penetrating of the verbal structures *a priori* forces them to restrict themselves to the painterly means. Consequently, an artistic work process becomes possible, which does not

> need to fall back on extra-medial categories. In this work process, subject and means of the analysis always remain identical, and what is analyzed is at the same time the instrument of the analysis. The analysis does not take place in the theoretic superstructure, but only in the production process of the investigation, whereas the theoretic inflexion is the embracing attempt of systematization, exclusively crystallized by the artistic practice. The analysis reconnaîtres [sic] the dependence of a painterly result, i.e. a painting, from the specific kind and composition of the means which are needed for its articulates [sic]. In "analytic painting" the artwork is realized as an open happening, its particular components become visible in the painterly result by virtue of the production process. In a strictly analytic method, the complex appearance of the artwork is divided into separate phenomena, so that their causal references come to view in their most elementary forms of cooperation.

So far, Honnef's description – in its ambiguous way – does seem to cover Dippel's definition. This would allow for the inclusion of several artists from *Fundamental Painting* in his show as well as in later shows of the Italians. However, it is non-descript on the kind of "phenomenon" the painting should or should not create. It will be this point that distinguishes some of the Fundamental works from the Analytical ones as described by Corà.

Furthermore, in his text for *Analytische Malerei*, Honnef defined eight criteria for Analytical Painting, the somewhat umbrella term for all kinds of new painting in the 1970s, including Fundamental Painting: The painting takes shape during the process (as opposed to being a concept merely executed), and solely the artist determines the fruition of this process. The painting becomes a "reflection about painting pictures," in which the process remains traceable. The painting shows a "dialectic relation between painterly materials" and is an "analytic, artist's statement."[55] The painting examines the language of painting, its structures and regularities, mechanisms and connections, while it is neither influenced by tradition nor favors any particular directives. Finally, the painting needs an "active observer," meaning an observer who actively perceives it with contemplation.

Honnef concluded that "The painterly results of 'analytic painting' are manifestations of visual thinking: They lead to an elementary, i.e. unusual way of seeing." Although less specific and detailed in description – notably leaving out any specific definitions on the individual painterly elements, materials, and tools –, Honnef's definition of Analytical Painting approaches Dippel's definition of Fundamental Painting. In fact, Honnef who coined the term "Planned Painting" for a new kind of analytical painting in the 1970s did not limit it to any poetic or emotional elements. This specification was made in the later text of Italian origin and often designated as "Analytical Abstraction." Yet, all of these shows (Honnef's from the mid-1970s as well as the more recent ones of Italian making) were differing arrangements of accumulated works of the most varied painterly results. Also, when scrutinizing the definition of "planned" or Analytical Painting, which are not defined specifically by Honnef yet specifically by Bonomi and Corà, a clear difference is visible – in particular between Fundamental Painting and the Italian kind of painting from the 1970s. Thus, we can safely say that a distinction can rightfully be made between Fundamental Painting and that of the more profuse German-Italian making.

Even if Fundamental Painting might fit into Analytical Painting in Honnef's original sense of the term, it remains an identifiable kind of painting found in the North of Europe, which strongly connects with 1960s New York Minimalism, and it is apparently the opposite of the Analytical currents of southern European countries – an interesting fact that we will come back to again and again. The organizers of the show *Fundamental Painting*, who wished to define the "new" current in painting of the 1970s – or at least one of the currents, keeping in mind that Fundamental Painting is not "nouvelle peinture," for example –, specifically excluded most of the artists proposed by Honnef and by the Italian curators from the well-defined, smaller group entitled Fundamental Painting. The latter group was made up of mainly northern European and American artists, whose works are of a more specific character.

Similarly, we may conclude that Fundamental Painting is a mentality which is rather specific to the Northern European (meaning artists from Great Britain, the Benelux region, and partially Germany) and American spirit, which excludes all and every reference to problems outside the painting medium. Fundamental Painting is void of sentimentality, illusions, poetics or ideologies. It is a painterly process strictly defined by the painterly essence of painting which is non-objective and two-dimensional, and based on the painter's intuition, void of any unnecessary peripheries. The fact that Fundamental Painting is a mentality (which by definition stays with a person throughout life) as well as a complex approach (beyond its apparent simplicity) calls for prolonged research. This is further supported by the fact that most pioneering Fundamental painters are still active today and still working within the same concerns, although the visual results have gained in freedom throughout the years.

Further chapters will show who are these painters that started their inquiries in this direction as early as 1972, and their works will be studied more closely. We will then see just how such a Fundamental work and its elements function. Furthermore, the "fundamentalness" of their processes as well as their resulting works will be verified, which will once again emphasize their distinction from the artists of Analytical Painting. Finally, we will outline the history and origin of this mentality.

2 THE IDENTITY OF FUNDAMENTAL PAINTING

Fundamental Painting is based on a defined set of elements and tools, which are both characteristic and necessary for such an approach. In the introductory text of the *Fundamental Painting* catalogue, Rini Dippel informed us that her definition of Fundamental Painting followed Douglas Crimp's description of the work by the American Minimalist painters in his groundbreaking article of 1973 entitled "Opaque Surfaces" in which he explained that:

> This muteness or blankness obtained in Opaque painting is the result of various strategies. These I want to enumerate tentatively under the terms of a narrow definition of painting as a surface exhibiting a particular *format, size, scale, color, line* and *texture*, all of these contingent on the *materials* used and the *manner* in which they are employed. Although we are concerned here with a group of painters of quite disparate tendencies, bound together almost exclusively by their commitment to anti-illusionism.... (258)

Both Dippel's emphasis on certain basic painterly elements being the sole focus of Fundamental Painting as well as her belief that it reflects more a mentality than a predefined group draw clear parallels with Crimp's description. Moreover, *Fundamental Painting* at the Stedelijk Museum in 1975 was built around not only the works but also the creators of Crimp's Opaque painting: Robert Mangold, Brice Marden, and Robert Ryman. Together with Agnes Martin, these painters who were central to the Amsterdam show would soon be dubbed the painters of Minimalism.

The painting of these four US artists is part of the American phenomenon called Minimal Art. However, this term primarily refers to three-dimensional works whereas these four artists are purely painters. What's more, they should (also) be included in the international phenomenon called Fundamental Painting. Supporting evidence for the common characteristics of Minimalist painting and Fundamental Painting at large comes to light when Rini Dippel's definition of Fundamental Painting is compared to the random definitions of Minimalist painting by authorities in the field. For example, in *Minimalism: Origins*, Edward Strickland defines Minimalism as "a style distinguished by severity of means, clarity of form, and simplicity of structure and texture" (4), while Dippel writes on Fundamental Painting that it is a "a basic commitment regarding the formal principles of painting," where the "canvas must be treated with human means, hence without complicated artificial devices" (FP 10 and 13). She also lists a number of neutral formats such as a rectangle or a square as characteristic of this kind of painting.

Strickland concisely details the characteristics of Minimalist painting as follows:

> Minimalism ... makes its statement with limited, if not the fewest possible, resources, an art that eschews abundance of compositional detail, opulence of texture, and complexity of structure..., monochromatic canvases ... gridded or otherwise diagrammatic paintings.... It tends towards non-allusiveness and decontextualization from tradition, impersonality in tone, and flattening of perspective through emphasis on surfaces (neutralization of depth cues in painting or of the space/substance...). (7)

This is reminiscent of Dippel's words expressing that Fundamental Painting's focus of interest is on the traditional painterly materials and inherent elements of painting, that "texture is characteristic for the material that is used to create the surface," and that "most of these artists ... restrict themselves to a single color." Fundamental Painting is "anti-illusionist painting, in which moreover all compositional elements are absent" (FP 14, 13 and 12). As for line, Dippel points out the novelty in comparison to its traditional use when she explains that: "Line is usually employed either to suggest an object in space, or to delineate space itself.... However, for these painters line constitutes the edge of the form of the canvas, or it is a reference to that edge...." She discusses Martin's grids to illustrate her point. Moreover, while trying to explain Fundamental Painting, she cites point five of Van Doesburg's manifesto: "The technique employed must be mechanical, i.e. exact, anti-impressionist" (FP 14 and 12).

Thus, Fundamental Painting limits itself to the utmost anti-illusionist concerns i.e. "painting in a strict sense: on a flat plane, without representation and without image." Nevertheless, this definition by Dippel should be read in combination with the opening quote by Robert Morris from her catalogue text: "Simplicity of shape does not necessarily equate with simplicity of experience" (FP 10). This painterly commitment to Fundamental Painting – Dippel states over and over again in her texts on Fundamental Painting – is not a defined group of artists but a mentality. Likewise Strickland notes: "The painters ... had little in common in terms of their aesthetic; what they shared was an impulse ... to formal and stylistic purification of means in order to determine how much or how little was essential" (24). Thus, both formal elements and mentality together form the framework for Fundamental Painting as well as for Minimalist painting on both sides of the Atlantic. (For this reason, besides referring to Rini Dippel and her role model, Douglas Crimp, this study will refer to Minimal Art specialist Edward Strickland – as well as to Frances Colpitt, the authority on the critical perspective of Minimal Art, who in her book *Minimal Art: A Critical Perspective* similarly points out that "the artists ... never considered themselves as being a group" [3]).

In this context, the words of Robert Pincus-Witten – written three years before the show *Fundamental Painting* and a year before Crimp's publication – come to mind. His article "Ryman, Marden, Manzoni: Theory, Sensibility, Mediation" in *Artforum*

June 1972, explains what painting like that of Ryman or Marden is similar: "Ryman is interested in painting as theory…. Marden, on the other hand, is interested in painting as the expression of sensibility and as a result, he is committed to maintaining an inherited tradition. Both artists have concentrated their issues so closely, however, that they can be viewed as the opposing faces of a problematical region of discourse" (50). He goes on to explain that their painting can be considered as issuing from not only the painting of Malevich and Mondrian but also that of Agnes Martin. Hence, Martin (who is indeed a generation older than Mangold, Marden, and Ryman) would mark the beginning of Fundamental Painting, while the younger New York Minimalists would delineate a range of possibilities within Fundamental Painting. Accordingly, Dippel writes in her text for the catalogue of the show *Fundamental Painting* that "the paintings of Ryman, Marden, Mangold and Martin may be seen as the introductions to the four 'chapters' in the exhibition" (10).

2.1 Elements and tools of Fundamental Painting

The exhibition *Fundamental Painting* shows a subdivision into several categories of Fundamental Painting – reminiscent of Douglas Crimp and notably Robert Pincus-Witten. Such a grouping into two strands of Fundamental Painting, then further into subgroups of these, becomes apparent from the various curators' notes (see chapter 1.1.). On the one hand, there is a sort of "core group" around Ryman and Marden that explores the material used and how paint is applied. On the other hand, there is an opposing, more "painterly," group around Martin and Mangold that strongly emphasizes the shape of the canvas and the figure on the canvas, categorized under the term "form/sign."

The core group includes three subcategories. One is entitled "more or less monochrome" including Ryman (assigned the terms "paint/technique" and "medium/canvas"), Girke (listed as "working optically"), Berghuis (simply called "color"), and Smits, as well as Richter (as part of the "historical context" or "surrounding group"). The second is labeled "concerning the plane." It comprises Marden (indicated by the word *surface*), Zeniuk, and Berthot (referred to as "frame/edge"). The third is dubbed "focus on color" and includes Jackson (associated with the words *color* and *environment*) and Van Koningsbruggen (associated with "non-color" and "positive/negative form").

The latter more painterly group is likewise divided into subcategories. The first is called "grid," formed around Agnes Martin. It includes Rosenthal (with the additional mention "lines/grid"), Renouf (referenced as "grid of the structure"), and Rajlich (said to be "between Martin and the real painters" meaning "between Ryman and Martin"). The second is "figure/shape" which includes Mangold (with the mention "shape of the canvas and figure on the canvas") and Charlton (the keyword here being *ratios*).

Cane is listed separately in a subcategory called "canvas/figure." It is unclear which of the two main groups he belongs to. Considering the curators' preliminary exhibition notes, he most probably was meant to be part of the core group. (Wéry is not included in the preliminary divisions. Yet, based on the final exhibition layout, she is apparently associated with the second group.) (See Fig. 1)

Hence, several subgroups have joined the four core divisions around the four Minimalists. The main categories "monochrome" (around Ryman) "plane" (around Marden), "grid" (around Martin) and "figure" (around Mangold) are joined by the somewhat more general category of "color." Following the above logic, and in line with Pincus-Witten's concept of Ryman and Marden's denoting the opposite sides of Fundamental Painting's range, with Martin being considered the most painterly artist: The second main group built around Agnes Martin should lead back to the core group (also the first main category). However, it is not to be confused with the group representing the historical context, which includes Malevich and Mondrian, as presented in the educative room and by the works from the collection hung in further museum spaces. The actual hanging of the show – although also largely determined by space and size issues – follows this categorization relatively well (Fig. 2), albeit in reverse order.

The works by Ryman introduce the show. Richter and Van Koningsbruggen are put side by side. Marden leads to Girke and Zeniuk. Berthot's work is grouped with Berghuis and Smits, while Rajlich and Jackson each occupy a space of their own. Cane is contrasted with Charlton. They, in turn, give access to works by Mangold. Works by Rosenthal, Wéry, Renouf, and Martin, each hung in a separate room, close the show. (Please note also that Rajlich is mentioned several times as "in between Martin and Ryman." Accordingly, his works, which form a link between these two main groups, are hung at a turning point in the exhibition's itinerary.)

However, we should keep in mind that this division into subcategories is a curatorial, art-historical endeavor. While comparing and contrasting the various working notes of the curators, which are kept in the archives of the Stedelijk Museum Amsterdam at the City Archives, we can see that the subdivisions were shifted from time to time – even though the final choice of Fundamental painters saw relatively few changes in the later phases of preparation. This is not too surprising, due to the nature of Fundamental Painting. As Dippel claims, it is a specific mentality; and the nature of this mentality is that all Fundamental painters work with the basic painterly elements. Yet, while sharing a common mindset of working on canvas with painted brushstrokes and possibly including some line drawing, they each create according to their very personal approach. Dippel communicates this very clearly in her introductory text when writing:

> The four 'chapters' in the exhibition mentioned earlier should be interpreted in very general terms. Every classification is artificial, and this one, based as it is upon visually

> observable results, certainly is. As far as the mentality is concerned, painters who seem at first to be poles apart may well have a close affinity, while conversely an external similarity can only be superficial. (FP 12)

Rather than following the above curatorial categories, let's have a closer look at the Fundamental painters' painterly elements listed by Dippel. This will allow us to discover their individual use of the basic elements: format, size, scale, color, non-indicative line, form as figure, and texture. Dippel also lists the use of painterly materials and tools, a process that is predefined but modified by intuition, the tendency towards flatness in composition, the paintings' non-objective nature, and finally, the effect on the viewer of Fundamental Painting. The "artificial" categories proposed by Dippel seem indeed to define a very specific kind of painting that reflects the mentality called Fundamental Painting (which – not to forget – issues from and at the same time includes Minimalist painting). Her categories combine both European and American results, fit the historical framework, and reflect the American concepts published on this kind of painting.

2.1.1 Format

As a first fundamental element for "painting qua painting in a strict sense," Dippel notes: a neutral format, meaning a square or a "near-square" rectangle (FP 10 and 12). She does not specify why, although this is a crucial consideration when contemplating Fundamental Painting. In his referential article, Crimp writes that "[o]f all rectangles, the square is undoubtedly the least allusive, the most neutral" (258). When the format is (almost) square, it has a lack of conventional orientation. It neither incites a horizontal nor a vertical reading, the way rectangular formats do. Namely, the Western viewer will see a rectangular painting within the context of the European history of painting. As Göran Hermerén states in *Representation and meaning in the visual arts*: "There is no 'innocent' eye; seeing is an active process, not a passive one, and it involves interpretation" (37). Even if unconsciously, such a viewer associates any rectangular format with the traditional landscape format or a typical (full-size) portrait painting.

In 1974, one year before the exhibition *Fundamental Painting*, art critic Barbara R. Reise wrote in reference to the square:

> [It] is certainly a "known" image: it has existed as a man-made construct since before the earth-measurement geometry of Euclid, "proved" by Pythagoras. Since that time it has been more apparent in cartography and architecture than in the visual arts, where it has had little structural or meaningful significance outside the art of ancient and imperial Rome, Albers and the 1960s New York art of André, Flavin, LeWitt, Mangold, Agnes

> Martin, and Ryman. Perhaps this is related to the peculiar character of the square as stable, mute, inert: self-centering itself powerfully as something "other".... Certainly it is unlike the circle, triangle, and rectangle, – whose geometric shapes have accrued cultural association with infinity, the trinity, death, human verticality, and the horizon(tality) of landscapes. The square somehow remains an extraordinary primary abstraction of physicality: and as such it is perfectly sympathetic.... (32-33)

In fact, the square is perfectly compatible with the Fundamental painters as a presence in and of itself. It functions as an *alter ego* to the viewer – just like Michael Fried claimed in his 1967 text "Art and Objecthood," where he compared Minimalist artworks to "the silent presence of another person" (16). The viewer of the (square) work can enter into a visual dialogue with it on a primary level of reality ("face-to-face"), not as with something requiring a sequential reading, representing something else or something beyond.[56]

Also Frances Colpitt, a contemporary authority on Minimalist painting, agrees with Dippel on this preference for the neutral format and touches specifically upon the formal characteristic of it, when writing in retrospect that "painters of the sixties shared a commitment to the single unified image," and specifying "(the rectangle ... being the most satisfactorily neutral)..." (35). Hence, the neutral format correlates to the "unified image." Colpitt refers to the book *Art and Visual Perception: The New Version* from 1974 – almost contemporary with *Fundamental Painting* –, where Rudolf Arnheim discussed this instantaneous function in art as being parallel to Gestalt theory of perception. This is reminiscent of writings on Minimal Art from the late 1960s which often referred to Gestalt, notably texts written by Minimalist sculptor Robert Morris, in particular, his "Notes on Sculpture" (See Colpitt 97-98).

The word *Gestalt* in German means "shape" or "configuration," as in the essence of an entity's complete form. In Gestalt theory, recognizing a commonly known shape is part of the fundamental nature of human perception, not a result of deduction. (Remember Reise's mention of the square being a "known" format.) It therefore follows that, based on Gestalt, Fundamental Painting with its square, near-square or rectangle format – visually simple forms from geometry – is not only instantly perceived but also instantly recognized as such. Such an observation infers that a Fundamental painting is right there, in front of the viewer. It is at once completely within the viewer's field of vision, notably due to the basic fact that a canvas is a two-dimensional surface. It immediately communicates its form with all its *drum und dran* ("lock, stock and barrel") to the viewer

From this initial "unified image" impression, the interplay of painterly elements unfolds over time. This concept of an instant, unified – or rather unitary – first impression followed by a slow unfolding and discovery is in line with the Gestalt theory of perception, which actively strives for unity and order thereby claiming that vision goes from the general to the particular and not the other way around. At the same time, this effect relates to Theo van Doesburg's *Manifesto of Concrete Art*, cited by Dippel, that reads (point 4): "The construction of the painting, as indeed that of its elements, must be simply and visually verifiable" (Qtd. in FP 12). The painting should be recognizable at first glance as well as form a unity, meaning that all elements work together so that no painterly element predominates. In this context, we note that the saying, "The whole is greater than the sum of the parts," is often cited as the essence of Gestalt theory. Similarly in Fundamental Painting, the various painterly elements and results surface over time after the initial "general view" of the painting as a particular format has been grasped. This is what Fundamental painter Robert Mangold in an interview with his wife Sylvia Plimack Mangold called the "seeing-viewing-experiencing" process (60) – which will be explored more in detail as this study progresses.

Thus, the choice of format plays a central role in Fundamental Painting. Although the square had already been utilized by former painters for various reasons throughout the history of art, it is appreciated by Fundamental painters in the mid-1970s as an easily accessible, neutral format. This was the case, as Crimp notes on format, in Minimalist painting (and therefore by extension also in Fundamental Painting): "One senses immediately that shape has been brought under control by these artists. It is not arbitrary, but instead exists in a fixed relation to the strategies at work.... [F]or Opaque painting, the format is predetermined by the necessities of opacity and how best to achieve it" (258).

With "opacity," Crimp means the way the other elements unfold after the initial visual contact with the painting, in order to achieve "the painted *equivalent* of sculpture's objecthood, i.e. surfaceness ... to give to the painted surface an equivalent literalness to that which Minimalism had imparted to the sculptural object" (258). Colpitt makes a similar remark when writing: "Because ... most paintings [are] flat, relations are forced out of internal structure to surface and shape" (75). Surfaceness, referring to the flat nature of a painting by definition, is a recurring term in Crimp's article which merits detailed discussion to establish its relation with the other internal elements in Fundamental Painting. These choices of format, their workings, and the results will be shown as this study progresses in revealing the painterly elements in Fundamental Painting.

First, let's see how considerations on format manifest themselves in the works exhibited at *Fundamental Painting*. In relation to the works of Robert Ryman – the pivotal figure in the *Fundamental Painting* show – which are always square or near-square, Robert Storr explained in a 1993 catalogue on the artist that "the obvious focal point implied by the coordinates running between the four equal sides of four equal corners, allow him to operate around and especially off the center without ever requiring him to fix it in any explicit way" (17). This slow revelation of the painterly elements is therefore also a result of the un-centering of the square canvas, which in its turn relies on the compositional all-over aspect or balancing act with painterly elements. At the same time, the square format "prevents readings of a fictive extendibility" (Crimp, 258). The viewer's attention stays on the painted surface.

Moreover, Martin, Rajlich, and Wéry work with near-square formats, which function in a similar way. However, when the artists add a painted or drawn grid, their work becomes, in the viewer's mind, infinitely extendable in space. Wéry arrives at a similar effect through horizontal line structures. These painters insist on this "fictive extendibility" that Ryman thwarts by keeping the support visible in order to emphasize the factual object (the artwork) and its flatness. (Renouf, in turn, keeps the grid-like weave of the canvas visible.) This is why Dippel, in her notes on "Gereduceerde Schilderkunst," positions Rajlich "between Ryman and Martin" (1). Rajlich combines both systems. Besides using a grid like Martin, his works have an unpainted edge with dripping lines of paint at the bottom, similar to Ryman's.

Stephen Rosenthal's picture planes, left without stretchers, are loosely hung on the wall to announce their materiality in a similar way, although this somewhat contradicts the flatness of the painted plane. Then again, Jerry Zeniuk and Raimund Girke work, as Ryman does, emphasizing the "surfaceness" of the painted plane inside a rectangular format. Their formats are clearly vertical rectangles. This still leaves them neutral. Yet they can be associated with a traditional full-length portrait for the European viewer.

In relation to the rectangular format, it is interesting to note that Gerhard Richter spontaneously expands on the concept of format in his artist's statement for the *Fundamental Painting* show:

> I use [the technique] in its most conventional form (oil paint on canvas on a wooden stretcher) and therewith accept the usual definition of a rectangular plane as the carrier of images to be hung on straight walls in artificial spaces (architecture) – easily viewed over and well lit. Painting is as little affected by this as literature is by its usual binding….[57]

Although it seems as if it is a conscious denial of the importance of format which is so characteristic for Fundamental Painting, this statement can also be read as an acceptance of the most "fundamental" format of painting – the rectangle.

As for Brice Marden, who likewise uses rectangles – both horizontal as well as vertical –, Crimp notes another interesting functioning of this format: "the possibility of extendibility of surface is vitiated by the use of polyptychs whose panels refer only to one another" (258). It is another safeguard to avoid the painting creating an illusion or feeling beyond that of the two-dimensional object. Jaap Berghuis, Kees Smits, and Robert Mangold also use multi-panel arrangements. Marden's principle is likewise echoed in Alan Charlton's *Paintings with a Central, Vertical Division*. In his so-called channel paintings of 1974, Charlton took the "framing" a step further, when he enclosed the "image" in a gray rectangular, central panel within a second panel which took on the role of the frame.

The viewer unconsciously associates this with the Renaissance tradition of Leon Battista Alberti's "window onto the world," searching for a scene "beyond" the canvas plane within the boundaries of the frame like looking through a window. In this light, it is not surprising that instead of writing a statement for the exhibition catalogue Charlton chose to quote fellow artist Alberto Giacometti: "The adventure, the great adventure, is to see something unknown appear each day, in the same view. That is greater than any journey round the world" (Qtd. in FP 26).

By leaving an equally wide space between the canvas shaped like a frame and the central canvas, Charlton both contradicts and comments on the traditional way of seeing art. While anchoring the work firmly in the viewer's space, he points out the realness of the physical canvas – the "objecthood" of the work (see also 3.2.1). As Rini Dippel wrote in her notes "Gereduceerde Schilderkunst": "Alan Charlton's painting functions as a bas-relief, for which the choice of formats and their ratios are essential."[58]

Similarly, Jake Berthot, Louis Cane, and Edda Renouf all insert a kind of frame-like border into their painted planes. The plane inside the drawn rectangle which is parallel to the painting's edges reads as a picture within a frame. Their paintings refer to painting's traditional format and likeness, while positioning themselves as an object; as the visual frame is exactly the same in color and structure as the plane inside, frame and painted plane must exist on the same level – as an object in the viewer's reality.

Richard Jackson, then again, works in the opposite way. He fuses the painting directly with the wall in order to make it part of the viewer's space. He also sticks the study (a drawing) onto the painted wall as well as the piece of canvas on stretchers he has used to smear the paint across the plane. The viewer instantly recognizes the reversed canvas as a painting and the drawing as an artwork although they are not. With these attributes, Jackson's painting becomes somewhat of a three-dimensional entity, where it is unclear which is the actual artwork. As Dippel writes in her notes "Gereduceerde Schilderkunst," Jackson is "[t]he only artist in the exhibition, who creates a kind of environment" (2).[59]

In the curators' notes to the exhibition *Fundamental Painting*, there seems to be some confusion regarding format – the outer shape of the artwork (canvas) – and form – as in any painted or drawn figure. They made numerous notes on the artists mentioned under the category entitled "form/sign" which, in particular, refers to the painterly group represented in the second half of the exhibition's itinerary. This group is divided into the subcategories entitled "figure/form" and "grid" (both largely referring to the use of line). Yet, Rini Dippel mentioned

Robert Mangold – next to Charlton – as those who are still working with form. She wrote: "Robert Mangold: ..., pure concentration on the shape of the canvas and the figure on the canvas; basic metric forms – the square and the circle and parts thereof – and the possibilities of these within the chosen framework of the format of the painting..." (1).[60]

Mangold has a highly individual way of handling a format other than a neutral square or rectangle. In fact, he uses the workings of perception in order to question format and form. The outline of the shaped canvas interacts with the drawn figure on the canvas in order to confuse the viewer. Regular geometrical shapes are seen initially, then at a second glance, the shapes push and pull against each other, distorting one another. Circles are broken. Squares are skewed. Visually the "seeing-viewing-experiencing" process, as the artist calls it (Schiff 60), questions the way of seeing, the knowledge of geometrical forms, and how they "fit" together – the correctness of the composition.

In a similar fashion, Dippel in her notes on "Gereduceerde Schilderkunst" categorized Van Koningsbruggen under *format*, specifically as working with "positieve en negatieve vorm" ("positive and negative form;" 2). In Van Koningsbruggen's canvases, the original painted form is always stamped on an adjoining canvas, repeating itself or creating its opposite. The form indeed dominates the painting as a figure on a ground. What's more, some of his paintings are not rectangular but shaped – into other geometric forms. Their edges might echo the shape of the geometric form within. Yet, as these shaped canvases are neither small, medium, nor monumental, they function rather like a sign on the wall.

All in all, it can be said that the Fundamental painters impose strict limits on format (as well as on painted or drawn form). They opt for the neutral, unified canvas, which allows for activating the picture plane through decentralization, while occasionally applying multi-panel groupings in order to keep the painting within its painterly medium. Similarly, the frame as traditional delimitation between the real world of the viewer and the imaginary world of the canvas-as-window is explored as a means of delimiting the painting. The "right" choice of format – as already hinted at in relation to the decentralized reading of Ryman's squares and to the works by Robert Mangold – makes the increase in the play of differences within the format possible.

At the same time, repetition – that is, exploring the same format (for example, the square canvas) over and over again, using also the same other constants (the painterly elements) over and over again – allows for the maximum difference between the results while using the same painterly proposition. In Fundamental Painting, the constraint of a fixed number of constants (in the form of the chosen painterly elements) does not limit the difference but rather exacerbates the multiplication of variables, encouraging differences in results. That's why Fundamental painters often stay true to their chosen format over the years. Their work becomes a research on painting itself, explored through a single hypothesis tried out in a serial or modular fashion.

2.1.2 Size and scale

The question of size goes hand in hand with that of format and is, according to Rini Dippel, the second most significant characteristic of Fundamental Painting. She notes that Fundamental Painting often uses a medium size that can be easily taken in all at once. This is not surprising when we consider that the desired effect of the initial glance – as previously discussed – is one of instantaneously perceived unity, in line with the Gestalt theory of perception that Fundamental Painting seems to at least remotely follow. Dippel writes: “No enormous canvases à la Pollock and Newman (with the exception of Cane), in which one can and must lose oneself, but neither are there easel paintings. The size of the works is usually aligned to human proportions” (FP 13). The format accordingly needs to fit within the viewer’s field of vision. Yet at the same time, it must be accessible up close to allow for a slowly unfolding exploration of the canvas which is crucial to Fundamental Painting’s “seeing-viewing-experiencing” process – as will be detailed later on.

Dippel’s role model in the field of Fundamental Painting, Douglas Crimp, obviously included the same characteristic when he wrote about the size:

> Almost without exception the size of Opaque painting is midway between the easel picture and the mural-size canvas; it is less easy, therefore, to see these surfaces in the terms of Alberti’s “open window” or the engulfing ambiguous space of recent formalism.... Because of Opaque painting’s inherent suspicion of painting itself, it constantly attempts to situate itself outside the expected conditions of traditional painting, whether that tradition be considered in terms of the Renaissance or the early 1960s. (258)

Thus, not only a neutral format but also a neutral size are considerations that Fundamental Painting has, in order to set itself off from the painting that came before it. This way, Fundamental Painting can better approach its new objective of “surfaceness.”

A wall text in the 2011 exhibition at the Kunstmuseum The Hague quoted Marthe Wéry as saying: “[When you paint something big] you can really experience the victory over the surface as a means of expression in the most basic sense of the term.” Both shape and size, therefore, are “brought under control” by the Fundamental artist to enhance “surfaceness.” Dippel writes that “big” in Fundamental Painting terms rather means human size in height and width which should engage the viewer’s entire field of vision – as opposed to the dimensions needed for Abstract Expressionist canvases that engulf the viewer:

> Working on a large scale was essential for painters like Newman in order to evoke the infinite, the "Abstract Sublime." These [Fundamental] painters of today [1975] relate to the painting in a very different way…. They confine themselves to sizes which bear a specific relation to the human body – without any deeper, hidden significance, however. Their attitude is very practical: the canvas must be treated with human means, hence without complicated artificial devices. (FP 13)

As for considerations of size, however, the perceived dimensions (the scale) are, for the artist, more consequential than the actual ones, since scale is felt rather than empirically measured. It is the viewer's experience of the object that determines scale. Frances Colpitt, an authority on Minimalist painting, postulates on this subject: "The loose restriction to human size, however, has less to do with anthropomorphism than with scale. By presenting an object about the same size as the spectator, a more active relationship is established between the two" (70). By using the size to convey a scale similar to the spectator, a sense of one-to-one dialogue is evoked – like two beings in private conversation, neither dominating nor engulfing the other. [61]

This can also mean small-size paintings. Namely, a larger object includes more of the space around itself than does a smaller one, as Minimalist Robert Morris wrote in his "Notes on Sculpture" (Part 2, 218-19). Smaller paintings are more intimate, inciting a more private relationship with their viewer. As Colpitt puts it: "Smaller objects force the spectator into a closer physical appreciation of detail or 'surface incident'" (87-88). Out of this consideration, Fundamental Painting relates to human size – without necessarily mimicking the latter, but by creating a dialogue between the painting and its viewer.

Already in the spring of 1974, Barbara R. Reise explained this in an article published in the magazine *Data*:

> Scale is a relational property of physicality. It has to do with the degree of interval, the difference in size, between things…. [A]s it is in the long Renaissance tradition, that "scale" is based on the humanistic pictorial mirror or hand-to-arm-to-body-to-painting (or sculpture) relationships of size; [today, in the mid-1970s] rather it is the parameters of the painting, the *thing-itself*, which gives the basic size against which everything else is relative. "Everything else" can be the size of a single brush used over the whole surface, or the ridges of impasto left from between stiff bristles of a brush, … or the wall or the room of the painting, installation, or even the different size of another similar "thing-self." (35)

Once again, the Fundamental artist's choice seems to lead to Crimp's so-called surfaceness. Crimp writes on scale:

> Traditionally, scale has functioned aesthetically in both real and illusionist senses.... In Opaque painting there is no fictive scale because one cannot enter into a relationship of imaginative proportion with the painting. Staying on the surface, one is aware only of real scale, the proportion of the painting to one's self; and it is precisely this appropriately one-to-one ratio which Opaque painting exploits by limiting itself to the size of the human figure. (258)

Thus, in the paintings of Agnes Martin and Tomas Rajlich, which are (near) square and where the entire picture plane is covered by a grid pattern, the notion of scale takes on a whole new dimension: namely that the modules relate to each other. Firstly, the actual canvas as a square is seen as a final large-scale repetition of the grid module. Secondly, the individual module relates to the expansion of a rectangle made of several modules. The smaller the grid modules are, the smaller the evoked scale is. (In the works of Martin and Rajlich, these grid modules are only a few centimeters square.) This kind of reading is achieved by using modules traced by hand, which draw the attention of the viewer into the painting (or rather across its surface). In their industrial-looking yet hand-drawn grids, "there are infinitesimal differences in the lines and edges, but all of them subordinate to the repetition of the grid," as Briony Fer once remarked (47). The small size of the module therefore turns the human-size painting into a more intimate encounter, the way a small-scale painting would. This offers a perfect combination of both the use of scale in terms of a good middle size as described above and the advantage of small works in approaching "surfaceness" to the maximum.

All the canvases in *Fundamental Painting* (except those of Louis Cane, who works with a monumental scale, and Richard Jackson, who creates something of an environment) have a human scale. The works by Berthot, Girke, Mangold, Marden, Martin, Rajlich, Richter, Ryman, and Zeniuk all more or less reflect a person's height and rarely surpass the width of outstretched arms. Ryman, Rajlich and Martin also create small-sized works, while Renouf, Rosenthal, and Wéry tend to work on smaller, more intimate paintings in general. Berghuis and Smits work with smaller, adjoined panels, which again associates the painting with human scale. Van Koningsbruggen's works are neither really small nor human scale but rather something in-between. This is in line with this artist's own view that he does not belong in the exhibition *Fundamental Painting*, as an undated note sent by Rini Dippel to Edy de Wilde concerning an inlay into the exhibition catalogue reveals.

Thus, in Fundamental Painting, scale is human for the sake of its one-to-one dialoguing quality. The initial view is that of a unitary, human-scale entity presenting itself in the viewer's space. Subsequently, a visual dialogue unfolds between the painting and the viewer as two equal entities. The painting does not create an atmosphere but presents itself as a kind of *alter ego*. The viewer is face to face with a flat plane without any internal scale as there is no longer a "window onto the world" (as there was in figurative painting with a linear perspective).

Consequently, the scale in Fundamental Painting is external to the work, determined by the viewer's relation to the (very real) painted surface. Its size and internal elements are actively used for their ability to create scale, in a way that promotes a detailed reading of the painting. Notably, the grid with its dual character (modular and at the same time expansive) has unlimited potential to create this desired intimate dialogue with human dimensions. An intimate size and scale are opted for, in order to trigger the viewer's contemplation of the details in the painting in front of him. The viewer is dialoguing, as it were, with the work on the subject of the painterly elements and ultimately on painting as painting.

2.1.3 Color

According to Rini Dippel, the third characteristic of Fundamental Painting is color. She writes that the Fundamental painters prefer neutral, sober hues appearing in monochromatic combinations, more specifically:

> When different colors are used in juxtaposition, they tend to suggest various layers of depth. Most of these artists, whose object is to make the plane exist as a plane, restrict themselves to a single color. When more than one color is used, they either occupy a field of their own (Marden) and/or are applied in successive layers. A monochrome, muted surface often conceals numerous layers of color. Some painters (Marden and Berghuis) make this method very explicit at the edge (lower or sides). (FP 13)

Edward Strickland, a specialist on the origins of Minimal Art, agrees that: "Specifically in painting, recurrent Minimalist qualities are … monochromaticism…" (23). He specifies further that: "A single pigment might be applied uniformly across the entire surface" (12). Yet, this preference for neutral hues does not mean that the choice of color is unimportant – on the contrary.

The choice of color is well thought out, in order to respect or even assure the unity of the flat picture plane. As Frances Colpitt, who is the reference on painting of the 1960s and 1970s, declared: "Color was not decorative, expressive, or symbolic, but an integral aspect of formal definition" (29). Color – or the lack thereof – is an important element in the perception of Fundamental Painting. The non-colors of a Fundamental Painting are preferred for their "resistance to interpretation" (Colpitt, 29). They are chosen precisely to avoid any mimetic, emotional, symbolic or metaphorical function. Dippel writes: "For Ryman, Martin and Girke this means using predominantly white, for Marden it is blues, grays, ochres, for Richter,

Charlton, Smits, it is gray, for Berthot green-gray, for Zeniuk gray-black and brown shades" (FP 13).

The exception to the rule is Marden's use of several colors. His painted panels are unmistakably colored and juxtaposed in such a way that incites an associative and spatial reading *a priori*. This is, in turn, neutralized by the non-specificity of the colors as well as by the cleavage lines separating adjoined panels, in order to emphasize that the painted plane is indeed a flat object. The other Fundamental artists use color differently.

For example, "Mangold's colors are unusual but specific….", as Dippel writes in her notes entitled "Gereduceerde Schilderkunst" (2).[62] His paintings are yellow, blue, red and the like; however, they are neutral in their associative qualities. As the titles of his very early mature works indicate, their planes are reminiscent of redbrick walls or the areas of sky visible between buildings. His other hues are commonplace like paper-bag beige, for instance. The choice is made in view of its commonness, while the hues (especially in combination with the shapes of and on the canvas) act as a trigger for the viewer to perceive them unconsciously with an associative richness.

Fundamental Painting participant Marthe Wéry, whose works have relatively pure basic colors, followed a similar strategy. Wall texts at a recent exhibition quoted her saying: "I need to use color as a spur…," and she continued: "Nothing in the world is as familiar to us as colors: they give the world form, depth and beauty. But nothing is as ambiguous as the words we use to describe and compare our perception of color." Again, this is a reference to the simultaneously associative yet non-specific qualities of colors. Agnes Martin's works are limited to pastel tints of red, yellow, blue and gold. Their application is highly transparent like watercolor on a dense white ground, imbuing the works with a hardly visible color aura. Also, some of Louis Cane's canvases are chromatic color planes in brown, dark purple or even muted shades of the primaries, next to black. Lastly, Richard Jackson created a work in the exhibition space, composed of "brightly-painted canvases to form new paintings in a process which emphasizes the physical identity of the painting" (FP 13). As Dippel admits: "This exhibition [did] not go so far in its fundamentalist approach as to refuse to 'admit' some exceptions as far as the use of color is concerned" (FP 13).

In fact, as Dippel wrote in "Gereduceerde Schilderkunst": "All mentioned artists do use color, but often in a 'hidden' way…. Zeniuk uses colors like red and blue, but processes them into grays, Ryman uses colors underneath his whites…" (2).[63] Frances Colpitt specified about painting in the Fundamental era: "More prominent were neutral or industrial colors that had no natural or emotional associations, but were rich in their reductive subtlety" (28-29). The most powerful interference can be achieved with flanking (like Marden's), while the color underlying a non-color as well as the non-color gray *per sé* – as used by other Fundamental artists – creates this "reductive subtlety."

An understanding of how color perception works is needed in order to really understand this. Light, which travels in the form of waves, stimulates our visual perception faculties, making us perceive these as color. Color has three basic elements: hue, chroma (saturation) and value (brightness). Hue issues directly from the difference in wavelength. It is linked to saturation, which indicates the level of purity of a color – the higher the complexity of wavelengths, the more distinct the color (or chroma). Finally, color has a value, also called brightness. It designates the luminance of an object, meaning the amount of light reflected by the colored surface. In painting, there are three primary hues: red, yellow and blue. All other hues of the spectrum can be composed by mixing these three primary colors. Adding white or black paint modifies their value, creating a tint or a shade respectively. Chromatic colors are subject to all three attributes, while achromatic colors (white, gray and black) when pure do not have any hue, just saturation and brightness.

Non-colors are nevertheless recognized as unique in human perception. Besides, they seem to approximate chromatic colors in the way human beings perceive them, depending on their surroundings. Gray seems to be the most prone to this, as in terms of paint it is rarely a truly achromatic mixture between pure white and black. The human eye can detect even the slightest hint of color. For example, Gerhard Richter speaks of this discovery when discussing his dynamically brushed gray canvases in his letter to Edy de Wilde:

> As I painted a few canvases gray in the beginning (about eight years ago), I did it, because I did not know what to paint or what there was to paint; and it was clear to me while doing it, that such a sorry reason could only have senseless results as a result. However, in time I noticed qualitative differences between the gray planes as well as that these did not show anything of the destructive motivation. The paintings started educating me. By generalizing the personal dilemma, they annulled it; the misery became a constructive statement, of relative perfection and beauty, thus painting.
>
> Gray. It simply has no message; it neither triggers emotions nor associations; it is neither visible nor invisible really. It tends to communicate un-obviousness so well, to represent it, and in such a way that is almost illusionist, just like a photographic image. And it is adapted as no other color to represent "nothing."
>
> To me, gray is the welcome and only possible reference to indifference, refusal of speech, lack of opinion, lack of presence. But because gray – just like a lack of presence etc. – can only be real as an idea, I can only produce a hue that means gray but is not. The painting then is a mixture of gray as fiction and gray as visible, proportioned color plane.[64]

So, Richter chose gray for its neutral character, at the same time as he was attracted to its capacity to encompass the entire range of possibilities of "what to paint." In his wish to paint "nothing," he painted something unspecific. The color gray also seems to have made his painting into something beautiful, which seems to match the definition, in his view, of painting as art. In the end, his choice was a rather conceptual one.

Around the same time, in the late 1960s, painter Alan Charlton also recognized this special character of the color gray and made the use of smooth gray planes his trademark. He painted his first gray monochromatic paintings in 1969, as he writes in his letter to the author (4). Since then, the smooth, monochrome, medium-gray, acrylic-painted, rectangular panels on 4.5 cm stretchers have become his prototype works. He chose this color for its commonness, as it is a "very basic, standard, industrial color," just as he chose the other elements for the same reason, as for example the size of the stretchers which corresponds to the "standard timber that is used in normal construction in England" (*I am an artist who makes a grey painting,* 02:57-02:59 and 02:48-02:53). They are the basics of a painting but are very common, nevertheless. They convey a certain literalness, objecthood (the equivalent of Crimp's "surfaceness"). Yet, Charlton points out in relation to his works that "the paintings are not only monochromatic, but also gray" (Qtd. in Lemoine 306).

In the video *I am an artist who makes a grey painting*, he explains the reason why he chose the color gray as follows:

> [I]t was a not so much an accidental choice, because it grew very much out of wanting to make a painting out of very ordinary materials.... [I]t was a very ordinary, regular, down-to-earth color. It wasn't until I actually started making the paintings that I felt that the color gray itself actually held something more to me than just this. Because using that, the logic, I could perhaps have chosen a brown or a black or, in fact, any type of industrial color. But it did have a special stillness which was important to keep in the painting and, to reflect now, it was almost like the painting was already half successful just by the choice of color. And so I knew from that time, it always held a fascination that I could do different things with it. (13:35-14:52)

These words indicate the importance of the seemingly neutral color choice. In being the non-color closest to a chromatic hue, gray has a multi-sensation to it. Most probably, a human being can discern tenths if not hundreds of different shades of gray corresponding to the chromatic hints in the paint mixture.

Moreover, in reality colors are not just perceived by the viewer due to their intrinsic, physical properties. Their perception is also subject to the interrelation of colors and even heavily depends on the presence of other colors. The viewer may not be aware of seeing all those colors or color nuances, yet he takes them into account unconsciously. This connects to the use of color in a "hidden way," as Dippel writes in "Gereduceerde Schilderkunst" (2). Notably, Dippel adds: "In order to avoid all misunderstanding, let me state that color is important to virtually all artists in this exhibition, even if they limit themselves to white, gray or muted colors. Brighter colors have often been painted over in a lengthy process so as to be almost invisible" (FP 13). Most artists in the exhibition paint several layers of color, which are either overpainted by a non-color or have a neutral color as a result. Namely, a similarly rich yet neutral effect or viewing experience is achieved when applying layer after layer of colored paint only to cover it with a dense white veil or fuse it into an inconspicuous gray. This is what imbues Fundamental paintings with their "reductive subtlety," as Colpitt calls it (29).

In the Amsterdam exhibition, this especially concerns Raimund Girke, Robert Ryman, and Jerry Zeniuk, while Marden also excels at color layering (next to his flanking color panels). Their works, unlike Charlton's purely gray panels, make viewers sense the bright hues underneath the white, gray, or brown-black surface layers. The delicate application and mixing of hues unconsciously renders an animated associative experience in front of the non-color panels. While Girke and Ryman conceal their colors, Zeniuk mixes them into the matte gray covering the canvas in such a subtle way that the canvas structure remains visible. In his "gray and dark-brown to black monochromes that show an opaque surface (the weave structure of the canvas remains visible through 25 layers of wax),"[65] he evidently uses the gray shades as references to other hues, pulling his paintings even more towards the chromatic "feel" (Dippel, "Gereduceerde" 1). Marden uses a similar wax mixture to create a smooth color plane. The matte, dense visual quality of the colored plane blocks the viewer's sight like a flat wall (eliminating atmosphere).

In an artist's statement of 1971, Girke talks at length about the working of the non-colors in his canvases, which as nothing else shows the incredible richness of experience that these non-colors can convey. He muses:

> The dismissal of colorfulness, multi-coloredness, in favor of monochromaticism means more intensive possibilities for working on color, the limitation of quantity results in an increase in quality. Instead of many colors, which fight each other for a privileged position, a single color appears as a ruler, 'gets its due,' is free and can reach its full intensity.
>
> I abandoned multicolor in favor of a single color, and – as a logical result –
> – I abandoned this one color in favor of the non-color range black-gray-white.
>
> Black-gray-white is a for a large part still unexplored colorfulness, full of secrets and discoveries. Only when I push black into the finest gradations across numerous variations of gray all the way to white, the color that outshines all, when the color plane is set into motion by a continuous change between light and dark, black-gray-white becomes color (and does not stay just in the graphic range).
>
> White – cold and heat simultaneously – a personification of the pure, of light and brightness. Black and gray are servants, their task is to bring the white into a soft waving motion, aided by structure to imbue it with a continuous motion across the entire

picture plane, to modulate it sensibly and as a support to make white shine in its full brightness. Black and gray as opponents emphasize white and underline its shine....

The world of the monochrome offers infinite possibilities, a new character within given limits. Color is limited to itself, free of all boundaries, becomes a life of its own and opens itself up now in all its power. (Kultermann, n.p.)[66]

Concerning, as Dippel states, "the work of Jaap Berghuis, in which color – albeit very subdued – plays a role" ("Gereduceerde" 1)[67], an extract from an interview with the artist by assistant curator Dorine Mignot on 27 February 1975 is reproduced in the exhibition catalogue. Berghuis explains: "[I do determine] also the color, blue or yellow, and whether it will be the very first layer or one of the intermediate layers, and I also determine whether I shall use color at all, or make a gray painting. Color and brushstroke have nothing to do with mood" (19). So, again, we see that the choice of color (or non-color) is an important consideration in Fundamental Painting – and that it is not an expressionist one but a formal one. Berghuis even specifically mentions his conscious involvement with color as one of three themes in his painting.

Another noteworthy remark made by Berghuis, which is valid for all Fundamental painters in whose works the canvas edges remain visible, is that "[t]he edge of the canvas is of course important because you can often see traces of underlying colors there" (FP 19). It is, so to speak, a sort of guideline for the viewer's unconscious perception of color underneath the gray surface of the painting. (This recalls the point from Van Doesburg's manifesto cited by Rini Dippel in the context of *Fundamental Painting*, namely that the viewer should be able to visually recreate the painterly process.) Color, then, is indeed a conscious choice. It is accepted but often subdued or otherwise controlled, so that it avoids creating an atmosphere and the painting simply remains on the picture plane.

Raimund Girke, in his artist's statement, also points out this necessity of a visual reproduction of the painterly process in combination with the other important elements in painting and the role of (non-)color. Namely, he points out the fact that besides appearing as a color, at its base, color is a material:

[T]he connection between successive, almost indistinguishable layers of paint results in almost homogenous colors and an extraordinary density and intensity of color. The layered structure emphasizes, besides the paint as material, also the process of painting itself, and leads to ostensibly quiet color, whose [sic] latent energy becomes noticeable only gradually. Color starts having an effect in the field of near-invisibility, of what is only just tangible (FP 31) [68]

Once more, the color choice is proof of Colpitt's notion of "reductive subtlety."

The richness of possibilities offered to the artist by a non-color as well as the working with color as a material is a central element in the white (near-)square paintings by Robert Ryman, the central figure around whom the exhibition *Fundamental Painting* was created. As Dippel informs in "Gereduceerde Schilderkunst": "Out of all participants, Robert Ryman has most researched the possibilities of paint, the surface … the techniques …, limiting himself mainly to white paint" (1).[69] Notably, Ryman uses different whites in his paintings. Depending on both the chemical composition of the white and on the brand, white is never the same white.

Each white has its specific color characteristics inherent in it. As Barbara Reise wrote in an article on Ryman's work in 1974:

> White paint is not only "neutral" in terms of its compositional potential. White as a material property is the most *physically positive* of all pigment colors. It reflects the most light. It is the most visually responsive to the physical atmosphere, to the colors and light of the context. As such it is the most sensitive physical color as material of different surfaces – reflecting light (in shiny surfaces), absorbing it (matte), or refracting it into shadows between strokes of thick impasto or pieces of paper,… [I]t presents itself as nakedly, as directly, and as purely as does the linen, copper … cotton, to the viewer's visual and tactile experience. (35)

Reise continues to write on the color white in painting – especially Ryman's painting –, on white paint as material:

> "There are whites and whites: no color which is all color – and different in each particular case. For we are not speaking of a 'white light,' but materialistically: of white paint.… Ryman has used all of these different whites according to their individual color characteristics. But he has also used these differently colored white paints in terms of their physical nature to further differentiate the colors that we see" (33-34).

The apparently simple layering of hues, finally covering them over with white or another non-color, can be done in different ways. For example, in the exhibited *Untitled* (1960) by Ryman, the painted white surface is executed with such thick paint and animated brushstrokes that the multitude of underlying colors – notably a marine blue and ocher yellow – are clearly visible between the thick, white strokes. Thus, here the use of paint in monochromatic application does not so much highlight the two-dimensional unity of the surface, as it brings out very much "the realness of paint … not as pure color but as marker of its effects" (Hudson 61-62).

This possibility is especially evident in sober tonalities, as mentioned in relation to Jerry Zeniuk's dark structured planes with the canvas structures shining through. It can likewise be seen in the paintings of other Fundamental painters: for example, in Edda Renouf's paintings that show a rather matte, coarse haptic quality or Stephan

Rosenthal's scratched planes which channel the paint. Van Koningsbruggen, then again, takes the sentence literally. His statement for the exhibition *Fundamental Painting* reads:

> At a certain point, as I was painting a painting with a brush and black and white paint I noticed that some paint was stuck on my brush. The paint on the brush had a similar pattern as the paint on the painting. In fact, the brush became a painting. Later on, the right painting became the brush for the left painting.
>
> In fact, I was not interested how the idea (the painting) ended up. One paints with paint, so unexpected and unplanned things happen, luckily. A stain is created on the upper left or the lower right. I do not have control over that and I do not want this [the control] either.
>
> For example: I have a black painting and a white painting, both the same size, and I rub them against each other from left to right. Then I leave my studio.[70]

In the case of Van Koningsbruggen, the effects made by the paint itself more than those made by the painter constitute the paintings.

Fundamental Painting participant Louis Cane perfectly summarized in his artist's statement for *Fundamental Painting* the cognitive process of the artist painter, concerning the complexity of the so apparently banal choice for a lack of color and the important factor that working with color pigments inherently implies (the manipulation of paint). The fact that he included it so prominently by itself shows the importance of such a consideration for the Fundamental artists. Cane writes:

> <u>The profession of painter, another view on color:</u>
>
> What to say first, if not: "See my way of treating color and you will see how I 'treat' the rest," or: "Color is the 'royal way' that I take to modify the rules and the constants." In fact, the profession of painter could be the profession of color; and I can very well imagine the subject of this profession, the subject of this practice. Call on color and tell it: "What do I do with you whom I do not know?" and it replies: "Oh well, figure it out yourself any which way you can, after all it is not my problem, if you discover me to be a language,..." This is what painting basically is: to apprehend color, in order to recognize the language that I make it speak, in order to know of myself why I have this desire to speak through it.
>
> This language is that of a painterly subject and, when it speaks in color, in the first place it indicates to me the form of the desire that I will have and dream about, with what I call the versatility of color. This means, with its apparent absence of senses, it is an absence that turns it into 'a material that is easier to work with,' as it hasn't the power to resist its use. One does not even have to 'think before using it' anymore, or at least this is what I thought some time ago.

> Yet, more specifically and considering my path (my attitude) in relation to this, I am forced to reconsider the preceding proposition; because, in fact, as a painter "to see color" demands not only to work with the "technical" means that it possesses, but it also demands to acquire knowledge about the transformations of these means, by way of exactly this relentless addition that is the "illustrative power" of color,... In this sense, it is forcibly color that we should have put in order. The profession of painter has made it into "a part of things." But in the end, is it not this the "real" work of the profession of a painter? Is it not something that, in relation to color, takes into account a capacity of discernment to be exercised within the infinity of the color "range" – the profession of a painter? That which testifies <u>qualitatively</u> of the relationship that I entertain with <u>an abstract quality</u>: color. (1-2)[71]

Color – or paint – is a central, crucial element in painting. Without the availability of paint to be put on the canvas plane, there would be no such thing as the history of painting. In this context, also the words of Fundamental painter Tomas Rajlich that a painting must be painted and not drawn highlight the importance of this painterly element in painting (Broos, n.p.). Basically, color is the language of painting, and – as Cane specifies – a painter must not only be aware of its technical implications but also of its effects on the viewer.

Fundamental Painting is an enterprise that has made it its program to start from scratch with painting, to discover a painting's elements in detail from the very basics. Like a little child learning to walk and talk, the Fundamental painter "learns" about painting, growing ever more with his artwork, continuing the Fundamental quest into ever more richly facetted propositions. In terms of color, this also means discovering each single color and its attributes one by one, starting with the non-colors which only hold two out of three color attributes. The perception of several color fields side-by-side (e.g. Marden), or the discovery of the associative possibilities of ambiguous tones, as well as the understanding of the effects of (unperceivable) overlapping shades are all part of this quest.

Tomas Rajlich confirms the expansive possibilities of this in an interview with Kees Broos:

> I basically started with white and light-gray paintings. Despite the use of a little bit of green or gray-blue, the result was nevertheless a gray-white painting. Still, I cannot help it – and this grew on me slowly while working – that I very much like paintings in color.... But one cannot just change like that, although the evolution is there that – in comparison with a few years ago – the paintings are more colorful.... – because, oh well, color belongs to painting after all.[72]

The nature of the Fundamental Painting exercise is reflected in: the obsession with color – or rather the initial need for and sufficiency of neutral color –, the discovery of the richness of non-colors and non-specific colors in relation to each other or in layers, as well as the concern with application of color and its visual experience (the unified plane, without an atmosphere nor emotion), and the recognition of color as paint (as material), and the experience of the viewer in all this. In his key article, Crimp summarizes these workings of color as follows:

> In Opaque painting color is kept as neutral as possible.... Where color is used ... it is usually extremely muted, kept non-specific and entirely even; it eludes both description and association. Furthermore, it is never used to assert an optical effect; rather it is dictated by the necessity of opacity. (259)

Again, color as a physical effect of the paint functions in favor of "surfaceness." Color, both as color and as material, is a crucial element for contemplation by the Fundamental artist and his communication on painting (be it the activity, the object, or the history) with the viewer. The "language" of painting largely defines the painter: Fundamental, analytic, non-illusionist, or anything else.

2.1.4 Line

The fourth characteristic of Fundamental Painting as listed by Rini Dippel is line (FP 14). While considering this, the thought of line as the representation of a figure or form may automatically come to mind. This is not appropriate for Fundamental Painting. However, line is still one of its valuable elements precisely in how it can convey flatness versus illusionism on a painted plane. The words of *Fundamental Painting* participant Louis Cane show the importance of this painterly element:

> It always seemed to me that drawing is what guides my work, meaning that which subjectively positions me and corrects me in the contradiction of the dualities form/support, color/white or painted/not yet painted, etc. .... The drawing, this first draft, this pre-draft, is a first step that determines the projection towards the other, towards its possession.... Thus, I remember that an old professor of painting advised me: "Grab hold of the figure tightly with your drawing and you will master composition." To follow this "advice" ... I still hear the word <u>compromise</u> instead of <u>composition</u> and the word <u>destiny</u> instead of <u>drawing</u>, because it is "the drawing" after all that decides the destiny of the painter's canvas.... that which makes him feel alive: his language. See here, then, my language strongly resembles a seductive enterprise, yet it does not for that matter say less in its role as one of the inherent specifics in painting and, I almost forgot ..., as inherent to the profession of a painter. (Statement 2-3)[73]

Following Cane's train of thought, the choice of what to do with line determines the destiny of the work – and of its creator. In his case, the chosen language of painting is Fundamental Painting – painting about painting, non-illusionistic, without representing any subject matter beyond itself.

Line, formed in Fundamental Painting, is used to adopt viewing habits and to contemplate the traditional use of drawing in painting – to represent a figure. Robert Mangold is probably the most obviously concerned with such an interplay. His drawn "figures" push and pull against the form of the shaped canvas itself. The viewer muses upon the correctness of recognized, geometric figures, contemplating possible options as to their positioning in space, which could account for their apparent distortion. In his artist's statement for the show, Mangold writes:

> A principal involvement in my work during the last ten years has been my concern with structure, the relation of the interior structure of the piece to the exterior shape. Edge line to inner line. A desire to make the picture a clear unity of shape/line – color/surface. A piece that would present itself directly, totally to the viewer, with all its information right there. (FP 37)

In actual fact, Fundamental Painting uses figure as form. At the same time, Fundamental Painting assigns line the role of keeping the pictorial space (flat) on the canvas's surface and, thus, of positioning the painting in the viewer's space.

Another Fundamental painter, Marthe Wéry, started using line to play with the contrast between figure and ground in her works just after her return from Montréal in 1972 – the "year of rupture: abandonment of form in order to entirely take possession of the surface of the support" (Letter).[74] She did this by drawing many lines very close to each other onto a monochrome picture plane, which is so near in hue to that of the lines that visually the drawn elements fuse into the ground as does the ground into the drawn elements. This is explained by a wall text of a recent exhibition which quotes her: "My entire work is an elementary attempt to experience the surface. Elementary in the sense that I try to explore its essentials. In its simplest structure, a line is a surface." Line is assigned a novel use or – one could even say – eliminated as line for the sake of surface. Here again, we are reminded of the Fundamental painter's goal of "surfaceness," as formulated by Douglas Crimp.

A similar interchange is achieved in Edda Renouf's white grid-painting entitled *Horizontal Point-Line Progression* (1975), which reads like a white grid on a white ground; but in which the square modules (the potential voids between the grid lines) are actually the painted part, and the grid is constituted by the sections of ground remaining visible all around. Similarly, in Tomas Rajlich's *White Painting* (1973) the squares are painted by hand. They form a (painted) contrast to the (supposedly) traced grid. Yet, in fact, the grid is drawn with a painted brush, meaning it was also painted.

In addition, the grid is so large that the line turns into a surface, like in Wéry's case. (The viewer questions which patterns are painted by hand and which are not, as well as what is drawn and what is painted.) The traditional element of illusion (the grid) is used for the sake of flatness. All these are questioning the definition of painting itself (as opposed to that of drawing) through their visual play of painting – an approach seen over and over again in Fundamental Painting.

Strickland, an author on Minimalist painting, writes on the subject of line as form: "Form in Minimalism is characteristically reduced to undifferentiated holism or all-over pattern: the field and/or the grid or other regularized geometrical schemes" (12). He adds: "Specifically in painting, recurrent Minimalist qualities are … regularity of contour … and rectilinear symmetry…" (23-24). By invoking symmetry, the eye is led back to the center of the painting – as seen when discussing the preference for (near-)square format – , at the same time being led away from it by this very line. This "trick" succeeds in making the viewer explore the picture plane, looking for the various pictorial elements that confirm that a Fundamental Painting is indeed a painting. The modular grid structures and unifies the picture plane further. In view of this, the grid is a recurrent and valuable characteristic of Fundamental Painting.

Brice Marden recalls its specific use in painting: "The grid has always been just a way of measuring space and showing that different things can be happening in that space and on the plane simultaneously" (*Blocks* 1:20-1:29). Minimalist sculptor and mural painter, Sol LeWitt, once pointed out that the Minimalist grid comes from the art of painting, where it has been traditionally used to invoke perspective and turn the two-dimensional picture plane into a reflection of the three-dimensional world (Cit. in Colpitt 60). The grid is, therefore, by definition an element of painting that is used in Fundamental Painting – which wishes to work exclusively with the basic painterly elements – in a novel way. Composed of identical modules, it turns the indicative qualities of a traditional, linear perspective-grid with diagonal lines into a visually non-indicative one made of only perpendicular lines, thereby preserving and indirectly reinforcing the two-dimensionality and unity of the picture plane, as Rosalind Krauss explains in "Grids." In the exhibition *Fundamental Painting*, this can be seen in the works of Agnes Martin and Tomas Rajlich. Both use a linear grid-pattern to visually anchor the painting firmly onto the two-dimensional surface plane. In their industrial-looking yet hand-drawn grids, "there are infinitesimal differences in the lines and edges, but all of them subordinate to the repetition of the grid," as Briony Fer once remarked (47).

Tomas Rajlich even explores the "perfect" Fundamental Painting grid. In his works from the 1970s, we see "visual" grids, which are constructed by way of merely painting the small square modules at regular intervals, plus a second kind of negative grid created through applying masking tape (in the form of a grid) to the unpainted canvas and then – after having painted over it in a gestural manner – removing it. In Rajlich's works, there are also grids that are drawn (cf. the works of Agnes Martin), grids that are painted, and "industrial" grids that are printed onto the support. Thus, the various grids used by Rajlich can be not only positive or negative but also hand-painted, industrial-looking and/or actually mechanically-made designs. As a conclusion to these explorations into the grid, Rajlich explained in an interview with art critic Kees Broos in 1975 (parts of which are reproduced in the *Fundamental Painting* catalogue) that "graphic line does not belong to painting," because "a painting must be painted, not drawn."[75]

References to illusionism and to the use of graphic line make paintings a sort of mixture between painting and drawing – and therefore a bit off-axis in terms of the scope of Fundamental Painting. For Rajlich's works, this means, as he himself explained, that:

> In the last paintings, the grid has become no more than a construction within the painting. The earlier pieces, up to a year ago, still gave an impression of spatiality; optically there was a space on the surface of the canvas – which I myself considered wrong. Everything should happen on the surface, I want to eliminate the illusion: that is why I kept the grid. All the layers that are painted over it are applied on the principle that they should remain as much as possible within the plane of the grid.... The grid is there as an element, it helps to keep the painting within the surface. It is used, just like paint and linen, as an element in the construction of the painting. (FP 50)[76]

So, in Fundamental Painting line, especially in the form of a grid, is used with a view to evoking flatness (Crimp's "surfaceness") in a non-indicative way, instead of in the traditional sense.

Besides indicating flatness, when used in the form of a regular grid pattern, line evokes an external scale by visually expanding the painting along its gridlines (vertically as well as horizontally) *ad infinitum*. This sense of infinite expansion anchors the painting in the viewer's environment and proposes it as an object, instead of as traditionally a "window onto the world." It becomes a flat plane on the wall's plane. At the same time, it conjures up a sense of intimate scale – an internal kind of scale, as discussed before – by way of the modules in relation to a random set of modules, and finally, to the painting itself (a rectangular shape and with that, the largest module). Rini Dippel called this: "the purest art of line that was ever made, in which every hierarchy of forms is lacking and only the tension of the rectangles formed by the grid in relation to the square canvas is tangible" (FP 14). The paintings now activate the "seeing-viewing-experiencing" of the viewer without any implicit or actual movement.

This solicited interaction with the viewer (to be revisited later) is one of the fundamental elements in Fundamental Painting. Once again, the ways the Fundamental painters work lead the viewer to Michael Fried's "objecthood" of the artwork, and subsequently to Douglas Crimp's "surfaceness" in painting. Similarly, line can be used in a non-indicative manner by way of factual cleavages that appear visually as lines and thus correspond to the "objecthood" – the "surfaceness" – of the painting. Marden's multipaneled works create these lines automatically, as do the multipartite paintings of both Jaap Berghuis and Kees Smits. The works of Robert Mangold specifically contain both visual lines – "literal divisions" in Dippel's words (FP 14) – and "real" (drawn) lines. Jake Berthot also places these two kinds of perceived lines side by side. In this play of contrast, illusionism is subverted by stressing the real existence of the object. As Colpitt explains: "Illusionism is the result of either a transparent picture plane or the apparent continuation of a ground beneath an overlaid figure, while recognition of the physical existence of the support means that surface, as well as shape, must be viewed as a single palpable thing. The two perceptions are in conflict" (103).

In her dissertation on Robert Ryman, Susanne Hudson perfectly summarizes this concern when stating that painting in the 1970s opened up illusionism to part-by-part associations and interactions within real rather than pictorial space (157). She goes back to Rosalind Krauss – a major art critic from the 1970s –, who claimed that painting at the time "had been focused on justifying or legitimating the internal structure of a given work – a structure made visible by the articulations of a surface ... – by means other than those of mimesis or illusion," and that this *telos* was evinced in the engagement with the literal, that is "with the purging of illusion from the work of art by making everything about it external.... Literalism was an attempt to make the work ... stop at its surface. In order to do this, all divisions of the surface had to be experienced as the actual separations of the material of the surface" (*Bachelors* 99). Thus, "more than anything else," Krauss said, it was "focused on surface, and where the surface stops, which is edge" (*Bachelors* 99-100).

This statement is echoed in Dippel's text in the exhibition catalogue, in which she takes Brice Marden's "unfinished" lower edges of some of his painted panels as an example of a reference to the edge. Such "unfinished" edges can also be seen in the work of Tomas Rajlich and Jaap Berghuis. In this context, Dippel's role model Douglas Crimp, wrote about line: "In almost all traditional painting, line functioned either to delineate an object in space or to delineate space itself; that is to say, in almost every case, line was the exclusive prerogative of representation.... Line is employed in Opaque painting, if at all, as the edge of shape or as equal and logically referent to that edge" (259). Call it literalism, objecthood, surfaceness, or what you may, incontestably all critics seem to agree that painting of the Fundamental era set itself a goal in employing this particular reminder of two-dimensionality in the painting experience – notably with the use of line (be it drawn, a grid, an edge, or even a runny paint line).

Fundamental artists Stephen Rosenthal and Edda Renouf took this "surfaceness" even more literally in their use of line, arriving at a kind of intermediary form between factual and drawn line. Rosenthal not only included "horizontal lines in ink over a transparent acrylic layer" (FP 14) in his works, but also included lines that arise from his scratching into this painted layer, while following the structure of the material. Taking a similar yet opposite approach, "[the] French-American Edda Renouf works with the grid of the weave. Structure and texture are created by way of removing a few threads out of the weave of the canvas" ("Gereduceerde" 1).[77] Renouf uses the line inherent to the canvas's weave. She highlights its existence by pulling threads out of the woven structure to form counter-structural linear patterns on the painted surface. These, in turn, highlight the physical reality of such a picture plane.

Consequently, the choice of being for-or-against the use of line is as vital to Fundamental Painting as the choice of being for-or-against the use of color. Edward Strickland also addresses this unusual concern with line when he writes in *Minimalism: The Origins*: "Specifically in painting, recurrent … qualities are … elimination (in monochrome color-field) or geometrical simplification (in grid or panel paintings) of line;" and he explains how these lead to an "anti-illusionistic flattening of surface" (22-23). Notably, Jerry Zeniuk, Raimund Girke, Gerhard Richter, and Richard Jackson have no use for line; while Alan Charlton's and Brice Marden's monochromes stand out for their smoothness and use of edge as line; Martin's and Rajlich's works are characterized by grids. Line is an extremely versatile, painterly element and particularly remarkable in its capacity to suggest three-dimensional illusion as well as to offset it.

In the language of Fundamental Painting, line takes on many likenesses and becomes a tool to question and offset this illusion. Line can be drawn directly on the canvas, made from a cleavage visually perceived as line, or even created from various physical aspects of the painting. Line leads the viewer's eye and activates the viewing experience, even – or especially – when it instills a certain regularity or symmetry to the picture plane. Line has become a painterly element (not a drawing element). It has lost its traditional illusionist role. It unifies the picture plane and keeps it flat or even pushes it out into the viewer's space. Line structures the spectator's vision, leading the eye, while indicating scale and underlining the painting's object-like quality. Moreover, the use of a linear grid (inherently painterly) masterfully combines the use of non-indicative line and a commentary on illusionism (the traditional element in painting). While turning line into a surface, the painting becomes truly painted instead of being drawn. All in all, the question of painting, or what painting is, is visually posed to the viewer by the work itself – echoing the concern with painting as the ultimate basic yet all-encompassing form of painting, common to the Fundamental approach.

2.1.5 Texture and facture[78]

Rini Dippel mentions texture in the works of *Fundamental Painting* artists in her note entitled “Gereduceerde Schilderkunst.” She lists Edda Renouf in this context and mentions Robert Ryman as the painter having most “researched the possibilities of paint, surface….” Yet, she also mentions Alan Charlton’s “gray monochromes, painted totally smoothly” and that “Brice Marden’s apparently cool reduction seems to come from the painted panels with an extremely smooth surface (painted with a palette knife)…” (1).[79] This choice of extremely smooth surfaces does not, at first, appear very logical regarding Fundamental Painting’s values.

Fundamental Painting’s role model, Crimp, writes on texture:

> Texture, like scale, has both actual and virtual readings. The problem with much of so-called flat painting, which sought to expunge texture, is that in equalizing the structure of the surface, the viewer apprehended the ‘texture’ of atmosphere. In revealing a specific texture of paint *qua* paint or stroke *qua* stroke … or layer *qua* layer…, the viewer apprehends the structure of the surface as being actually on that surface.

Crimp adds that “it does not matter whether the texture is smooth … or relatively rough…. What matters is that texture is apprehended as an actual characteristic of the material used to create the surface” (259). Consequently, opting for both a smooth or a rough surface is – as is the case for choice of color, use of line, and the like – a delicate enterprise in order to keep the picture plane flat.

Berthot and Cane strive to counteract the potentially illusionistic quality of the smooth picture planes of their paintings by incorporating a kind of frame-like edge painted in the same hue. Alan Charlton relies on the actual object-like qualities of his works which have always consisted of smooth, gray monochrome panels, covered from edge to edge, explaining in the video recording *I am an artist who makes a grey painting* from the 1980s that, for him, the panels must be smooth to arrive at creating a Fundamental Painting:

> The intention was to try to develop different grays…. In fact, this developed into being more concerned with how they were painted rather than the different grays they were using. By applying the paint thinner, this enabled that the surface of the canvas started to play an active role in the structure of the painting, and so therefore everything was becoming equal, which is always my intention: that the canvas, the shape, the wood, the size, everything should uniformly fit together. (06:49-07:30)

In Charlton's works, the smoothness plays a critical part in the balancing act between the basic painterly elements – which is really what Fundamental Painting is all about.

When viewing his paintings, the viewer discovers that besides their characteristic grayness and smoothness, Charlton's works either are multi-paneled pieces or, thanks to their shape, include the wall they are hung on within their composition. This systematically prevents the gray planes from creating any hint of atmospheric perception. Then again, Brice Marden – likewise painting smooth gray canvases – makes the painted plane visually dense by way of mixing in wax so that it appears like a wall. Jerry Zeniuk uses the same principle in his gray, dark brown, and black paintings, exhibited in the *Fundamental Painting* show.

Marden moreover leaves an "unfinished" edge at the bottom of the canvas, a kind of drip line, where the different layers of paint and their colors can be read. As mentioned before, Berghuis and Rajlich incorporate such an "unfinished" edge in their paintings too. In an interview with Kees Broos, Rajlich clarifies this lower edge drip line border:

> If you paint all the way to the edge like I do, while the painting is propped up against the floor, then you cannot reach the bottom part very well and a somewhat unfinished ridge is created. Yet, it is precisely this ridge that helped me to keep the surface of the painting really flat. The painting, which is covered with a painted layer, has drippings along the ridge at the bottom, which optically determine the position of the painted plane. Optically, this bottom ridge indicates that there is no more depth within the canvas.[80]

Once again, "surfaceness" appears to be a main painterly consideration.

In contrast to Charlton's and Marden's smooth planes, Rajlich's paintings are obviously painted with a brush – the large and dynamic strokes clearly visible –, and also the works of Kees Smits and Jaap Berghuis show a vigorously painted, all-over structure. The brushstrokes' texture unifies the plane and manifests the hand-painted quality of the painting. However, it must be counterbalanced to respect the need for "surfaceness." In order to keep dynamic brushwork on the painted plane, Rajlich uses both the drip line and the grid. Smits and Berghuis opt for multi-panel groups where the cleavage between panels reveals the flatness of the support they are painted on. Richard Jackson directly fuses his painting with the wall, while Gerhard Richter's and Raimund Girke's paintings show no desire to counteract the brushstroke patterns covering their paintings' surface.

It can also be the material of the facture itself that insists on the flatness of the picture plane. In the works of Robert Ryman whose paintings like *Untitled* (1960) present gesture as an essential and integral part of the painting, it is the dynamic, impastoed application of the paint which stabilizes the otherwise open, overall structure of the picture. Moreover, Jerry Zeniuk prefers to use the material itself as a tool to counteract any potential atmospheric effects. Dippel informed us in "Gereduceerde Schilderkunst" that "Jerry Zeniuk … works in 'encaustic' (wax and pigment): gray and dark-brown to black monochromes that show an opaque surface (although the canvas' woven structure remains visible through 25 layers of wax)" (1).[81] He uses very thin paint, which allows for the canvas weave to push through the painted layer.

Zeniuk doesn't use the paint (like Ryman) but the carrier to flatten the picture plane. Similarly, Agnes Martin's paintings let the canvas structure shine through. Robert Mangold's also let the weave shine through. However, their texture can be anything from even and smooth to very liquid and transparent. He chooses his surfaces depending on all other painterly elements in the picture so that the best balance is achieved. Rosenthal, on the other hand, first creates the structure of the picture plane by scratching lines into it, and then works with the effect this has on the paint (channeling its flow). Then again, Edda Renouf's "surfaceness" is brought about by the process of unraveling the canvas and then painting over the rough structure which has been formed with very thin paint.

Renouf writes in her artist's statement of March 1975, reproduced in the exhibition catalogue:

> In my painting I start by looking at the weave of the unprimed linen canvas by holding a newly stretched canvas up to the light. I forget myself and am led by what I see in this weave: a natural grid – a play of horizontals and verticals which are sometimes slightly uneven and undulating, not strictly geometrical. I pull out certain threads, at times long lengths, at times short lengths. I then size and prime the canvas and paint with thin color glazes: dark blue, black, white, sienna red. By working from within, opening the structure of the material, I seek to reveal the life, the energy already inherent in the linen canvas and the paint. (53)

For Renouf, the use of structure as texture becomes a means of creating the painting. By purely basing her approach on the given painterly material, she is focusing on the fundamental elements of a painting.

An interesting point that arises from this contemplation of the material support is the intimate relation that the artist establishes with the canvas. By considering the fine weave – and, by adding a sort of highlighting, making the viewer consider it – an intimate scale is created, different from that of the painting's actual size. Confronted with this work, the viewer does not only sense the presence of the artwork as an object but also the individual character of the actual canvas as a material. In this context, the words of Marthe Wéry should be recalled that her "entire work is an elementary attempt to experience the surface" (*Wéry*).

In fact, Wéry voices a similar concern in notes on painting which were sent to the curators of the *Fundamental Painting* show in place of a statement:

> The 21st of August, 1974: Difficulty to separate technique and spirit. Above all, it is important to activate "something" along the lines of texture: this means to, first, recognize a basic material, or that a connivance has been established. For example, the paper: acknowledgement of its grain, then an inscription of my intervention on the most fundamental textural level of the material. My intervention is no longer simply situated at this level, it becomes an act of erasure or of modesty, as opposed to a tendency whose aim is to impose itself or to impose something. About the texture? It is a living thing, i.e. something that destroys itself. [My] Intervention is to extend that life, an attempt to suspend the process of its destruction.[82]

The artist's intervention therefore is a means to highlight the inherent characteristics of this painterly element: the material, the support. As Dippel writes in her catalogue text: "The texture is characteristic for the material that is used to create the surface" (14). For Fundamental painters the material of the support is an important factor in painting, the inherent characteristics of which are to be respected by the artist.

A passage from Kees Broos's interview with Tomas Rajlich shows the importance of considerations on structure in Fundamental Painting. Broos probes the artist: "You are typically someone who paints on canvas, but suppose you would be commissioned to paint a large wall in a building, how would you do that?" Rajlich answers:

> As to the technical side of it: I am used to acrylic on canvas. And it might sound strange, but if I were to receive such a commission, I would not paint directly on the wall. I might have the wall first covered with linen the way it's done with wallpaper, for example, and then paint on that, because I believe the structure of linen to be essential to my paintings. Hence the use of this material to try to achieve the smallest possible illusion of any space.[83]

Thus, the structure (support) as well as texture (paint) and facture (application) are key elements to Fundamental Painting. The nature of the surface determines the character of the painting and makes it unique, bringing it to life. Its considerations are comparable in significance to the artist's considerations on the other elements – format, color, line, and the like – and once again, contribute to its "surfaceness." These elements all have to be typically "painterly." The picture plane can be anything – smooth, pasty or impastoed – and the structure of the canvas may be visible or not, as long as the potential atmospheric reading is contradicted by emphasizing the "objecthood" of the painting. This is for example done through the use of multi-panels, drip lines, or grids; reworkings of the support material; paints applied as material, and the like. Rough structures have the additional advantage that they incite a more intimate dialogue with the viewer. The fine weave or brushwork of the canvas beckons the viewer to approach, thus inciting a more intimate scale for a larger canvas (cf. grid patterns). In Fundamental Painting, what is important is the emphasis placed on the texture of the support of the painting as well as that of the painted surface. Both structure and gestural traits unify the picture plane. Due to the considerations concerning the texture of the surface and the facture of painting, the Fundamental painting is pictorial but also a material fact.

2.1.6 Tools and materials

In the context of the texture and materiality of a painting, the canvas as a structure has revealed itself as having an important role. In a text on Cézanne, what Yve-Alain Bois writes in this regard is also central to Fundamental Painting: "Since the time of [Leon Battista] Alberti, the picture plane is assumed as transparent in painting, but the condition *sine qua non* of this transparency is that the supporting ground be covered over without reserve" (42). Fundamental Painting contemplates painting as painting by considering the bare canvas – a fundamental element of a painting. In the same way, it considers color not only as hue but also as non-illusionistic, material paint.

In Fundamental Painting, the ground is treated as something to see, as opposed to something to cover. The bare canvas or its surface structure is, at times, exposed to set it off against the other painterly elements. Similarly, different canvases with different types of weaves might be chosen by the artist, because the ground has an unquestionable effect on the appearance of the paint spread upon it. The canvas structure might even push through and show the materiality of the painted surface. In this context Suzanne Hudson, scholar on Robert Ryman's painting, points out: "Neither figure (painting) nor ground (support) is ultimately privileged, although the viewer's act of engagement with the painting becomes active and self-determined" (104).

The "discovery" of the range of possibilities of canvas itself as a special element in determining the texture of a picture plane (in combination with the concept of color as material in its own right (and not just as a means to create an illusion) is another aspect featured consciously in Fundamental Painting. Equally, all other tools and materials have been brought to the forefront and are meticulously scrutinized for their role in painting and their possible contribution to the "fundamentalness" in painting (point number 8 on Rini Dippel's list of characteristics of Fundamental Painting) (FP 14). Fundamental artists have chosen to insist on these inherent elements and traditional workings of painting without any of the concerns of creating illusions or evoking meaning. Rini Dippel notes on the importance of the materials and tools:

> It was Ryman in particular who drew attention to the enormous range of possibilities offered by materials such as paint, bearer, and brushes alone. There are many types of different bases, too: cotton, linen, cardboard, hardboard, plywood, steel, copper, synthetics, etc. And many different kinds of paint: oil paint, synthetic paint, enamel, combinations of wax and oil paint or pigment. The tool is, as a matter of course, the brush – in a variety of shapes and sizes – but also the spatula (Marden), the roller (Mangold), the sponge (Smits), the hand (Zeniuk) or the painting itself may be used as "brush" (Jackson, Van Koningsbruggen). (FP 14)

In addition to using the painterly elements in novel ways in order to rediscover painting, Fundamental painters use the painterly materials and tools to such ends. Both elements and materials as well as tools are key to the creation of the desired visual effects. Moreover, they allow the painter (and the viewer) to simply gain awareness of the scope of all that is (or can be) "typical" painterly material.

Following the same logic, Colpitt informs us that "Minimalist painters of the sixties ... quickly turned to the new materials and techniques..." (23), in addition to their focus on traditional pictorial materials. Lucy Lippard already wrote in her article "As Painting is to Sculpture: A Changing Ratio," published in *American Sculpture of the Sixties* in 1967: "The recently developed acrylic paints were well suited to ... 'cool' painting, for ... reasons of brilliance, purity and impersonal functionalism borrowed from technological or industrial sources" (34). And Strickland elaborates: "Specifically in painting, recurrent Minimalist qualities are ... eschewing of gesture and concomitant erasure of facture; ... technical equalization of texture (beeswax mixes, spray paint, rolled enamel, acrylic matte, absorbent or impermeable surfaces)..." (22-23). The reasons behind this preference for smooth planes of a good number of Fundamental painters were discussed above. Most Fundamental painters – namely: Berghuis, Berthot, Cane, Charlton, Girke, Renouf, Richter, Rosenthal, Ryman, Rajlich, and Wéry – however work with the relatively traditional types of paint (be it oil or acrylic), canvas (be it linen or cotton duck), and the traditional brush whereas Marden's spatula and Mangold's roller, while also being painterly tools, are much less orthodox.

Colpitt points out: "Unlike sculpture, Minimal paintings were not fabricated outside the studio.... [P]aint application was the responsibility of the artist alone. Nevertheless, the 'look' of fabrication was evident in most paintings" (23). The new appearance of acrylic paint on the market in the mid-20th century (besides the focus on all the other kinds of painterly materials and tools for sale) was a defining factor in the new use of paint as a material and the confirmation of painting as an object. Yet, clearly only the artist can be named as the instigator of this quest for the essence of painting. It is this necessity of the creative process by the artist alone that is important and not whether traditional or new painterly materials are used, or how the result will look – as long as process, materials, elements and result all are undeniably implicated in the field of painting.

The point here is – as Hudson writes in *Robert Ryman: Used Paint* – that since the mid-1960s, the works are "about the nature of paint: the paint [is] the content of the paintings, as well as their form" (175). There are various ways to apply paint: for example, it can be spread slowly or vigorously, applied in dabs or long strokes, smoothened out, or stuck to the surface like chunks of matter, but also the paint can be allowed to drip randomly. In Fundamental Painting, such experimentation with the materials and tools remains visible in the result. The final painting accordingly communicates something about their inherent nature to the viewer. For example, Robert Mangold's early surfaces are smoothly, almost industrially, covered with a roller. In these early works, this is a necessity in view of reaching the perfect balance, as they are relatively colorful, hold geometric figures, and are executed on shaped canvases. In contrast, Tomas Rajlich's (almost square) paintings are truly brush-painted. The artist told Kees Broos in interview: "The principle of painting is, in my understanding, after all something that one should be able to do with all his power, not necessarily all emotions, but with all his will."[84] An underlying grid, for example, allows him to do so without abandoning the Fundamental principle. Each type of paint application shows the chosen tool's *raison d'être* in the context of the particular painting.

It must be remembered that Fundamental Painting is an exploration of painting by the painter in the process of doing it, and that this process should be easily reconstituted by the viewer when confronted with the work. In his statement for the *Fundamental Painting* exhibition already quoted in chapter 2.1.3, Raimund Girke explains very well the delicate process of deciding how to use materials and tools, taking into account the viewing experience. Namely:

> Determined elements in the working process are the materials: they demand specific approaches which must remain intelligible. The free range of the brushstrokes which are adjusted to the dimensions of the plane creates a more or less activated painted plane, and the connection between successive, almost indistinguishable layers of paint, results in almost homogenous colors…. Besides the paint as material, the layered structure emphasizes also the process of painting itself…. (FP 31) [85]

The viewer needs to be able to recognize the character (the specificity) of the tools and materials that constitute the painting. This applies to the use of all painterly tools and materials in Fundamental Painting. It concerns both the support and the picture plane – not just the paint. The criterion is that these materials and tools be painterly, that they create the desired painterly effects, while their application is the sole responsibility of the artist. The inherent qualities of all materials and tools involved in the process are just as important elements in the construction of a painting as the painterly elements of the composition with color and line. They have a character of their own, which is very particular to each of the applied materials as well as typical for the tools used. As Marthe Wéry said, according to wall texts at a recent show: "Materials – paint, paper, canvas, wood – are living things."

In Fundamental Painting, this most genuine, inherent element is sought after by the artists; and it resurfaces in dialogue with the viewer. The materials (and the tools used) communicate something to the viewer about the painting process as well as about the object-quality or materiality of the painting itself. Again, the artists' choices are made in view of "surfaceness." Dippel's role model Crimp wrote on this subject: "Material is, of course, paramount in an art which depends on its substance being apprehended as actual.... It is the properties of the materials used as materials ... that the viewer keep his attention fixed on what, specifically, he is seeing (and *that* he is seeing)" (259).

2.1.7 Process

The previously outlined considerations about materials and tools make up a fundamental part of the painterly process – number 8 on Rini Dippel's list of characteristics of Fundamental Painting (FP 14). In this process, the components of painting (support, paint, brushstroke and so on) are brought to the foreground. The mode of their application is crucial in this regard. It is indicative of how these paintings come into being. In this context, it is useful to recall Colpitt's statement that even in "cool" Minimalist painting, the act of painting remains the responsibility of the artist.

Charlton, for example, wrote: "I paint the canvas with a brush as smooth and even as I can, not leaving any sign of a hand gesture. However, somehow, it is important that I have painted it (I would never spray the paint on)" (Letter 2). Namely, as Dippel informs the reader of the *Fundamental Painting* exhibition catalogue: "The work is carried out according to plan, but at the same time it is subject to the influence of the action involved. It is interesting to note that many painters themselves acknowledge the part that intuition plays in their work" (14). Words with a similar scope can be found in the 1975 exhibition brochure handed out to visitors: "A few painters strongly accentuate the thought-process that precedes painting, but in which intuition is not switched off" (1). Thus, while the painting process of a Fundamental painting is predefined, intuition plays an important role in its creation. The whole process can, in turn, be visually recreated by the viewer.

In this context, it should be remembered – as Nancy Spector pointed out – that:

> Ryman's convictions have come from the experience of making paintings, and not vice-versa. He is not concerned with "shoulds," with aimed-for results, with theories.

> For him the crux of painting is in the making. With every work he knows beforehand what materials he will use and he knows what he is going to do with them. There is no question that there is a considerable investment of thought and intention at the start. But the way every decision is carried out, each touch of the paint to the surface, and the whole visual result, are still unpredictable. ("Ryman" 15)

These words on Ryman perfectly summarize and describe the Fundamental Painting process.

As Raimund Girke's, Edda Renouf's, and Marthe Wéry's statements on the texture of the support (discovered in the preceding chapter) indicate, Fundamental painters work with painterly materials, staying true to their most inherent nature. Moreover, the tools (and materials) remain painterly, even if the artist incorporates something new on the market or finds a certain number of new uses for more traditional items. Fundamental painters are curious to know how each kind of tool or material and even each brand functions. For all Fundamental painters, the choice of the basic elements (material and tools) as well as the modes of exploring them in painting are strictly delimited. Within this context, learning about painting through the act of painting itself is paramount.

That said, Kees Smits, Richard Jackson, and Rob van Koningsbruggen, for example, focus more on planning their production process ahead of time. Smits writes in his artist's statement for the exhibition: "I determine the method of painting and the construction of the painting beforehand. After that the painting can be made non-stop. The painting must confirm the method and the construction" (FP 66).[86] Furthermore, Richard Jackson spent four days just measuring the exact composition of his ephemeral wall painting for *Fundamental Painting* before then executing it relatively quickly (De Carpenter). Rob van Koningsbruggen seems to leave the execution of his painting to the material (as tool) itself, by way of stamping a freshly painted canvas onto another canvas to obtain his finished work.

Agnes Martin's compositions, then again, just appear to her in her sleep or in her meditative moods, as we learn from a video interview with Mary Lance entitled *Agnes Martin: With my back to the world.* Then, she meticulously calculates the ratios of the grid needed before executing the painting. During the process of painting, she merely makes decisions on the intensity of color in order to assure the perfect balance. (There is a moment in the video recording, where one of the colors seems to be too light, so she adds another layer.) (00:04:18-00:06:40 and 00:40:52-00:47:02) The intuitive part in Martin's works is in the choice of the hue's intensity (and the thickness of the line).

Robert Mangold is equally contemplative and balanced in his approach: "The work progresses from idea to drawing, to more precise drawing, to small painting, to a full-sized work, a process which may take one month, or two, or longer. I like to have the idea around for a time, while I decide whether or not I wish to do it" (FP 37). The "doing it," however, is the sole responsibility of the artist and will still modify the concept. The informed reader knows how meticulous Mangold is in precisely balancing all elements: the thickness of a drawn line in relation to "literal divisions" (FP 14) – as Dippel calls the cleavage between panels –, the density of each color's paint, and the corresponding transparency of the canvas's structure, all adapted to the level of tension sought between figure and shape.

Fundamental Painting therefore is logical (not systematic), meaning that not all the steps are predetermined. Each compositional decision is contingent upon the decision preceding it. The inherent character of the applied tools and materials is allowed to unfold – revealing its very nature – during the painting process, in order to constitute painting that is indeed fundamentally painting. Besides being logical, Fundamental Painting is modular (which is not to be confused with serial). The difference between these two is best explained by Mel Bochner in his articles "Serial Art, Systems, Solipsism" and "The Serial Attitude," both published in 1967, in which he explains that modular ideas differ considerably from serial ideas although both are types of order.

In "The Serial Attitude" Bochner writes: "Modular works are based on the repetition of a standard unit. The unit, which may be anything … does not alter its basic form, although it may appear to vary by the way in which the units are adjoined" (28). In "Serial Art, Systems, Solipsism" he explains that in seriality there must be an incremental variation of units, regular and systematic:

> Seriality is premised on the idea that the succession of terms (divisions) within a single work is based on a numerical or otherwise predetermined derivation (progression, permutation, rotation, reversal) from one or more of the preceding terms in that piece. Furthermore the idea is carried out to its logical conclusion…. (100)

Hence, while seriality may be based on mathematics or numerical systems, modularity is based on the exploration of predefined elements in a predefined framework determined by the artist. We can say that Fundamental Painting is logical and modular (and not serial – regular and systematic).

This concept of a never-ending yet personal exploration of a standard module brings to mind Ryman's typical "white square" as well as Agnes Martin's and Tomas Rajlich's gridded near-squares. Moreover, Raimund Girke's, Jerry Zeniuk's, and Gerhard Richter's paintings – plus, to a certain degree, the works of Jake Berthot, Louis Cane, and Stephen Rosenthal – seem to indicate a certain modularity going on. (In a monologue filmed by Matt Bertler, Jake Berthot even explains that his kind of painting is a method not a system.) The exhibited canvases of each of these artists all look very much alike. Moreover, Alan Charlton's standard 4.5 x 4.5 cm unit, which all his works are built on, is perhaps the strongest proof of a modular basis to Fundamental Painting in the show.

In a video presentation of his works in chronological order entitled *Alan Charlton: I am an artist who makes a grey painting*, he explains that all his paintings "developed out of paintings that went immediately before them" (11:31-11:35). All these paintings are part of this same module, and the slightest hint of disappearance of this modular quality from his works is a threat. Namely, at a certain point he says: "The only thing that did worry me was that – although the edge of this painting is still 4.5 centimeters – that [sic] the importance of the module seemed to disappear" (07:30-07:39).

Moreover, the works of Marthe Wéry are modular. In her working notes of 13 January 1975 sent to the curators of *Fundamental Painting* instead of an artist's statement, she indicates 1974 as the year when her modular quest in painting began and writes extensively on the subject:

> My work of a painter is always almost mechanical and, therefore, entails constraints. Yet, it only looks mechanical. It is taken over by this corporeal tension of doing or by the project inscribed in the action. This project: to go all the way. All the way to the end of the line; all the way to the edge of the page; all the way to the end of a series of pages. Experiences themselves inherently repetitive....
>
> This process of questioning the space of a painting happened progressively. It was momentarily interrupted when there was a refusal to inscribe a figure on a surface but where, at the same time, there was the recognition of the space as totally a surface. A second break came about with an explosion or unfolding of a series of surfaces, in order to pursue an experience in and of itself, undefined because it was grounded in doing so, in a tension that always came back and was destined to be relived again and again.
>
> If the series become infinite through this, it is because it instills itself according to this experience and not – or just accidentally – according to the result. Should a series end, this end can only be a sign of the series having run its course....[87]

Although Wéry uses the word *series* while clearly describing a modular process, this passage illustrates the commitment as well as the complexity of the painterly act in Fundamental Painting which questions over and over again the act of painting itself and its inherent elements. Marthe Wéry's answer to the *why* of this *how* is most probably valid for all Fundamental painters: "I think I'm a pragmatist. I can only understand things, if I've done them myself. My mind isn't abstract, it's very concrete" (*Wéry*).

Wéry – like all Fundamental painters – explores painting by painting. An indication of how this works is given by Wéry's notes of 21 August 1974, also sent to the curators at the time:

Repetition: That is the very nature of the framework of things. The framework is always a repetitive phenomenon. This fact – for me – justifies staying with the framework of the line, which is sufficiently diversified, thanks to the basic material, so as not to appear exhausted....

What does this experience correspond to? First of all, there is the submitting to an event.... Then, to circumstance.... The framework and the framework sought is looking for coherence or to reach a sort of coherence. I finally have the impression that the act of repeating and repeating ... puts me in the best place to wait for what I am seeking. It is not possible to separate the technique from the mental outlook, nor from psychological existence, the impression of living mentally. There is a kind of agreement, which results in activating the object's tiny, little textures....

The series creates this movement. It is a repetitive interpretation that influences or initiates its viewer.[88]

Once again, we notice the importance of working in a modular way – researching in depth the same few basic elements of painting, their inherent characteristics – as well as of the role intuition plays in this process. Not in the least, the importance of its visual communication to the viewer is stressed so that he participates in this questioning of painting *per sé*.

A specific point in the definition of Fundamental Painting by Dippel, mentioned numerous times before, is that the painterly process must be readable to the viewer. Dippel writes in her catalogue text:

Nearly all 'fundamental' painters show how the surface of the painting is made. How long it has taken to paint it is more difficult to see, but it is obviously a lengthy enterprise in most cases. This way of painting implies that extra attention is demanded from the visitor. A concentration of looking that happens to be more difficult to achieve than with any form of realistic painting. (14)

Also her role model Douglas Crimp states on the subject that:

[T]his painting employs non-relational parts, if any; logical procedures of applying material or 'skin' to supporting surface; a straightforward and simple approach to the act of painting a self-critical responsibility for the surface which accrues. One senses the artist's presence in these works ..., not, that is, in terms of the artist's sensibility or personality, but in the more inclusive sense that we are shown how this surface is *made* explicitly. (259)

Therefore, Fundamental painters develop their paintings based on predetermined ideas modified by intuition, without an overall conceptual plan – hence Dippel's naming it Post-Conceptual. This enterprise is a complex one, with the sole responsibility at the level of the artist – hence Dippel's naming it Post-Minimal (see Chapter 1.2). Although all works are based on a similar starting point, each work emerges as a careful combination of its components. Each painting is subjected to new decisions regarding support (material, size), paint (consistency, reflectivity, color and tone) and its application, and with which type of paintbrush (or other tool or technique). At the same time, the artist respects the inherent painterly qualities of each and every one of them. Fundamental Painting is modular in that it is based on the same module of exploring painting through its sole painterly elements, while it is logical in terms of the artist's making a choice as to what to explore. It is also personal by avoiding a systematic progression of the research on each and every module. Intuition plays an important role in the discovery of the inherent qualities and workings of the purely painterly elements within the chosen framework – which is painting as such. Therefore, each work is handmade and the sole responsibility of the artist.

Fundamental Painting is logical rather than rational as each decision in the painting process issues from the preceding one.[89] The module (its repetition) is thus not a constraint but a base for variation, allowing for the detailed exploration of the fundaments of painting. Fundamental Painting is a kind of "learning by doing" of the painting enterprise. As Hudson noted, it is not just a process but "embodied thinking" (3) – or in Dippel's terms, a mentality. This together with its communication to the viewer – the connection of the artist with the viewer in a visual dialogue on the subject of painting as concept, item and process, with the painting acting as the intermediary – are inherent concerns in the creative act.

2.1.8 Composition

As Fundamental Painting focuses on the specific elements and their effects, these become its subject-matter, leaving the composition non-objective and imageless – two further criteria of Fundamental Painting as indicated by Dippel (12).[90] Various authors writing on the American part of Fundamental Painting, Minimalist painting, confirm and specify this notion. For example, Strickland writes: "Specifically in painting, recurrent Minimalist qualities are non-representationalism and non-referentiality...." Continuing on the subject of composition he adds: "avoidance or extreme simplification of relations; ... identification of image and surface; unvaried replication of pattern within the individual canvas and in series; ... concentrism..." (22-23). This connects with Colpitt's words when she writes: "Balanced or 'equilibratory' relationships between elements are no longer the source of composition. Instead, symmetry appeared to be the most obvious solution to achieving non-relational composition" (43). The mere interrelation of painterly elements, where none dominates, is substituted for traditional relational composition. For one, the symmetrical shape of the canvas in combination with all-over patterns (or avoidance of a figure and ground) already leads the viewer through the scrutiny of the canvas. The format visually pulls the eye towards the center, while the traces of the artist left in the paint pull it back away from the center over and over again, yet it keeps whatever is happening on the surface. Flatness or "surfaceness" as Douglas Crimp calls it, is an essential factor.

When we scrutinize the works in *Fundamental Painting*, almost all of them meet these criteria, notably the monochrome canvases of Berthot, Cane, and Charlton, as well as Marden's multi-colored, multi-paneled works which tend to unify image and surface. Even their colored works are mostly so non-descript that no particular reference arises. In addition, the grid-line paintings of Martin, Rajlich, and Renouf, as well as the line paintings by Rosenthal and Wéry clearly demonstrate all-over patterns. All tend to present themselves at first glance as a stable symmetrical entity and function concentrically during the viewing process. (Only the multi-panel works with heavy brushwork by Jaap Berghuis and Kees Smits show more of a progression than a symmetrical, concentric format. Curiously enough, Richard Jackson's mural does seem to respond to these criteria – in theory, but in practice it does not read as a balanced unity.)

Furthermore, Raimund Girke's, Robert Ryman's, and Jerry Zeniuk's clearly-visible surface incidents on the painted plane do not distract from their sense of unity through apparent symmetry and their concentric reading. Even Gerhard Richter's gray monochromes announce their presence in such a way as to largely respect this kind of arrangement, although their apparent brushwork disperses the view all round. Fundamental painter Raimund Girke writes:

> There is no more composition in the traditional sense. The entire painting is only one structural plane, which is subdivided into structural fields, but in which no more formal dominants appear. The various structural elements, which brings the color plane to life – a still but extremely penetrating life [sic]. Every ever so tiny structural element has a function in the whole as part of the structured plane, it is active and therefore indispensable.

And he continues commenting on his own work: "Different directional values of the single structural fields stand out and are hidden again by the mutual penetration and transparent layering. The world of the monochrome offers the infinite possibilities a totally new character within the given limits" (Kultermann, n.p.).[91] In Girke's works, as well as in those of his peers, composition as such is lost in this meticulous way of discovering painting and its efficient communicational format. The picture plane is visually activated by the way it is painted, dismissing traditional composition.

Robert Mangold's "Thoughts on my work" that formed his artist's statement for the *Fundamental Painting* exhibition, then again, contain a seemingly traditional concern with balance (although in relation to a similar structural field) and explain the purpose of it – the "seeing-viewing-experiencing" by the public:

> A principal involvement in my work during the last ten years has been my concern with structure, the relation of the interior structure of the piece to the exterior shape. Edge line to inner line. A desire to make the picture a clear unity of shape/line – color/surface. A piece that would present itself directly, totally to the viewer, with all its information right there. An effort to avoid any preciousness, any romantic involvement with paint or painting. An effort for a utilitarian kind of work, economical, whose organization or structure and color is dictated by the plan and purpose of the piece. I think it is important for work to be new, constantly shifting to avoid repetition; to this end I intuitively push the work, this way or that, into new ways of dealing with the things that involve me.

Mangold's "extreme simplification of relations" (Strickland 22-23) still incorporates lines that read at first glance like figures. They might provide for a tendency to see them as outlines but this is quickly avoided thanks to his fundamental concern with the painterly elements (format, size, color, line, texture) and their impact on the viewer.

Clearly, it is not about any image to be represented outside of this basic, direct communication of the inherent elements of painting. It is about the equal importance of each of these elements, put together in a unique way. It is about the unified image (in other words: unifying the overall image to have it communicate all its elements at once, then have them unfold) and about expressing it in the most efficient way. The viewer's modes of perception are solicited and tested by the painting, concerning any and all basic painterly elements in it – be they just optical tricks or actually material in substance. Although relationships are inevitable, simplicity can override the domination of the formal ones. (In contrast, Van Koningsbruggen's canvases composed of dominant geometrical forms are clearly referential and focused on form in the traditional geometrical sense.)

As Fundamental painter Robert Ryman explained in 1972, he "kept trying to make it more basic, more simple." He added: "I didn't want anything in the paintings that didn't need to be there, because anything that's in a painting that doesn't need to be there, shouldn't be there" (Kurtz 42). On a similar note, Stephan Rosenthal wrote in his artist's statement for the show as his goal: "To make a painterly statement about the properties of painting, the givens of painting without expressive accessories" (FP 60). Painting is simplified to just the crucial parts.

As to the results of this kind of approach, Colpitt comments: "[t]he consequences of non-relational organization were threefold: structures appeared increasingly anonymous as compositional decisions decreased; impact on the spectator was more immediate as fewer details were presented for scrutiny; and most important of all, there was a resultant unity and wholeness of the work of art" (46-47). Alternatively, it could be said that the limitation of means has a maximal effect in activating the picture plane and, thus, bringing back the language of painting to the direct, elementary dialogue between the artwork and its beholder. This thoroughly defines Fundamental Painting.

Part of the intimacy with the viewer is not only thanks to the systematic absence of a subject in a composition (traditional, Renaissance-like approach) but also to the systematic absence of the frame. Considerations on the frame are a crucial part of Fundamental Painting. As Colpitt writes: "Once the painted image was made to stretch across the length and height of the picture-support, the concern with the figure's relation to the ground was replaced by an attraction to the relationship of pictured image to the framing edge of support" (50). Traditionally the frame creates a separation between the reality of the viewer and the reality inside the painting (the "window onto the world" effect). It makes the painting appear as a window to look through, separating its illusionist image from the wall – as well as from the viewer's space which, in turn, focuses the eye within the picture, to be exact –, at the same time that the frame delimits the painting as an object, as something separate from its environment. Fundamental Painting – which strives for "surfaceness" – aims to abandon this window-like quality and present the painting as an entity in its own right. Therefore, the frame – or lack of it – always comes into question among the fundamental (and Fundamental) painterly elements.

In a number of works by Alan Charlton in the *Fundamental Painting* exhibition, the *Untitled* (1974) series, the question of the frame takes on a central role. The paintings are each constructed of a central gray panel that has a traditional horizontally-placed, rectangular format, reminiscent of landscape painting, and another canvas as a kind of detached frame with similar horizontally-placed rectangular contours and the same gray tonality, placed all-around the central canvas. Between the two parts, a void of exactly 4.5 cm (Charlton's standard pictorial unit) reveals the wall behind. In this way, the painting instantly incites a contemplation of the frame in painting while at the same time linking the painting inseparably with its environment. Last but not least, by way of the bare wall, it insists on the object-like quality and flatness of the picture plane.

However, the other artists in the show (except for Agnes Martin) do not use a frame at all. As Colpitt writes: "The frame of the painting, which sets it off and distinguishes it from ordinary objects at the same time that it underscores the window-quality of painting, disappeared a generation before the sculptural base" (35). The non-framing of the painting positions it within the viewer's reality. This allows for the mostly monochromatic paintings to appear as flat "reliefs" on the wall. By dismissing the frame, Fundamental Painting pulls the relationship between painting and beholder into the spotlight.

In paintings that show a grid pattern, such a composition in combination with the absence of a frame facilitates an easy mental repetition and expansion of the work's grid beyond the canvas. In the mind of the viewer, the grid can be expanded equally *ad infinitum* to all sides. This way of working once again connects the painting to the reality of the viewer, while at the same time insisting on the work's two-dimensional quality and therewith on its objecthood. Hence, the absence of frame in Fundamental Painting is crucial for the self-contained one-to-one dialogue between artwork and beholder.

Following these ways of working and the other discoveries encountered by the various artists, Fundamental Painting seems by definition to focus on the painterly basics of painting and the direct dialogue with the viewer concerning them. A key element in this seems to be indeed Douglas Crimp's "surfaceness" (258). Flatness – or more precisely the inherent two-dimensional nature of the picture plane – is a recurrent fact in Fundamental Painting. In terms of composition, this means, as Colpitt once masterfully summarized, that:

> Pictorial depth was also treated symmetrically. In traditional painting with deep space, forms were strategically located so that the eye was guided through the painting in depth. Depicted objects were thus in an asymmetrical relationship to the picture plane. Such a painting cannot be sensibly switched from back to front. In contrast, non-relational, symmetrical balance induces flatness.... Like a laterally symmetrical painting without a top and bottom, foreground and background no longer have any meaning. A view from behind the "scene" would be the same as from the front. (44)

With these considerations in mind, when we turn back to the enumeration of characteristics of Minimalist or "opaque" painting by American historians like Edward Strickland and Douglas Crimp and to our previous research into the elements of Fundamental Painting, flatness becomes an important value to preserve instead of a condition to start with (as also specifically pointed out by Dippel). It is an inherent feature of a canvas, for its inherent connotations. In Fundamental Painting, in which each element is given equal importance – be it part of the material, concept, or process –, a new kind of balance is achieved; and the seemingly minimal content evokes a maximal impact. Letting go of the traditional frame around the picture plane (or incorporating it as part of the painting surface) is part of this process, since it positions the painting as an entity in and of itself in the same reality as the viewer's. The picture plane (imageless, non-relational, symmetrical or concentric) insists on its objecthood instead of some illusionism through its ways of applying the basic painterly elements and the basic painterly materials. As a result, all that the viewer can discover in the painting – all the pictorial effects of the painterly elements – is right there on the two-dimensional picture plane. Hence, this plane is indeed by definition a painting.

The painting now is a unified plane. It is an activated structural field – visible at one glance – which takes into consideration the viewing habits of its beholder. A reduction of relations between elements within the painting increases the importance of the relation between this painting and its spectator. As Colpitt puts it: "In Minimalism … the relationship of parts (figure to ground, image to shape of the support in painting…) is internal; external relationships are on the other hand set up between the object and spectator" (41). The dialogue on painting is already inherent in the painting, yet comes into being in dialogue with its viewer.

2.1.9 The viewer

In the end, Fundamental Painting is not just about painting but about the viewer too, who then becomes the final painterly element in Fundamental Painting. We can summarize the previous chapters on the elements of Fundamental Painting as follows. To quote Suzanne Hudson:

> Painting becomes a less static or grounded medium and a more fluid, material site for the continual testing and reworking of conventions and the effects that these conventions or properties produce. What a painting *is* becomes inextricable from what a painting *does*. It all starts with paint, but paint alone is not sufficient to produce a painting; it is necessary but not sufficient. A painting needs paint, a support, a delimitation of that support in the form of an edge, a wall (a viewing context), and someone to see it – to register as a painting…. (105-106)

According to the Fundamental Painting mentality, the dialogue with the viewer or, at least, the communication of the painterly elements to the viewer is a crucial element – as has been suggested in previous chapters.

In the artists' statements for the *Fundamental Painting* show, we find a number of hints as to this importance of the viewer – and the viewer's ability to recreate in their mind the creative act of painting. For example, Stephen Rosenthal's words are illustrative of this idea of making a painting and of the viewer's recreating or decoding it visually:

> To make a painterly statement about the properties of painting, the givens of painting without expressive accessories.
> To define states of material as they are confined to the process of application.
> To make optical objects….
> To make physical concretion contingent upon optical consciousness….
> To place the substratum of painting on the surface.

To make visible a narrow range of values on the periphery of awareness....

To make painting a code, as part of a visual system far from its point of conception. (FP 60)

Kees Smits, then again, states: "Every painting is ... a parallel image, of my actions while making the painting."[92] The scope of Fundamental Painting is to involve the viewer in the contemplation of the basic elements of painting, leading them to recreate the creative act itself.

Yet, there seems to be more to this than just the recreation of the working process through the recreation of the painterly elements. For example, in an interview filmed at Art Cologne 2016, Richard Jackson explains about his early Wall Paintings like the one exhibited in *Fundamental Painting* that "the idea was to expand painting, make it bigger, make it a kind of walking-through experience rather than just a flat thing on the wall. [....] They have to come to it and figure it out, how this works. You know, how the system worked...." (06:18-06:50) Brice Marden puts it as follows: "That space [of a painting on the wall] is the expression of the vision of the painter. The painter strives to make his expression explicit because he wants to affect man" (FP 42). Thus, the perception of a painting comes down to (the experience of) its beholder.

In *Agnes Martin: With my back to the world*, Agnes Martin says something similar: "I don't see why we would consider it [her work] spiritual. [...] It just is everyday an experience." (00:50:1-00:50:24) Also, Alan Charlton's statement taken from Giacometti, "The adventure, the great adventure, is to see something unknown appear each day..." (Qtd. in FP 26), indirectly points to the visual nature of painting. Furthermore, in *Arts Magazine* art critic Dore Ashton notes, in relation to the works of Jake Berthot from the same years as exhibited in the show, that "painting, to be a work of art, must be a self-contained metaphor. The metaphor ... gathers speculation and emotion into an artfully condensed unit."

Whether it is in terms of conveying feeling or in terms of being reminiscent or revelatory of something to the viewer, the artwork triggers something in its beholder. The painting is finished under the scrutiny of its viewer, and not just because "beauty is in the eye of the beholder." In fact, the viewer seems to be the final element in painting. What's more, the viewer is a living element and therefore this discourse becomes interactive. Fundamental Painting is founded upon the basics of painting in the traditional sense, while at the same time it avoids looking like at a traditional painting.

Robert Mangold says it all with his coined term "seeing-viewing-experiencing," and he adds: "If it's done right then the final object is really somehow much more important than the idea" (*View* 7). The viewer is central to painting now, yet the focus is more on the painting itself (as opposed to Abstract Expressionism, which was all about the viewing experience). Colpitt brings it to a point when writing: "Where process issues concern the work of art as a *physical object*, internal and external aesthetic issues pertain to the *perceptual object* as it is experienced by the spectator" (41).[93]

For one, there is the purely factual kind of a perception of the painting, whose experience now encompasses real space. As Alan Charlton stated in a video monologue on his lifetime work in the 1980s, entitled *I am an artist who makes a grey painting*: "With all the paintings the space inside and outside the painting is as important as the painting itself" (09:57-10:02). That is to say, the space of a Fundamental painting, which is by definition flat, is in the viewer's space.

Agnes Martin explains the interaction with the viewer in her work: "looking at art is like 'a simple direct going into a field of vision as you would cross an empty beach to look at the ocean'" (Wilson 48). It is not simply a matter of the viewer looking at the view before him, but of their entering into and moving across a field of vision. The horizon cuts the sky but this is not fixed: it is always relative to the spectator's altering viewpoint. The distance that visually maintains the horizon in its proper place collapses or unfolds as soon as the spectator moves, while the horizon seems to merely move up and down – not back and forth. Similarly, paintings like Martin's stay flat on the surface, although they change in reaction to the viewer's movement. Thus, this kind of painting is more "across" than "in" space, as Conceptual artist and art critic Mel Bochner once remarked ("Excerpts" 70).

"Surfaceness" is crucial in this context, as we have seen from previous discussions on the insistence on painting as a two-dimensional entity. Colpitt explains:

> Lateral symmetry (across the picture plane, as opposed to through it in depth) forces the spectator to change his or her viewing habits: no left to right scanning is encouraged. Reading is adirectional, and so relationships between one area of the canvas and another do not occur. Lateral symmetry implies imaginary quadrants of left and right, top and bottom. An axis, either centrally vertical or horizontal, is created to which the eye gravitates but tends not to cross. (44)

Although symmetrical, one part of a Fundamental painting cannot be substituted for any other part due to its slight variations by virtue of its hand-made nature. This means that the painting is not to be interpreted as an object in a room but as a concrete surface, a surface that is real as opposed to a "window onto the world."

The painting acts as a manifestation within the viewer's reality. The Fundamental painting is a surface that can be read: it exists in real space and in a situation. Space when presented as flatness incites a more detailed reading by the viewer of its pictorial elements, thereby establishing a dialogue between the two entities. Colpitt describes this as follows: "The form is completely given at once. What unfolds in time is the experience: a series of changing perceptive states based on the relationship of the viewer's body to the object." (97) And she specifies: "The awareness of the duration of the experience is especially pronounced since the spectator does not give him- or herself up to the object, but retains a persistent awareness of self as separate from the object of contemplation." (95)

Crimp puts his finger on the point *how* and *why* this relation to the viewer is so vital when he writes:

> In Opaque painting there is no fictive scale.... Staying on the surface, one is aware only of real scale, the proportion of the painting to one's self.... It should be emphasized that this relationship does not lead to a latent illusion of anthropomorphism; rather it functions to make the viewer aware of his own cognitive activity ..... (258)

The dialogue between viewer and painting offers more than the sum of its parts; it seems to provoke a heightened sense of awareness.

Marthe Wéry, in the working notes of 21 August 1974 she submitted to *Fundamental Painting*, describes the result of her relation to the painting and the link to the viewer as follows:

> It is simply something that lives, that transforms itself in living.... It is, in any case, something that gives the impression of participating in the deepest pulsation within the nature of things and by this fact, without doubt, of oneself. A sort of pact that is made and that lives – or is provoked. Whatever part of it remains must, in principle, in turn, foster it once again, as long as one remains open.[94]

Moreover, Alan Charlton writes in 2012: "The 'presence' of the painting is what I try to do, this is more important than how it is made or painted, the feeling (emotion) between the viewer and the painting is vital. This is the 'art'" (3). This subject of a "pulse of the nature of things" or the "art" in Fundamental Painting – the *je ne sais quoi* of it all –, which issues from the combination of artwork and viewer, will be taken up again later in the chapter concerning the significance of Fundamental Painting.

2.2 The Fundamental mentality

Now that we have explored Fundamental Painting in detail, we are in a better position to compare and contrast – to validate or invalidate – the curators' choice. By reviewing the lifetime works of the artists in the show – one by one – for their Fundamental qualities or treatment of format, size, scale, color, line, and texture; by considering the artists' use of materials and tools, their process, and their approach to composition; and finally by retracing the viewing experience created, their artistic proposition can be checked against the Fundamental mentality. Now that we have a detailed overview and have had ample opportunity through decades to reflect on it, we are better able to assess Fundamental painters' works of the time and the oeuvre of these artists. Accordingly, their validity as adherents to Fundamental Painting can be tested.

The perseverance of their mentality in painting is, by now, known. Consequently, this chapter will highlight the unique Fundamental touch for each oeuvre or, the one thing that makes it run counter to this painting vein. It will become apparent that not all artists included in the 1975 show, *Fundamental Painting,* have remained true to this current, while some other artists (notably from the larger group of Analytical Painting that the organizers of the show at the Stedelijk Museum Amsterdam specifically excluded at the time) can now be included. Thus, we hope that with this chapter the correctly circumscribed historical fact of Fundamental Painting's existence is given its due.

The works of the four Minimalist artists in the show – Robert Mangold (1937), Brice Marden (1938), Agnes Martin (1912-2004), and Robert Ryman (1930-2019) around whom the exhibition was built – show a rather diversified range. Nevertheless, they do seem to exemplify the full range of Fundamental Painting. Ryman – listed in the show as being both the Fundamental Painting's core and its predecessor – indeed seems to be the Fundamental painter *par excellence*. As a researcher, he meticulously explores each and every nuance of each and every painterly element. Mangold could be seen as a more traditional kind of Fundamental painter, carefully balancing each and every element in an almost scholastic way. He pushes the limits and gets as close to a traditional kind of understanding of the elements as possible, without giving in to their traditional use. This becomes notably evident in his use of color and figure.

Similarly, Marden tends to position himself in line with the continuum of the painting medium throughout time. While visually proposing a thoroughly Fundamental kind of painting, he hints at the inclusion of a metaphysical element, as his statement for the exhibition catalogue indicates. His works are more about the "feel" of non-referential colors than about the visual rendering of the artist's processes and the workings of the painterly elements. Martin admits outright to creating her painting according to a "vision" and for that – in line with her generation – leans towards Abstract Expressionism.[95] Also her luscious hues are unlike the Fundamental preference for neutral colors. Having said that, her preconceived, industrial-looking, utterly flat compositions and human scale canvases make Martin a Fundamental painter.

As Robert Pincus-Witten seemed to sense already in 1972, Fundamental Painting comes from Agnes Martin's type of painting and fans out from Ryman's "painting as theory" to Marden's painting "as the expression of sensibility," in line with the tradition inherent to the medium. Yet, these painters' artistic issues are so specific and so concentrated that they all belong to the same "problematic region of discourse" (50), as seen in Part Two. Marden, and Mangold are still exploring it, as Martin and Ryman did until their death in 2004 and 2019 respectively. As the previous discussion of the use of each element in the artists' works exhibited in *Fundamental Painting* has shown, the painters that seem to fit into this framework as delimited by these four American Minimalists are Alan Charlton, Tomas Rajlich, Raimund Girke, Edda Renouf, and Marthe Wéry.

Charlton (1948) most certainly offers the most factual (almost conceptual) approach to Fundamental Painting. His materials, tools, and processes are never varying. His elements are reduced to the absolute minimum: 4.5-centimeter stretchers, a human-scale format divisible by 4.5 centimeters, and smoothly applied (no facture) gray paint without any drawn lines. His intuition is merely let loose for the choice of format or gray tone for whichever series he's creating. His artistic intervention dwindles to a barely perceived act. Still, the creative process is the sole responsibility of the artist. Most of the variables are to be found in the interaction with the viewer.

The inherent elegance of his paintings might also nudge them over to the other side of the Fundamental Painting range, close to Marden's. For over four decades now, he has been painting his smooth gray modular canvases. His works have become ever more elaborate, with multiple panels. As the viewer approaches the paintings (perhaps moving from side to side) the proportions visually vary. The relationship between the various canvases shifts. A dynamic is achieved within the work, which – curiously enough – one sees as a whole and not as a series of separate unrelated gray rectangles, despite the reiterating bare wall between the panels. The experience, which unfolds after the initial mental register, is based on the particular relationship of each viewer to the work.

As opposed to Charlton's work, the experience of Tomas Rajlich's (1940) paintings is purely visual, focused on the painting inside the painting. His is the most dogmatic (painterly) in his Fundamental approach to painting. Facture is an element to be examined in all its likenesses. The artist's touch is inherent to his (near) square canvases of human scale, with his trademark modular grid or ridge of bare canvas and dripping-paint lines. However, Rajlich's work has evolved since the mid-1970s. The canvases present more variations on the vertical rectangle instead of the (near) square. The varieties of the grid (drawn, painted, negative form) and its placement (over and under the paint) have been explored, gradually making way for ever more emphasis upon the edge. Today, bare canvas surrounds the work like a frame. This is a response to the question of what a painting is, demonstrating that a painting can even be a bare canvas as long as it is part of the unified picture plane. The artist's touch has become less gestural but the hand-painted quality of the painting is never abandoned.

Rajlich's subdued palette has given way to a wide range of shimmering colors. Notably, in the 1980s he started working in gold pigments (cf. Agnes Martin's small-scale painting *Untitled* [1961] executed with oil and golden ink on canvas in the *Fundamental Painting* show) and has been using shimmering paints ever since. More recent work incorporated mother-of-pearl, aluminum foil, or metallic sparkles into the paint. Colpitt writes on this subject: "Industrial colors, particularly metallic ones

… connot[e] a certain functionalism. Such surfaces reflect light, rather than absorb it, and affirm the flatness of the picture plane and the actuality of the object" (29). Thus, Rajlich's lifetime work has moved closer over time to approaching flatness ("surfaceness"). Also, it is evident now that light is the final creative element of painting and that there is a continuous (re)creation of the painting each time it is seen, again and again. Multiple decades of such painting have still not exhausted the possibilities of his Fundamental Painting.

Next, Raimund Girke (1930-2002) was a quite painterly Fundamental painter, who never abandoned his quest. The likeness of his paintings hardly changed over time. Only in his later works, dark colors – especially blue and black – entered the scene, and his brushstrokes became more gestural. Thus, his lifetime oeuvre was modular as a whole. His early paintings' surfaces are very delicate in their facture, which is not counterbalanced with an emphasis on the object. The surface modulation has an utterly visual quality. It does not look palpable; rather he allows his white and light-gray canvases to fuse into a colored plane that is more sensed than taken in visually. His works are a step in the direction of a slightly elusive rather than factual kind of Fundamental Painting, dangerously close to Analytical Abstraction. (Remember the quality of the latter to elude its visibility by creating an atmosphere through color, especially white.)

Finally, Edda Renouf (1943) and Marthe Wéry (1930-2005) seem to adhere to the more metaphysical kind of Fundamental Painting judging by their texts on the inherent life of materials in painting and the communication of this "living" painting with the viewer. Both Renouf and Wéry (until her death in 2005) consistently continued creating works that at first glance visually do not differ much from the works exhibited in *Fundamental Painting*. They hold true in all categories specified as characteristic for Fundamental Painting. Yet, their tendency to use color in their works relatively often (Wéry even using bold primaries outright) makes them rather stand out. This is reminiscent of the color use of Brice Marden, who, at the time, was likewise starting to allude to the metaphysical. However, unlike the Abstract Expressionists, neither Renouf nor Wéry were trying to specifically allude to the metaphysical and thus their work remained Fundamental.

While the aforementioned artists all take factual approaches, including a possible metaphysical angle, Jake Berthot (1939) is different in that he takes a subjective approach in working with emotions as opposed to the objective viewing experience sought by Fundamental painters – and therefore retrospectively cannot be included among them. Dore Ashton writes in *Art Magazine*:

> Berthot belongs to the family of painterly painters who make no pretense that "real" life can somehow alter that nature of art, make it more legible, more accessible to the

> quick take. He remains within the great tradition in which the boundaries of the painted surface are definitive. Everything occurs within.... The metaphor, as it has always functioned in both painting and poetry, gathers speculation and emotion into an artfully condensed unit. It can never be a slice of life for it has been abstracted from life and fashioned to catch up a host of indefinable thoughts and feelings into a single, striking image. The range of expression available within the metaphor is always greater than the stuff of the metaphor itself. It is to the problem of range of feeling that Berthot most consistently addresses himself. (33-34)

Hence, Berthot's paintings are a metaphor for feeling. They communicate something subjective about the artist or the viewer, albeit undefined. This excludes him from the Fundamental mentality. Accordingly, since the exhibition his work first gained referential titles, then became a kind of tile mosaic of colored planes, and finally, by the mid-1980s, reached his ultimate style – blurry landscape painting – which he continues today.

In fact, a large number of artists in *Fundamental Painting* have turned out not to have been so Fundamental at all. As Alan Charlton writes in his letter in 2012: "The Fundamental Painting exhibition was very important. However, shortly afterwards painting changed to figurative/wild painting. Many of the artists in that exhibition also changed with the fashion" (3). Together with Jake Berthot, the artists Richard Jackson, Gerhard Richter, Louis Cane, Jaap Berghuis, and Kees Smits, in retrospect have revealed that they did not have the Fundamental Painting mentality after all. Stephen Rosenthal and Jerry Zeniuk, then again, are a disputable inclusion to the *Fundamental Painting* show. And Rob van Koningsbruggen (1948) had already at the time personally renounced his place in the exhibition.

According to an undated note sent by Rini Dippel to Edy de Wilde, the statement printed in the inlay to the catalogue was supposed to read: "As this catalogue goes to press Rob van Koningsbruggen has announced his withdrawal because he cannot, after all, agree with the concept underlying this exhibition." When we consider his works in view of the above characteristics of Fundamental Painting, one must agree with the artist. His canvases, either rectangular or geometrically shaped, are neither small nor relate to the human being through their scale. They function much more like signs on the wall. Plus, the execution of the paintings was not exactly the responsibility of the artist. As he says in his statement, he had no control over the final application of the pigments; neither did he want to have it. He did not research paint as a material, nor did he seem to work with the materiality of the other elements in painting in a visual way. On the contrary, his line has a clearly descriptive, contouring function. His composition is similarly rather conventional. It is neither self-referential, symmetrical, concentric, nor unified. His later works are similar and definitely not congruent with the Fundamental approach. Nevertheless, a number of works were included in the *Fundamental Painting* show "thanks to the cooperation of the collector Christiaan Braun," as the inlay to the catalogue informs the reader.

Furthermore, the inclusion of Richard Jackson (1939) in the exhibition, which director Edy de Wilde insisted on despite the curators' reservations, seems to have been a mishap. In the chapter on format, it was pointed out that Jackson created more an environment (a sort of monumental mural) than a human-scale painting. Moreover, his work was brightly colored. He also used a canvas on stretchers as his tool to smear the paint across the wall – an object reminiscent of a painting but traditionally not used to create the painting. Intuition was virtually absent in his carefully planned execution. Furthermore, despite a concentric and diagonally symmetrical composition, Jackson's work did not read like a unified image.

In an interview with the author on 25 August 2011, Rini Dippel stated that director Edy de Wilde wanted Jackson to be included. The curatorial team was uncertain what to do with him in the context of the exhibition. The curators' questioning of his place in Fundamental Painting is illustrated by Dippel's questions in her notes entitled "Gereduceerde Schilderkunst:" "Possibly still most comparable to the colors of Johns? Or a totally individual 'input' of the West Coast of the USA? … art creates art" (2).[96] The evolution of Richard Jackson confirms that he is not an artist committed to Fundamental Painting. In later years, his works evolved into brightly colored environments – sculptural and interactive.

Also Gerhard Richter (1932) did not stick to the research into painting by way of painting. His artist's quest has been a conceptual one concerning the image. The texts accompanying his gray paintings of the mid-1970s already indicate this interest. In the passages on both format and color from his artist's statement, his interest seems to tend towards the conceptual implication of the specific choices and not the actual formal research into these elements. He seems to want to communicate nothingness rather than painting. Plus, the application of the painterly elements does not indicate a Fundamental process. For example, the illusionist potential of his brush-stroked plane is not counteracted by indicators of flatness nor emphasized by a concentric reading aid.

Similarly, the notes of the curators concerning the selection for artists to be included in the *Fundamental Painting* show bear witness to the difficulty of including his work in the Fundamental Painting mentality. In an undated, early meeting note of the curatorial team of *Grenzen van de schilderkunst* (Limits of Painting) – which is later to become *Fundamental Painting* – on the concept of the show ("Opzet"), "some works by Gerhard Richter" are listed as part of the historical context of the show. In another undated note on the exhibition *Grenzen van de Schilderkunst* which also refers to the concept ("1e Opzet"), Richter is included in the "tangent figures" to the "core group" of Fundamental painters. Then, in a letter by Dippel to De Wilde dated 10 January 1975, it seems that the curators were discussing whether or not to include Gerhard Richter in the *Fundamental Painting* exhibition at all; Gallery owner Konrad Fischer who represented the artist strongly felt they should. Finally, Richter was included in the exhibition, and his works were hung in room 39. In view of this indecisiveness of the curatorial team on Richter's place in Fundamental Painting, we can cite the critique uttered by Winfred Gaul in his letter addressed to Edy de Wilde, which arrived at the museum on 18 March 1975: "The presence in such an exhibition of someone like Richter, who does not analyze the materials of painting, but treats styles ironically, is utterly incomprehensible."[97]

Also the works of Louis Cane (1943) are disputable. Already at the time, his canvases stood out in the *Fundamental Painting* exhibition with their coloring and monumental size. In France, in the early 1970s, he was known as the theoretical writer and editor of the Supports/Surface periodical rather than as one of the visual artists of the group. With hindsight, we know that his works at the time of the show had a somewhat Fundamental appearance, but that most of all his other creations were far removed from that. In fact, since the mid-1970s he has mostly painted in a figurative manner. Given this as well as the fact that both the organizers of the exhibition and others with theories on 1970s painting tend to separate the French kind of new current from the more Nordic ones, it would be safe to say that Louis Cane is not a Fundamental painter.

The trouble with Kees Smits's (1945) works, which (if we believe the preparatory exhibition notes) the curators were equally unsure whether to include or not in the *Fundamental Painting* show, lies mainly in their viewing experience as well as their execution. His multi-panel compositions painted over in a dynamic gestural pattern read rather like a sequence than a concentric and unified composition. The skewed balance between elements as well as the lack of symmetry do not allow for a detailed reading of the surface. The relatively imposing color does not help in the balancing either. Also, the use of a sponge instead of a proper painterly instrument for their execution as well as their non-stop execution according to a preconceived plan do not hold entirely true to the Fundamental mentality. The works of Jaap Berghuis (1945 to 2005) pose a similar problem regarding inclusion into the Fundamental Painting category. It is only that Berghuis has no preconceived idea of the painting before execution.

Finally, both Stephan Rosenthal (1935) and Jerry Zeniuk (1945) are dubious inclusions in Fundamental Painting. Their works at the time of the eponymous show did largely respond to the criteria of this mentality in painting. Especially Zeniuk's works were fully congruent with the Fundamental approach, except maybe for the fact that he used his hands to paint with. Although painters are known to have used their finger to make the odd stroke at times, painting with your hands is not inherently painterly. Rosenthal's works from the 1970s then again show a number of inconsistencies. First of all, the loose hanging of the works in the show was unfortunate in view of the aim of flatness or "surfaceness" in Fundamental Painting. Also the linear structure (obtained by scratching) which covers his canvases does not encourage a concentric or centrally-focused reading.

When viewing the evolution of the work of both artists in retrospect, we discover an equally problematic discrepancy. After pursuing his kind of Fundamental painting style for a number of years, Rosenthal switched to painting that allowed "the particularity of each image to reach the brink of the recognizable without going over it" as Ben La Rocco put it on the occasion of his 2008 show at Margarethe Roeder Gallery. Zeniuk, on the other hand, came up in the 1980s with his trademark color blotches. Ever since then, he has been creating rectangular canvases with differently colored, uneven spots distributed across the bare canvas surface. Both artists have redirected their scope, if it had ever been Fundamental to begin with. For this reason, Rosenthal and Zeniuk do not belong to the "real" Fundamental Painting vein.

However, it must be stated that Jerry Zeniuk is of a different opinion. He is virtually the only artist that was included in the 1975 show who today designates himself as a Fundamental painter with those very words: "I see myself as a Fundamental painter, a Formalist." (And he accepts Stephen Rosenthal as a fellow-painter who was dealing with the same kind of reductivist painting in those days.) At the same time, in the same telephone conversation with the author on 1 December 2012, he explained his painting does not come from the same vein as Ryman's. According to Zeniuk "Ryman is paint, paint staying on the surface," his works are about an idea. Zeniuk's own works, he believes, are more than that. He claims they are about color and come from Cézanne and Mondrian. This allows for his more recent works (of colored spots on bare canvas) to be a continuation of his monochromes from the 1970s, he concludes. The artist simply describes it as a "clearer" version of the "unclear" 1970s paintings. He is concerned with painterly issues and if this is understood correctly, one can see that it is neither decorative, sentimental, nor atmospheric. It is about color in relation to surface, on the one hand very pictorial while on the other still very materialistic. So, from this viewpoint, Zeniuk might be considered a Fundamental painter, who is on the other end of the scale (the "painterly" group) from Ryman (the "core" group).

In the end – retrospectively –, the true Fundamental painters in the 1975 show *Fundamental Painting* were the four American painters of Minimal Art, around whom the exhibition was conceived, and five European artists. Furthermore, the show included two painters who deviated from the Fundamental path in mid-career and four artists who were incorrectly included in the show by its curatorial team. Another three artists were added to the group show due to pressure exercised on the curators by lenders, galleries, and the museum director. All the artists' texts from the 1970s connect to painting of the Fundamental kind, even though their works might not be consistent with their words.

Therefore, today, we can agree with Dutch art historian and critic Philip Peters who wrote in 1993 on the subject of the *Fundamental Painting* show that:

> It is doubtful whether nowadays it would occur to anyone to present such a motley company under the same label, except for the fact that some of the artists shown then at the Stedelijk belonged to more or less the same generation. And if it were done, the label now would be probably completely different. I well remember 1975 and that exhibition at the Stedelijk and at the time I thought the grouping together completely acceptable. Now the artist [sic] are in a different phase of life and at a different stage of their career and developments inside and outside art over almost twenty years make us view their work differently. In other words, the work then has been given another context by what was done afterwards and our way of looking, of considering has changed.

At the time, these eighteen artists (take or leave a few) might have seemed to form the perfectly congruent Fundamental Painting vein. Even their works and texts from the time show a common mentality (as discovered in Part II) in quite some detail. Yet, in retrospect, the Fundamental Painting label still holds true for only about half of them. These are the true Fundamental painters, for the nature of a mentality is that it does not change over time and stays with one for life.

2.2.1 The range in Fundamental mentality

In retrospect, it would be more evident to pinpoint who the "real" Fundamental painters are and to identify others of this mentality, who were in their first hours in the mid-1970s and persist until today. Let's have a closer look at how the show divided up the various Fundamental categories. There seems to be a range in line with Robert Pincus-Witten's view, who writes that this kind of painting issued from Martin and was represented by a range from Ryman – painting as theory – to Marden – painting as sensibility (50). Indeed, some kind of range like this can be found when comparing and contrasting the works of these three American Minimalist painters. It is a range stemming from a kind of Abstract Expressionist, painterly painting – which, however, does not create atmosphere but stays flat along the surface. The range spans a theoretical, meticulous discovery of painterly materials to the discovery of the life (the feeling) within these materials, all the while respecting the painting as a two-dimensional entity by definition.

The explanation for these highly personal modes of Fundamental expression might be found in the personal background of each artist. Agnes Martin is a generation older than Ryman and Marden. Chronologically, this makes her part of the Abstract Expressionist generation. As she states in the video documentary entitled *Agnes Martin: With my back to the world*, she considers herself "the last Abstract Expressionist," explaining: "I'm not a Minimalist; I'm an Abstract Expressionist. I believe in having my emotions recorded in the painting." (00:33:30-00:34:00) As we learn from the same film, the works appear to her during her states of meditation. (This might be related to the fact that she suffered from schizophrenia, although she adamantly defended that her illness had no relation to her work.) She believes in inspiration, while she has let go of all facts and preconceived ideas, because these will not lead to learning the truth about life. (00:35:22-00:37:30) It strikes a chord with the mysticism of the "abstract sublime"[98] that the Abstract Expressionists such as Mark Rothko and Barnett Newman consciously preserved in relation to their very painterly, imageless painting.

The space in Martin's paintings (unlike theirs) is flat on the surface and moves depending on the position of the viewer, the same way a horizon moves between the flat vision of water and sky while one moves across a plane. She explains this sensation of space in interview, *Agnes Martin: With my back to the world*, how she discovered this driving out of New Mexico and seeing the plane (00:26:07-00:28:02). However, Martin's obsession with large expanses of water and her fascination for the "ocean [which] is deathless" (Glimcher between 200 and 201) shimmers through already in her earliest life choices. Before she became a professional painter, she worked in a children's daycare center of the Liberty – the largest dock on the Swan Island in the Willamette River –, and upon her arrival in New York City in late 1957, she settled at 27 Coenties Slip, Manhattan's former busiest and largest dock, attracted by "the open expanses afforded by the river" (Haskell 101). It is also a recurrent theme in her written notes (Glimcher between 16 and 17) and work, as for example in her movie *Gabriel*.

Robert Ryman, originally from Tennessee, went to New York City in 1952 as a musician. In the early years, he played Bebop on the tenor saxophone in bars around the city, as he explains to Barbaralee Diamonstein-Spielvogel. In the same manner that jazz exploits a variation on a theme, which can be represented in module-based scores, his white paintings could be seen as similar variations on one square base module.[99] Ryman says himself, he believes that music "had an influence on [his] approach to painting, because you play it on a structure, and you learned your instrument, and then you played within this structure" (*Art:21* 1:00-1:10). His knowledge of painting came from visiting museums and, eventually, his job as an attendant at the Museum of Modern Art allowed him to sit and look at paintings all day. His learning, therefore, is primarily formalist. Accordingly, his paintings are very much focused on the formal elements and on what happens visually if these are worked in one way or the other. Ryman intensely explores paint and other materials until, at a certain point, he decides that the painting is finished. This is painting as theory, or rather as a kind of scientific research approach.

Lastly, there is Brice Marden, a generation younger than Ryman. Marden attended the Boston University School of Art (1958-1961), where he studied under Reed Kay who is known to have stressed that "a serious artist is well acquainted through experience with the properties of materials" (Mancusi-Ungaro 113). Marden did not have any interest in the debate on the "objectness" of artworks that prevailed in the 1960s, as he informed Carol Mancusi-Ungaro in an interview on 1 October 1992, yet questions of scale, depth of support, and the like did matter very much to him. However, he contemplated them intuitively, not theoretically (111). Considerations about his work are very much in the area of sensibility.

Yet, his early monochromatic paintings came out of a thorough painterly process. In an interview on 21 December 2005, he admits his work is "a combination of intuition and formality" (Mancusi-Ungaro 111). Already, Marden's canvas was primed in view of wanting "a real surface, a paint surface" and even at this early stage, "it was important that [his] hand be involved" (112). Marden would make his own paint mixtures based on wax in order to arrive at a perfect surface, as he writes in his technical statement (*Marden* 28). The surfaces of his gray paintings from the late 1960s do matter. They are smooth but very much handcrafted. The circular smudges, that can be vaguely discerned at the edges of the paintings, sometimes testify to the artist having smoothed out the painted surface with a spatula. Imperfections due to an uneven canvas surface remain and are accentuated by the many layers of paint.

Besides the fact of being a surface, these reminders of the artist's intervention – these barely visible traces of its handmade quality – are central to Marden's work. In a 1988 article by Saul Ostrow, Marden called the layers of paint in these works "veils of feeling." As he explained, "It seems as though, because the early paintings were just one color, one could say one color, no feelings – but instead of no feelings they were all this feeling. Each layer was a color, was ... a feeling that related to the feeling, the color, the layer beneath it" (32-33). Marden does not mean some emotional feeling or sensitivity of the spectator but the actual visual feeling of the paint, experienced by the spectator in its presence. It is about the visual feeling of each individual flat surface.

Robert Mangold, the fourth Minimalist painter falls in between the two extremes – Ryman's theory and Marden's sensibility – already detailed above, as defined by Pincus-Witten. The curators of the *Fundamental Painting* show categorize him within the "painterly" group, i.e. with a somewhat more "traditional" direction. His works manage a balancing act of all their elements, while at the same time respecting each and every one of these with their own inherent qualities, which recalls the approach of non-objective painting at the Bauhaus. Mangold's approach to painting is both theoretical and intuitive. Mangold had been a student at Yale when the school was under the strong influence of Josef Albers who was a professor there for many years. Congruent with the Bauhaus education Albers passed on, Mangold's lifetime work has been very much concerned with the comprehensive analysis of each and every one of the painterly elements. He has explored the inherent qualities and working of each of them, prioritizing one or the other in different series over the years. The application of each and every element – the fluidity of a layer of paint, the thickness or color of a certain drawn line, and the like – is meticulously decided upon by intuition in order to make all elements work in a perfectly balanced way so that none of them dominates even the slightest bit.

Taking a closer look at the other artists exhibited in the *Fundamental Painting* show who were found to be the "true" Fundamental painters, a similar range from Ryman to Marden (the core group of the show) can be discovered, originating in painting like Martin's (according to Pincus-Witten's definition of the American branch). The curators categorize Stephen Rosenthal and Edda Renouf in the "painterly" group, because of their linear structures, while Tomas Rajlich is considered as something in-between – both painterly and "core" fundamental. They group Alan Charlton with Robert Mangold as working with figure or shape, and they place Raimund Girke and Jerry Zeniuk among the core ranging from Ryman to Marden, at the respective ends. Marthe Wéry was not yet included in the show at the time of the curators' considerations on categorization. (Given the final placement of her works in the exhibition spaces, it can be assumed that her work was likewise considered part of the painterly group under Agnes Martin.) In this context, it should be noted that the curators originally not only divided the show into two veins, but also added another "tangent" group to the "core" category. It is interesting, with hindsight that the artists included in this tangent group could more than be justified as such for they turned out not to be true Fundamental artists at all. (See also chapter 2.1.)

Based on the study in previous chapters of the application and effects in Fundamental works, we can find a similar range but a slightly different division from the one made by the curators at the time. In retrospect, Rajlich seems to have been correctly positioned in between Martin and Ryman. His early works are definitely a rather theoretical research into painting in their monochromaticism and application of paint. At the same time, Rajlich's use of the grid functions in favor of flatness and scale as does Martin's. His later works in ever-brighter colors are instantly appealing and slowly reveal their subtler beauty. Their reflective materials shimmer like a stretch of water. They remain very much Fundamental but still seem to touch upon the metaphysical element of Abstract Expressionism (in a similar way that Martin's small golden painting included in *Fundamental Painting* does).

Stephen Rosenthal's works, then again, appear to echo Ryman's work. Especially his stretched canvases of later years – painted in a thick pasty white, under-painted with other hues – show such reminiscence. Moreover, the works of Girke and Zeniuk hung in the exhibition recall Ryman's non-colors under-painted with colored layers combined with Marden's matte, opaque surfaces. Like Ryman, Zeniuk uses gesture to show the materiality of the surface. Girke also values the visibility of the process, like Ryman, but his white canvases do little to counteract the facture of their surface and keep it flat. In this sense, Girke leans towards the sort of color field found in Abstract Expressionism.

With hindsight, the curators' placement of Zeniuk on Marden's end of the Fundamental range should have been replaced by Renouf and Wéry. Both of these female artists seem to be working with the revelation of the color and material's inner life. Especially Wéry's colorful canvases approach Marden's color scale and concept of "feel." This interest in the feeling of a color can also be found back in the work of Alan Charlton (as seen in detail in the chapter on color). Gray has an ambiguous color aura, emanating from the smooth canvas plane, which may be only held flat on the surface by multi-panel groupings. At the same time, Charlton seems to be the most dogmatic painter – which fits well the modular, theoretical approach of Ryman's end of the range, too. Finally, Charlton's work even corresponds to Mangold's shaped canvases, in his making them appear like a relief on the wall – as the curators suggested in "Gereduceerde Schilderkunst" (1).

On the whole, it is noteworthy that the reason for arriving at a Fundamental expression might be found in the personal circumstances surrounding each artist's artistic activities – like with their American peers. For example, Rajlich's painting sprung from his arrival in 1969 in the Netherlands whose transparent skies and endless water expanse, as well as painting tradition and newly-Americanized surroundings offered a multitude of formalist impulses. Charlton, on the other hand, claims to have found his style that same year in a radical turning away from traditional painting as taught at the art school in London, as he writes in his letter to the author (3-4). Girke came to his monochromatic painting style very early, influenced by Informel but primarily fascinated by panel painting – which makes him a self-developed formalist. Renouf, Rosenthal, and Zeniuk with their mainly American background had a head start. The same goes for Wéry who came to her Fundamental style during a prolonged stay in Canada, where the art of the neighboring country was easily accessible.

All in all, the four American painters detailed above indeed form the framework of Fundamental Painting (painterly, and from sensible to theoretical) which defines the two "opposing faces of a problematical region of discourse," as Robert Pincus-Witten put it (50). Moreover, this framework also holds true for the selected European Fundamental painters who, sharing a Fundamental mentality, all fit the category of Fundamental Painting (as delimited by the Americans) in their own way. Possibly, the European Fundamental artists differentiate from their American peers due to the versatility and multi-applicability of the former's works, within the art-historically determined range of Pincus-Witten. Anyhow, all of these highly individual artists (European and American), coming from various backgrounds, found each other in a common mentality and produced a pool of works that – on a formalist level – presents a surprising number of similarities, with an even more astounding variety. Ultimately, it all comes down to the concept of painting by definition, notably the surfaceness of the medium.

2.2.2 The Fundamental mentality at large

In retrospect, it should be more straightforward to pinpoint other artists of Fundamental Painting, who started working in this vein around 1970 and endured. But now that FunJdamental Painting is defined and its long-term adherents identified, we must keep in mind that Rini Dippel called it a mentality and wrote at the time that the *Fundamental Painting* exhibition was by no means all-comprehensive. Having explored Fundamental Painting in detail, this study can now identify several artists who, although not included in the show, deserve to be now included in this current.

Scrutinizing the proposals of the *Fundamental Painting* curators as well as the numerous shows on the non-objective current of the 1970s, we see that a few names in particular come up that seem to herald a Fundamental Painting potential. Notably artists in the Italian groupings of Analytical Painting are highly likely to fit in, due to the latter's relation to this current (see chapter 1.2.3). Shows concerning Analytical Painting have over and over included a few participants of *Fundamental Painting*. The artists concerned are: Alan Charlton, Raimund Girke, Tomas Rajlich, and Jerry Zeniuk. This is not surprising, as these four painters indeed seem to be the core European Fundamental Painting adherents.

However, Vincenzo Cecchini (1934) who only sporadically appeared in the Italian shows, can also be added to this European group of Fundamental painters. Already in 1973, he was included in the exhibition *Un Futuro Possibile – Nuova Pittura*, which combined contemporary American and European painting. In 1975-76, his works were part of the show *Concerning Painting....*, and in 1977-78, of *Bilder ohne Bilder*. More recently, in 2000, his works were shown in *Suoni della Superficie* which – once again – compared and contrasted works by both European and American painters from the Fundamental era. Still, Cecchini's lifetime work remains largely unknown to the public. Also during the whole selection process for *Fundamental Painting* back in 1974-75, he had remained off the curators' radar – as the various preliminary curators' notes attest. (Probably this was partially due to the fact that he had always led a life away from the limelight in a small coastal Italian town.) His relatively early elimination from the shows on Italian Analytical Painting might be due to the fact that his rather Fundamental approach differed from the Italian Analytical spirit at the time, so his inclusion in the former only makes sense in a much larger context.

Cecchini started his Fundamental oeuvre about a decade before most of the other European Fundamental painters. His work has presented medium or large-scale, almost square, monochromatic rectangles in neutral colors. Their surfaces are clearly hand-painted. The ambiguous nature of the colored layer is often dissolved by fine strips of paint (variously colored) along the edges folded around the sides of the stretchers, indicating the layering of various colors. Moreover, spots of bare canvas along the edges remain visible at times or are left bare on purpose. All this underlines the objecthood and "surfaceness" of the painting. Another feature of his work is that Cecchini often presents his works in the form of diptychs or triptychs in similar shades. This process illustrates the variations on a theme in a modular way. His works from the nineties are executed in more fluid paints, often forming a kind of straight, angular line (obviously hand-painted) from one canvas edge to the other. It is not a descriptive line, yet it questions the "surfaceness" of the picture plane, while anchoring the monochromatic plane onto the edges of the canvas. All things considered, his paintings are in line with the characteristics of the Fundamental mentality.

There is yet another potential Fundamental painter, Marcia Hafif (1929-2018), whose name was among the artists suggested to the curators of *Fundamental Painting* by gallery owner Michael Sonnabend, but who was neither included in the show at the Stedelijk Museum Amsterdam in 1975 nor in other European shows. Today, her work seems even closer to Fundamental Painting than some of the works by other artists who were included in the show. Hafif has written extensively on the Minimalist painters as well as on the European Fundamental Painting vein, which underlines her interest in this kind of painting. Despite his disagreement with the view that Hafif is a Fundamental painter, a telephone interview with participant Jerry Zeniuk on 1 December 2012 shows that her work fits in with Robert Ryman's kind of painting – around which the show was built. On her personal website, she explains her lifelong work which she started in 1972, as a "project of examining the methods and materials of Western Painting in the form of works of art."

In the mid-1970s, Hafif made a series of canvases gradating a non-color or presenting a range of colors from the same paint (brand, type…). Around the time of the Fundamental Painting show, she was manufacturing her own paint. She mixed pigments in linseed oil and then covered both ready-made and prepared canvases with these homemade paints. Every element thus refers back to the definition of painting itself. In a similar fashion, she studied the effects of various techniques like egg tempera, encaustic, watercolor, glaze, and scumble in wall painting. Hafif studied painting by painting, discovering the workings of various formats, sizes, supports, paints, colors, textures, and so on. Her series are modular – by nature. Contrary to the more painterly group of Fundamental painters, her work is based on an idea. As she once herself declared, she did not know what the result will be, but she knew how to get there.[100] (This recalls Ryman's painting as theory).

Like the Fundamental painters, Hafif factored in the viewer's experience – as an element which is an integral part of her painting. In her article "On Composition," she writes: "The convention, painters must address, is that of the wall as a location for painting, the vertical of its side edges, the horizontal of its ceiling and floor, which echo the top and side edges of the painting, creating a 'page' upon which we work, the enlarged field of the new composition." Her (mostly) small or human-scale paintings on canvas – often multi-partite – are meant to interact with their environment. They are meant to be hung at eye level so as to unify the series and the wall – cf. the initially unified artwork facilitates the unfolding of the viewing experience over time. In "Why Paint, 1989" Hafif wrote: "*An Extended Gray Scale* [1973] is hung in sequence with narrow spacing through the rows [,] can be installed above and below or a section can be displayed separately. The large *Mass Tone Paintings* [1973-74] represent History Painting or Portraiture. The Table of Pigments, or elements of paint color is displayed in rows and blocks but each work can also be seen alone. *The Neutral Mix Paintings* [1976] are intended to be hung above and below each other in [19th century] Salon Style." (Note the reference to formats reminiscent of traditional genres among other things.) Thus, each series has its own needs in terms of hanging in order to incite the proper, associative viewing in their beholder.

In 1989 Hafif intrinsically defined her own painting as Fundamental painting when writing in the above article:

> I have come to accept it [the term *monochrome*] as a means of referring to paintings which are not necessarily of just one color, but whose predominant characteristic is that of a square or rectangular, flat, painted surface without geometric divisions, depicted images or the suggestion of deep space. The absence of these devices is what makes certain paintings not only monochrome – other paintings may be as well – but also radical, that is, going all the way toward a unified surface.

Hafif's paintings are modular, always rectangular (almost square), monochromatic, frameless, and flat. They also respect the criteria of being taken in at first glance as a whole and of interacting with the viewer. Her work, furthermore, defines the variety of traditional and indispensable elements of painting, thus making it a Fundamental oeuvre.

This fact – in addition to the Fundamental motivation to paint in times when the medium seems obsolete – is perfectly summarized in her article "Why Paint?" from the late 1980s:

> Having taken into consideration ... the consensus decision of the art world that painting was no longer acceptable as an art form, it seemed necessary to move my awareness to a second level.... I thought it could be possible to paint on another level, one providing a certain distance in order to look at the paint rather than at its subject. It would be possible to paint 'as if' one were painting, using the materials and techniques of painting, without referring to a separate subject.... Thus I do not paint with the intention of making a painting as such, but I work from the outside using traditional methods and materials to discover a new image.

It is this passage which reveals that her works are not conceptual – as often thought – but painterly, and therefore, fit perfectly into the Fundamental Painting mentality (according to its definition in Part II). In 2019, for the first time, also the curators of her retrospective show at the MAMCO in Geneva used the term "fundamental" for her painting in their Journal.

Thus, as announced by Rini Dippel and corroborated over time, Fundamental Painting is a mentality that reaches far beyond the walls of the *Fundamental Painting* show. In retrospect, even though a few of the artists presented turned out not to belong to the Fundamental current, at least two other artists – European as well as American – should be added to it. This brings the total up to about thirteen representatives of the Fundamental mentality across two continents, including at least two generations of painters of both genders. Given that the Fundamental mentality links together such a relatively large group of painters internationally and that it has been going on for half a century, Fundamental Painting can, without hesitation, be deemed significant.

3 THE ORIGINS OF FUNDAMENTAL PAINTING

Rini Dippel writes in her catalogue introduction to *Fundamental Painting*: "New painting? 'It's in the air,' but it doesn't fall from the sky" (11). Fundamental Painting is a way of "learning by doing" for the artist who is exploring painting in the act of painting. But it is also based on what the artist knows about painting in general, as participant Louis Cane comments in his artist's statement for the 1975 show:

> Today, little by little, I feel as if I am beginning to take part in such things, which simply means that the artist-painter takes possession of his own means, from the moment he becomes capable of not forgetting the biography of his own practice. SHI TAO says in his own notes on painting (1641-1717) concerning receptiveness and knowledge that it is receptiveness that leads and knowledge that follows. Considering this while keeping in mind what I'd just said, I willingly admit that SHI TAO is right. He is right not only because his phrase is supported by the truth of practice, but also because, in that way, he seems to be suggesting I pay more attention to my own receptiveness, so that I won't limit myself to just having the knowledge of others. It's like that, as I see it, time spent painting can become time spent to actually understand.[101]

In order to learn how painting works, the artist must be receptive to the past (to painting's formal elements) and curious about the medium. Artists can only be ahead of their time by so many steps, but to be able to do this one must first know what came before. In this context, the words of Suzanne Hudson on the work of participating artist Robert Ryman are highly significant: "Because of his practice's longevity … questions of historical recapitulation matter,… Ryman's practice is not divorced from aesthetic or social history…. But any claims for connection to that history must be grounded in the particularity of paint and the effects that it fosters, painting by painting" (17).

Painting before the time of Fundamental Painting is significant to the Fundamental painter not so much because of its external issues but because of its inherent ones, that is its formalist actions. Kees Broos's interview with Tomas Rajlich illustrates this. It ends with the artist's words: "Painting, as a pure visual activity, has to do with seeing – viewing a lot. Perception is more important than explanations."[102] Likewise, Ryman's interview with Barbaralee Diamonstein-Spielvogel points to the value in analyzing painting visually, over and over again. For example, he explains that as a guard in the Museum of Modern Art he looked at a number of painters that helped inform his vision – Matisse, Cézanne, Rothko, Mondrian: "It always had to do with, not so much what they were doing, but how they were doing it … how they were putting things together, and why. [….] It was much more the how they did it and why they did it, than what they were doing" (00:53:14-00:53:40). Also his *Fundamental*

Painting catalogue statement states that Ryman is talking of "the seeing of painting. This 'seeing' can be so complex that the possibilities for painting are endless" (64).

The show *Fundamental Painting* originated around Ryman, as Dippel noted in interview of 25 August 2011. The artist specifies:

> It's hard to describe a painting. You can describe [it] to a certain extent, but it's always more than that. Always. The more is the part that matters. In the *Red Studio*, for instance, Matisse was using an image of the studio in order to make a painting. The studio was the "what," but the "how" was how he did the painting; that's what I am talking about, and that's the important part. (Carrier 632-633)

This goes for all his Fundamental Painting contemporaries as well, because their painting is by definition about the actual act of painting. This *how* of painting which led to Fundamental Painting will be closely examined next.

Rini Dippel ends her text to the *Fundamental Painting* catalogue with a brief paragraph entitled "The limits of painting." It starts with the phrase: "The limits of painting appeared already to have been reached in 1918, when Malevich painted a white square on a white square canvas, and Rodchenko did the same with black on black," and concludes with the phrase: "The painters now shown are carrying on the research into and with the true plastic means, and each is reaching his own conclusions." In between, Dippel very briefly traces the history of the "end" of painting. It would be taking her text "far afield here to examine all the major spheres of influence" (15), but they can and should be examined in the context of this study.

More insight into these "spheres" is given by an undated text, preserved in the exhibition archives of the Stedelijk Museum Amsterdam, entitled "Gereduceerde Schilderkunst" in which Dippel writes:

> In the case of some artists, we could speak of a new, cool romanticism, an attitude that strongly differs from the Informal Art, Lyrical Abstraction and Action Painting of the 1950s, even if, at times, their outward results show superficial similarities.
>
> This essential painting (cf. Naomi Spector) could not have come about without Minimal Art and Conceptual Art (we, therefore, sometimes speak of Post-Minimal painting). The reductive as well as the planned aspect – or rather the consciously planned – connect these painters with both of the former currents. For some, the serial and the modular are also important.
>
> Divergent influences are valid for the various artists. For most, however, Ad Reinhardt was a major predecessor, as well as Frank Stella and Jasper Johns, and further back in history, Malevich, in particular, (more than Mondrian). (1)[103]

The orientation text for the exhibition was entitled "Teksten van en over abstracte schilders van vroeger en nu, met betrekking tot de tentoonstelling *Fundamentele schilderkunst*" ("Texts by and on today's and past abstract painters, relative to the exhibition *Fundamental Painting*") and could be taken home by visitors as a kind of exhibition brochure. It names the following artists and currents as showing "raakvlakken en verschilpunten" ("similarities and differences;" 2) to Fundamental Painting: Kazimir Malevich, Theo van Doesburg, Barnett Newman, Mark Rothko, Ad Reinhardt, Antonio Calderara, Informal Art, Yves Klein, Piero Manzoni, Jasper Johns, Ellsworth Kelly, Frank Stella, Minimal Art, Conceptual Art, and Robert Ryman. These same texts are posted along the walls of the exhibition entry hall, as the installation photographs testify (Fig. 23). The curators of *Fundamental Painting* were trying to point out the influences so that the visitor of the exhibition could have an informed visit.

With all this in mind, we will be shortly taking a closer look at these origins (in the form of the history of the painting medium), as well as at Fundamental Painting's social context. The paintings from the *Fundamental Painting* exhibition and the various curators' notes will be used to trace the main points that led up to the Fundamental current in the history of 20th century painting. The approach will be from a more aesthetic (formalist) rather than theoretical point of view, in order to remain true to the nature of Fundamental Painting. It will include indications by the participating artists, and their influences – in line with the origins of the so-called end of painting.

3.1 The early beginnings

Although the curators of *Fundamental Painting* typically start their discourse on 20th century non-objective painting with Malevich, the possibility of his arrival at a monochromatic painterly proposition takes us a step further back. The path towards non-objective painting – and finally Fundamental Painting – finds its beginnings in the late 19th century. At a time when photography was slowly expanding, painting entered a new phase. Painting did not end but found a new beginning. The scientific discoveries of the 19th century resulted in studies like Michel Eugène Chevreul's *De la loi du contraste simultané des couleurs* (published in 1839), which influenced painting in France – such as Impressionism in the 1870s, followed by Post-Impressionism in the 1880s. These painters wished to capture light accurately on the canvas, seeking to render its changing qualities. With the discovery of various components in the composition of light, the refraction of color started to play a central role in painting. The idea of representing a passage in time in a static work was also an important element in this. What's more, works were largely composed in "real time" (outdoors), rather than being completely pre-sketched and then painted in the studio. The creative act (intuition) gained in prominence. As in Fundamental Painting, the subject was determined in advance, but the details were created in the act of painting.

From a formalist point of view, this resulted in an open composition. Such composition was characterized by centrifugal forces, which cause the viewer to focus upon the entire representation. This would translate into artists adopting unusual angles (over traditional perspective), and painting directly with colors (rather than using linear composition) – as embodied by Claude Monet's painting *Impression, soleil levant* (1872/73), from which Impressionism takes its name. The subject represented appears blurred. It diminishes in importance. Painting was now more about the rendering of light through pigment, than about rendering subject matter. The Impressionist canvas manifests itself as a multitude of colored brushstrokes, which means the paint (and the facture) is visible as a material. This was very different from the smooth surfaces of traditional painting.

It is accordingly here that painting started being Modernist. It is the linguistic elements of painting (form, style, color, line, and so on) that confer meaning to the painting. The technique (with its various elements tending towards flatness) emphasizes that it is really an object and not an illusion. "I'm art," these paintings seem to say. They refer to the now as opposed to the past. This new approach to painting would eventually lead to Fundamental Painting, almost a century later.

Based on these new premises, Post-Impressionism takes on the form of a number of individual explorations into painting, where the artist, in search of a more ambitious kind of expression, pushed further the limits of working with the inherent elements of painting. This kind of painting is no longer dominated by considerations of rendering figure and perspective in the academic sense. Color is not used locally anymore but as an arbitrary and expressive element – vivid colors reign. It is due to the influence of art from non-European cultures such as the aesthetic qualities of Japanese and African Art that composition is flattened out into such two-dimensional color fields. The brighter the color and larger its area, the more of it the viewer perceives.

In addition, the preferential use of high vantage points creates a compressed depth and makes the picture plane appear almost parallel to the canvas. Such viewpoints used in painting make the viewer much more aware of his own position in relation to the canvas. The viewer is much more aware of the materiality of Post-Impressionist paintings. This is due to their flatness – their loss of a "window onto the world" continuation of our three-dimensional reality – and their colorful presence, but also due to the visible brushstroke at times.

The painting now is an instance in the viewer's reality. The subject matter loses its primary role. It is painting which comes from seeing and inciting viewing. The canvas reflects the interventions of the artist, whose use of arbitrary color for its expressiveness influences the perceived scale. All these issues will become the main theme in Fundamental Painting: implication of color choice, materiality of the painting, open composition or flatness ("surfaceness" as opposed to a "window onto the world"), preconceived painting modified by intuition, the physical relation of the viewer to the work, – and "presence" of the painting which is evoked by factors like scale.

Some of the earliest examples of Post-Impressionist works with major innovations in terms of formal treatment of the painting are Georges Seurat's (1859-1891) *Sunday Afternoon on the Island of the Grande Jatte* (circa 1884), and Paul Cézanne's (1839-1906) *Bathers* (circa 1885), Paul Sérusier's (1864-1927) *Le Talisman* (1888), Vincent Van Gogh's (1853-1890) *Room in a Café* (1888), and Paul Gauguin's (1848-1903) *Vision after the Sermon* (1888). Seurat's painting is still very stylized in carefully chosen color combinations, executed in a careful "pointillist" technique – positioning dots of primary colors side-by-side to visually create complementary colors. The interesting point is the size of the painting at approximately 2 x 3 m. This size is traditionally reserved for monumental commissions, while the depicted figures in Seurat's painting give it a human scale. The fact that Seurat painted the frame around the painting in the same colored-dot technique, dematerializes it and makes it part of the viewer's space. It is a step towards the abandonment of the frame altogether, as seen in Fundamental Painting.

Cézanne's and Sérusier's works stand out for their Cloisonnism, a subcategory of Post-Impressionism which was characterized by its flat patches of color. Cézanne's work is dominated by his typical hatching stroke (mostly regular), which functions as a constructive stroke that creates color blotches almost independent of the subject. Sérusier's is an early example of the autonomy of color. At first glance, the composition appears to be arbitrary, uneven, built up solely from brushstroked color patches. The viewer, on looking closer, discovers the subject – which is a side issue.[104]

Van Gogh's and Gauguin's compositions also work with large color planes yet use strongly delineated contour lines – and their arbitrary color renders a mood (like in Abstract Expressionism half a century later). On a formal level, these works depict a very shallow space – they are very flat. All these Post-Impressionists were aiming for a visual unity of surface, each through their own particular kind of paint application. Flatness is an inherent part of this development. In this respect, it's worth noting the later developments in Fundamental Painting, which include: its commitment to the unitary surface, its choice of human size and aim at Crimp's "surfaceness," and its considerations on the functioning of the frame, as well as the importance of the painting process and its visibility.

The above context calls for a digression. A quote from the beginning of Louis Cane's artist's statement for the exhibition *Fundamental Painting* reveals just how aware Fundamental painters were of the formal innovations that had already taken place around 1900:

To tell the truth, I believe that a large part of painting, constituted today by what is exhibited in the galleries, follows ostrich politics. Plunged into ignorance, it pretends that there is nothing to know. From the least possible, it puts on exhibits of the least possible; simplicity turns into simplisticism. And there you are, that's about what I was thinking as I left the Cézanne exhibition at the Orangerie (1974). "Subtle" work, intelligent, well-dosed color, which, in fact, points to something else than the words that I apply here. Thus, this "organization" of color and drawing, which in Cézanne's work reveals a multiplicity of technical means, at the same time indicating detail (in the sense of taking a detailed view of something) also reveals the contradictions that for the artist come into play through that which is called the profession of a painter. The "profession of a painter," see here a term that, not so long ago, evoked a useless constant to me, something I believed to have come from "old painting." Now, I'm wondering about this point, because today I find myself asking more and more just what baggage I could have laid on this term? How is it possible that I need to reactivate and reproduce this knowledge to make my painting "progress"? In other words, what comes from all this if not a fresh attitude on the subject, which determines a fresh understanding of color, drawing, shapes, and the "time spent painting"?[105]

Cane's words are not only remarkable in the way they link Fundamental Painting to the artist's cultural environment, but also how they reveal an interest for Fundamental painters in painters like Cézanne and beyond.

The actual conspicuousness of such technical elements in Cane's works (indicative details) is imperative in relation to the concept and process of painting. Furthermore, Jerry Zeniuk emphasized several times in a telephone conversation on 1 December 2012 that his painting stems from that of Cézanne. Ryman, in an interview with Barbaralee Diamonstein-Spielvogel, explained that he started painting because looking at painting made him interested in it. In his position as a guard at the MoMA, he would spend all week looking at Matisse, then spend a week with the Cubists, such as Picasso and Gleizes, then Cézanne and the like. It is important to underline the fact here that Fundamental painters look at painting not so much from a historical point of view but from a formalist one. They are interested in the *how* not the *what* – as Ryman put it – of painting before their own. So, let's continue this formal review of painting up to the 1970s.

Henri Matisse (1869–1954), who seems to have incited a certain fascination on Ryman, is the founder of Fauvism, which questioned what art is. He simplified color even more. He switched from the Neo-Impressionist technique of juxtaposing complementary colors (imitating our perception of color) to applying color in an arbitrary or structural way. This means that he used color as color (not as color in nature). He was clearly fascinated by angular color patches – fragments of painting – as expressive units. In his Fauve works, like *La Grande Desserte* (1905), color as a flat surface takes over in combination with thick line (mutating into somewhat of a plane, cf. Marthe Wéry). The ambiguous, flat color space of the picture gives it strength (presence in front of the viewer). Matisse's interest was formal. He obviously wanted to say the most with the least by getting rid of all the fringes (cf. Fundamental Painting's reduction to the crucial painterly elements). In his painting, formal qualities carry the significance. There is no need for narrative. He has made color and form meaningful in their own right.[106]

Around the same time, André Derain (1880-1954) started using the bare canvas as part of the picture, for example in his *Self-Portrait* (1904). Georges Braque (1882-1963) soon followed, letting the bare canvas shine through in his Le Havre paintings from the Fauve era. Maurice De Vlaminck (1876-1958), then again, worked with vivid brushstrokes in high impasto. The support had thus become part of the image and the painted surface had become a material fact – as would be developed further in 20th century painting and Fundamental Painting where the plane becomes the picture. Fundamental Painting likewise uses the bare canvas in its search of the key inherent elements of painting, as well as it uses pastuous paint to impart its materiality. With regard to gestural brushstrokes, let's remember Tomas Rajlich's words that painting should be done with all your might (with elbow grease), that painting (activity) is by definition an integral part of painting (object).

Next in our survey of early 20th century European art is Cubism, as mentioned by Ryman. In its various phases from 1907/08 through 1914, it is one more step closer to Fundamental Painting where the surface is the image. In Georges Braque's *Great Nude* (1908), volumes defy gravity and there are hardly any neutral voids anymore. All the space around the subject is activated by Braque's brushwork and color patches, yet his former, bright Fauvist hues are leaving ever more space for the less saturated even neutral ones. Cubism soon adopts a dull, neutral color palette, stemming from the logic that this will draw more attention to the subject matter (cf. preference for neutral colors and monochromatic painting in Fundamental Painting). There is no more negative space in the compositions. Figure and ground fight for priority of sorts.

The pictorial space of this painting moves towards a flattened, bird's-eye view, thus looks more two-dimensional, although analytical Cubism tries to render a subject from multiple viewpoints simultaneously. This stems from an interest in the then much-debated fourth dimension, which was said by some to represent time – to capture a three-dimensional object moving through space in time. Cubist painters sought to render these four dimensions on a two-dimensional canvas. Formally, the interesting element in Cubism – in relation to Fundamental Painting – is the use of a grid (mostly centralized and vertical) as a sort of scaffolding to hang the pieces of the fragmented subject matter on, in order to render these various viewpoints and dimensions together.

The various planes hanging from this grid are seen from different angles and thus have multiple light sources. The motive merges and submerges. Cubist painting still depicts "normal" subject matter and respects the laws of gravity as well as the logics of the real world. Yet, Cubism poses questions about reality and the way art talks about reality. Thus, after the decomposition of color that started with Post-Impressionism and the liberation of color from subject (Fauvism), Cubism abandoned the wide color palette and decomposed the subject.

In the same period, Fernand Léger (1881–1955) in his *Nude Model in the Studio* (exhibited at the Salon des Indépendants of 1913) quite seriously dismembered the subject, Cubist-style. More importantly, instead of taking standard fine-grained canvas, priming it, and painting on it in smooth layers, he took coarse-grained canvas and painted directly on it with very thin paint – even leaving pieces of bare canvas along the bottom. Reminiscent of the Post-Impressionists, his work conveys this idea of it being a painting rather than an image. Léger favored the material and technique over the subject. He had a visible preference for the tactile quality of volumes (rather than colors) in his painting. It obviously did not matter what he painted but how he painted it (cf. Robert Ryman's statement on the importance of the *how* not the *what* of painting).

Meanwhile Wassily Kandinsky (1866–1944) is rumored to have had an epiphany in 1910 when moved by viewing Monet's painting of haystacks upside down. Although in German Expressionism, content and focus on line traditionally reigned, he realized that color and form alone could move the viewer (Lindsey and Vergo 363). In 1912, his book *Concerning the spiritual in art* was published. Kandinsky believed that the tangible, sensible world did not really matter – that the ultimate reality was spiritual. (The Theosophical concept of "Maya" means that what we think is real is actually illusion; our visible world is but a mirage.) Painting was supposed to elicit a relief from this "fake" world – leading the viewer into a world of higher feeling. The bottom line is that Kandinsky wanted to render visible "the inner sound of things" (Rebay 28). As becomes obvious from his chapter on "The Language of Forms and Colors," for him all colors and forms had expressive meaning in their own right beyond that of any particular physical reference.

Color was for Kandinsky visibly more important as form (unlike his German colleagues). His works of this period moved ever more away from being representational, and in 1911 he started to work on two types of images: "impressions" and "improvisations" (Rebay 98). The creative act of an "impression" came from something in the real world or from a sensation based on reality, while an "improvisation" was the product of purely autonomous creativity – a composition of inner feelings. Soon Kandinsky's line stopped being descriptive and became autonomous. The entire composition was activated by throbbing areas of color and line. In a different way,

Fundamental Painting would look for the inherent nature of painting and use the painterly elements of color and line – line as in gesture rather than the traditional graphic line – to render life to the painting.

So, around the turn of the 20th century a number of painters – who we consider significant in Western art today – worked through color, line, and form, until each of them found the visual analogue which was sufficient for them. Thus, step-by-step, together they took painting forward. The painterly process and the result gained the upper hand over the historical ideas. Painters now painted directly onto the canvas with a tendency to render a moment in time, be it in terms of a visual or other experience, rather than to portray some figurative subject matter. Moreover, the painters now conceived of color as light; the way the viewers see was questioned. Arbitrary, autonomous color and form as well as expressive, non-descriptive line now formed the independent content of painting so as to uncover the expressive inherent nature of these elements beyond any subject matter portrayed. At the same time, the painterly elements thus gained independence from portraying nature, while the painting itself gained in materiality and spatial flatness. Paint as a material thanks to visible brushwork, the use of bare canvas or considerations on its structure, variations in size in relation to the effect of a painting, and considerations on the elimination of the dividing frame were now part of the painting enterprise.

With Cubism, visual notions of a canvas's natural two-dimensional surface emerged through the painters' activities. The neutral void disappeared. The grid as a main compositional element entered the scene. In the search of a unified canvas, the image started fusing with the painted surface. This arrival at a kind of painting in which color is form and the surface plane is part of the content is the beginning of an "Ariadne's thread" which guides the viewer through the labyrinth of early 20th century painting to Fundamental Painting. (Further pioneers of non-objective art besides Kandinsky and the stimulating currents for Fundamental Painting, as defined by the curators of the 1975 show, will be discussed in detail in the following chapters.)

From a historical perspective, the separation of color and subject matter disintegrated the act of painting itself. All these painterly discoveries around the turn of the 20th century led to a key revolution: the shift from abstract to non-objective paintings. The main point is that the first non-objective paintings initiated the "end" of painting, creating a predicament: What are the painters to paint now, when there is only paint left on the canvas? Léger's work provides a clue: the *what* to paint becomes the *how* of painting.

3.1.1 The non-objective and the "end" of painting

The beginning of the "end" of painting brings us to Kazimir Malevich (1878–1935) as a key figure in relation to the new current in 1970s painting. As mentioned before, the curators of *Fundamental Painting,* in line with other art historians, started their history of monochromatic painting around World War I (WWI) with Malevich, who they proposed as a predecessor of Fundamental Painting. With this aim, they cited his declaration given below in the brochure that accompanied the show:

> When in 1913, in my desperate search to liberate art of the ballast of the figurative, I fled towards the square and made an image that did not represent anything more than a black square on a white ground, the critics – and with them society – sighed: Everything we loved has gone missing. We are a desert.... Before us stands a black square on a white plane. (2)[107]

As these words show, Malevich was definitely leading painting away from figuration and towards color and form – towards non-objective painting.[108] This marked the first "end" of painting according to many critics, but it might just have marked a new start (for painters). Several other "ends" of painting would follow over the 20th century, each time followed by the "resurrection" of painting including that of Fundamental Painting.

According to the curators' brochure for *Fundamental Painting*, the subject matter in Malevich's first Suprematist painting, *The Black Square* (1913/1915) – currently at The State Tretyakov Gallery in Moscow (Inv. No. 11925) – gave way to a simple geometric figure. Malevich no longer represented an object. He painted a painting. This point is clearly stated in his 1915 Manifesto *From Cubism and Futurism to Suprematism: The New Realism in Painting* (for the brochure of an exhibition in 1914). It provided a discourse on the formal innovations and teachings he had taken from Futurism and Cubism, which were still observing external subject matter and then deconstructing the objects they saw into fragments:[109] "Painters should abandon subject and objects if they wish to be pure painters" (Harrison and Wood 173). Malevich went on to write in *The Non-Objective World* that: "The black square," which is a shape that technically speaking does not exist in nature unless imperfect, in his picture is "full with the absence of any object" (10).[110] This echoes what Dippel writes: "For Ryman it [the square or a near-square] is the perfect form. For Malevich it also represented the perfect form, but unlike the often pragmatic (at least outwardly so) approach of today's painters [and their self-centric paintings], Malevich conceived of the square as the 'first step of a "pure creation in art"'" (FP 12).

Suprematism, coined by Malevich, indicates an art purified from all representation and representing the "supreme" reality instead. It is painting consisting solely of geometrical shapes, colors and facture, and is supposed to be an expression of pure energy (cf. Marden's "painting as sensibility"). A constant factor in Malevich's Suprematist works is a white ground. The floating geometric forms against a white background indicate the lack of gravity in an infinite space. It seems to be an attempt at pointing out the invisible structures ruling our world.[111] Namely, at the time that Malevich invented Suprematism, the art world was under the influence of new theories on the fourth dimension and, like a number of his peers, he wished to "render visible the invisible."[112]

During the *Fundamental Painting* exhibition, a number of Suprematist works by Malevich from the large compendium of works bought in 1958 by Willem Sandberg – the then Stedelijk director – were exhibited in room 48. Amongst them was the painting *Suprematist Composition (with Eight Red Rectangles)* (1915). As its title says, it presents eight red rectangles which are completely flat. These have different sizes but are painted in exactly the same red, without any variation of intensity in hue, tonality or brightness. They are positioned on an equally flat white ground covering the entire picture plane. The only variations of the surface are found in the brushstroke patterns. These rectangles, positioned almost – but not entirely – parallel to each other, seem to vibrate, hovering in space. The image seems to have captured them in spirited movement and frozen them in time. Optically, these red rectangles have minimal depth, like pieces of colored paper on a white plane.

Another painting from the Stedelijk Museum's collection, *Yellow Quadrangle (Dissolution of Sensation)* (1917/18), in contrast, seems to incorporate traditional perspective. A yellow rectangle is positioned diagonally along a white ground covering the entire picture plane. The rectangle's diagonal placement and its yellowness fading away (finally fusing with the white ground on one side of the rectangle as if there was some sort of foreshortening) both suggest a recession into space. This perception is based on what has been most viewers' traditional way of seeing, since Byzantine reverse perspective and the Renaissance's use of linear and atmospheric perspective in painting to render objects in space.

In this way, Malevich attempted to construct visual analogies for the invisible in painting. The key feature here is that the artist's feeling (or sensation) can be expressed in paint and re-considered or re-experienced by the viewer. This approaches Dippel's criterion of Fundamental Painting that it should be possible to recreate the process of painting for the viewer. (Although, in this case, the viewer does not so much recreate the process as feel the sensation of paint itself as it covers the canvas.) Being non-representational and non-referential, the painting loses its function as a substitute reproduction of everyday reality. Yet, it still represents the reality of the painted (or painting) itself.

Formally, the importance of Malevich to painting is, to cite his own words in "From Cubism and Futurism to Suprematism: The New Realism in Painting," the insight that "Color and texture in painting are ends in themselves. They are the essence of painting, but this essence has always been destroyed by the subject" (3). The critical and ironic point here, though, is that Malevich did not only abandon the subject but also chromatic color. In his famous *White on White* (1918) painting, in the MoMA Collection since 1935, Malevich uses only one kind of white paint. (Depending on manufacturer's chemical constituents – such as lead or titanium – white comes in different nuances.) Thus, it is only thanks to the different orientations of his brushstrokes that the white square stands out against the white ground. White is, thus, not used as a color but as a material (with a textured surface). Facture was used here as the decisive element in the painting. Its importance will be exploited again in Fundamental Painting.

Accordingly, in the exhibition brochure to *Fundamental Painting,* the text on Malevich ends with the words: "Especially for Robert Ryman, this work was of great influence" (2).[113] Ryman actually explores differences between nuances of whites in his paintings. The importance of color and texture in relation to painting – painting as object – is clear and has already been discussed in depth in this study (in relation to both Ryman and the other Fundamental painters). Ryman uses paint the way Malevich uses paint, meaning paint as material rather than paint as color. He comments: "As it is, the way I [Ryman] use white it's more as a neutral paint, in order to make other things in the painting visible, color for instance" (Storr 44). This is precisely what Malevich had done in his *White on White* by focusing on two different kinds of facture with the exact same white paint.

Another important feature of such a choice and treatment is the effect on the viewer. As Donald Judd – the father of and main literary authority on Minimal Art – explained in his celebrated article of 1965, "Specific Objects:"

> Almost all paintings are spatial in one way or another.... Except for a complete and unvaried field of color or marks, anything placed in a rectangle and on a plane suggests something in and on something else, something in its surround, which suggests an object or figure in its space, in which these are clearer instances of a similar world – that's the main purpose of painting. (76-77)

Ryman takes this fact of painting and takes Malevich's *White on White* further – literally into the viewer's world – by painting the square canvas white and using the wall of the then popular "white cube" gallery as a ground. Gary Garrels quoted Ryman in 1989 as having explained: "The wall plane is actually part of the painting and it extends out three or four feet .... The wall space ... is essential for that line that develops from the edge of the panel of the painting with the wall. If you were to see any of my paintings off the wall, they would not make any sense at all." By incorporating the surroundings, the painting is (nearly) unspatial. Yet, in both Malevich's and Ryman's work, "the composition of space, however radically it rejects gravity, is implicitly pictorial," as Frances Colpitt once put it (30).

In a nutshell, Malevich's monochromatic *White on White* explores the expressive possibilities of white based on its facture which catches light in different ways. The "pure" canvas that Malevich strives for is never blank. Similarly, the manner in which notably Robert Ryman works with white – as specifically mentioned in the curators' note – is also very painterly. In many works, his play of light across the impasto brushwork shows his concern with the tones and nuances created within the white. Accordingly, as we learn from Phyllis Tuchmann, Ryman is adamant that his paintings are not at all monochromes (Reise 37). This is also partially true when considering that Fundamental Painting works with all basic painterly elements equally. This allows for the Fundamental painters' interest in the canvas itself as a material and, therefore, also as having a certain color of its own.

In both Malevich's *White on White* as well as Ryman's "white square" paintings, white is more sought after for its suitability in crafting a surface than it is for adding color. Their paintings are monochromatic, but they do not come from the concept of painting a monochrome. In this context, also Ryman's following words are worth noting:

> It's not really monochrome painting at all…. The white just happened because it's paint and it doesn't interfere. I could use green, red, yellow, but why? It's a challenge for me to use paint and make something happen with it, without having to be involved in reds, greens, and everything which would confuse things. But I work with color all the time. I don't think of myself as making white paintings. I make paintings; I'm a painter. White paint is my medium, there's a lot of color involved. (Reise, 34-35)

The curators of *Fundamental Painting* write in the exhibition brochure on this subject: "Around 1918, Malevich painted not only a white square on a white ground, but also other white shapes on a white plane, and (together with Rodchenko) made an issue of monochrome being a main point" (2).[114] Alexander Rodchenko (1891-1956) painted *Black on Black* in 1918, the same year as Malevich's *White on White*. While the former is a monochrome, the latter is merely monochromatic.

In September 1921, Rodchenko participated in the Moscow exhibition, *5 x 5 = 25* intended as the farewell to painting. In the exhibition, Rodchenko showed the most radical painting to date, a triptych entitled *Pure Red Color, Pure Yellow Color, Pure Blue Color,* and signed the Productivist Manifesto with the declaration that the end of painting had been reached (Weibel 196). His three canvases are rectangular planes, monochromes void of any subject, form, or line. They comprise only one color each and it is always a primary: red, yellow, or blue. Rodchenko described these works in 1939 as follows: "I reduced painting to its logical conclusion and exhibited three canvases: red, blue and yellow. I affirmed: it's over. Basic colors. Every plane is a plane and there is to be no representation" (Tate, room 7). "Pure" color is the essential material of this painting, which in its tripartite likeness is represented as an object. Note this work still comprises color – several colors – and the facture of the planes is not even. The planes do not even coincide precisely with the edges of the rectangular canvas. (This would lead to future attempts to radicalize such monochromes even more.)

Thus, the question of the monochromatic or the monochrome entered the art history scene. In Russia, a lot had been written on facture in painting. In 1912, artist David Burliuk's article "Faktura" (facture) defined the polarities: "unitary" versus "differentiated" surfaces. In 1914, with his book *Faktura,* Vladimir Markov retorted that facture came from the variety of materials used in icons and congruently meant the contrast between spiritual and worldly spheres. Artists (at least in Russia) were thus aware of facture in painting.

Another important work in the *5 x 5 = 25* exhibition was Olga Rosanowa's *O.T. (Green Line)*, dated 1917. It is believed to be the first painting to truly have abandoned the distinction between figure and ground. The green stripe optically exists on the same plane as the white ground, which tears the green stripe at its borders. The entire picture plane is a juxtaposition of color planes, but the whole surface remains flat (unlike the color planes in Cloisonnism). Its flatness is induced by the dominance of facture over color. The history of painting (its formal side) now had moved from the "emancipation of color to the emancipation of the plane," as Peter Weibel put it,[115] aided by the attentiveness to facture. (Half a century later, this would lead to the "emancipation of the wall"[116] in Fundamental Painting [Weibel 201 and 204].)

Notably, facture also marks the difference between Rodchenko and Malevich. Benjamin Buchloch writes in "From factura to factography:" "Quite unlike the traditional idea of *faktura* or *facture* in painting, where the masterful facture of the painter's hand spiritualizes the mere materiality of the pictorial production ... the new concern for *faktura* in the Soviet avant-garde emphasizes precisely the mechanical quality, the materiality, and the anonymity of the painterly procedure of empirico-critical positivism" (87, note 6). Judging by their works, Rodchenko consciously aimed at avoiding any painterly quality in facture, whereas Malevich was more influenced by facture's tradition in icons and the spirituality it conveys. Rodchenko's paintings – unlike Malevich's – are made from a desire to make the "last" painting.

Peter Weibel writes: "Color became the last element in a historical kind of painting, facture the first element in a new kind of painting" (199).[117] The richness of the opposition in different uses of facture, as seen with Malevich and Rodchenko, would incite further research and become a pivotal element throughout 20th century painting. Insight into the working of facture would liberate painting from the opposition between tradition and The Atomic Age with its highly technological character, as an interest in the possibilities of materials and methods surged. By the time of Fundamental Painting, it was topical precisely because of this polarity.

Consequently, while the beginnings of this "new kind of painting" are to be found in Kandinsky's search for spirituality (by way of color and line), in the hands of Malevich, painting is a medium that "feels" real. The facture itself makes the painting both part of reality (not an illusion) and the responsibility of solely the artist himself. With Malevich, the concept of painting a picture – a "pure" picture not an image –, which would dominate the 20th century, entered the scene. The visual implications of a non-objective evocation or suggestion now were a main consideration. Thanks to Rosanowa, line came close to becoming plane and, in turn, plane approached the image. Color and texture now started dominating all previous painterly concerns. In their paintings, the painter's spiritual touch is contrasted with their sense of objecthood.

At the same time, the discourse on painting monochromes begins with Rodchenko, which would become a new and remarkable phenomenon throughout the 20th century. It is not to be confused with the development of painterly monochromatic painting, as represented by Malevich, which would likewise be a major theme. Monochromes mark the "end" in painting, while monochromatic painting – to which Fundamental Painting belongs – issues from these alleged ends. Together, this interplay between the "end" of painting and a new beginning (issuing from it) is a dominant phenomenon in Postwar painting. Fundamental Painting would be yet another new beginning – as Rini Dippel writes in the eponymous exhibition catalogue.

3.1.2 Art Concret

The WWI period was a particularly fruitful one in the Netherlands, where a number of artists from other countries were living at the time due to its being politically neutral. Artists there pursued non-objective painting, turning away from the turmoil and the art that would be used for propaganda. A key moment was the formation of De Stijl, towards 1917. Together with Suprematism, it marked the beginning of a geometric tendency in 20th century art. This was a group of visual artists and architects, including painters Theo van Doesburg and Piet Mondrian, who played an important part in the history of 20th century painting. As pivotal figure Theo Van Doesburg (1883-1931) wrote in the introduction of the first issue of De Stijl's eponymous magazine in fall 1917: "This periodical wishes to make modern man receptive to what is in art, awaken the perception of beauty. The artist is to produce [a] purely plastic work of art and prepare the public for it." In Paris of the 1930s, this led to the so-called Art Concret – founded by Van Doesburg and named by the curators of *Fundamental Painting* as a predecessor to this common painterly mentality.

To understand the influence of Art Concret on Fundamental Painting, it is necessary to take a closer look at De Stijl. De Stijl was influenced formally by Cubism yet philosophically by mysticism. A book entitled *New Image of the World* by Theosophist and mathematician M.H.J. Schoenmaekers was a key influence. The basic argument of the book is that, fundamentally, nature always works in regular ways and that complementaries shape the world. Following Schoenmaekers's ideas on ideal geometric forms, rejecting material reality as it appears to the five senses, and moving from abstraction to the non-objective, key representatives Van Doesburg and Mondrian radically limited their painterly means to a minimum. In due course, they would produce works with a simple, repetitive geometrical composition, using only straight lines in non-colors and flat zones of pure primary colors: yellow (radiating), blue (receding), and red (floating).

In the 1920s, especially Van Doesburg, who was the ombudsman and central figure of De Stijl, promoted the formal propositions of the Dutch group and kept on developing them. At the same time, Mondrian was developing his own work in a similar but different direction. Both artists were by then living in Paris. Van Doesburg's endeavors led to a new form of the geometric linear composition in primary colors and non-colors in 1930 called Art Concret. He was highly influential on the French scene until his untimely death in 1931. During that period Mondrian left for London before moving to New York in the late 1930s. We will see the impact of painting in the US on Fundamental Painting in the next chapter.

The *Fundamental Painting* exhibition brochure informed the visitor: "In his manifesto of Art Concret, dated April 1930, Van Doesburg lists a few points, which show similarities with the state of mind of the painters in this exhibition."[118] The few coinciding points listed in this text were incorporated in the exhibition brochure, as we see in the following artist's statement by Van Doesburg:

> The artwork must be entirely thought through and formed in the mind before it is executed.… The painting must be entirely constructed of purely visual elements, i.e. flat planes and colors. A painterly element does not have any meaning beyond "itself", and as a result, the painting has no other meaning than "itself." The construction of the painting, just like that of its elements, must be simple and visually controllable, i.e. anti-impressionist. (2)[119]

The same remark can be found in Rini Dippel's text for the exhibition catalogue with the additional information that Fundamental Painting and Van Doesburg's Art Concret mainly differ on two crucial points. The first is whether art is universal, and the second is whether it is seeking "absolute lucidity" (12).

If we take away the first one, a utopist desire for a universal art, this rigid conceptual preconception of the canvas recalls, more than anything else, paintings by

Alan Charlton. The other Fundamental painters seem to emphasize more a result that has been modified by the creative process, as seen in the previous chapters. In fact, curators informed the visitor in the exhibition brochure: "Van Doesburg, nevertheless, emphasizes the rational approach of the painting much more than do the artists in this exhibition, for whom intuition is also essential" (2).[120] This role of intuition in changing the preconceived composition during the painting process brings us back to Mondrian.

Piet Mondrian's (1872-1944) texts that appeared in *De Stijl* (later revised for his 1920 book *Le Néoplasticisme*) show an absolute conviction that the movement had the answers to the world's problems. Mondrian was convinced that the viewer, when experiencing directly the paintings, could not but be receptive to De Stijl's criteria and its impulses. The idea behind this was an iconic picture in a state of dynamic harmony (without any spatial movement, neither across the plane nor across the space) creating the same harmonious environment for the viewer. Over almost three decades, he focused on perfecting such a visual proposition in a formalist way to reach the desired goal. This concept of the viewing experience, with a non-objective use of colors and forms, would be found later in Fundamental Painting.

Mondrian's typical Neoplasticist paintings are dogmatically restricted to modular units that create a composition out of the basic rectangular unit in different sizes, later including a black grid line that functions as a plane in itself (cf. Alan Charlton's basic painting module of 4.5 x 4.5 cm, the multi-panel compositions of Kees Smits, or the grid patterns of Tomas Rajlich and Agnes Martin). Due to the visual differentiation in the directed movement of red, blue, and yellow, a "push & pull" effect is created. The various zones counteract each other. Through such works, the De Stijl artist and his peers strove to express a universal and utopian ideal of order and spiritual harmony which would be have a calming effect on the viewer. Yet, the harmonious dynamism in Neoplasticist works – a term coined by Mondrian and which designates his works from the De Stijl period and afterwards – was not a preconceived theory for painting, as the first issue of the *De Stijl* magazine announced.

On the contrary, as with Fundamental Painting, Mondrian's Neoplasticist works were only created in the actual act of painting. Any principles underlying such painting arose from the creative act itself. The evolution of Mondrian's oeuvre is a good example of this. His base module created by his signature grid – also of crucial importance to Fundamental Painting in the 1970s thanks to its ability to keep the painting on the surface – was a product of a long and slow process. Under close scrutiny, individual works from the Neoplasticist period reveal retouches and corrections in lines and plane. Mondrian's last and unfinished painting entitled *Victory Boogie Woogie* (1942/44), created in New York City and today at the Kunstmuseum The Hague, is even partially composed of rectangular pieces of tape in primary colors instead of being painted. This most probably illustrates Mondrian's painterly process as that of a preconceived composition which was then reworked and perfected in detail during the creative act. (Note also, for example, the conception of line as plane, found back in works by Marthe Wéry.)

What's more, in his very last painting *Victory Boogie Woogie* (1942/44) Mondrian returned to suggesting a third dimension by way of an overlapping grid structure – yet without including space. By using a painted grid that was partially modified by squares of colored tape, Mondrian achieved a new kind of "surfaceness" in painting. Jerry Zeniuk, amongst others, claims that "without Mondrian [his] painting would not exist." In a telephone conversation with the author on 1 December 2012, he explained that "Mondrian invented somewhat of a new space, that did not exist in painting before – a conceptual kind of space, not a naturalist one."

Moreover, in *Victory Boogie Woogie* (1942/44) Mondrian does away with the boundary between art and life (cf. Fundamental Painting). The painting's shape – a perfect square lined up along a 45-degree angle to the edges of the wall and hung from one corner – exploits the perceived diagonal.[121] Having no frame, the flat, non-objective canvas acquires a visually dynamic direction (known to the European viewer as that of painting's traditional linear perspective). It starts relating its edges to the corners of the wall, making the painting appear as a figure on a ground. It enters into visual interaction with its viewer. Mondrian's last work thus heralded the richness of painting to come, in particular that of Fundamental Painting. Hence, Dippel's statement made in her notes entitled "Gereduceerde Schilderkunst" that "Malevich (more than Mondrian)" was an influence must be dismissed as incorrect.

In any case, the lessons of De Stijl – and later Art Concret – were important for Fundamental Painting. Not only because of the points made in writing by Van Doesburg but also because of the visual effects of their acts. De Stijl introduced the notion of "static dynamics" started by Malevich – who was still using traditional spatial implications – in a truly flat, modular composition: The typical De Stijl composition that is a centralized grid pattern that expands out into the viewer's space due to its proneness to repetition, but does not allow the eye to leave the canvas. Its concept limited the painter's palette to a few basic pre-selected colors which highlighted their universally objective yet sensitive effects on the spectator. Likewise, De Stijl introduced the concept of line as a painterly element – line as plane in the form of thick grids. Mondrian, then again, showed the possibilities (and richness) of a rigid, geometric, preconceived concept, which was overruled by the act of painting as well as a new spatiality in line with the medium's flatness. This shows how this early 20th century geometric movement led to Fundamental Painting in the 1970s.

3.2 Painting as Painting

In the first half of the 20th century, the elements of painting were gaining independence one by one. The painting as well as its painterly elements could now exist, each in its own right. "The concept of facture appears where color as material of painting already appears to be obsolete. This concept therefore makes more things, than just objectivity and color (monochrome) superfluous, in turn making the easel painting itself superfluous. At the same time, it liberates painting from the prison of painting, opening up new possibilities in terms of choice of material and method," wrote Peter Weibel in his article "Das Bild nach dem letzten Bild" ("The image after the last image") (199).[122]

This focus on the inherent characteristics of the material and elements was specifically promoted at the Bauhaus art school in Germany. Through its teachers, Bauhaus was highly knowledgeable about and continued the ideals of the Dutch De Stijl as well as Russian Suprematism and Constructivism. Van Doesburg also taught at the Bauhaus in the early 1920s, and his Art Concret spin-off remained influential. As mentioned before, Van Doesburg found an untimely death in 1931, and the school was moved from Weimar (1919-1925) to Dessau (1925-1932) to Berlin (1932-1933), finally closing in 1933 under the pressure of the slow rise of Fascism (which promoted propagandist figurative art forms). The upshot of these events was that the non-objective idiom disappeared from Europe. However, Bauhaus principles in painting could continue to be promoted by its main teacher and painter Josef Albers – who had gone to the US and chaired the art department at Beardsworth College (and later Yale University).

In the United States, American abstract art had never ceased to develop over the 20th century from the work of its pioneers Marsden Hartley (1877-1943), Arthur Dove (1888-1946), and Georgia O'Keeffe (1887-1986) in the 1910s. Its further development incorporated influences from Europe which were a direct result of WWII. New York City which had already been proclaimed the new capital of art was also a major influence, through the work of artists like the Abstract Expressionists and Frank Stella (1936). Abstract Expressionism established "not only the independence of New York from Paris but its predominance," as Edward Strickland put it in *Minimalism: Origins* (3). And, as Erwin Panofsky wrote in 1955, "no European scholar … could remain blind to the fact that the United States had emerged as a major power in the history of art; and that, conversely, the history of art had assumed a new distinctive physiognomy in the United States" (326).

This "new distinctive physiognomy" continued in Minimalist painting as well as Fundamental Painting at large. It is not surprising then that Dippel, in her account of the beginnings of Fundamental Painting, mentioned the exhibition "Arte come Arte" at the Centro Comunitario di Brera in Milano, which opened in Spring 1973.

It included the American Minimalist painters Robert Mangold, Brice Marden, Agnes Martin, and Robert Ryman (part of the *Fundamental Painting* show), as well as the American Abstract Expressionists Barnett Newman and Ad Reinhardt, Frank Stella, and a number of artists of Post-Painterly Abstraction (incl. Ellsworth Kelly). Therefore, here the "newest" generation – which would define Fundamental Painting – was shown together with and linked to older generations already working in the same direction.

One of the most renowned Postwar American painters, Barnett Newman (1905-1970), took up the mission of making a new beginning in painting, which was based on his belief that: "Only an art free from any kind of the geometry principles of WWI, only an art of no geometry, can be a new beginning" (*Newman* 179). Though he voices his dismissal of prewar European currents like Suprematism, Neo-Plasticism and Bauhaus, in doing so he also automatically builds on this basis. In retrospect, he should indeed be considered as a source of such new departures in painting. The exhibition brochure text of *Fundamental Painting* informs the viewer that: "With formal means, like format, combinations of color, outline of color plane, which are positioned vertically next to each other each time, Newman wants to imbue his work with a metaphysical meaning. His titles are indications to the interpretation of his work. The painters in this exhibition are far removed from references to the metaphysical, the infinite, the abstract-sublime…" (3).[123] Nevertheless, Newman is proposed as a predecessor to Fundamental Painting, due to his painterly proposition – while, at the same time, pointing out that it is a formal parallel that disregards the metaphysical (although this is not entirely correct, as we will see in Part 4).

Newman is most famous for his "zips," as the artist calls them in "Barnett Newman speaks about his art" – reminiscent of Rosanowa –, in his human-scale as well as monumental-scale works, constructed from large all-over fields of flat color. Both works in the Stedelijk Museum collection, *Who's afraid of Red Yellow and Blue III* (1966-67) and *Cathedra (*1951), were hung in room 42 during the *Fundamental Painting* exhibition. They have straight "zips" that read rather like a narrow color band – as opposed to Newman's earlier "zips" indicated by irregular edges only. These "zips" are meant to unify the painting, flatten it out and expand it by echoing the edges, he explains in the aforementioned video interview; but they are perceived as a color field. Namely, "the concept of the field is the single most important innovation in Minimalist monochromaticism," as Strickland writes (57). (Abstract Expressionism, Color Field and Hard Edge are included in his concept of "Minimalist monchromaticism.")

Newman's "zips" visually anchor the viewer in the expansive color plane of the painting, facing him like a kind of entity for dialogue. According to Newman's words from 1949 cited in the *Fundamental Painting* exhibition brochure, he does not want to "reach the world of fantasy and abstraction through reality, but by way of non-reality, the chaos of ecstasy, to reach something that incites the feeling which is experienced when realizing total reality in one single moment" (3).[124] Painting is no more an abstraction from reality but reality itself, constructed from color shapes and reaching the viewer at one glance (cf. Fundamental Painting's initial visibility at one glance, then the slow unfolding of the experience, and finally the heightened awareness of one's own reality – which will be discussed in detail in Part 4).

In relation to another renowned Abstract Expressionist, Mark Rothko (1903-1970), the *Fundamental Painting* exhibition brochure tells the reader that he is like Newman a "color-field" painter, "who wants to incite emotions by way of color fields, as opposed to the action paintings of the 1950s, which are about the emotional value of the act of painting."[125] Note that the curators of the exhibition wished to highlight that Fundamental Painting does not express the transcendence of the artist when painting – a clear reference to the kind of enlightenment that the Abstract Expressionists wanted to achieve –, but rather is made to set off a cognitive reaction in the viewer.

In the exhibition brochure, the curators continue their discussion of Rothko as one of the predecessors of Fundamental Painting with a descriptive note on his use of color as form and texture: "In colors that do not contrast much as they are close together on the color scale, Rothko paints rectangles hovering over a background. Although their parameters are parallel to the edges of the canvas, the outer limits of each rectangle are fuzzy since the colors are not applied equally anywhere, but unevenly in somewhat transparent, fluffy brushstrokes one over the other" (3).[126] The curators thus emphasize the tactile factor of the Abstract Expressionist works. This is congruent with the origins of Fundamental Painting being more visual than theoretical – and Charles Wylie's words of 2006 that "It was Rothko's form, not his content" that impressed the pivotal Fundamental painter Robert Ryman (13).

In the same vein, Fundamental painter Brice Marden comments on Rothko in the video "Brice Marden on Newman and Rothko.":

> Rothko's works, for me, level painting in paint.... With Rothko, it is more up front – how the paint is.... It gets tighter and tighter, and it's right up there, and then, you know, you've got Ryman. You know, Ryman is this kind of weird extension on Rothko, the late Rothko's.... They're *so* close, *so* up front to the surface.... And it is not much of a jump from that to the Ryman's.

It should be emphasized here that these few sentences fully cover the link between the predecessors, and Fundamental Painting. Plus it should be noted that *Fundamental Painting* participant Tomas Rajlich also mentions Rothko as something "to be close to" in his interview with Kees Broos. All are aiming at "Painting for painting's sake," pursued throughout the 20th century, as the painters of Post-Impressionism already longed for,[127] and which towards the late 20th century would culminate in Douglas Crimp's "surfaceness."

Ad Reinhardt (1913-1967) is the third American Abstract Expressionist to be specifically mentioned as a predecessor to Fundamental Painting in the exhibition brochure. During the *Fundamental Painting* exhibition, his works are hung in the hallway over the staircase. Already in the mid-forties, Reinhardt stated that "[t]he content [of non-objective painting] is not in a subject matter or study, but in the actual painting activity" (Rose *Art-as-Art* 49). And in 1953 he established his *tabula rasa* of painting *Twelve Rules for a New Academy* (published in 1957) and proclaimed his own canvases to be the last paintings. Thus, Reinhardt inherently dismissed the possibility of future painting, including that of the Fundamental kind. Yet, at the same time, he voiced the "Six General Canons" in painting that also define the Fundamental approach: "No realism or existentialism.... No impressionism.... No expressionism.... No fauvism, primitivism, or brut art [sic].... No constructivism, sculpture, plasticism, or graphic arts. No collage, paste, paper, sand, or string ... no '*trompe l'oeil*', interior decoration, or architecture" (Rose *Art-as-Art* 205-207).

Chief curator Rini Dippel writes on Reinhardt and his link to the show in the exhibition brochure:

> Reinhardt dismisses all that is not essential in his art, in order to penetrate into its being. First he makes red and blue paintings, and then from 1953 until his death he paints square black canvases, in which a Greek cross becomes visible after close scrutiny. "I am painting, the last painting that anyone anywhere can ever make." Moreover, Reinhardt's theoretical publications on art make it evident that he is concerned with the purity of art, art as art: "Everything is in motion, going somewhere. Art must be silent." "The only thing that can be said about art is that it is one. Art is nothing else than art. Art is not what is not art." In this exhibition painting as painting is discussed. (3)[128]

Thus, according to the curators, as Fundamental Painting is about painting as painting, it is comparable to Reinhardt's concept of "art as art," similarly limiting itself to the essential – and being nothing else than painting.

Stewart Buettner, in his thesis on *American Art Theory: 1945-1970*, sees Ad Reinhardt as *the* predecessor to posterior painting. He writes: "Reinhardt's painting and thought marks the progress from Abstract Expressionism to an essentially comprehensive formulation of formalist practice and theory" (139). Further in the essay, he writes: "Reinhardt's definition of art was strict, admitting only traditionally accepted tools and media while eliminating everything which had a meaning greater than the compositional arrangement of forms on canvas" (140). Buettner also points out the continuity between Piet Mondrian, as representative of De Stijl (their more restrictive *Manifesto of Art Concret* used by Rini Dippel as the base for *Fundamental Painting*) and later non-objective painting. He writes: "In his painting and his ideas about art, Reinhardt represents the ultimate in the way of a painter concerned with the purity of conception…. Partaking in Mondrian's vision (but not his mysticism) he sought that in art which had to do with essence" (141-142). In this context, let's remember once more the words of Robert Pincus-Witten from his article "Ryman, Marden, Manzoni: Theory, Sensibility Mediation" in the June 1972 issue of *Artforum*, in which he claims that the kind of painting called Fundamental today can be considered as issuing from not only Malevich and Mondrian, but also from Abstract Expressionism.

Again, Reinhardt sought to create the ultimate painting, and Fundamental Painting used this last step as a steppingstone. Frances Colpitt brought it into focus when she wrote in *Minimal Art: The Critical Perspective* that:

> Reinhardt represents conscious reductionism: the deliberate elimination of detail and relationships in affirmation of the art of painting. The symmetrical composition and close-valued hues of the black paintings, … were influential in their purity…. The artist's astringent polemics in the name of unity, illustrated by "the one painting … monochrome, one linear division in each direction, one symmetry, one texture…." that he produced over and over again from 1960 until his death in 1967 parallel Minimal theory of that decade. (Colpitt 31; Qtd. from Rose 56)

Remember that the show *Fundamental Painting* was built around the four American Minimalist painters Mangold, Marden, Martin, and Ryman, and that: "Late in his career, Reinhardt termed his painting 'minimal,' borrowing terminology then in its infancy to explain the extent to which he had limited the formal elements found in his painting" (Buettner 141).[129]

In contrast to the instantaneity at a first glance which Newman pursued, Reinhardt's black paintings need time to visually unfold. It's only after some time has elapsed that the Greek cross emerges in the three-by-three square composition in various blacks. In this way, they relate to the viewer – to his senses –, taking up a very intimate dialogue with their beholder, without relating to anything else. They hardly even relate to the space surrounding them – undisturbed by a frame to keep it flat. Painting is not about the geometry anymore. Geometry now merely is a means to an end. The works of Barnett Newman and Mark Rothko are still about the viewer. Ad Reinhardt has taken a further step. The "seeing-viewing-experiencing" of his Black Paintings is about the unfolding of the canvas at one with the viewer.

Reinhardt's canvases are only about themselves and the viewer's perception of them. This is congruent with Reinhardt's definition of "art-as-art" as distinct from anything else. The beholder is merely the final necessary element in this. The unfolding of the canvas in the eye of the beholder in Reinhardt's black paintings pinpoints the moment of reality in this kind of painting. It is a reality in art. Reinhardt relentlessly defines "arthood" as being in contradiction to everything else, be it psychology, religion, or life itself: "Art is art, and everything else is everything else" (36).[130] Similarly in Fundamental Painting, the viewer plays a crucial role in the accomplishment of the painting. It is about the coming together of viewer and artwork, and accordingly it is also different from anything else. The "seeing-viewing-experiencing" of the painting by the viewer creates an event in reality, a situation. In other words, their painting exists only in such a situation, not on its own.

Yet, there is a difference between Reinhardt's black paintings and Fundamental Painting. Reinhardt's black paintings are not visible at one glance. They unfold in time. The Fundamental image also unfolds its detail over time, but it is true to the unified image. It first presents itself all at once to its interlocutor. Thus, the influence of Abstract Expressionism on Fundamental Painting in terms of both Newman (with his visibility at first glance) and Rothko (with his surfaceness), as well as Reinhardt (with his "arthood") are exploited. Fundamental Painting is both a kind of painting for painting's sake as well as it is an art of looking. It is the experience of the painting through painting – through form, texture and other painterly elements, through the two-dimensional surface. Fundamental Painting is clearly the continuation of the non-objective idiom, its formal teachings as refined in Abstract Expressionism, and the concept of art as art. These paintings are reality itself and they are the centerpoint of the viewing experience.

3.2.1 Objecthood

Abstract Expressionism is a direct starting point of Fundamental Painting. As Robert Ryman stated in an interview with Phyllis Tuchmann: "During the late '40s, '60s, Rothko was the first …, to make the point that painting was an esthetic object. That point was made over and over again through the '60s (I'm talking about abstract painters)…" (Qtd. in Reise 37). At this time, this characteristic of offsetting illusionism in postwar 20th century painting became known as "objecthood", as coined by art critic Michael Fried who defined it in his legendary *Artforum* article "Art and Objecthood" in the summer of 1967. His aim was to distinguish an artwork's self-referential presence from that of a plain everyday object.

Fried systematically tried to "wrench art from a realm of mundane presence – the space of mere things and the dispiriting temporality of the workday world – and thereby to salvage its possibility for presentness. It is a claim for the perpetuation of modernism and its self-determining subject," as Hudson put it (156). Or as Colpitt put it: "The rejection of mimesis and reference, and a concomitant emphasis on materiality, led artists and critics to the notion of objecthood, a status preferable to that of either painting or sculpture, and more specific than 'art.' To refer to a work of art as an object, in the sixties, meant that it was a nonrepresentational, concrete, and real thing existing in the world, without illusion or formal prototype" (107). In other words, this means that through painting's inherent two-dimensional nature it should be interpreted as a real, physical surface as opposed to a "window onto the world" (more on this subject in the chapter on Minimal Art). Thus, in the choice of other artists as forerunners to Fundamental Painting, the curators' conviction that it finds its roots in Ad Reinhardt's "arthood" or the notion of "objecthood" at large, which in painting becomes Douglas Crimp's "surfaceness," is a logical one.

In the spirit of this keyword *objecthood*, the curators of the exhibition *Fundamental Painting* added the paintings of Jasper Johns (1930) as one of the 20th century influences on Fundamental painting. The brochure reads:

> In 1959, Jasper Johns wanted to make a painting with a circle as a subject. He drew the circle with a flat, revolving stick or mechanic arm. Once the circle was drawn, he did not think it fair to remove the stick. The circle on its own would be an abstraction on a linen canvas. Pinned down with the creative device or mechanic arm itself the painting became an object again: a preliminary draft for making a circle (*Device Circle*). All of a sudden, the subject, the title, and the form of the painting coincided.[131] (5)

The Fundamental painter does not so much want to arrive at "objecthood" as at the "surfaceness" of a painting. The painting's object-like quality, in the end, is the paint.

The curators, defending their inclusion of this artist, added to their above quote, Leo Steinberg's quote on Jasper Johns: "For over 20 years, Johns has been occupied with the issues that are now being discussed by the painters in this exhibition. In particular, with the how of painting – the mixing of paint, the application of paint and the use of wax – as well as the question: 'What is a painting?'" (5).[132] John's work *Untitled* (1964-65) from the Stedelijk Museum collection hung in room 46 during the exhibition. The Stedelijk Museum writes about this work on its website:

> In this work, Jasper Johns appears to refer to the various theories of color that many painters have struggled with over the centuries. The stenciled letters R(ed), Y(ellow) and B(lue) are a reference to the three primary colors, which have also been used to paint the three largest sections of this work. The three predominantly white rectangles, with a different color on each end, allude to the secondary colors, which can be seen elsewhere in the same work. Together, they form six of the seven colors of the rainbow, which also appears three times in the painting. Painters' tools are also a central feature of this work, as can be seen from the broom in the yellow-painted section on the right, the handprints in the yellow and blue areas and the repeated use of the ruler.

Indeed, this interest in the painterly materials and components of painting is also to be found in Fundamental Painting, albeit in a totally different way.

Besides discussing the main Abstract Expressionists, while staying in the context of "objecthood," *Fundamental Painting's* exhibition brochure included a mention of Color-Field painter Ellsworth Kelly (1923-2015):

> The most important elements in Kelly's work are form and tension. For some time, he used to make organic forms that were cut off by the edge of the painting and seemed to continue beyond the picture plane. He works a lot with the contrast black-white, but also with bright colors red, yellow, green, and blue. In recent years, his forms have become geometric again; sometimes he sidetracks from the usual rectangular outlines and makes paintings in the shape of triangles and trapeziums, which are made with several canvases put together. In this way as well as with his use of color, he sometimes reaches illusionist effects. This is how he emphasizes that a painting is both an object and an illusion at the same time.[133] (5)

In fact, Ellsworth Kelly, who lived in Europe in the late 1940s and early 1950s, "smuggled" illusionism into his works which thrive in "objecthood." He strove to make a non-objective painting without abandoning abstraction.

However, the paintings as they are hand-painted present themselves as a painting instead of just a plain object. His works are simply abstractions of shapes of groups of objects transferred from everyday life in the real world, yet they are made so as to be flat so as to avoid any reference to their origin – not even in the title. In the late 1950s through the mid-1960s, Kelly created works that dissociated the outline of a form from its surroundings by presenting the latter in a primary color (or green) and totally flat. During the *Fundamental Painting* exhibition, his work *Blue Green Red I* (1964) was hung in room 42 adjoining the exhibition spaces. This title gives no hint as to the origin of this willingly non-compositional composition.

The painting is a horizontal rectangle, covered by a straight vertical yet wide band in blue, while the green and red areas do not form perfectly straight rectangles. It is a rounded indistinct shape in red. The rest is entirely covered in green in such a manner that it does not correspond to any closed shape. Although hand-painted, these shapes have smooth even colors and hard edges. They look mechanically drawn. The informed viewer knows that the color sequence in Kelly's titles follows a fixed pattern: He tends to list the color of the ground last (Hudson 136). Therefore, in this painting red should be the ground and green, the figure which seems to sweep over the red one, like a long curtain resting on the floor. This effect is intensified by the fact that the blue rectangle, recalls a stretch of sky seen through a window. The viewer's mind, thus, interprets the perfectly flat and even areas of colors as a layered, thus three-dimensional, arrangement. The viewer cannot help but compare it to such situations drawn from real life. Yet, such an association is not at all made to be distinct by the artist on purpose: "If Kelly's panels can be said to be about anything, they are about the anti-illusionistic use of color as form," as Strickland once noted (73).

Robert Mangold's first mature works *Walls* (1964-65) and *Areas* (1965-67) are reminiscent of Kelly's. As their titles indicate, the hardwood panels suggest fragments of buildings alternating with expanses of sky visible along New York's skyline of high-rises. The *Walls* are spray-painted in industrial colors, giving them the familiar air of construction materials, while the *Areas* are spray-painted in a bicolor mist with only the subtlest gradations, yet still enough to suggest a traditional atmospheric perspective. The panels of both the *Walls* and *Areas* are shaped and joined together, which gives them a further architectural quality, be it positive (substance) or negative (space). Mangold's work *1/6 Gray-Green Curved Areas* (1967) belongs to the nine works by this artist hanging in room 33, as part of the *Fundamental Painting* show. His later works are more subtle interplays on "objecthood" with a hint of illusionism being neutralized (working with a "push & pull" visual tension similar to Kelly's.

Accordingly, the note that in "the works in this show, forms of illusionism are avoided,"[134] was added to the curators' statement concerning Kelly in the exhibition brochure (5). Although Kelly dedicated his artistic quest to being rid of having to invent a composition for abstraction, the evolution of his works is the opposite of Mangold's. After an initial period of illusionism offset by "objecthood," Kelly seems to have been resigned to an anti-compositional quest and started making "primary structures," It's a term taken from the show *Primary Structures* curated by Kynaston McShine at the Jewish Museum in New York in spring 1966: Basic forms in (mostly) primary colors that testify to their formal invention – and spatiality. Through making such comparisons and contrasts, the curators of *Fundamental Painting* tried to draft a definition of Fundamental Painting – of what it is and what it is not.

Last but not least, the exhibition organizers cite, in the exhibition brochure, Frank Stella (1936) amongst the American predecessors. Their text refers to the work entitled *Newstead Abbey* (1960) which is part of the Stedelijk Museum Collection (Inv. No. A 27018). For this *Fundamental Painting* show, it was hung alongside works by Newman and Kelly in room 42, giving access to the exhibit that started with works of Robert Ryman. *Newstead Abbey* is composed of symmetrical, vertical stripes (whose width is determined by the thickness of the stretchers) running down the length of the canvas that together angle off into right-angle kinks that include the stretchers themselves, causing an indentation in the edge of the canvas. The lines formed by the gaps between these stripes of gray paint are simply segments of bare canvas showing through. The curators conclude that: "By opting for only one color and symmetry, Stella consciously tries to exclude any pictorial depth. Thanks to the relation between structure and shape (in this case, the stretcher and the stripe have the same width), the absence of any pictorial depth of field, and the visibility of bare areas of canvas, Stella stresses the idea of the painting as an object" (6).[135]

This painting – with its light gray – as well as its given description recalls very much the painting process adopted by Fundamental painter Alan Charlton. Since his early years in the Academy, Charlton painted gray canvases. This choice of color comes from his desire to paint with the most basic materials. Gray is a plain and industrial-looking color, adapted to both everyday purposes as well as art. This so anonymous non-color – often used for industrial drawings – evokes a large spectrum of sensations, due to its unique inherent chromatic qualities. This "multi-sensational" quality together with the hand-painted application of the smooth gray plane forms the artistic element in Charlton's work. Similarly, the duality of industrial appearance yet artistic quality is felt in numerous other Fundamental paintings.

Like Stella, Charlton and a number of other Fundamental artists conceive their "composition" beforehand, and then the work is merely painted out. However, despite their works' industrial look, the painters do hand-paint their canvases. Brice Marden's evenly monochrome panels emanate a similarly subconscious personal-appearance like Charlton's. Agnes Martin's fine regular grids, at closer scrutiny, show signs of their hand-drawn nature. On the other hand, Rajlich's canvases use the grid that can be expanded *ad infinitum* to keep the gestural brushwork (which insists on the painting as a painted entity) on the wall's plane and in the viewer's space. They are a combination of a preconceived idea and a spontaneous painting act. In all cases, the artistic touch is counterbalanced by the negation of illusionism in the canvas. And – no matter how equal or industrial-looking it may be – having the artist actually paint the canvas is indeed an important element of Fundamental painting. The painting is the artist's responsibility.

Another important factor of Fundamental Painting – at large and especially evident in the work of Charlton (following Stella's lead) – is the conscious choice of format. The canvases may be rectangular as in traditional painting, but this is a conscious choice not a given one. In the case of Stella and Charlton, the canvases are not just rectangular but shaped, and the paintings' compositions are also directly coordinated with the stretchers. Stella, for example, opts for stretchers made out of wooden laths that are wider than the regular stretchers used for painting, since they can lift the flat canvas off the wall and thus emphasize the painting's object-like quality. Furthermore, the width of the painted lines between the strips of bare canvas echoes the width of Stella's stretchers, thereby relating the painting's "composition" to its proportions as an object. Similarly, Charlton's stretchers are made from standard 4.5 centimeter wooden slats available in almost any hardware store in the UK. All the formats of his canvases (including the gray surfaces of his pictures) are, in one way or the other, variations on this 4.5 centimeter module, determined by the standard width of a wooden lath. Each and every painting, therefore, is based on a single base-module that is interrelated – again – with the object-quality of the painting.

By way of their "objecthood" – the relation between the materiality of the painting and its "design" –, these paintings become part of the viewer's reality. Stella's early striped canvases achieve this, not only thanks to this interrelation between the material and pictorial elements of the canvas itself, but also by relating the composition to the space around the painting. Stella commented about this kind of composition in his Pratt Institute lecture of 1960: "A symmetrical image or configuration placed on an open ground is not balanced out in the illusionistic space. The solution I arrived at – and there are probably others … – forces illusionistic space out of the painting at a constant rate by using a regulated pattern" (Qtd. in Rose, "ABC Art" 59). The flat and expansive composition (symmetrical both sideways and up-and-down) invites the viewer to imagine it continuing (and repeated endlessly) off the canvas, onto and along the wall.

Charlton's gray paintings exhibited at *Fundamental Painting* relate to their environment by incorporating the wall in their compositions. The paintings are composed of two panels. One is rectangular while the other forms a kind of frame around it, leaving a gap of 4.5 centimeters so that the bare wall is visible in between them. In this way, their flatness is also defined by fixing their depth at no thicker or thinner than 4.5 centimeters – the size of the stretchers –, which is the basic module of their composition. It is this manner of creating a painting from the basics in an objective way that interests Charlton. It is very close to Stella's endeavor to create a perfectly "objecthood"-like, flat painting. By showing the "skeleton" of the painting (stripes on a bare canvas, thickness of the stretchers) as well as emphasizing its "objecthood," the artists anchor their works in real space. Likewise, other Fundamental artists use a similar system to try and anchor their works to the viewer's space. The grid is an often-used device to arrive at this goal (Martin, Rajlich). It functions the same way as Stella's strips of bare canvas that the viewer perceives as expanding onto the wall. In the case of Robert Ryman, the painting is more an echo of Malevich's *White on White* as it appears on the wall as a white square on a white ground. It is all a question of hanging or being in a particular situation. Stella's striped paintings were the first to really deal with issues of placement (as well as shape) in relation to the viewer. Stella was equally concerned with the actual process of painting, as was Rothko before him who insisted that his painting should be hung very low – or even be laid on the floor – in order to relate correctly to the viewer (Rubin 37 and Anfam 72-75, Fig. 76-86). This is Stella's share in the heritage necessary for Fundamental Painting to come about.

The lateral symmetry created straight across the picture (rather than into some illusionist depth of field) in Stella's Black Paintings series was a revolution in the understanding of viewing habits. It dismisses any hierarchies between the various parts of the picture and prevents a directional reading from left to right. The composition has become non-relational and flat. The viewer's eye constantly gravitates towards the central axes, yet it is also pulled away and incited to discover the human touch of this industrial-looking painting. In Stella's flat symmetry, no part is exchangeable in the end. In these and other ways, a painting interacts with the space around it – as also Rudolf Arnheim in general and Frances Colpitt in particular have described (390 and 44). Anchoring the painting in the viewer's reality so as to create a meditative and harmonious interaction with its beholder is a principal quality of Fundamental Painting as well.

This sense of their being an interface with the surrounding space – and therefore with the viewer – is to become a key element in painting after Stella, in particular in Fundamental Painting which by its very nature focuses on the inherent elements of painting. Stella's lateral symmetry incites a surface reading rather than a sense of looking into a fictive space or creating an atmosphere. As Charlton says in an interview with Doris von Drahten, he mainly works with the "Erfahrung zwischen einem selbst und dem Bild" ("experience of painting itself;" 233) while Robert Mangold coined the term "seeing-viewing-experiencing" for his own work – which says it all (Schiff 60). The canvas interacts with its viewer, like an entity in the same space (as opposed to modifying that space by creating an atmosphere). Stella's canvases like Fundamental canvases have an objective presence – literally as well as figuratively – which is non-intrusive yet stimulating.

The curators hinted at the workings of the artist's (visual and technical) choice on the spectator, emphasizing that Stella – following and molding the American Postwar trend – is interested in painting as painting, meaning painting as a "necessity" (not painting as symbol, as a "window-onto-the-world," or as any other traditional variants).[136] The concept of the "objecthood" of painting – already hinted at with Kelly and Johns – comes up again. Last but not least, the painting's relation to its beholder is again crucial as explained in Stella's well-known statement when questioned by Bruce Glaser: "My painting is based on the fact that only what can be seen is there.... What you see is what you see" (58-59). From that point onwards, painting is focused more and more on the relationship between the viewer and the artwork – moving from a focus on the viewer to a focus on the painting, as achieved in Fundamental Painting.

3.2.2 Postwar art in Europe

The show *Fundamental Painting* does not only cite postwar American predecessors and influences. A number of European artists are also of importance to Fundamental Painting since it is largely a European phenomenon. As we have seen at the beginning of Part 3, the tendency towards non-objective art started to be explored in the early

20th century. When painting gained independence from its subject matter and color was dissociated from it, painting became independent of painting in the traditional sense. Without a recognizable subject, there was no longer a need for traditional compositions (i.e. forms of perspective), and the canvas could become a playing ground for painting as painting. Such painting about painting reached its apex in the United States shortly after the Second World War, while in Europe only a few trials in that direction survived due to mid-20th century political events.

The curators of *Fundamental Painting* wrote on this subject in the accompanying educative brochure:

> In the 1950s, almost simultaneously in the USA and Europe, forms of abstract painting – for which it is characteristic that the paint is applied spontaneously, emotionally, and without a plan – surged. In America it is called Abstract Expressionism and Action Painting, in Europe Lyrical Abstraction, Informal Art and Tachism. In the case of the American painter Pollock, there is no more composition; the paint lines and spots fill the entire picture plane in an equal manner. The European Informal artists often paint almost monochrome paintings, elements of form disappear forevermore, and the painting has no center. The surface structure of the painting is important. Sometimes, there is an external similarity in painting style to the painters in this exhibition, but mostly – in their case – careful planning preceded the painting.[137] (4)

The curators of *Fundamental Painting* again used comparison and contrast to explain this kind of painting. The important comment given here is that – although gestural – Fundamental Painting is not the result of an impulsive kind of gesture but a premeditated one.

However, is this difference really that significant? Jackson Pollock (1912-1956), who is specifically mentioned as a representative of the American side and implicitly portrayed as an impulsive painter, is maybe closer to Fundamental Painting than his European counterpart Georges Mathieu (1921-2012). Although he is often assumed to have simply splashed his canvases at random with paint in different colors, a video of the artist in action shot by Hans Namuth shows that he poured his drip paintings in an intuitive and well-considered fashion (as opposed to the physical, high-speed splashing act of Mathieu working on an action painting). Pollock's resulting works – the surface of which is almost entirely covered with a densely interlaced, drip-line pattern – reach a groundbreaking new kind of flatness and painting proposition. The all-over composition instills a new kind of "surfaceness." (Once again, this confirms the advancement of American painting over that of Europe after WWII.)

Pollock's lines are non-descriptive. They become the image. When a painted line is so light that it has no material thickness (depth) whatsoever – the surface of the painting remaining visible below these linear patterns –, the viewer knows that the entire action happens on the two-dimensional canvas plane. Figure and ground seem to fuse. Pollock created a thoroughly non-relational kind of composition, in which the overall form of the work overrides any particular importance of single elements. On a similar note, artist Robert Morris explained in his "Notes on Sculpture – Part I" in this regards that "art objects have clearly divisible parts which set up relationships," going on to say that "certain forms ... do not present clearly separated parts for these kinds of relations to be established in terms of shapes." According to Morris: "Such are the simpler forms which create strong Gestalt sensations. Their parts are bound together in such a way that they offer a maximum resistance to perceptual separation" (51). The Gestalt-like workings of Fundamental Painting were mentioned earlier: the painting is instantly recognized as such by the simplicity and recognizable capacity of its proposition. After the viewer's initial encounter with the painting, it slowly starts to unfold in more detail while retaining its unity.

In contrast to Pollock (part of the American postwar trend), the curators mentioned the European postwar painters who tended to work on monochromatic compositions which were centrifugal and centripetal yet not centered. (Note this quality, which was discussed in relation to the preferred – square or almost-square – format of Fundamental painters.) An example is Antonio Calderara (1903-1978) cited by the curators in the exhibition brochure. They explain:

> Since 1959, Calderara dismisses representation of reality. "I choose horizontals and verticals, because they do not exist in nature." He simplifies the forms down to geometrical planes and limits himself to a handful of colors, that, even so, he manages to imbue with much intensity and luster. The color seems to catch the light. Calderara achieves this with an interdependence of form and color, measure and order, in his works. "I would like to paint the Void, which is the Universe, the silence, the light: Measure, order, harmony, the infinite." Calderara's paintings evoke a large spatiality and, in this sense, are forms of abstract illusionism.[138] (4)

It is interesting to note how the curators discuss Calderara's work. The last sentence in the above passage informs the reader that it is "abstract illusionism," creating a sense of vast spatiality – or rather a color illusion like a cloud. This is an about-face to the opening statement on Fundamental Painting, claiming that all illusionism should be avoided. For this reason, Italian Analytical Abstraction is taken by the curators as different and separate from Fundamental Painting, precisely because of its spatiality and its alleged tendency towards illusionism. Furthermore, the curators claim that Calderara is – like the American Abstract Expressionists – looking for the revelation of something spiritual. (In fact, the Abstract Expressionists were looking to incite an experience of transcendence in the viewer through art.) Fundamental Painting might have a metaphysical dimension, but it is not a primary objective of Fundamental painters.

Yet, the works of the Fundamental painters do assimilate the basic idea of Calderara's non-objective paintings of the 1960s and 1970s, which have delicately nuanced color fields. Their pastel hues, reminiscent of the atmospheric perspective of the artist's earlier sun-kissed Italian landscapes, have an air of cloudiness over them. They seem to radiate light. Notably the works of Robert Ryman and Tomas Rajlich take up Calderara's interest in light, which is the ultimate element in the creation of painting. Even Alan Charlton states in *Immagine della Luce* that "[l]ight is very important to [his] paintings. It is one of the elements.... The light is important because it changes the painting.... At different points in the day, the painting has a different feeling" (00:00:01-00:00:18). Without light, the beholder would not be able to perceive color nuances and surface incidents. The viewer would not be able to see at all. In order to be perceived by the viewer, a painting needs light: Our vision is created by light. As Impressionism already heralded, an integral element of painting is light – and in that sense light is noteworthy to Fundamental painters.

Ryman and Rajlich, especially in their later paintings, consciously work with light. In the early 1980s, Rajlich switched his palette from a range of non-colors (white through gray to black) to pure gold. He continued following the same logic of a visibly hand-painted brushwork kept on the surface plane in combination with a grid (underlying or overlapping) or with drip lines along the bare canvas-border below, but opted for a light-reflective pigment. As before, metallic pigment can function in favor of "surfaceness." It makes the painting change at every instant and live under the impact of light. It changes with the times of day – and reacts under artificial light sources. The character of the painting in this way adapts to its environment, so that its creative process continues beyond the artist's intervention. It stays in constant flux, forever. Since the late 1980s, Rajlich has been working on this proposition in an ever-increasing range of colors and shimmering materials.

Ryman, on the other hand, continued working on almost-square white paintings for over half a century. They are executed in different whites – depending on tonality, chemical composition and variants with manufacturers – and under-painted in an assortment of other colors. When hung as the artist intended them to be, these paintings, surprisingly, also react to light. Their white surfaces seem to radiate color. For example, on the top floor of the Hallen für Neue Kunst in Schaffhausen, Switzerland, a retrospective selection of works by Ryman – hung by the artist himself – was on permanent display from 2008 until the venue's closure in 2014. The works interacted with the light in this white-walled space with rooftop windows and with the ochre floor, with patches of different shades in the repaired areas. The light fall brought out the under-coloring of the paintings, while the large expanses of white walls and ochre floor influenced the viewer's vision – on a subconscious level. After a while, the viewer would start (mentally) seeing haloes in pastel colors emanating from the white canvases. Ryman's works are therefore activated by the ultimate element, light, in the eye of the beholder.

Likewise, European master of white painting, Zero artist Piero Manzoni (1933-1963) is indicated by the curators as one of the forerunners of Fundamental Painting – yet for different reasons. In his 1956 manifesto "Per la scoperta di una zona di immagini" ("In benefit of the discovery of a zone of images"), he promoted total artistic freedom. The curators chose the following quote from 1960 for their educative brochure, however:

> Notwithstanding if it is about the representation of an object, a fact, an idea, or a dynamical phenomenon: the only value of a painting is in its existence, total being. Nothing needs to be said, just to be; two harmonizing colors, or two tonalities of the same color, already form a foreign element for the meaning of an unequal, limitless, absolutely dynamic plane. The infinite is monochrome (a single color), or rather, colorless – and is not a monochromaticism, in which every color relationship is absent, in fact, colorless? (5)[139]

Manzoni's statement is a confirmation of a painting's power of being and a plea for monochromatic paintings in non-colors. The concept of the mere "being" of an artwork would reappear in the context of Fundamental Painting (while his mention of an idea would be of importance in the context of Conceptual Art later on).

Manzoni worked on his "achromes" from the late 1950s through the early 1960s [1962]. These are supposed to express "pure energy." They are collages (or rather wall structures) made of plaster and various other materials – artistic, industrial, everyday, organic or other –, white or covered smoothly with white paint. In room 45, during *Fundamental Painting*, the Stedelijk Museum Amsterdam showed Manzoni's *Achrome* (1959) from its collection (A28686). Painted with kaolin (China white clay) that dries extremely slowly, the canvas was created not so much by the artist as by itself, meaning by the pressure of its own weight on the surface. Manzoni was convinced that the artist should put as little as possible of himself in the painting. As indicated in his manifesto, he considered it a space for freedom – the freedom of the object in question.

This was an attempt to banish every kind of potentially illusionist element from painting. Formally, Manzoni's white structures function as wall-hung objects. The fact that they are white avoids compositional complications due to color relationships (that distract from other elements). He claimed that it is only this way that the painting respects the freedom of the mind of each individual viewer to evoke all kinds of images. He believed his *Achrome* to be absolute. It is simply there for the viewer to see. A decade before *objecthood* was coined in the United States, Manzoni seems to have arrived at a similar concept. His idea focused, though, on the viewer's freedom of association, rather than on the artwork itself. Still, Manzoni's work is illustrative of the workings of a painting in dialogue with its viewer (the "seeing-viewing-experiencing" process sought in Fundamental Painting), although – unlike the Fundamental artists who are first and foremost painters – Manzoni was a conceptual artist.

From 1958, he was part of the European artists' group Zero that took its name from a magazine (published 1958-1966) and stood for a network of like-minded artists. Notably, it included the Frenchman Yves Klein (1928-1962) who was a promoter of colored monochromes. He claimed all credit in this regard, even nicknaming himself "Yves le Monochrome" ("Yves the Monochrome").[140] Klein was an artist who would fully explore the issues of monochromatic painting, using notably his trademark color IKB (International Klein Blue) – a saturated blue hue –, as well as gold, and sometimes pink. His paintings stem from the Oriental concept of the void: as not being empty but full with the immaterial.[141] Klein wished to represent "a void; then a profound void, then a very deep blue" (Qtd. in Watt 107).

Proposing Klein as a major European (albeit indirectly Japanese) influence on Fundamental Painting, the curators of *Fundamental Painting* wrote on him in the exhibition brochure:

> In 1957, Yves Klein exhibits 12 monochrome paintings in ultramarine blue, which he considers to be the most perfect expressions of the color blue. With it, he wishes to represent the Infinite and the Immaterial and at the same time refers to the cloudless sky. Yves Klein "the Monochromatic" also paints single-color pink and golden works. For him, the colors have a symbolic and mystical value: thanks to the pure color, he experiences total liberation. According to Klein, color should only represent itself, void of any psychological traditions. As for the format, he chooses a rectangle, which in his understanding stands for a colored plane which is unlimited (as opposed to a delimited colored shape). In order to paint as anonymously as possible, he abandons brushes and takes up a roller; a personal distance to the painting is of great importance to him. This mysticism which connects Yves Klein to his work is totally absent in the painters of this exhibition.[142] (4)

The freedom of form, color, and artist's execution are mentioned here. Once again, the formal aspects of painting prior to Fundamental Painting are highlighted.

Klein used color in its own right, avoiding the emotional or associative aspects (cf. Fundamental painting). He opted for blue, which optically is the color of emptiness – the void of an airy expanse –, or gold (cf. Martin and Rajlich's later works) which is optically the color of sunlight – and which is hermetically sealed and reflects back at the viewer. Similarly, he hand-painted his paintings, while limiting personalized brushwork to a minimum by using industrial tools. A typical work for the artist, Klein's *L'Accord Bleu (RE10)* (1960), a matte monochrome in International Klein Blue color including a number of sponges over-painted with the same hue, from the museum's collection (A 23546), was hung in room 45 during the *Fundamental Painting* show.

The rough surface texture and sponge attachments give this work – as well as Klein's other monochrome paintings in IKB – an unusual depth. Formally, it represents a new kind of "objecthood" in painting (before this notion is defined by American critics). Also, the rounded corners of this and similar works aid in perceiving the painting as an object on the wall. While attempting to be equivalent with space, Klein's paintings, in fact, dispense with pictorial space. In 1965, Minimalist artist and critic Donald Judd noted the importance of the absence of compositional space in Yves Klein's blue monochromes: "Almost all paintings are spatial one way or another. Yves Klein's blue paintings are the only ones that are unspatial, and there is little that is nearly unspatial, namely Stella's work" (*Complete* 182). Fundamental painter Tomas Rajlich stated to the author on the subject of Klein in 2012: "The Yves Klein exhibition at the National Gallery in Prague [1968] had a defining influence on me. It confirmed that it was possible to do totally different things than those considered to be acceptable art."

Consequently, the European postwar influences on Fundamental Painting, as cited by the curators of the show, motivated the Fundamental painters in their treatment of painterly concerns – not unlike the ones spotted in American postwar painting. The curators' compare-and-contrast approach started off with American Action Painting: non-relational composition, "surfaceness," the unified canvas, and the Gestalt-like viewing experience were brought to mind once more. The discourse on the European predecessors to Fundamental Painting indicated their interest in surface structure and the de-centralization of the canvas. The function of a painting as a well-considered surface for interpretation by the viewer – subjective but emotionless – was being addressed.

In their discourse, the curators highlighted the importance of monochromaticism, be it colorless or colorful. The examples stressed color as a painterly element in the work for its own sake, at the same time underlying Fundamental Painting's deviation from Analytical Abstraction. It has become clear that painters, at that time, were working towards a new kind of freedom in painting, which was unmistakably created by an artist's hand yet strictly avoided any personal influences beyond the workings of the painterly elements. These developments traced the beginnings of "objecthood" and the abandonment of – both pictorial and illusionist – space in painting, where the monochromatic void was filled with the fullness of painterly elements for their own sake; and light was discerned as the ultimate painterly element in painting. Notably, Yves Klein was identified as a crucial influence on Fundamental Painting for his treatment of space. The fact that all these kinds of paintings simply "are" – the meaning and importance of which will be discussed in Part 4 – forms the framework for Fundamental Painting.

3.2.3 Minimal Art

After the reductivist trend towards the absolute in non-objective painting on both sides of the Atlantic, in New York in the 1960s it reached its crux and became what has been coined Minimalism. In Amsterdam, the 1975 show on Fundamental Painting exhibited the Europeans grouped around their American counterparts – the painters of Minimal Art: Robert Mangold, Brice Marden, Agnes Martin, and Robert Ryman – who, in fact, chronologically preceded them. Therefore, it is relevant here to have a look into Minimal Art – specifically its painting vein –, and outline the background to Fundamental Painting. As for the painting itself, it follows that the inherent elements of painting (discussed in detail in Part 2) apply as much to Minimalist Painting as to Fundamental Painting, because they share the same origins. Thus, it is more how this phenomenon came about than its content that concerns us here.

This phenomenon was not a self-proclaimed group but rather a mentality. In *Minimalism: Origins*, Edward Strickland informs the reader that "the term Minimalism itself remains both a stylistic and chronological abstraction, particularly in the areas of painting," because it "*really* began only around the time the term hit the art magazines in 1965" (5), although artists – especially painters – might have been toying with such considerations for some time beforehand. Notably, from 1959 through 1965 the adjective *minimal* already appeared in Donald Judd's articles in *Arts Magazine.*[143] It's worth noting on this point that, today, Minimal Art belongs to the most valued currents of the 20th century and that the term is inseparable from Donald Judd – in reference to the importance of both his texts and his lifetime work.

From the early 1960s, Donald Judd was making wall sculptures that hover between being two- and three-dimensional objects, and in the middle of the decade, he reached his now trademark style of regular, geometric serial structures in metal. Judd commented on his work from this period in "Specific Objects:" "Three-dimensionality is not as near being simply a container as painting and sculpture have seemed to be, but it tends to that.... [t]he new work obviously resembles sculpture more than it does painting, but it is nearer to painting.... Color is never unimportant, as usually is in sculpture" (1-3). These artworks exist not only in space but also in the viewer's space. Ironically, his later works – which include Plexiglas planes within a protrusive wooden or metal framework – reflect the scene of the moment like a mirror, thus creating the ultimate "traditional" painting of the viewer's world. The definition of painting and its position in our reality is a theme even in Judd's ambiguous structures.

He is one of the artists who wrote about art – their own as well as that of their peers –, just like Carl André, Mel Bochner, Dan Flavin, Sol LeWitt, Robert Morris, and Robert Smithson. The reasons why this generation of Minimalist artists wrote critical articles, like no other artists before them, are numerous but undetermined. Yet, taking the critical environment into account, it might be assumed that these artists had a need to explain and bridge the gap in criticism. Art critics of the time ventured into the discovery of Judd's structures as well as other Minimal Art approaches only several years later and, more often than not, adopted a negative stance.

Most known for their regular articles on the subject are Lucy R[owland] Lippard, Barbara E[llen] Rose, Michael Fried, and Clement Greenberg. Lippard and Rose were supportive of the phenomenon, while Fried and Greenberg were rather not – although they would be influential to the Fundamental kind of painting. The pivotal point in all of their discourses was that non-objective painting is moving towards (or being reduced to) the essence. Lippard – Robert Ryman's spouse at the time (1961-1967) – was the most educative on and positive about Minimal Art. (She would be the only one to remain true to it over time even though her actual fields of specialization are Conceptual Art and Feminist art.) Frank Stella's spouse (1962-1969), Rose wrote the article "ABC Art," published in the October issue of *Art in America* in 1965, which became the defining text of Minimal Art and coined its name. (In later decades, she would turn her interest towards other American currents as her book *American Painting* illustrates.)

Michael Fried (1939) goes down in history for coining the term *objecthood* for the Minimalist era, which situates itself at the (alleged) end of a genuine trend towards "anti-illusionistic" artwork (Cf. The curators' criteria for Fundamental Painting in the exhibition catalogue [10]). It builds on Ad Reinhardt's "arthood" and slightly precedes Douglas Crimp's notion of "surfaceness" (as seen in chapter 3.2.1). The same year, in 1967, art-historian Sheldon Nodelman wrote in "Sixties Art: Some Philosophical Perspectives:"

> Perhaps the most important and comprehensive – and certainly the most obvious – change in pictorial structure between the nineteen fifties and sixties has been the definitive renunciation of illusionist representation. This renunciation is the culmination of a long development toward the dissolution of the fictive world of space and objects 'behind the picture plane' (74).

Two years later Fried gave this novelty a name.

Although he coined the trademark term so central to the discourse on Minimal Art today, Fried also struggled with this new kind of art. In fact, by differentiating art from objects by way of "objecthood," he tried to extract these new art forms from the sphere of mere objects and imbue them with a timeless presence. Fried seems to have been at a loss as to how the timeless element in art after Abstract Expressionism could exactly be explained. Like Rose in "New York Letter" (63), he speculated on the metaphysical nature of presence in painting to allow for a connotation of "art" as opposed to the realm of everyday objects. In the 1960s and 1970s, the object-like qualities of untitled paintings (following on the large, atmospheric color planes of the 1950s which bear names hinting at the spiritual realm) gave him little to go by in defining the metaphysical component and keep them in the realm of art. Following Greenberg's lead in terms of a historical continuity and an essence that makes art art, Fried did not adhere to the notion of reductivism and considered painting to be a more complicated cognitive enterprise. He adamantly defended Modernism and its evolution in the field of the non-objective and emphasized the significance of the viewer's experience. It turns out that he was right.

Fried was a follower of Clement Greenberg (1909-1994), with whom the concept of a "real" surface – as seen in Fundamental Painting – began. As early as 1940, in his "Towards a New Laocoon," Greenberg promoted the reduction to painting's essential elements as the goal in 20th century painting and traced the connection between the first non-objective painters and the postwar era. In his "Modernist Painting" of 1961, he explained his conviction that "the first mark made on a canvas destroys its literal and utter flatness, and the result of the marks made on it by an artist like Mondrian is still a kind of illusion that suggests a kind of third dimension. Only now it is a strictly pictorial, strictly optical third dimension" (90). Thus, from his point of view, 20th century non-objective painting's focus on flatness of the support brings along a certain "optical third dimension" – a space that can be traversed only with the eye, as opposed to representational space (and as opposed to an object or sculpture that unfolds in real space). This concept of an "optical third dimension" is a visual experience found in the presence of Abstract Expressionist painting. On one hand, it opens up the picture beyond its material likeness, and on the other hand it links with the tradition of perspective in painting (cf. Mondrian's new kind of space in *Victory Boogie Woogie*). Fundamental Painting insists on the flatness of the painting and reduction to its elements yet also on the two-dimensional nature of the canvas and its asymmetrical, and unspatial reading.

Still, Clement Greenberg, whose writing was a major influence on the "reading" of painting in his time, was hesitant in the face of the Minimalist generation. This was despite the fact that, in the end, he would stand for the one step in painting that would be the one step from Abstract Expressionism to Minimalism. Greenberg wrote extensively as a formalist on the evolution of non-objective painting and its meaning to the history of painting. In "Modernist Painting," he argued that elements like "the flat surface, the shape of the support, [or] the properties of the pigment" were brought into painterly consideration with Modernism and that the strategy of subsequent non-objective painting was to "transvalue" these inherent values (86; and Hudson 115). (Based on previous chapters, this holds true.) As he wrote in "After Abstract Expressionism," he believed it to be a reductive enterprise aimed at arriving at "the irreducible essence of pictorial art," which "consists in but two constitutive conventions or norms: flatness and the delimitation of flatness" (Fried 168-169, note 6).

Interestingly enough, in the light of Fundamental Painting, Greenberg saw the painting of his time to be a kind of reformation of those elements and meanings that had always been inherent to painting – as Hudson points out (115). In 1960 he wrote in "Modernist Painting" on a visionary note: "I cannot insist enough that Modernism has never meant, and does not mean now, anything like a break with the past. It may mean a revolution, an unraveling of tradition, but it also means its further evolution. Modernist art continues the past without gap or break, and wherever it may end up it will never cease being intelligible in terms of the past" (92). In Greenberg's eyes, the (postwar) evolution of non-objective painting was not so much a "dematerialization" (as Lippard called it)[144] but on the contrary a focus on art – a wish to render the picture first and foremost a painting (cf. Stedelijk Museum Amsterdam curator Rini Dippel's statement on Fundamental Painting not being something new but a mentality taking a new look at the tradition of painting).

Furthermore, in a 1962 essay entitled "After Abstract Expressionism," Greenberg argued:

> The aim of self-criticism, which is entirely empirical and not at all an affair of theory is to determine the irreducible working essence of art and the separate arts. Under the testing of modernism, more and more of the conventions of the art of painting have shown themselves to be dispensable, unessential. By now it has been established, it would seem, that the irreducible essence of pictorial art consists in but two constitutive conventions or norms: flatness and the delimitation of flatness; and that the observance of merely these two norms is enough to create an object which can be experienced as a picture; thus a stretched or tacked-up canvas already exists as a picture – though not necessarily as a successful one. (The paradoxical outcome of the reduction has been not to contract, but actually to expand the possibilities of the pictorial: much more than before lends itself now to being experienced pictorially or in meaningful relation to the pictorial….) (131-132)

Accordingly, although Greenberg strongly believed in the 20th century evolution of the painting medium (towards "surfaceness"), he remained skeptical of the evermore reductivist approach. He did not question the claim to art of contemporary painting, but he questioned its claim to quality.

In fact, the pivotal point in the discourse of everyone – Lippard, Rose, Fried, and Greenberg – was that non-objective painting was moving towards or being reduced to an essence. Lippard never defined it. She hinted at this being its two-dimensionality, following Greenberg's lead. Fried called it quality, a notion that also Greenberg had touched upon. On a similar note, Rose believed that it had to do "with finding out how little one can do and still make art," as she wrote in "Looking at American Sculpture" (35). In the hands of the foremost contemporary critics of the Minimalist era, the theory thus became not whether or not "art is art", but that "objecthood" is not an object. The question shifted to aesthetics and became one of whether any artwork is good or bad art. As Fried wrote in "Shape as Form," "one might say, that modernist painting discovers the essence of all painting to be quality" (27, note 11).

Listening to the critics, we see that quality ("being art") depends on the presence or absence of a metaphysical element. The artists' focus is elsewhere. It is this aesthetic connotation – this affection for the metaphysical component – that renders 1960s art criticism problematic to the Fundamental Painting generation. Yet, it confirms this generation's validity as a next step in the history of painting (and, as Part 4 will show, it is not necessarily incompatible with it from an objective point of view). It must be pointed out that Fundamental painters and curators in 1975 were adamant about not wanting to have anything to do with the spiritual of the Abstract Expressionist generation before them. However, now that they have established their own space in history, this is no longer an issue. In hindsight, it can be said that Greenberg and his peers, in avoiding all reference to spirituality in art and in focusing on painterly qualities instead, inadvertently created the required discourse which paved the way for later developments in painting.

Notably, Stewart Buettner in his *American Art Theory: 1945-1970* claims that Greenberg was pivotal in building the non-objective painting idiom of the first-generation Abstract Expressionists, with Newman and Rothko. He writes:

> Greenberg stood in a position to actually dictate the fundamentals of the formalist aesthetic by sheer weight of his influence as a critic.... Greenberg enunciated the essential characteristic of formalist painting, which stood clearly in the line of European painting from Cubism to Constructivism.... Working as the heir to the advances of twentieth-century European art, the modernist painter [1960s New York], above all, respected the purity of a medium so that the materials or techniques used by other art forms were not incorporated into painting. It was the attainment of this purity which established the quality of the work of art.... Since two-dimensionality was the "only quality which painting shared with no other art," it became the absolute criterion against which all painting was judged. (146)

This brings us back to the basis of Fundamental Painting, to Douglas Crimp's "surfaceness." Thus, it is this kind of discourse that prevailed at the time of *Fundamental Painting*, opposing those few critics who felt tempted to write about Minimalism and the numerous artists who felt obliged to defend it in writing. The works had been "in the air" for a long time. In the end, Fundamental Painting is a discussion that is unconcerned with any theory outside that of the painting.

On a curatorial level, the pioneer show on Minimalist painting was undoubtedly *Systemic Painting*, curated by Lawrence Alloway, which was held at New York's Solomon R. Guggenheim museum (21 September through 27 November 1966). It traced the correspondences of American geometric currents, with special attention given to Hard-edge and Minimalist painting. Works by Robert Mangold and Robert Ryman were included, while works by the somewhat younger Brice Marden – who was just starting his career with a first solo show at Bykert Gallery – were omitted; also no works by Agnes Martin were included.

A Dutch show, curated by Enno Develing, at the Kunstmuseum The Hague two years later (23 March through 26 May 1968), traveling to Düsseldorf and Berlin, was the first to use the title *Minimal Art*. However, it only showed sculptural works. Similarly, the brochure of the *Fundamental Painting* exhibition informed the viewer about Minimal Art as follows:

> Minimal Art: A term for an art current (second half of the 1960s), the works of which have a "minimal artistic content." Large, basic geometric forms that exclude associations with nature are characteristic for it. The work is often composed of a series of similar forms, chosen more intuitively than rationally (a difference from the European geometric tradition). The relationship with their environment is important; the works are, for example, presented without a pedestal. In terms of color, there is a preference for white, gray, and black, or the color of the material (see Carl André). Their quality of subdued form and color, which is supposed to increase the viewer's concentration onto the work as such, can be likewise recognized in this exhibition. The "minimal" sculptors focus on form as form, the same as the painters in the exhibition focus on painting as painting.[145] (6)

Obviously, the curators of *Fundamental Painting* considered Minimal Art to be sculpture rather than painting (possibly referring to the Carl André floor piece installed in the stairway during the show). Nevertheless, they still approached it from a visual viewpoint: the intuition-based (often modular) proposal, its relation to the surroundings, the artists' preference for non-colors or inherent colors of the material, as well as a ban on all "fringes" that could distract from the artwork are all characteristics that can be found in Fundamental Painting.

It is in line with what Frances Colpitt notes at the very start of her thesis *Minimalism: The Critical Perspective*, namely that this terminology (Minimal Art) "is restricted to those artists who shared a philosophical commitment to the abstract, anti-compositional, material *object* in the 1960s" (1). She refers to both sculpture and painting. Her statement is specified in the words of Naomi Spector, who has written on the change in painting brought along by Minimalism that:

> Traditionally it was what was done with the paint that was of interest, not the paint itself. Whether the visual result was representational or abstract, the paint was still used towards certain ends outside itself, whether they were illusional or not. Even "non-objective" pictures used the paint to express emotion, convey ideas, embody theories of art, or achieve a kind of spiritual transcendence. But with Ryman, particularly after the early sixties, the paint stood only for itself. It was asked to speak for itself alone, to be itself with its own full complement of inherent qualities. At the same time, the other physical, visual components of the paintings came to be of aesthetic concern in just the same way. Even those elements which usually were kept "behind the scenes," which we habitually do not see – such as the sides of stretchers, the signature, the way canvases are attached to stretchers, and much more – entered the aesthetic arena. Everything visible counts with Ryman, and everything about a work has been made to count visually. (12)

Note the similarity with the mention on "painting as painting" in the aforementioned curators' quote in the exhibition brochure to *Fundamental Painting*.

Accordingly, Robert Ryman (1930-2019) is the only artist participating in the exhibition *Fundamental Painting* who is also mentioned in the exhibition brochure listing of predecessors or influences on this current. In fact, as Rini Dippel explained in an interview on 25 August 2011, the exhibition found its origins in wanting to build a show of contemporaries around him. In the exhibition brochure, Ryman was cited with the following statement:

> There is never any question of *what* to paint but only *how* to paint. The how of painting has always been the image, the result.... the square format is important. To me it seems to be the most perfect form.... White paint is my medium. It does have to do with color (namely the color of the support, the carrier, which is always visible somewhere.)[146] (7)

From these words, the reductivist spirit can be sensed in terms of reducing the painterly elements and input to the minimum – notably format and color. Painting is appreciated for it object-qualities. Note that while this working with the basic elements of painting does imply reduction, neither reduction nor objectness is the goal. The elimination of unnecessary elements is driven by the deliberate focus on the *how* of painting. Similarly, Ryman's spouse, Lucy Lippard, preferred the word *rejective* over *reductive*. (Lippard wrote in "After a Fashion:" "rejective art [a term I prefer, to 'minimal' or 'reductive' because it does not imply attrition]" [623].)

With Ryman as a "father figure" to Fundamental Painting, it likewise makes each and every element that used to be considered visually virtually meaningless, meaningful. In fact, this drive for "objecthood" makes painting even more attractive to the artists who are painters at heart. As Colpitt points out, in 1967 already Lippard wrote that these painters were mutually "occupied with a further progression of painting, despite the contention of some critics and artists that painting is obsolete." She adds that "Mangold was aware of the critical objections to painting, but he countered [in a 1978 interview with Robin White] that 'one of the reasons people gave for saying that painting was dead [its capacity to be immediately and wholly perceived] seemed like the very thing that made it extremely unique and important'" (Qtd. in Colpitt 32). "Objecthood" meets "surfaceness." Dippel writes on Fundamental Painting: "The painting is what it is, it does not represent more than what is there to be seen – this tautology (which is irritating to many people) may be traced back to certain statements made by Minimal [sic] artists" (FP 13).

All in all, though, we should keep in mind that Fundamental Painting (incl. Minimal painting) is born out of painterly questions and its effect comes out of painterly means. It is not born out of critical notions – which change periodically – nor out of considerations on the metaphysical element in painting (inherent to Abstract Expressionism), both of which are indispensable in painting for most of the contemporary critics. As Judd noted in a 1980 interview with Frances Colpitt, artists in the 1960s rarely agreed on anything theoretical (Colpitt 3); and as Edward Strickland wrote in *Minimalism: Origins*: "The critics' medium is words; consequently, they may tend to classify the painters on the basis of theirs, listening to what they say rather than watching what they do" (60). This study hopes to avoid making the same mistake.

Still, as far as painting goes, Minimalism is a mid-1960s American phenomenon, which – as both Edward Strickland and Kenneth Baker defined it – extended well beyond its decade, reaching Europe some years later. Such dating coincides with the beginning of Fundamental painting and is congruent with Dippel's statement that the Fundamental kind of painting had been "in the air" for at least a decade, by the time the show opened its doors in Amsterdam in 1975. As Clement Greenberg claimed, painterly concerns are formalist, and – although it was the era of Minimal Art – the painters actually did develop their works in line with painting by painting – as their lifetime works have shown. In fact, in Part 4 the reader will learn that, looking at the paintings, eventually both opinions seem to pan out and are not necessarily irreconcilable. Fundamental painters simply inserted themselves into this context in a formalist way, while being able to maintain the metaphysical element in art by overtly avoiding the whole metaphysical question. In doing so, one of the qualities that position Fundamental Painting firmly in both the history of painting as well as in that of aesthetics becomes clear.

3.3 The Fundamental era

Fundamental Painting hit the art scene in Europe in the 1970s. As Rudi Fuchs wrote in *Cronaca* in 1976:

> Painting is an activity (a skill) inside our culture. The content of painting (as with all other things) thus continually mutates. Such changes constitute our history; and this no one can ignore. Content is expressed through form…. The paintings were completely hand-painted – at the moment when other artists turned to other expressive means (video, photography, language, their own body, light). This cultural context in itself gives handmade painting its specific content. Previously (more than with Mondrian) there was a very conscious and voluntary choice for painting – for painting in terms of slowly watching for something to appear through the acts of one's own hands. (Cortenova, 64)[147]

In fact, opening any art history book on the 20th century confirms Fuchs's statement that in the 1970s the majority of artists turned to expressive means other than painting – or, at least, non-objective painting.

In H.H. Arnason's referential *A History of Modern Art*, for example, the chapter on this period is given the title "Pop Art, Assemblage, and Europe's New Realism" – in other words, figurative painting and other art forms. (Note in this context that in her famous article "ABC Art" of 1965, Barbara Rose designated Pop art as "the reflection of our environment" and Minimal art as "its antidote."[69]) Arnason's following chapter is entitled "Renascent Constructivism, Post-Painterly Abstraction, Op Art, Kinetic Sculpture, Minimalism." Note the word *renascent* in this listing is used in terms of geometric art (partially referring to sculpture), while the term *post-painterly* implies turning away from the painting tradition. The latter category refers almost entirely to American art. Finally, Kinetic Sculpture has hardly anything to do with painting with the brush either as it mainly concerns three-dimensional forms. Op Art could also mean sculpture although painterly techniques do persist. Minimalism then again, only refers to 1960s New York and mostly "primary structures." The chapter does, however, embrace the four painters of Minimal Art, included in *Fundamental Painting*.

As for the 1970s, Arnason (1986 edition) designated the era as "The Post-Minimal Seventies: from Conceptual Art to Public Monuments." Apparently, the few painterly expressions that made it into the previous subchapter were as quickly swiped away. The title further indicates a clear dominance of conceptual and architectural art forms for that time period: subchapters include "performance art" and "earth and site works." Moreover, the following chapter, still dealing with the 1970s, leaves little hope for Fundamental Painting (or any other non-objective painting), although it admits a sort of acceptance for a multitude of art forms therein. It is entitled "The Pluralistic Seventies: From the New Illusionism to Pattern, Decoration, and New Image Art." Thus, after the fifties marked by the non-objective painting on both sides of the Atlantic, the next decades were absolutely overrun by other art forms especially in Europe. Robert Ryman in an interview of the time with Barbaralee Diamonstein-Spielvogel claimed that: "It's only a small world, visual painting. There are always a few people that are interested in it, but it is never a mass thing" (00:48:58-00:49:24). This confirms that – by the 1970s – avant-garde, non-objective painting was no longer the focus in the US and in Europe.

Secondly, an art historian specialized in American Minimal Art of the 1960s, Frances Colpitt, commented on this chronological action-reaction in a similar fashion to Fuchs. She wrote:

> In general, monochrome had become a legitimate, if not widely practiced, approach to painting in the 1950s.... For many young artists, Abstract Expressionism appeared to have exhausted all the relevant painting issues. The alternatives were now the rejection of two-dimensionality altogether for the "primary structure," "specific object," or "unitary form," or the monochromatic canvas, which substituted non-illusionism, clarity, and singularity for traditional composition and pictorial space.... For artists who began to show around 1965, painting seemed again viable because of the great proliferation of sculpture in the preceding two years. (31-32)

This turn to painting, precisely since most artists turned towards other media in the 1960s in the USA and 1970s in Europe, has already been confirmed by Robert Mangold (*View* 8).

About the appeal of painting in a period when this medium was considered obsolete, Gerhard Richter similarly stated in his letter to Edy de Wilde from 1975:

> I am fascinated by this kind of reduced painting in general; because I believe that, with lots of scrupulosity and great prudency, it attempts a rightness or rather a definitiveness of painting, and in that, it aims for quality, which tends towards what is valid and general. This appears important to me, in the context of a mindlessly blooming productivity, which is becoming ever more definitive. (FP 57)[148]

Also, Jerry Zeniuk mentioned in an interview with the author that at the height of Minimal Art a show took place including painting like Robert Ryman's, but that very few people were informed. He explained that the visual arts were breaking up in all directions, while painting was on the sideline and painters were asking themselves where it was going. This is why, according to Zeniuk, these few painters returned to the basics, reducing painting to its elements – which, in turn, opened new possibilities for them.[149]

It's also worth noting an outcome from a survey conducted with the visitors of *Fundamental Painting.* This indicates that 58.2% of visitors saw "a connection between the Fundamental and other phenomena in society" of the time. One of the most frequently given explanations for this was that "there [was] a need for sobriety and simplicity in society" and that "in the entire society there [was] a tendency towards reviewing all anew, returning to the roots" (Steen 10).[150] Maybe this is what Franco Sborgi in "Traces for analytical painting" called the "need for painting," notably across Western Europe in the 1970s (160). In fact, all these considerations show the importance of Fundamental Painting as a conscious choice for painting in its time and as a necessary continuation of art throughout time.

In art criticism, this relation of painting to its era is often considered in reference to Minimal Art (which includes the New York painters participating in the *Fundamental Painting* exhibition). For example, Frances Colpitt also writes that "Minimal Art lay dormant through the 1970s, rejected by the end of that decade, as hardline, authoritarian modernism by younger, pluralist artists" (3). Although at first this seems contradictory, in retrospect, knowing the importance of Minimal Art, this leads to the same conclusion. Namely, that 1970s Minimalist and Fundamental Painting is important in the course of history due to its choice of and focus on the basics of the traditional painting medium while most other artists were following other directions.

Thus, painting emerged from the 1970s despite the prevailing environment in art, and such works – both American and European – were brought together in the show *Fundamental Painting* in 1975. Reaching back to the tradition of painting itself, Fundamental Painting was a conscious choice not only for painting but also specifically for the hand-painted canvas. (As seen in previous chapters, it is important for Fundamental painters that they execute the painting themselves, even if sometimes their "handwriting" might not be visible.) In the 1970s, artists in the USA as well as Europe explored the idea of painting as painting, on a painterly more than theoretical basis. Thus, it must be concluded that Fundamental Painting has a fundamental interest in painting – as it has always existed. It is an exceptional phenomenon in its time, but it is also important despite its era, as it follows continuity over the ages.

3.3.1 The path to Fundamental Painting

Fundamental Painting of the 1970s followed the longstanding painterly tradition, although this medium had gone out of fashion. It was a conscious turning back to painting due to the pluralistic environment, as well as providing a continuation within the painterly tradition. Art historian and critic Lynda Morris differentiated between two extremes in painting, based on the dominance of either of the above considerations. One year before the *Fundamental Painting* show in Amsterdam, in her article "Strata" she commented on the difference between the 1960s American choice for painting and the somewhat posterior European one.

She wrote that for the United States, painting of the Fundamental era was a continuation of the postwar situation. Her view was that the environment in the late 1960s – moving towards other art forms, especially Conceptual art – "left a natural space for painting to continue to question its own function." Morris suspected that Europeans approached painting less directly and more intellectually than their American peers. She spotted a demographical shift here, namely that in Europe artists were dealing with painting as a reaction to their environment. In Morris's words, the European situation was "a complex attitude towards the function of art and in this context the function of painting" (76).[151] (On a side note, this confirms the cohesion of Fundamental Painting on both sides of the Atlantic. European Fundamental painters tended towards the formalist approach of their Minimalist peers, in so doing separating themselves from the more theoretical European contemporaries like Analytical Abstraction.)

Morris also added that the Europeans were more inquisitive, but the Americans produced more results (Review 12).[152] As the *Fundamental Painting* show was built around American artists (as the "founders" of the current) and featured a number of European artists who came to this idiom slightly later, this calls for a closer look at Morris's conviction. All the more so, as the importance of painting in the 1970s in an environment geared towards other new art forms reappears in the exhibition brochure of *Fundamental Painting*. Besides Minimal Art, the curators also cited Conceptual Art as an influence on the current:

> Conceptual art precedes the breakthrough of a new mentality, in which also traditional ways of seeing are at stake. It searches for freedom of perception. Daniel Buren describes Conceptual Art as an abstract-theoretical research on the essence of the concept of art. Many others see it as an art form, in which the material object is replaced by something immaterial, namely an idea. The ideas often concern projects that can be perceived by the senses; they appeal to the imaginative powers of the viewer. The artwork is completed as it were in this spirit. Many painters in this exhibition emphasize the importance of the thought process, which precedes their "manipulation with paint." (6)[153]

Note the emphasis on artists' thinking about ways of perception and Conceptual Art (the art environment of the time) preceding this new mentality, their own thought process, and the result in relation to the effect.

It has been shown how Fundamental painters, who are fully aware that they are observing while they are painting (and conscious of other painting), meticulously manipulate all painterly tools in order to reach the desired results. In particular, we must not forget that Kees Smits, Richard Jackson, Rob van Koningsbruggen, and Alan Charlton planned their paintings beforehand and then merely executed the work according to plan; Agnes Martin and Robert Mangold also worked using a preconceived plan, even though intuition plays a part in the creative process. The above quote furthermore emphasizes the importance of the notion of "art," its essence (cf. the definition of painting as such) and the necessary interaction with the beholder of the artwork (cf. Fundamental Painting). In addition to the concept of an idea preceding an artwork (linking Conceptual Art to Fundamental Painting), note the curators' reference to the rise of a new mentality as well as to the interest in traditional perception.

The assumption is in line with what the art historical books from the time (for example Arnason, first published in 1969 [1986 edition]) indicate: After WWII, New York became the new capital of the arts, and Abstract Expressionism – painting for painting's sake – was the major revolution in art. Namely, as a result of the WWII, the United States experienced an influx of revolutionary European artists, which formed a new source of inspiration. As previously discussed, this situation produced formalist painting like Abstract Expressionism and Minimal Art. It was a continuation, in Morris's words.

Meanwhile in Europe, Paris had resumed its leading role and the Nouvelle École de Paris reigned during the postwar years (or European Conceptual Art, as Daniel Buren claims, according to the aforementioned curators' note). Its heterogeneity of styles, often grasping back to the prewar geometric idiom, exemplified Morris's statement that the Europeans had a searching attitude. Thus, we can assume that Morris's aforementioned conviction is valid: In the 1970s in the United States, Fundamental Painting was a continuation of postwar painting despite the environment that was turning away from this medium, while in Europe it was a return to painting (after a short break) through the influence of their American counterparts.

3.3.2 The Fundamental character

At this point, we need to look again at prewar events in relation to the early 20th century revolutions in art. A brief outline of the European and American situation leading up to Fundamental Painting will enable us to assess their differences in motivation as well as the results. Furthermore, as seen in previous subchapters, the early 20th century revolutions in abstract and non-objective art are important to Fundamental Painting: turn-of-the century and early 20th century art in France, Constructivism, and Art Concret, based on De Stijl, to name a few. This means that the pre-WWII art environments in the European centers that are home to Fundamental artists, like Germany, UK, the Netherlands, and France, are key to this discourse.

A second point is that postwar American revolutions in art are equally important to Fundamental Painting. As Edward Strickland put it: "After the next War [Second World War], Abstract Expressionism established not only the independence of New York from Paris but its predominance" (3). Exactly this prewar and postwar situation, the national artistic traditions, and their respective evolutions (cut short by the war in Europe), seem to have significantly influenced the direction that painting in Europe would take in the 1970s.

On the continent, the 1930s was a decade of figurative art, notably because it was well suited to the political atmosphere. Realist styles were preferred by Communist and Fascist regimes alike for their clarity in conveying a message to the people and in glorifying their nation. It was the totalitarian states – such as Russia, Germany, and Italy – and their art that seemed to offer a way forward to the artists, once the Depression had discredited democratic market structures. Thus, the 1930s was the decade of Socialist Realism and other figurative artistic currents, which were either well-suited for propaganda or possibly for opposing the current situation with a non-explicit artistic form. More specifically, in the U.S.S.R. of that time where the new abstract (geometric) form language had initially been used for propagandist purposes, in the 1920s the new economic-based policies were implemented; and the future head of state, Stalin, decreed in the early 1930s that Socialist Realism was a state policy.

Over the next few decades, this spread to the U.S.S.R.'s satellite countries (including Czechoslovakia). After WWII, Communism gained a dominant position in Central and Eastern Europe and, as dictatorial nations before, it favored figurative art styles that allowed for propaganda. For example, Petr Nedoma, director of the Rudolfinum stated at the occasion of a show on this theme: "Socialist Realist art at the end of the 1940s and the beginning of the 1950s didn't arrive in Czechoslovakia from nowhere – it had a real basis in the art of the 1930s and 1940s. While Czechoslovak artists of that era did not form a communist 'front,' as they called it, their work was often left-wing, and socialist propaganda was accepted. Socialist Realism was the outcome of a tendency seen in the 30s and 40s."[154] Any progressive movements were dismissed as they represented a threat to the *status quo*. In Central and Eastern Europe, early 20th century non-objective idioms died out.

When asked about the countries which were researched for including artists in the *Fundamental Painting* show (all Western-European, mainly from Northern countries), Rini Dippel stated that certain nations just did not provide the right conditions for Fundamental Painting (for similar reasons as in the East). She used Austria as an example. Besides its National Socialist past and related art forms, it had a traditionally "heavily emotional" and expressionist kind of art, so it is not surprising that the show's curatorial team did not find any Fundamental Painting there. Moreover, Spain (under Franco) did not produce anything in that direction for similar political and art-historical reasons, according to Dippel. Spain is a country of expressive, Surrealist art. It was not therefore just political developments in the mid-20th century that influenced the course of painting in Europe.

In the neutral countries of the Netherlands and Switzerland, as well as in post-WWI France and Germany, the environment allowed for a sporadic survival of abstract (especially geometric) non-objective art forms. Yet, this would not last long. The German Bauhaus (founded in 1919 by Walter Gropius) nevertheless represented the few abstract tendencies on the continent in the 1920s and early 1930s. Bauhaus was influenced by visionary teachers like Lászlo Moholy-Nagy, Josef Albers, and Wassily Kandinsky, and guests like Theo Van Doesburg. Notably, Albers – best known for his color theories today – is known to have promoted working with any material according to its nature, choosing the most inherent and least intrusive option [cf. painting for painting's sake], in his Foundation course. The Bauhaus was first moved twice, then in 1933 closed down entirely by the Nazi regime under the pretext of its producing "entartete Kunst" ("degenerate art").

The exhibitions *Die erste grosse deutsche Kunstausstellung*[155] and *Entartete Kunst*[156] of 1937, which were followed by a bonfire for burning all abstract and non-objective art in the courtyard of the main fire station in Berlin-Kreuzberg, marked the definitive, forced victory of figurative art forms – across (totalitarian) Europe. Even in the neutral neighboring country of the Netherlands, abstract and non-objective art no longer had viability with the rise of Fascism. Artists had largely forgotten the Dutch De Stijl, after the emigration of its main characters Piet Mondrian and Theo Van Doesburg to Paris (in 1919 and 1923 respectively); and, after the capitulation of the Netherlands to German National Socialist militia in 1940, the country was heavily destroyed and culture stifled by a *Kulturkammer* (cultural chamber) and governmental involvement.

Van Doesburg's and Mondrian's new home would be France, which was one of the last European countries by the 1930s that was still inspired by the early 20th century abstract and non-objective teachings. During the 1920s, Van Doesburg had heavily promoted De Stijl's ideals in Paris (until his premature death in 1931) and arrived at an even more dogmatic version. This was published in April 1930 as a Manifesto entitled *Base de la peinture concrète* in the first issue of the magazine *Art Concret* (which provided the foundation for the curatorial concept of the 1975 *Fundamental Painting* show). Under the influence of the former De Stijl artists amongst others, Paris produced the artist group Cercle et Carré (1929-1930) – reserved for geometric artists – followed by the more inclusive Abstraction-Création (1931-1937). Notably, also former Bauhaus member Wassily Kandinsky was then living in Paris (until his death in 1944) and participated in this group. Due to the concentration of abstract and geometric artists from all over Europe, the distinctions in France between the various idioms faded away. Finally in the late 1930s, Abstraction-Création disbanded and the non-objective idiom disappeared with it. The École de Paris with painters like Henri Matisse, Pablo Picasso and Georges Braque, Amedeo Modigliani, Raoul Dufy, and Maurice Utrillo dominated the scene.

As WWII approached, the leading European artists and promoters of the early 20th century revolutions in art dispersed. Those who did not die relocated – for example, to the UK and USA. Consequently, by the outbreak of WWII, little or nothing of the abstract and non-objective idiom remained in continental Europe. The Soviet Union and the various European countries which had succumbed to Fascism aggressively put a halt to abstract tendencies in art and turned to realistic forms. In other countries, like the Netherlands, the non-objective idiom was slowly forgotten or cut short by the war. In France, a heterogeneous grouping of immigrant painters exploring abstract and non-objective forms survived for a while, only to equally disappear. Nevertheless, these pre-WWI cultural differences will prove to be significant to the Fundamental idiom.

3.3.3 The influence of WWII

The arrival of WWII changed the artistic scene completely and, notably due to the emigration of important artists to the UK and the USA, New York became the new capital of art. Stewart Buettner explains: On an external level, in the first decades of the twentieth century, American artists were less distracted by personal and political conflicts and more devoted to understanding their human environment than their European counterparts. Also, by the end of the 1930s and given what was happening in Europe, sympathy in the USA for Communism and other political extremes disappeared (and accordingly the tendency towards figurative art). The *Partisan Review* and *Art Front* (the artists' union's monthly) turned their attention to "revolutionary art," including abstract art, according to Buettner (28), and almost all major postwar non-objective painters – like Jackson Pollock and Ad Reinhardt – were employed by federally funded art projects. The abstract idiom was thus spreading.

Moreover, the arrival of revolutionary European artists, like Bauhaus teacher Josef Albers and De Stijl painter Piet Mondrian (1938-44), enriched the already fertile ground of abstraction in the United States. Josef Albers had already left for the USA after the closure of the Bauhaus in 1933 and took up a teaching position at Black Mountain College (and later Yale University). He influenced a whole new generation of painters (Buettner 128-131). As Minimal Art specialist Edward Strickland wrote: "Albers is the principal link between European geometrical abstraction and Minimalism" (28). Strickland's statement is based on Robert Pincus-Witten's article on the groundbreaking show *Systemic Painting*, where he writes that Albers's "pertinence to the square format favored by Systemic painters" is "more than obvious" (43). Also Buettner in his thesis *American Art Theory: 1945–1970* claimed that "following the spirit of … Albers, perception became the absolute criterion of formalist painting" (148).

Piet Mondrian, then again, had left Paris for London in 1938 and arrived in New York in 1940 (where he died in 1944). Mondrian was a very active member of American Abstract Artists, writing and lecturing on the European non-objective ideals in painting in New York in the early 1940s. Almost half of his influential writings (reprinted as *Plastic art and pure plastic art, 1937, and other essays 1941–1943* in 1945) stem from this period. On this subject, Buettner wrote in his thesis that "the art and thought of the American Abstract Artists ran counter to the attitudes engendered by Abstract Expressionism and … were largely ignored between 1945 and 1960. In emotional restraint, clarity of form, precision of concept and execution … this type of abstraction stood as the antithesis to the emotionality and painterliness of Abstract Expressionism" (127).

The United States had exactly enough history in abstract art which enabled artists such as Albers and Mondrian to become catalysts for American postwar formalist painting, as Buettner indicates in his thesis. He identifies a number of factors as foundational and which were in place in the early 20th century in the United States, and which would lead to the height of postwar painting in New York. For one, "the American were seldom theoretical" (15) (cf. Lynda Morris, who claimed that the Americans produced more results whereas the Europeans took a mainly theoretical approach). They simply – consciously – sought to arrive at a style that is specifically American, Buettner observes. Some borrowed heavily from European aesthetic theory – in general rather than depending on any one group or artists.

Also relevant is the fact that "the attitude of the American artist towards materials remained one of respect and moderation" (23). Furthermore, Buettner writes: "In painting especially, artists were concerned with presenting their own physical activity, a concept that was of little apparent concern for the European artists of the period…. Tied to, and almost inseparable from this was the increasing need for more expansive surfaces on which to paint" (15) (cf. Fundamental Painting's painstaking interest in the materials and processes in relation to a canvas of human-scale). In America, the definition of beauty lay in the process not the product, as Buettner put it (31).

Also, art was defined ever more in terms of a meaningful experience, narrowing the gap between art and life. The aesthetic theories of John Dewey's *Art as Experience* of 1934 were significant in this and had "made their impact on both European and American artists," as Buettner pointed out. Yet again it was Josef Albers who was considered to exemplify this kind of European artist (58). It would be these attitudes of postwar American artists that make American and European painting (abstract and non-objective) so different from each other.

The prewar European 20th century tendencies which had sporadically continued in abstract art like Bauhaus and De Stijl mainly transferred to the USA. Here, they were assimilated based on the US attitude towards materials, processes and the creative act as an activity and experience. Postwar America developed new American tendencies in abstract art, including Abstract Expressionism, Minimal Art and, with that, part of Fundamental Painting. Meanwhile, the European abstract artists passed through a soul-searching period after WWII, and were set back by at least a decade – as Morris stated. Towards the late 1960s or even 1970s, some finally turned their attention to what was going on in the USA. The delay in development caused by this (post)war rupture produced Fundamental Painting in Europe slightly later than it occurred in New York.

3.3.4 Postwar Europe in view of Fundamental Painting

In her article "Strata," Lynda Morris mentioned that the Europeans had a questioning stance while the Americans were more result-focused in their work, and that the European approach to painting was a reaction (Review 12) while the American approach denoted a painterly continuity. She was referring to the deep-rooted decision of European artists for a return to non-objective painting after its disappearance around WWII for various reasons, which were other than painterly. In Western Europe after the horrors of WWII, artists wished to turn away from the figurative vein. They were convinced they could no longer paint the way they had before.

In the European countries which had come out of the war as democratic nations, artists began searching for a new form of visual language that would prevent the political situation of the 1930s and 1940s from ever happening again.[157] Artists from North-Western European countries turned their attention to non-objective art, rediscovering De Stijl, Art Concret, Bauhaus, and similar directions. The Netherlands, Germany, France and the United Kingdom, in line with their political situations and pre-WWII evolution in art, would be the ones to find the way back to the "cool" non-objective ideal. (Note that a parallel with the nationalities represented in the *Fundamental Painting* show seems to be taking shape. The North-Western European character of Fundamental Painting, as specified by Rini Dippel, does not seem as random a coincidence as it previously had.)

Yet, these European artists had little knowledge of the "geometric" idiom. Either, they were too young to remember the height of such movements in early 20th century abstract painting, or they had had little interest in it, having worked exclusively in a figurative way during the interbellum. Meanwhile in Eastern and Central Europe, due to their very different political perspectives, art was in stagnation, with the same figurative styles of the prewar years. Consequently, the postwar abstract and non-objective idiom was stylistically very changed.

For one, there were the former Fascist countries, Germany and Italy, which produced a new non-objective current. Germany, having started and lost WWII, would see its artistic life recover quite slowly. In 1951, artist Bernhard Myers wrote in "Postwar Art in Germany" that German museums had hardly any Modern art, due to the destruction or sale of such works by Hitler's regime. Furthermore, he wrote: "The shortage of books and periodicals on art is so serious that museums and university libraries are often far less equipped than the average American university teacher's private library" (255). As to the possibility for artists in Germany to view Postwar painting "in the flesh," Myers noted: "[I]t has not been possible to show the German public the scope and level of art in the US… [T]he very decent show of American paintings offered by the Stedelijk Museum in Amsterdam somehow did not get to Germany" (256). He was most likely referring to the show *Surréalisme + Abstraction* from the collection of Peggy Guggenheim held at the Stedelijk Museum Amsterdam in 1951 which travelled to the Palais des Beaux-Arts in Brussels, as well as the Kunsthaus Zürich. The first *Documenta* (1955) in Kassel would be the first large-scale postwar exhibition of Modern art, taking up all art forms presented in *Entartete Kunst*.

At the same time, Myers specified that there was considerable interest among the European artists to see such recent developments, while also confirming that WWII was instrumental in sparking it. He wrote: "We may assume that the preponderant interest in various forms of abstraction, chiefly abstract surrealism and abstract expressionism [not to be confused with American Abstract Expressionism], represents an attempt to escape from the unpleasant realities of a bombed out world" (251). It's worth noting that these postwar styles are related to a tradition in painting based on a meticulous interest in realistic rendering, expressiveness, and the drawn line. In fact, regarding art in Germany itself, Myers notes that "German art is escaping into various types of abstraction or into gentle lyricism," (252)[158]

In 1957, in Düsseldorf, Galerie Schmela opened its doors with a solo show by Yves Klein, possibly influencing the formalist side of painting as well as underlining the lyrical nature of monochrome painting. In 1958, Germany was amongst the first European countries to host a large-scale show of American postwar art. The show *The New American Painting* started its tour at the Kunsthalle in Basle on 19 April 1958, then travelled to the Galleria Civica d'Arte Moderna in Milan and the Museo Nacional de Arte Contemporáneo, Madrid, before arriving in Berlin. There, it was exhibited at the Hochschule für bildende Künste. The show continued to the Stedelijk Museum, Amsterdam; the Palais des Beaux-Arts, Brussels; and the Musée National d'Art Moderne, Paris; finally reaching its last station, the Tate Gallery in London, in late February of 1959. It was curated by Dorothy Miller (the Museum of Modern Art's first curator) and was organized and financed by the United States. It included works by Barnett Newman, Jackson Pollock, and Mark Rothko.

That same year, a one-man show of works by Jackson Pollock toured Europe: Rome, Amsterdam, Hamburg, Berlin, and Stockholm. The *XXIX. Biennale di Venezia* (1958) showed works by Mark Rothko; and in 1961 Whitechapel Gallery in London and the Stedelijk Museum in Amsterdam showed his first solo (travelling to the Palais des Beaux-Arts in Brussels, the Kunsthalle in Basle, the Galleria Nazionale d'Arte Moderna in Rome, and the Musée d'Art Moderne de la Ville de Paris, 1962 through 1963). It's also worth noting here the countries toured by all these shows in relation to the nationalities in *Fundamental Painting* (and Analytical Abstraction at large).

During those same years, in a rebellion against abstract artists at large, Germany produced a group called ZERO (founded 1958, dissolved in 1966). It was founded by a number of artists, who considered that postwar European art had too much "ballast" and wanted to start from scratch. In concept – if not in practice –, ZERO's purist aesthetics were mainly voiced in the form of kinetic light objects. Although ZERO was reminiscent of Fundamental Painting's return to the basics of painting, it rather more influenced three-dimensional art forms in 1960s Germany. The press release to the show *Minimalism Germany 1960s* at Daimler Contemporary in Berlin in 2010 explained:

> In the early sixties in Germany, a new kind of Minimalism developed that was initially largely independent from the developments in America at the time. This German Minimalism was, in many cases, stimulated by, but also in conflict with, Concrete Art and the European Zero avant-garde, which drew attention to it from 1957 on, starting in Düsseldorf, with unusually staged exhibitions and spectacular projects for public space. The steles, cubes, and picture objects produced by the Zero artists, which lay in the space or stood in front of the wall, represent a significant new step for German art in terms of quality around 1959/60. The Düsseldorf Kunstakademie played an important role in the transition to a specifically German Minimalism from 1962 until around 1970. In the sixties, it provided many of its students with a basis for examining minimalized sculpture.

Accordingly, no German predecessors or influences would be specifically mentioned by the curators of *Fundamental Painting,* although several German artists were invited to participate in the show.

Yet, given the fact that a number of German artists participated in the *Fundamental Painting* show, and that Josef Albers – and with him the Bauhaus teachings – influenced American pre-war and postwar painting, it seems only logical to mention Germany's history here. At the same time, it has to be said that in retrospect German artist Gerhard Richter did not share the Fundamental mentality. The recent works of Jerry Zeniuk, who spent most of his early career in the USA, cannot be classified 100% within this current either. (This might, in fact, be the result of a dual background: his early years in New York City were influential on his Fundamental work, the later years in Germany leading him into different directions.) Only the Fundamental nature of loner Raimund Girke cannot be denied, although his non-colored planes sheer close to Analytical Painting. In fact, the German environment in the 1970s tended towards a revival of painting, yet mainly produced a kind of painting that can be designated as "geplante Malerei" (Planned painting) or Analytische Malerei (Analytical painting) – in accordance with Klaus Honnef's curatorial practice. It interacted with the Italians' contemporary painterly endeavors in Analytical Abstraction and was, thus, equally excluded by the curators of *Fundamental Painting*.

Also Italy did not have a favorable history in abstract art to go back to. Italy had been ruled by Fascist politics and corresponding art forms for decades. Going further back, to Futurism and even further back to the Old Masters, Italy's continual focus on color to address emotion in the viewer can be underlined as some of its roots. The fact that Italy did produce some kind of non-objective painting in the 1970s – seen earlier in the overview of shows and discussions concerning its artistic environment – was most likely due to the surge of the non-objective idiom in Italy after WWII, which was, as opposed to the other European countries, for the first time.

For one, Italy produced the group Forma 1 (1947-1951) that, according to its manifesto, consisted of visual artists who were both "formalist and Marxist" (cf. the later French group, based on Marxist-Leninist ideologies, whose theoretician was Fundamental painter Louis Cane). Secondly, it produced a group called Movimento Arte Concreta (1948-1958), made up of a new generation of Italians (a few from Forma 1) and of a number of artists from Switzerland, where the non-objective mentality had survived during WWII. Switzerland, which as a neutral country did not take part in either World War, encouraged the influx of a number of European (and native Swiss) artists fleeing Fascism – for example, influential artists, members of the Bauhaus, and Swiss-natives Paul Klee and Johannes Itten. Due to this and notably the efforts of artist Max Bill – former Bauhaus guest-teacher and link to Abstraction-Création – the knowledge of prewar, non-objective tendencies was preserved. (The continuity provided by the Swiss environment might be the reason why the Art Concret concept in Switzerland had remained relatively close to its basics, producing very "geometric" results.)

Furthermore, the American art collector Peggy Guggenheim became an influence for Italian artists. In 1948, she exhibited her collection at the occasion of the Venice Bienniale for the first time. The pavilion showed Abstract Expressionism – and other Modern art styles. In 1949, the collection would be exhibited at the Palazzo Strozzi in Florence and the Palazzo Reale in Milan, and soon after permanently at her new Venetian home, Palazzo Vernier dei Leoni, which was open to the public on a regular basis since 1951. That same year, the group MAC was founded in Milan with an aim to combine all Italian groups concerned with abstraction and non-objective art, including: Arte d'Oggi, L'Art Club, Spazialismo, Origine, and Movimento Arte Nucleare (D'Orgeval 31).

Similar to De Stijl and the Bauhaus, MAC comprised not only artists but also architects and designers. In 1953, it merged with the French Groupe Espace to become MAC/Espace, whose name already indicates a primary interest in three-dimensional objects or installations. Movement through space or time was also a key element of Futurism – an early 20th century Italian movement. This group and its traditional roots might be the reason for Italian artists' acceptance of a spatial element in later painting which is not quite Fundamental. Although MAC, as its reference to Art Concret indicates, specifically tried to exclude "lyrical" art, it connects with the atmospheric qualities of 1970s painting in Italy.

Italy produced the atmospheric and lyrical kind of monochrome painting as described by Bruno Corà in *Pittura70*, specifically excluded by Rini Dippel from *Fundamental Painting*. The curators of *Fundamental Painting* cited postwar artists Antonio Calderara and Piero Manzoni amongst the predecessors. When citing Italian postwar artists as predecessors to Fundamental Painting, the curators did this specifically to point out this very difference. Klaus Honnef confirms the unique theoretical approach of Italian postwar painters in *Kunstforum*, writing that "... the Italians researched it [the posed problem of painting in the 1970s] by using the Theory of Aesthetics and Structuralist Linguistics as their testing probe" (127).[159] Besides, as Honnef stated, relations with postwar Germany (in particular Winfred Gaul) influenced 1970s Italian painting. The appearance in the 1970s of Italian Analytical Abstraction, which would take quite a different course, starts making sense.

Now that we have analyzed Germany and Italy as possible sources of Fundamental Painting, we turn to France. France was an occupied German protectorate during WWII – but with a less restricted South. It still remembered the prewar heterogeneous group École de Paris (including a number of abstract and non-objective painters from Abstraction-Création) and produced an equally heterogeneous group entitled Nouvelle École de Paris after WWII. Besides the Nouvelle École de Paris, the Parisian galleries Denise René and René Drouin staged shows of prewar abstract and non-objective painting as early as 1945. Also Action painter Georges Mathieu organized a number of shows including American contemporary artists. For example, in 1948 he exhibited works by Jackson Pollock, Willem de Kooning, Ad Reinhardt, and Mark Rothko at the Galerie de Montparnasse. Magazines like *Art d'aujourd'hui,* led a vivid discussion on the preference for "warm" or "cool" abstraction (Mathieu 61-62, 28). And, over the following years, the Salon des Réalités Nouvelles (founded in 1939 in Paris, reactivated in 1946, and still in existence today) promoted abstract and non-objective art.

In fact, the Salon des Réalités Nouvelles tried to reestablish the dominance of abstract and non-objective art in postwar France, as its Statutes show. In the late 1950s, a section entitled *geometry* was created, which would soon be renamed Constructivism, then Art Concret, then "art constructive" ("constructive art"), up to 1977 when it became just *painting* (D'Orgeval 24, 35). This relabeling shows a certain retrospective approach to painting in the 1970s which did not herald anything new.[160] Also the fact that Ellsworth Kelly, living in France at the time, was not admitted to the Salon des Réalités Nouvelles, although it was said to be open to all abstract and non-objective tendencies, underlines this suspicion. His monochromatic works from the year 1950 were not acceptable to the leading Parisian artistic committee, consisting of artists and other professionals in this field, who did not consider them art (D'Orgeval 35). Apparently, the postwar American approach was too extreme for the committee after all.

Secondly, the fact that the only "new" group of painters in France was most likely BMPT (1966-1967), likewise shows a lack of American influences. It consisted of artists Daniel Buren, Olivier Mosset, Michel Parmentier and Niele Toroni. They were a group of conceptual painters. Each of the artists had a "trademark" way of painting, like a symbol on a monochromatic ground: verticals or horizontals, squares or circles. Their approach demanded that they decline communication of any kind of message and transmission of any kind of emotion through painting. The search for the prewar geometric idiom, given a thematic orientation through a theoretical discussion on "warm" vs. "cool," and the self-centeredness of Paris (acting out of its old status as the world's capital of art) might be the reason why French artists were largely uninfluenced by formalist impulses from overseas.

The French participant who was finally chosen for *Fundamental Painting*, Louis Cane, was in retrospect not a true Fundamental painter. This is not surprising, as Cane was part of the French group Supports/Surfaces (1969-1972) – the last avant-garde movement that France produced, as fellow painter Claude Viallat argued in 1991. The group questioned the basics of painting theoretically (remember Lynda Morris), which is different from reducing painting to its indispensable elements. As Klaus Honnef specified in *Kunstforum*, "… the French artists and theoreticians – numerous of these held both positions in the employee Union – approached the posed problem [of painting in the 1970s] mainly out of an ideological or psychoanalytical view…." (127) [161] It was not a formalist approach.

This could be the reason, though, why Louis Cane's artist's statement fits the Fundamental theme so well, while his works tell a different story. Postwar art in France also does not seem to correlate to the development of Fundamental Painting. The curators of *Fundamental Painting* mentioned the Art Informel vein of the Nouvelle École de Paris to point out the continuation of painting in Europe after the war; in the same breath, they specified that this kind of painting might look like, but was not equal to, Fundamental Painting. This distinction is due to the fact that Art

Informel did not result from a thought process on painting: even the art of loner Yves Klein who, like Kelly, was refused by the Salon des Réalités Nouvelles – now renamed Réalités Nouvelles-Nouvelles Réalités – and whose painting did seem to have been an influence, was not primarily a painter. Thus, it is understandable that the curators of *Fundamental Painting* specifically scrutinized but did not find any candidates from the 1970s *Nouvelle Peinture en France* show. (The other French participant in *Fundamental Painting* was Edda Renouf, who was actually an American living in Paris.)

In this context, we should also note that Serge Lemoine – a French authority on Art Concret – in "Un siècle d'art concret" located "the spread of Art Concert after 1950 in Europe, in particular, in France, Switzerland and Italy" (13).[162] This is the link between Switzerland, Italy (plus Germany in terms of Analytical Painting), and France indicated above. Curiously enough, this excludes the Northwestern European countries that also eventually had a revival of prewar non-objective currents and were the generators of European Fundamental Painting. Possibly, their approach was different because they were able to not look back but continue forward on that basis. Conversely, Lemoine's words confirm Rini Dippel's suspicion that the "new painting" in those countries was different from Fundamental painting.

With this in mind, it can be concluded that besides the USA, the countries actually producing Fundamental Painting in the 1970s were the Netherlands – the home of De Stijl – and the United Kingdom. It is worth recalling here that it was in London in 1905 where Annie Besant had published her influential book *Thought Forms* which led artists such as Kandinsky to create abstract art. London was also home to the Cornwall group which had had close ties to India (still under British rule) where abstract tantric art had flowered for almost a millennium. Members of the Cornwall group included artists Ben Nicholson, who worked in an abstract manner during the interbellum, and Constructivist Naum Gabo, who settled in the UK from 1936. Gabo was one of a large number of European artists fleeing the Fascist mainland, who had been hunted for their "entartete Kunst" ("degenerate art") style. Together with architect Leslie Martin in 1937, they produced *Circle: International Survey of Constructive Art*, which identified them as a group of likeminded artists who wished to apply Constructivist principles to art, advocating mathematical precision, clean lines and absence of ornament. It should also be noted here that Piet Mondrian (two of his paintings were included in the *Entartete Kunst* show) also spent 1938-1940 in London before moving to New York City. During his stay, his works were exhibited in leading galleries, including Peggy Guggenheim's on Cork Street (see Grant).

Thus, London developed a focus on non-objective painting, leading up to WWII. After the war, as early as in 1948 the Institute of Contemporary Arts in London staged the show *40,000 Years of Modern Art*; and Ben Nicholson – together with artists like Anthony Hill and the couple Kenneth and Mary Martin – was a key figure in reviving the De Stijl idiom in the UK in the 1950s, by taking up the discussion on an international level (Fritz-Jobse, 12). Accordingly, although Fundamental painter Alan Charlton stated that he started painting his gray paintings to escape the drawing and painting of the figurative styles of other artists, as taught in art school, the ground for non-objective painting was also being prepared in the UK.

Finally, the Netherlands, one of the countries most heavily destroyed by WWII, had a long tradition of painting– ranging from the Northern Renaissance, through the Golden Age, to Van Gogh and De Stijl – and a relatively recent history in the "cool" geometric vein, which would be revitalized after WWII. Already before the war, the Stedelijk Museum in Amsterdam had staged the unique panoramic exhibition of up to date non-objective art forms entitled *Abstrakte Kunst* (Abstract Painting). It included works from Constructivism, De Stijl, Art Concret, and Abstraction-Création, and showed a number of British artists as well as some artists working in the "warm" non-objective vein. (Note also here the natural importance of North-Western Europe in this overview, which is also found in Fundamental Painting.) However, after the WWII access to information on these developments was scarce. Old magazines, black-and-white pictures, and artist writings from the early 20th century were all that the postwar painters had to go by, at best. Until the 1950s, Dutch artists remained in relative isolation. Artists had to start on the non-objective idiom from scratch.

Yet, under the lead of Willem Sandberg, prewar curator and postwar director of the Stedelijk Museum in Amsterdam, the Netherlands would steadily familiarize itself with the major movements in art from the early 20th century in the years 1945 through 1951 and onwards. The Stedelijk Museum organized a series of groundbreaking exhibitions on 20th century revolutions in art (important to the non-objective idiom): Vincent van Gogh in 1945, Alexander Calder and Fernand Léger in 1948, Piet Mondrian and Bart van der Leck in 1949, and De Stijl in 1951. This was paralleled at the same time by a surge in artist initiatives in the abstract and non-objective vein in the Netherlands. The number was significantly more than elsewhere, producing groups like Vrij Beelden in 1946 (which means both "creating freely" and "creating in freedom") and Creatie (1950-1954).

In the 1950s, a new generation of "cool" non-objective art was established on an international basis as artists got back in touch and discovered their common longing for a new form of visual language. Initiatives (for example the group Nul ["zero"]) and magazines, like *Structure* run by the Dutch artist Joost Baljeu, were instrumental in this revival of the non-objective idiom. Thus, the Netherlands saw a true revival of non-objective art forms in the 1950s. At the same time, the Stedelijk Museum Amsterdam continued its exhibition program and acquired works by, amongst others, Henri Matisse, De Stijl, Constructivism, and Kazimir Malevich, exhibited in the new wing that opened in 1954. Surely, these actions paved the way for Fundamental Painting in the Netherlands.

Rajlich's words on his arrival in the Netherlands in the late 1960s highlighted the differences between countries: "Here [in Prague] the Klub Konkretistů was very radical at the time. Then I came to Holland and saw that, in comparison with their group Nul which created really radical abstraction, it was a somewhat silly Constructivism" (Skřivánek 13).[163] In the 1960s the Stedelijk Museum Amsterdam started exhibiting American art (notably Abstract Expressionism and Minimal Art), which guided the Netherlands back to its non-objective tradition and on towards a new kind of painting – Fundamental Painting –, influenced by a contemporary American impulse: Minimalist painting.

Thus, the countries that sheered close to the non-objective idioms of the early 20th century, which experienced a drastic decline (or change) in artistic activity as a result of WWII and benefited from a liberal postwar environment, made a new start in this direction. Based on the nature of painting before WWII and the national character of painting in general, postwar painting in these countries either tended more towards the "cool" non-objective idiom (open to Fundamental Painting)[164] or towards a more varied, "warm," expressive or theoretical form of non-objective art like Analytical Abstraction. In the end, the limited number of nationalities included in *Fundamental Painting* was due to the fact that the curatorial team did not find anything similar in more countries. Their choice no longer seems so randomly restrictive. Although Fundamental Painting reflects the personal mentality of each painter, on a historical level it already seems that it could only be "in the air" (FP 11) in the 1970s in certain countries, in North-Western Europe: The Netherlands including Belgium, France, the United Kingdom, Germany (plus Italy for Analytical Abstraction) – besides the United States, of course. Only those had a fertile ground that would enable the Fundamental painters to act on their proposition. Moreover, the fact that the *Fundamental Painting* show was a Dutch curatorial initiative including a number of Dutch artists seems to stem from this logic.

3.3.5 Important factors for Fundamental Painting

Thus, the *Fundamental Painting* show appears to have been a logical consequence of 20th century developments leading all the way up to Fundamental Painting, especially in the Netherlands – as well as the United Kingdom and other neighboring countries – due to the direct access to postwar American art in the 1960s and 1970s. This is a crucial point to differentiate Fundamental painters and their European contemporaries: the former's "live" access to American painting and the tradition of this vein. This is the reason behind the restricted number of nationalities – and, in turn, individuals – in the *Fundamental Painting* show. Such an observation can also be found in a text extract by Barbara Reise of 1974:

> This acceptance of the physical nature of painting as a matter of fact is characteristic of New York artists working in close physical association with the heritage established by Rothko, Newman, Pollock, and Johns from the 1950s: a heritage recently transmitted to some interested but sedentary European artists primarily through commercial galleries, theorizing critics, and art-magazine reproductions. The difference in paintings by artists of a similar age on both sides of the Atlantic can be seen in the contrast between the Parisian "Supports/Surfaces" group with its dependence on a verbal theoretical structure and the direct material importance of Brice Marden's surfaces, the image determination by a painting's physical parameters in Stella's early work, and the importance of canvas texture in the making of those irregularities of strictly orthogonal lines which are the fine excellence of Agnes Martin's work. Ryman not only accepts the importance of painting's material reality; he loves it, he revels in it, he uses it in ways which are most conservative of his material's essential pictorial properties, in procedures which manifest each stage of his encounter with the materials at hand. And his approach to the physicality of painting is not limited to an awareness of paintings only as traditional objects: he is also aware of the state of "objects" in contemporary art which are *not* "painting." "A lot of my paintings (I would say most, a lot) can not really be shown to anyone in the usual way of dragging a painting out of the closet or the storeroom and saying, here's a painting," he told Tuchman, "My paintings wouldn't work that way. You can't drag a Flavin, for instance, out of the closet and say, here's a Flavin. All you would see is a couple of tubes. It has to be on the wall, in a situation. Then it's complete." (37-38)

According to Reise, the difference between the American and the European contemporaries in the 1970s is primarily the result of direct contact with influential painting as opposed to indirect sources (cf. the chapter on postwar Europe) and an interest in painting as a material, its effects, and its existence as art within an environment.

These imperatives once again hold true in the light of Fundamental Painting when looking back at our previous review of the nationalities and backgrounds of Fundamental painters. It becomes clear that the few European Fundamental painters as opposed to others (ex. Analytical Abstraction) had access to revolutionary painting (especially postwar and contemporary American painting). They also had a formalist interest in painting and a direct physical contact with the act of painting without previous theoretical "ballast," as opposed to painting coming from a more theoretical stance. This set of givens seems to perfectly apply to the handful of Fundamental painters who have shown themselves to be true to this idiom across the decades. (This will be the implied younger generation of European painters that Lynda Morris must have been thinking of.) In Part II, their working with each and every single element in painting was discussed in detail, to show how the Fundamental painters know painting as material as well as painting as a definition, and that it is more important to them than painting as theory. First and foremost, they approach painting by looking at paintings and, with that, consider each painting as an object more than as a presenter of illusion.

In fact, the Fundamental painters whose works stood the test of time did indeed have access to important paintings. These were the Americans, who knew the collections of the MoMA (incl. Edda Renouf, born in the USA, and Jerry Zeniuk, who divided his time between Germany and New York City), and the Dutch, who were familiar with the collection and exhibitions of the Stedelijk Museum Amsterdam. Similarly, Marthe Wéry, a native of the Flemish part of Belgium and living in Montréal until 1972, had access to American postwar art. Charlton, then again, studied in London, where the Tate Gallery was building its collection of American postwar art at the time since the 1950s. In the 1960s and 1970s, the Tate Gallery had acquired important works by Barnett Newman and Mark Rothko. Also the Whitechapel Gallery showed a number of important temporary exhibitions, for example Mark Rothko's work in 1961. Raimund Girke lived in Hannover at the time, home of one of the most significant collections of Modern and postwar art, which was donated to the city by Bernhard Sprengel in 1969 and exhibited that same year at the Kestner-Museum. (Today, it is housed in the Sprengel Museum, which was opened in 1979.) This sort of accessibility is what makes the difference between those few painters that can be qualified as Fundamental and their contemporaries who cannot.

In this regard, Reise's text in fact indicates this parallel which also reflects Rini Dippel's opinion that a large number of non-objective European painters – notably the Italians, as well as the French participants of Nouvelle Peinture – should be excluded from Fundamental Painting. Indeed, as we have seen, they have different prewar and postwar backgrounds and a different exposure compared to the kind of "live" painting which leads up to Fundamental Painting. Therefore, they are different– a fact that was also inversely corroborated by Serge Lemoine's concept of "spread of Art Concret." Namely, as it seems that the Fundamental kind of painting comes largely out of formalist considerations, this excludes a large number of European painters of the 1970s (for example, the artists of Supports/Surfaces who worked from a theoretical standpoint) but not all – as the curatorial team of *Fundamental Painting* has shown us.

At the same time, the repercussions of WWII on the art world explain the timeline difference between the American and European Fundamental currents. The concept of a younger generation with a European background and their elder American influence corresponds perfectly to the Fundamental current, where the American models preceded the European ones by several years. This is the natural outcome of the European political situation, in particular WWII which interrupted the course of non-objective painting in Europe by over a decade. The ideas of the geometric current at large were slowly taken up again by artists in Europe after WWII, but only by the late 1960s did artists (and the public) in certain European countries have access to postwar and contemporary painting of American making. To return to Lynda Morris's statement, the increase in contacts between Europe and the USA is what allowed a younger generation of painters in Europe to develop a current of painting based on these postwar American concepts. Hence, European Fundamental Painting finds it starting point several years after its American contemporaries.

The various manifestations of the Fundamental idiom by the American and European artists participating in the 1975 show were detailed in Part II. Perhaps some artists were more process-oriented and some more result-oriented, as Morris claims – referring to the Americans and Europeans respectively. In fact, American artist and art critic Marcia Hafif likewise once explained to Jerry Zeniuk that some painters of the Fundamental kind knew the result but did not know how to get there, while others knew the way but not what the result was going to look like.[165] In any case, it has become evident at this point that both might also still correspond to a Fundamental mentality. However, a number of artists included in the *Fundamental Painting* show did not stand the test of time in the end. Some would be found to be indeed working from a more theoretical or probing standpoint, for example Louis Cane or Richard Jackson.

We must therefore conclude that in the end – although subject to external influences which determined the possibilities –, Fundamental painters show a similar interest in painting as painting. This goes for both European and American as well as younger and older artists. Formal knowledge of and contact with postwar American painting were key for painting to change instead of simply repeating itself. There was a prevailing tendency towards a Fundamental kind of painting which was more "in the air" in certain regions than in others. This is so despite the fact that the life's work of such artists tends to be more individual than national for the reasons developed previously, in Part 2.

The group of Fundamental painters, which we have defined and rectified, comprises about 12 to 14 artists in total. In the end, more Europeans than Americans are part of Fundamental Painting. Although the show *Fundamental Painting* was correctly based on the works of American artists as "fathers" of this current and supplemented by numerous European artists (who adopted this approach a few years later), it seems that "[t]he Europeans are more perceptive to painting in general…. There seems to be a lot of interest in painting, maybe more than here [USA]," as Ryman once noted (Diamonstein-Spielvogel, 47:55-48:16). That said, Fundamental painters overall share a mentality that is specific but at the same time profoundly connected to painting throughout the ages. Therefore, the importance and essence of the *Fundamental Painting* show – or rather the Fundamental mentality – might be best echoed in Frances Colpitt's words, when she writes on painting of the Fundamental kind: "Along with Ryman, these artists are emphatically *painters*" (32).

3.3.6 The future of Fundamental Painting

Fundamental Painting connects with generations not only in the past but possibly also leading into the future. For one, the pivotal figure of *Fundamental Painting* Robert Ryman was convinced that this is not the end but the beginning of a new era in painting, opening doors to generations to come. Already at the time of the *Fundamental Painting* show in March 1975, he expressed this conviction in his artist's statement:

> The basic problem is what to do with paint. What is done with paint is the essence of all painting. I am not talking of the technical process of painting, which in itself is important, but of the seeing of painting. This "seeing" can be so complex that the possibilities for painting are endless. As we know, it is not necessary to use paint to make an image, but most painters have used paint to make an image, either because they wanted to or because they could not "see" any other way to use paint. At times the aesthetic problems of painting can seem so elementary, there can be a risk of forgetting that painting, in the absolute sense, has only been in existence a relatively short time and the future of painting, the challenge and discovery of painting, is within the field of "absolute" painting. (FP 64)

In 1997, more than two decades later, Ryman reconfirmed his strong belief in the sustainability of painting in an interview with David Carrier:

> Painting will go on. Painting is by far not finished; it will never be finished, because it's too rich. The medium is so challenging. What could be more challenging than to have endless possibilities? I think that there is much more to be done. We will see things probably in the future we wouldn't have thought. Maybe it won't be like painting we know now. (631)

It is a question of the ability to see forever more in painting, to see that which we do not see today. Also Fundamental painter Alan Charlton has expressed hope:

> The *Fundamental Painting* exhibition was very important, however shortly afterwards painting changed to figurative/wild painting. Many of the artists in that exhibition also changed with the fashion. I think there is a return to thinking about painting in a more serious manner [today in 2012] and in that sense there is a new type of Fundamental Painting. (Letter 4)

So far, an evolution towards a more versatile (yet not resilient) range of Fundamental painting has become evident with the Fundamental painters from the 1975 show, as described previously. Notably, their work has gained in color. First Marden, Renouf, Wéry, and Mangold, then others have turned away from neutral hues. Starting in the mid-1980s, Rajlich first took up painting in reflective golden pigment and went on to explore a brighter, ever-widening range of hues. Zeniuk started working with color blotches (but his work deviated from the Fundamental current).

Other than color developments, Marden started working with all-over linear compositions of irregular grid patterns recalling architectural drawings, then in irregular linear patterns on even grounds in various colors. Both Zeniuk and Marden deviated in the mid-1980s, launching a new chapter in their work. Over time, versatility and a more intricate balancing of elements can be seen in all Fundamental oeuvres. This is not surprising, because experience and astuteness liberates creativity. As Fundamental Painting has become more elaborate, it is also more "perfect" and necessarily returns to the richness of its predecessors – traditional painting.

With the next generation (after the pluralistic 1980s and partially 1990s), a return to painting can be sensed amongst both artists and collectors (as for example Buchmann explains in "The (Re)Animation of Medium Specificity in Contemporary Art"). In recent years, part of this painting is non-objective, even monochromatic. However, the "fundamentality" of Fundamental Painting seems to be lacking. Even Robert Ryman's son, Cordy Ryman, who is likewise a painter and who has grown up around the pivotal figure of the 1975 exhibition, feels the need to incorporate foreign objects into his paintings and take them into the third dimension. Up to date, no painter from the younger generation who would do justice to the Fundamental title has yet entered the scene. If we believe Ryman and Charlton, Fundamental Painting was just the beginning of a new era in this medium. From my study, I believe that the future looks promising, but is not manifesting just yet.

Excursus: Fundamental Painting and the Czech Republic

As proposed previously, the history of certain countries does not make for a postwar environment which will have a Fundamental type of painting "in the air," be it for artistic or political reasons or both. In this regard, Czech art critic Jiří Valoch – one of the sporadic defendants of Fundamental Painting in the Czech Republic – stated in reference to Fundamental Painting and the Czech Republic in an interview of 13 December 2012 at the AVU in Prague: "It is something that was never here. We have missed the situation that would make us want to have such a thing here. We cannot have it, do not want it, and never will. We do not accept it. Here, we want art with a story."[166] Here are two key points, which correspond to our findings concerning the conditions for Fundamental Painting: The historical background and the contemporary situation.

It therefore does not seem coincidental that Fundamental painters come from countries which do have an early 20th century background in "cool" non-objective painting. At the same time, there are other countries that returned to this non-objective idiom after WWII, since they had the possibility to do so in the context of their particular political situation. A third important point, hinted at in Valoch's statement that the Czech "missed the situation," is – as recurrently evident and stressed – that Fundamental painters work from a formalist knowledge of painting.

Fundamental painters are curious about painting, looking at and experiencing painting. A prerequisite for this is the access to original painting of the kind that was cited by those artists whom the curators of the *Fundamental Painting* included amongst the predecessors. None of these three conditions for Fundamental Painting has been met in the Czech Republic. Considering the previous discourse, the Czech Republic never had a particularly large role in the 20th century evolutions in abstract and non-objective painting. Although Frank Kupka (1871-1957) is one of the fathers of non-objective painting, he lived in relative isolation and from 1896 onwards in Paris. The beginnings of abstraction and non-objective painting – as seen previously and as generally accepted in art history – are a Russian, German and Dutch story, partially coinciding in France and finding fertile ground in the UK and US.

When scrutinizing the referential *Dějiny Českého Výtvarného Umění*, abstract and especially non-objective art seems to be virtually absent. The early twentieth century in the Czech Republic was devoted to Symbolism and Cubism, and – as Vojtěch Lahoda writes in his "Melancholie, expresionismus a skupina Sedm v říjnu" ("Melancholy, Expressionism, and the group Sedm v říjnu") – in the interbellum, Czech art witnessed a return to Modernism and the Secession, with a hint of the Baroque and Medieval (75). Most significantly, Hana Rousová, in the referential catalogue *Linie, barva, tvar* (Line, Color, Form). whose goal was to "map specific Czech directions towards abstraction at the time," wrote: "So-called abstract art with its mainly formal aspects did neither then, nor now find enough fertile ground. Czech art is always anew connected to a certain theme..." (10).[167] Formalist painting is not in the Czech nature.

In the late 1930s, Czech art was influenced by Oscar Kokoschka (who was living in Prague), while the dominant style remained a classical, realist one (possibly with a Modernist touch). During WWII, Central Europe found itself literally in the midst of the crossfire, while the Topicův Salon aimed at showing more radical art forms. In 1945, Cubism and Surrealism reentered the exhibition scene. The slightly progressive background that the artists in the Czech Republic had to build on was obviously of an abstract and expressive nature, as opposed to the non-objective vein. After the Liberation, exhibitions of Pablo Picasso and the École de Paris were held, influencing the art scene. There was also an influential show in 1945 of Emil Filla's works from the late 1930s, a kind of Cubist Expressionism. Still, these were rather abstract and expressive styles. Only in 1946 could a retrospective exhibition of works by Frank Kupka, one of the few pioneers of abstraction, be considered a partial exception.

However, – to cite Vojtěch Lahoda from his "SVU Mánes a modernismus v letech 1939-1948" ("The visual artists' association Mánes and Modernism in the years 1939-1948") – as abstraction and non-objectivity was considered as something not at all topical in the Czech Republic at the time, it had no impact (Švácha 148). Contrary to the tendency in North-Western European countries towards non-objective art forms as a reaction to WWII, in the Czech Republic the main tendency had been towards Modern Realism – an art for the people. There, the state of shock led to another kind of modification in the essence and function of art. According to Miroslav Petříček in "Úvod: Svědectví o krizi moderního světa" ("Introduction: An Eyewitness Report on the Crisis of the Modern World"), after the war there was a turn from the Modern, as the human being turns towards himself, towards his obligation on earth (Švácha 12-13). Therefore, although Czech art turned back towards Paris as the prewar capital of art, it would – due to its history and postwar perception – take another direction than the art of the North-Western European countries discussed previously. As the Czech art scene was cut off from international happenings when a totalitarian Soviet state was imposed in 1948, the only abstract styles would be neo-Expressionist and post-Cubist, and at that, only surviving underground.

This troubled period through the 1950s was one of a heterogeneous subdued Modernism and Socialist Art. Collector Vincenc Kramář and others promoted the lyrical qualities of Cubism, but overall only a few "harmless" formalist additions enlivened Czech art. It was only towards the end of the decade that the situation opened up and looked to international developments a little bit more. The central exhibition entitled *50 years of Modern art*, at the Expo 58 in Brussels, showed an overview from Impressionism to non-objective art with a strong focus on French art and stimulated the first wave of abstraction – even non-objective art – in the Czech Republic. In the 1960s, the country sought a continuation in the evolution of Modern art, without further specification as to what this meant. The early 1960s saw a surge in Expressionism and Romanticism, and Vaclav Boštík became the pivotal figure in the new abstract sensuality. His works evolved into depictions of fields of energy created by the push-and-pull of colored light within an atmospheric pictorial space. (Note the similarities to the Italian lyrical works, belonging to Zero and analytical abstraction.)

The 1960s fell under the sign of Informal Art, following the Czech tendency towards introspection and content (but missing the existential drama of its French model). The decade was also witness to the rise of Neo-Constructivism, which was more in opposition to Informal Art rather than a continuation of the geometric tendencies of the past. Thus, the Czech geometric artists started again on the path towards abstraction, while still strongly influenced by their expressive and symbolic past and in the ban of French postwar developments. Fundamental painter and Czech native Tomas Rajlich commented on the period: "Before I emigrated, I worked on linear structures, which most likely originated from [Paul] Klee's drawings, because this was one of the artists, whom we at least knew something about in the isolation of the time."[168] As Jan Skřivánek wrote: "The Czech visual arts scene was not totally disconnected from these [Western] tendencies – for example, in 1968, an Yves Klein show was put on in Prague – however, it followed the cross-border evolutions only from the sideline and vicariously" (14).[169] Also Rajlich confirmed this when he stated: "The Yves Klein show at the National Gallery, however, was of defining influence on me. It confirmed for me that it was possible to do totally different things from those considered as accepted as art."[170] (Yet, it still took a move to the Netherlands to arrive at the Fundamental approach.)

Then, in 1968 the political events shut down all communication with the West, meaning with free Europe and – above all – the USA. As Skřivánek wrote in his article concerning the Western bloc: "At the end of the 1960s, classical painting was proclaimed dead. In the United States, the Minimalists celebrated their first successes, thereafter in Europe, the artists related to the international group ZERO (officially already dissolved at the time), which likewise had researched the possibilities of visual language stripped to the minimum [celebrated success]. At the same time, Conceptual Art and the neo-Dadaist Fluxus developed" (14).[171] Rajlich left for the Netherlands of which he says: "[Holland] certainly did also leave its mark on me. It is different from any other country and Dutch light is so right, Vermeer-like" (Skřivánek 16).[172]

Regarding this formalist remark, it must be remembered that the Czech Republic is the native country of Tomas Rajlich, one of the core Fundamental painters. Dutch critic Philip Peters sees a connection between the homeland of Rajlich and his paintings. In the 2008 catalogue to the artist's retrospective exhibition at the National Gallery in Prague, he writes: "I propose that Rajlich's work is actually an image, a blueprint, of Prague. The work of the last years accommodates the city on both sides of the river, the 'surreal' old town as well as the rational 18th century constructions" (46). The artist himself, on the contrary claims "Prague was not really important....", although he adds that: "On the other hand, then again, Ryman, for example, would never take up golden paint. I must most probably have a bit of Czech Baroque in me" (Skřivánek 16).[173]

Consequently, not only was the history and environment of the Czech Republic not beneficial to the development of a Fundamental kind of painting but also its final element – the knowledge and hands-on experience of postwar American painting – was impossible at the time. Just after WWII and into the 1970s, the Czech art scene neither had the background nor the possibilities for the creation of anything approaching Fundamental Painting. If anything, it turned toward a lyrical kind of abstract and non-objective art, reminiscent of the Italian analytical idiom that Rini Dippel specifically excluded from Fundamental Painting.

4 THE SIGNIFICANCE OF FUNDAMENTAL PAINTING

The significance of Fundamental Painting in the history of painting emerges naturally from the discourse of previous chapters. It is Modernism, in particular, which is most interesting for this discourse of emphasizing the painterly elements instead of the image expressed. Likewise the curators of *Fundamental Painting* position Fundamental Painting in art history, by tracing the origins of Modernism and then contrasting postwar Europe and the United States. In Part II of this study, it became evident how the formalist teachings in painting had been appropriated in Fundamental Painting. In Part Three, it became also evident that the main impetus was American postwar painting, which had firmly established formalist painting into the historical process. We can conclude that Fundamental Painting is a logical consequence of earlier 20th century painting and an international, European-American phenomenon. Artists from both continents seemed to display a similar mentality in the way they painted, while staying true to each one's individuality and national background. Fundamental Painting was an evolution thanks to as well as despite its particular context.

At this point, it is interesting to bring to mind the point made by the exhibition *Monochrome Malerei* at the Museum Leverkusen in 1960, curated by Udo Kultermann.[174] Art critic Bruno Corà claims that Kultermann had already seen in 1960 that contemporary painting at the time had appropriated and radicalized Piet Mondrian's, Kazimir Malevich's, as well as Wassily Kandinsky's, and Paul Klee's analytical and non-objective approach to pictorial elements (Bonomi 11). The show featured forty artists in all and included only a few predecessors to Fundamental Painting: According to Rini Dippel these were Mark Rothko, Yves Klein – along with several Art Informel adherents [notably Georges Mathieu] – and Piero Manzoni. Raimund Girke was the only Fundamental painter to be included. But if we accept Corà's remark, we could indeed say that Kultermann had already spotted a connection between the predecessors and representative of Fundamental Painting, amongst others, and non-objective approaches to pictorial elements of older generations of artists.

Notably, Kultermann's choice of words in the introductory text of the exhibition catalogue is remarkable in relation to a new, purifying trend in the painting of the time: purportedly his selection states the "fundamentalness" of liberating painting from every "servitude" in order to give it a conceptual entity, void of any relation to mimesis, to redefine painting at "zero" degrees. Rini Dippel in her introductory text to the *Fundamental Painting* catalogue specifies that Fundamental painters use monochromatic works to explore the inherent elements of the painting medium. This coincidence of wording could be seen as supportive evidence. It is a strong indication that Fundamental Painting was bound to happen around the late 1960s or early 1970s: and the hypothesis that Fundamental Painting forms a continuum in 20th century painting by connections with its predecessors and peers can be defended.

This consensus testifies to the existence of the phenomenon called Fundamental Painting. Previously in this study, it became evident that a new beginning based on Modernist breakthroughs (and more directly on painting of the fifties) was starting to emerge by the 1970s (FP 11). For European curators then, it materialized in the 1975 *Fundamental Painting* show which was built around four Americans. Following the discourse of its roots and particularities, the European part of Fundamental Painting is placed on a par with Minimal Art in the USA, an indisputably widely accepted art historical phenomenon. Thus, Fundamental Painting seems to be assured a place in the continuum of art history – and there is more.

Edward Strickland writes in his *Minimalism: Origins*: "Painting from [the caves of] Lascaux to the latest show is similarly composed of pigment applied to surface. Minimalist painting culminated the rejective purification of modernism by reducing the medium to its components and displaying those components overtly" (12). Indeed, the history of painting on panel or canvas goes as far back as Ancient Egypt and Ancient Greece. Even before the time of recorded history, there were many visual expressions of designs on surfaces which formed continuity in one way or other. The "how" in painting has always been there and is very valid in relation to Fundamental Painting. It is simply since the beginning of Modernism that this "how" in painting becomes the main theme in Western art. The culmination that takes place in Minimalist painting, as Strickland writes, can be directly transposed onto European Fundamental Painting and on its American counterpart. Consequently, this makes Fundamental Painting a genuine phenomenon in art, which follows Ariadne's thread of the evolution in painting throughout history, not only in formalist but also in aesthetical terms.

4.1 The meaning of Fundamental Painting

"The meaning of painting is painting," the central figure to Fundamental Painting, Robert Ryman, once stated (Variations, n.p.). Fundamental Painting is all about the consequences of painting. The Fundamental painter accepts traditional and inherent painterly materials and effects. Fundamental paintings are the manipulation with and the expressions of these painterly elements, ranging from support, via paint, to perception. Through this, these paintings become "something to see" (Ryman; Qtd. in Storr 164), painting to view – recognizing visual reality. At the same time these paintings are painting about painting – that which has and always will make a painting a painting.

Alan Charlton commented in this direction, when he said in *I am an artist who makes a grey painting:* "It's only after doing the painting that I fully understand what the painting is actually about" (15:19-15:24). In a letter by gallery owner Hannes von Gösseln to Geert van Beijeren of the Stedelijk Museum dated 5 March 1975, Jerry Zeniuk is quoted informing the curators of *Fundamental Painting*: "I find myself unable to make a statement which is meaningful and honest. To discuss my work technically is uninteresting and only part of the real process that does take place. To speak about art is to talk about ideas – and I make painting." Fundamental Painting is about painting: on the one hand discussing painting by the artist, on the other communicating something on painting to the viewer. It is the essence of painting, while the characteristic and final element of such a painting seems to be the *je ne sais quoi* found in every painting that makes it art.

For Fundamental painters, the painterly process – intellectually predetermined yet modified by intuition – has the upper hand over both the plastic form and emotional or aesthetic effects. The resulting work is "a set of evocative differences within a reduced set of material and practical givens" (Hudson 186). Suzanne Hudson explains, "the generic idea of painting is tested against its specificity as material consequences so that the question of what a painting is can be answered only by, in, and as painting" (113). As Mangold described it in an unpublished letter to David Carrier, dated 20 September 1994, such paintings are: "Answers for which no question has been asked," (Schiff 282, note 16). A Fundamental painting answers questions on painting. Nevertheless, it is both contemplative and human, not a "standing back and a 'take it or leave it' attitude," as Donald Kuspit writes in "Robert Ryman: Reductionism à Entropy" (89).

4.1.1 Fundamental Painting and the viewer

In order to visually discuss painting, Fundamental Painting needs an observer, someone to question it. This is where issues of process come into the picture once again. Fundamental painters are not concerned with just putting paint on a canvas, as generations before – Ryman once noted about himself (Storr et al. 164). They approach painting not considering the canvas as empty but as something in and of itself. As Hudson writes: "Painting in his [Ryman's] hands has continued as a series of propositions that are born out of an engagement with the materiality of paint, the properties of support structures, and notions of how such objects relate to their beholders in an exhibition space" (18). The act of painting of Fundamental painters makes their painting "something to see," as also Mangold writes in his "Catalogue Notes" (Storr et al. 164). This is the pivotal point in Fundamental Painting.

As this study has shown, this fact of Fundamental Painting being a kind of painting made for experiencing visually is inseparable from the fact that Fundamental painters are "bound together almost exclusively by their commitment to anti-illusionism" (Crimp 258). This common commitment to "opacity" seems to revolve around the "surfaceness" of the painting, as Douglas Crimp calls it. Out of this reasoning, Fundamental painters prefer a neutral format, which is often (almost) square. This makes it visually concentric and keeps the viewer's focus on what is happening on the surface (as opposed to in some pictorial space). The format and the painterly elements are the constants in this painterly proposition. Repetition of the same format and painterly elements – over and over again – allows for maximum variations in the results. It is a unified proposition: everything there is to see happens within a single visual field, upon a two-dimensional canvas (not separated by a frame), in a human scale. Accordingly, the happening is part and parcel of the viewer's own reality.

Line here is non-indicative as it comments on and dismisses its traditional illusionist functions. However, its inherent characteristic of leading the eye around the canvas is exploited to draw attention to the slightest details in the painting. This again focuses the viewer's attention on the painted surface. The richness of color is explored within its basic likeness: neutral tones. The primary nature of color is taken into account: both material and paint. Structure, texture, and facture (or its absence) are important elements as they actually create the surface. Fundamental Painting does not allow for anything expendable. Yet, the painterly elements in their inherent form (as a material) and the painterly tools with which these can be applied in various ways are as important as their traditional painterly effects which make them a part of painting. The "right" choice of each and every element, material, and its application greatly enhances the play of possible differences within the format. At the same time, it communicates something to the viewer about the process and the materiality of the painting.

A good example is the support. Traditionally, it had merely served as a base that became eclipsed in order to reveal a view within the fabricated pictorial space. It is now recognized in its own right. It is the surface of the "surfaceness" – a key factor in the artistic quest of Fundamental Painting. The painting insists on its inherent characteristic of being a two-dimensional plane. Notably, the use of geometric line patterns (especially grids), bare canvas, interventions to the canvas's weave, drip line borders, pastuous paint, and multi-panel constellations defines the painted image as congruent with this plane. The use of all these and other painterly elements is applied towards the goal of "surfaceness," which is more than an inherent attribute. It is a much sought-after value, because it is elementary in the viewer's experience of the painting.

Nevertheless, Fundamental painters let their paintings unfold without an overall conceptual plan. Each work emerges as a careful combination of its components. Each painting is subjected to new decisions regarding support (material, size), paint (consistency, reflectivity, color, and tone), and the application of paint (facture and type of instrument). Intuition plays an important role during the painting process in unveiling the inherent qualities and workings of these purely painterly elements within this chosen framework. The process is logical yet personal. The artist's choice merely establishes the framework for each new painting. It is a mentality, as Dippel has pointed out over and over again. The artist can only discover what painting really means by painting. The viewer is invited to join in and retrace the process.

4.1.2 Painting on painting

The Fundamental generation learns from American postwar painting that painting is primarily an art of looking – a viewing experience. As we have seen in previous chapters, American artists had historically learned to respect the materials and the creative process as frontier craftsmen, through which beauty could come into being. Art was considered to be first and foremost an experience. This concept would see a great revival in the 1960s. And so, postwar American painting only extended its metaphysical aspect, which at the same time was non-conceptual and simply paint-being-paint (i.e. objecthood or "surfaceness").

The Abstract Expressionists Barnett Newman and Mark Rothko, whose works tend to have a monumental scale, have highlighted the importance of the relationship between viewer and painting. In this context, size is an important choice. It influences the viewing experience and incites the level of reading of the painterly elements. Moreover, Newman has shown how a compositional detail like a "zip" can, in turn, influence the perceived scale or degree of intimacy of the dialogue between the artwork and the viewer. Rothko, then again, thrived in the "surface incidents" which could be read in his large color planes, to bring the painting from an enveloping environment to a detailed interaction (Colpitt 88). As Colpitt writes: "Most … monochrome painters in the sixties were concerned with external scale, the relationship of the size of the object to the size of the spectator and the environment. Because … most paintings [are] flat, relations are forced out of internal structure to surface and shape" (75).

Their peer, Ad Reinhardt, emphasizes in his multiple writings that painting is an activity and art is the result. The form of the painting at once present precedes its metaphysical content that unfolds in dialogue. Ad Reinhardt's *Black Paintings* are a prime example of this. At first glance, they are simply a black rectangle on a white wall (cf. Malevich's *Black Square* and Ryman's white rectangle on a white wall reminiscent of Malevich's *White on White*). In time these paintings reveal their "composition" and the multiple facets of black as a color. His paintings unfold slowly under the eyes of the viewer. It is an objective rather than an emotional unfolding. It is art as in the sense of an object with an essence wholly incomparable and unique. Reinhardt was instrumental in stating the "arthood," which differentiates an artwork from a plain object. It makes art be about the artwork – an experience in interaction with the viewer. (This concept of painting as an object in the viewer's reality, albeit different from other objects, is highlighted by the curators of *Fundamental Painting* through Jasper Johns's works, while the richness of visual interaction that can be triggered by a single image is personified in Ellsworth Kelly's work.)

Frank Stella takes a step further by combining all of these Abstract Expressionist revelations in the working of painting. Stella in his Black Paintings successfully fuses the industrial and the handmade: He uses industrial materials, geometric shapes, bare canvas, and modular composition, while the hand-painted nature and strong influence on the viewing experience of its beholder turns the painting into a painting per definition. In his early works, he both insists on the "objecthood" of painting and consciously plays with the obvious conclusions of the mind, like the tendency to repeat a pattern. In his symmetrical, a-directional canvases that interlace the image and the base, he subverts these traditional ways of seeing to actively force the viewer into questioning the canvas – about its materials and creation. All of these ways of working trigger the cognitive reaction chain in their beholder.

Douglas Crimp, on whose theories the exhibition *Fundamental Painting* was based, wrote on this subject:

> Traditionally, scale has functioned aesthetically in both real and illusionist senses. The actual large scale of formalist painting [i.e. Abstract Expressionist painting] is figured in terms of its proportion to the viewer and his actual space; thus, in turn, increases the fictive scale where an illusion of infinity is provided by the proportion of surface size to surface particle or incident. In Opaque painting …. [s]taying on the surface, one is aware only of … the proportion of the painting to one's self; and it is precisely this appropriately one-to-one ratio which Opaque painting [Fundamental Painting] exploits by limiting itself to the size of the human figure. [….] [I]t functions to make the viewer aware of his own cognitive activity, to make him apprehend himself in the act of apprehension. (258)

The authority on Minimal Art, Frances Colpitt, brings it to a point when she writes that the one thing that distinguishes such kind of painting is that "the spectator is given a new role as contributor of meaning, the result of what Foster described as Roland Barthes's notion of 'the death of the author'" (134).[175]

Questions about what the art in art is are posed visually. The Abstract Expressionists worked towards this focus on "surfaceness" that Fundamental Painting has achieved. The shaped canvas announces its nature by its flatness and "objecthood" and instills itself as a presence that interacts with its environment. While incited by Reinhardt and notably through the intervention of Stella (who was a generation younger), art of the Fundamental kind claims its place in reality – its objecthood and presence. It was stated earlier in this study that in relation to Fundamental Painting the middle-size, human-scale canvas is preferred. It interacts with its environment on an eye-to-eye level. This incites a closer inspection of Rothko's "surface incident" and thus, a more intimate dialogue between itself and the viewer (Colpitt 88). At the same time, the quality of the grid as an indicator of flatness and infinitely expansive figure comes up over and over again. The use of bare canvas also is known amongst Fundamental painters (Rajlich, Renouf, Rosenthal, Ryman). Fundamental painters, then, have learned a lot from the visual workings in relation to the viewer of Abstract Expressionism, perfecting it in terms of "surfaceness" and turning the focus from viewer to painting.

In short, the conscious creation of a "one glance" start to engage a dialogue between viewer and painting that turns into a "seeing-viewing-experiencing" of the canvas, directly reflects the influence of Abstract Expressionism on Minimalist and Fundamental Painting (See Chapter 2.1.8). The immediacy of Newman's late works as opposed to the individual sensibility and creation of an atmosphere of Mark Rothko's canvases – as well as the slow discovery of the elements in painting as heralded by Reinhardt – is reflected in Fundamental Painting and slightly echoed in both the American and European counterparts. Moreover, the Fundamental works touch upon "objecthood" or "arthood" as something in and of itself by their "surfaceness," as highlighted many times before in this study. The influence of Stella, too, can be found, namely in the non-relational compositions. As a result, in a visual dialogue the Fundamental painting always returns the focus onto itself.

Fundamental artists intuitively work their way through their research on the inherent qualities of painting, while informing the viewer of their quest in a modular fashion. In the end, each Fundamental work – and each body of works by each one Fundamental artist – visually poses this question on painting (or what painting is) to the viewer, by what it does. It echoes the concern of Fundamental Painting. The scope is to involve the viewer in the contemplation of the basic elements of painting. Anything that can distract from the link to reality and the environment (like color) is reduced to the minimum to allow for the other painterly elements to take center stage. Ultimately, the perception of painting comes down to its beholder.

The form is completely given at once, while the painterly elements, material, and process allow for an activated viewing experience. The painting has become a material fact, the experience of which unfolds in time – in the interaction between painting and viewer. Painting now is about the objective viewing experience of a subjective viewer, and the focus in this is on painting – as a single, unique object but also as a member of the family of painting over generations. Reminiscences of painting before Fundamental Painting arise, due to the fact that the formal part (the "how" of painting) has been inherent to painting since the beginning of time. It is a dialogue on painting between two physical presences on eye level: the viewer and the work – and the whole is greater than the sum of its parts.

4.2 The metaphysical in Fundamental Painting

As we have seen in the last part, Fundamental paintings are direct statements to the viewer, which slowly reveal their parts and how they are formed. They solicit both the visual and cognitive perceptive abilities of their viewer. The viewer is free to interpret the painting, according to personal experiences in relation to all painting known. Fundamental Painting thus is auto-referential, not only in relation to the particular work but also to painting at large. By approaching painting from a new direction and proposing the painterly elements handled in great detail, Fundamental Painting reminds its viewer that it is paint, color, scale, and the like, which we see first and last in a painting. And it leads its viewer back outward into the world – his own world, as Roberta Smith writes on Robert Ryman's paintings.

Hudson writes on this point – referring to Dore Ashton's "The Avant-Garde: Subtle, Cerebral, Elusive" (77): "*Time* asserted that Ryman's painting – and the art of his peers – was art because it made 'the viewer look, and feel, and think. The artist may speak from underground, but he retains, in an elliptical way, his traditional role'" (3). This means that Fundamental Painting concerns not only painting as object and painting as historical fact, but also painting as aesthetic revelation. This study does not pretend to cover the history of philosophy, but it does hope to come to a conclusive thought regarding its chosen subject: the philosophy of aesthetics in relation to painting (in the way it touches upon "seeing-viewing-experiencing"), in an effort to clarify the true significance of Fundamental Painting within the continuity of Art History.

4.2.1 The traditional role of Fundamental Painting

The traditional role of art includes having a context. The words of scholar Robert Storr are appropriate in this regard as he writes: "When we look at paintings, we are generally looking *for* something *in* painting, something that painting describes, or suggests, or evokes. It may be an image, a symbol, or an idea. Frequently it involves a synthesis of all three. Even in its most abstract form, therefore, painting has usually been *about* something outside or beyond itself…" (1). Fundamental Painting is about the experience together with the viewer involvement, self-reflective in many ways, as concluded previously. By being about painting, the painting is about the viewer's experience of painting and therefore painting at large. In this sense, the experience of Fundamental Painting is indeed about something beyond itself.

The following passage from John Dewey's *Art as Experience* – which as Buettner remarked was an influence on Postwar American painting – is interesting to note with regard to Fundamental Painting: "An experience has pattern and structure, because it is not just doing and undergoing in alternation, but consists of them in relationship.... The action and its consequences must be joined in perception. This relationship is what gives meaning; to grasp it is the objective of all intelligence. The scope and content of the relations measure the significant content of an experience" (25). According to Dewey then, the interaction between viewing a painting and the reaction of the viewer simultaneously is what makes the experience – and for that matter the painting – meaningful.

In this regard, as Dewey informs us, "a painter must consciously undergo the effect of his every brushstroke or he will not be aware of what he is doing and where his work is going. Moreover, he has to see each particular connection of doing and undergoing in relation to the whole that he desires to produce. To apprehend such relations is to think, and is one of the most exacting modes of thought" (45). This connects with the description of Fundamental Painting as a thought process of the artist and with its "arthood." Just as with generations before, the Fundamental artist delineates the parameters of a painting, while the viewer tries to uncover them. Painting has always existed within a given order – its composition having a set of rules, the pictorial elements determined by canons of harmony and the like. Fundamental painters have merely chosen to work in a way as essential and as removed as possible from any ulterior message, They merely propose the very basics of painting, its materials, elements, and effects that are per definition inherent.

However, by limiting itself to such basics and intensely "undergoing" the effects of the material in the painting process, Fundamental Painting is not only about the particular painting hanging directly in front of the viewer. It is also about painting at large. The viewing experience combines both the artist's and the viewer's personal history of experience of painting. It is determined by what the artist offers regarding knowledge on the formalist aspects of painting and by what the viewer receives or recognizes. The resulting painting incites the viewer to rediscover the meticulous nature of creating a Fundamental Painting, savoring the entire range of each and every painterly element – nothing more and nothing less. Ultimately, it is about a set of experiences, which are defined by the painting in combination with the viewer.

Fundamental Painting therefore does not only depend on its maker to unfold its true potential. It depends each time on what the viewer brings into the experience of the painting, perhaps based on a lifetime of experiences in viewing painting. In this regard, Dewey adds: "No one ever arrives at such maturity that he perceives all the connections that are involved..." (25). The experience is perpetually building; it can only be a series of partial experiences. Remember Alan Charlton's statement for the *Fundamental Painting* show, which in fact is a statement by Alberto Giacometti: "The adventure, the great adventure, is to see something unknown appear each day, in the same face. That is greater than any journey round the world." This seems to underline a perpetual nature and hints at the reason behind the timeless appeal of art (and hence Fundamental Painting). A Fundamental work teaches the viewer something new about painting but also about himself, each and every time. By being about itself, about the "how" of painting, Fundamental Painting is, at the same time, inherently about something outside itself, about something inherent to its viewer.

Ultimately, the experience is beyond both. The definition of "seeing-viewing-experiencing" a painting, as Mangold understands it, is of paramount importance in this context. In his studio notes of 29 April 1993, he writes: "When you view a painting you exist in relation to it. The relationship is one of seeing and being, not seeing alone, since it is impossible to separate seeing from being. It is the experience of seeing and being in front of a work which affects us." It might be a physical sensation. At the same time, the confrontation reminds us of our personal history, for example of similar experiences when encountering other paintings. The more complex "experiencing" after the "seeing-viewing" part – as Dewey indicated – is about "being," as Mangold writes in his notebook (Schiff 165). In Mangold's terms, as with science, the process of artistic creation and its re-creation by the viewer leads to an increasingly better understanding of being.

Thus, Fundamental Painting is about being – its own being and its viewer's being in relation to it. Accordingly and more specifically, Fundamental Painting is about nothing but itself. It communicates nothing but painting, thus it simply "is." Fundamental painting "is", just like the works of Malevich, Mondrian, Klein, Newman, or Rothko and the like simply "are." Already in 1960, scholar Sonya Rudikoff suggested that, "quite possibly, the art of our times is a witness to this, a witness to the irreducible nature of actuality. Out of experience itself come works of art which exist in themselves in the way natural objects exist, with no rationalized purpose or meaning, but, as is so often said, are simply *there*" (25). In contrast to the subjective nature of numerous other artworks in all kinds of media from the postwar and contemporary period that hit the viewer with an emotional impact, Fundamental Painting is "simply *there*" for the viewer to see, to experience. Yet, it is precisely for that reason that Fundamental Painting respects the traditional role of painting and art in general.

In brief, to put this in context, art has always been a means to an end. As centuries of philosophy of aesthetics teach us, it could be said that of old the artist was considered as a craftsman comparable to God the Creator, creating objects that were reflections of the spiritual realm (a kind of "recognition pieces"). Throughout the ages, artists consciously created artworks as instruments of revelations of something else. This something else which might have been in, out, or beyond the artwork, could be called the good, truth, beauty, or be designated with the name of a deity. In any case, artworks had to initiate the beholder or become a support for contemplation, making their viewer aware of what lies beyond. This path towards the revelation of absolute beauty was already described by Plato in his *Symposion*; according to him, only enlightened souls – beings receptive to this revelatory nature – could follow this path and reach revelation.

Thus, the philosophy of aesthetics throughout the ages has perceived that art is a slow discovery of something beyond the individual artwork itself. Thanks to art, the initiated viewer is led on a step-by-step path, along an ever-higher sense of awareness, towards revelation. The path is often one of slow discovery towards the understanding of one's own being, based on artworks that simply "are." It is timeless, absolute. It goes beyond immortality. The tradition of representation in Western civilizations (and of suggestion in Eastern civilizations) has supported artists who create works that aim at making the beholder aware of what lies beyond the visible aspects of nature and life (and that give hope). As Naomi Spector and *Time* magazine, amongst others claimed, the Fundamental painter seems to retain this traditional role.

Within the context of Fundamental Painting, the awareness of what lies beyond issues directly from the "seeing-viewing-experiencing" of a painting – a painting that simply "is." It is inherent to the viewer's experience of the painting. In her notes of 21 August 1974, Marthe Wéry described the experience in front of her kind of art as follows:

> The question of knowing if this is art or not is of little importance. I am very hesitant when using this term, which is becoming less and less specific. It is simply something that one lives, that transforms itself in living. It is, in any case, something that gives the impression of participating in the deepest pulsation within the nature of things and by this fact, without doubt, of itself. A sort of accord that is made and that lives wherever it is provoked. What remains of it must, in principle, in turn, incite itself again, as long as it is available.[176]

So, once again we encounter the notion in Fundamental Painting that the viewer is the final element in painting. The encounter is a never-ending give and take, in which from one comes the other. Hence this viewing experience of a Fundamental painting leads little by little to a heightened state of awareness of living – a heightened state of consciousness and possibly participating in the "pulsation" of all existence.

This sense of being that ensues from this complexity of relating to the painting is a slow discovery, in line with the philosophical concept of revelation. Accordingly, already in 1967 Lucy Lippard, in her famous article entitled "Silent Art" on contemporary painting of the Fundamental kind, wrote in reference to this viewing experience that "monotonal painting has no nihilistic intent," and she continued:

> Nevertheless, it demands that the viewer be entirely involved in the work of art, and in a period where easy cultures, instant culture, have become so accessible, such a different proposition is likely to be construed as nihilist. The experience of looking at and

> perceiving an "empty" or "colorless" surface progresses through boredom. The spectator may find the work dull, then impossibly dull; then, surprisingly, he breaks out on the other side of boredom into an area that can be called contemplation or simply esthetic enjoyment, and the work becomes increasingly interesting.... As the eye of the beholder catches up with the eye of the creator, "empty," like "ugly," will become an obsolete esthetic criterion. (63)

Note the reference to the traditional role of the artist-creator, and the Absolute nature of aesthetics.

In fact, like art throughout time, Fundamental Painting initiates the spectator on his path towards the Absolute. The important point to note from the history of the philosophy of aesthetics is that the artwork's traditional function has been to make a bridge from the viewer to that something else. This acceptance of the traditional function of painting can still be sensed at times in the words of Fundamental painters. For example, in "A Talk on December 5th, 1992 in New York" with collector Urs Rausmüller, Robert Mangold explained: "In our lives we can never really know anything about another person's existence, but art becomes a gesture to others, through meaning. The need for art is the need to bridge" (53). So, in congruence with history, he sees the meaning of art – including his own kind of painting – in its capability to bridge. In this tradition, Fundamental Painting is a form of communication between the artist and the viewer and therefore a kind of recognition piece towards something beyond – the "experiencing," the perception of beauty, and ultimately the awareness of being and the absolute.

Louis Cane in his statement for *Fundamental Painting* writes in a similar vein: "I make myself a certain idea of painting but ... in the end 'painting' is nothing else than an idea that I make myself of the other. This other, it can be a recollection even" (3).[177] The interesting addition here is his mention of recollection in this bridging process. To summarize: Any encounter, including our encounter with an artwork, triggers a reaction. It might be emotional or more factual or even lead to a higher sense of consciousness. In Fundamental Painting, when entering into dialogue, the painting clearly and slowly unfolds factual information on painting. The viewer becomes conscious of the range of the basic painterly elements and the vast range of possibilities they offer: the possibilities proposed by the artist and, possibly, at the same time, the recognition of these from a personal set of memories of similar experiences in painting. Thus, it creates a higher awareness of the viewer's life experiences in front of painting. Once again, this confirms our assumptions about the meaning of Fundamental Painting.

Fundamental Painting opens up awareness, following the tradition of art according to the philosophy of aesthetics. The Fundamental artwork still offers a sort of revelation and the artist keeps his traditional role. The viewing experience of a Fundamental painting leads the viewer to a heightened sense of consciousness. It is a kind of consciousness that is quite mundane: it talks about the viewer's own personal experience of painting, meaning not only the particular painting in front of him but also painting at large. It recounts both the viewer's and the painter's own history in relation to painting. It therefore connects to life, in the first place to the life of the Fundamental painting and its spectator. In the process, it triggers a sense of being and possibly connects to the all-encompassing pulse of existence, as Wéry indicates. In any case, it is a realm that issues from both the eye and mind of the artist and the beholder. So, the artwork is still a recognition piece, but for the sum of personal histories of painting from its creator and viewer(s). It functions in a traditional way and talks about "being," while *a priori* remaining in the mundane realm.

Fundamental Painting's awareness remains quite down to earth. It makes the viewer reach a sense of being, which, in this instance, is directly his own. It is a discourse on the viewer's own being in concrete terms. In this way, it must be admitted that the self-reflective Fundamental painting still leads the viewer to something beyond the painting and communicates something philosophical about existence. As Alan Charlton put it in his letter in 2012: "The 'presence' of the painting .... [...] is more important than how it is made or painted. The feeling ... between the viewer and the painting is vital. This is the 'art'. (3)" Yet, as opposed to many other types of art and philosophy over the ages, this is a sense of being anchored in the viewer's own reality. In the same way that Fundamental Painting has brought the space in the painting into the viewer's space, it has brought the metaphysical thought of as something beyond into the viewer's realm. Fundamental Painting takes up the traditional function of art and its attributes on a purely essential level.

Colpitt brings this to a head when she writes that what makes this kind of art special is its "philosophical underpinnings." According to her: "It expresses beliefs about the self and the self's perception of the world that are based on material – objecthood – and space as occupied by that material and the artist/viewer's body. It is the condition of objecthood that elevates the work of art, theoretically, from *mere* things in the world" (133). It is painting that is not looked into but looked at, as an alter ego with the same status and presence in the viewer's space as the viewer himself. It is interactive, inciting a dialogue. It addresses its viewer's perceptual senses, makes him consider his position in space, and activates mental activity related to seeing and being. It does not communicate anything about its creator, but it communicates something about itself, about its creation – what its creator did with it and what it does to its viewer.

4.2.2 Fundamental Painting as revelation

The concept of "being" in relation to art has been a recurrent theme in philosophy. Unfortunately, language lacks the means to describe the precise form of being that is sensed in the presence of such works. Across the ages, innumerable artists and philosophers have tried to verbally define this indefinable quality, which is inherent to art. Historically, in the fourth century BCE, Socrates proclaimed that beauty was part of being. Expanding on this basis, his pupil Plato forged the notions that have dominated Western art and philosophy ever since.

Plato's ideal was that of a divine origin, often referred to as beauty, truth, or goodness. Since, beauty has basically been linked to the concept of a divine presence. Beauty is a concept from the philosophy of aesthetics that is absolute. Real beauty is not the result of a subjective judgement but of a slow revelation. Beauty in the form of a tangible support can remind the viewer of this hidden divine presence. Since Plotinus, visual art has occupied this privileged place of a worldly referent and vehicle for conveying the intangible, which is more often than not described as abstract, non-objective and whose essence is unchanging. In fact, art has always been an intermediary for the revelation of being, and ultimately, it ideally becomes one with the beauty perceived in its presence.

Twentieth-century painters like Kandinsky or Mondrian drew inspiration from the artist's inner vision. Their art aimed to spark in the viewer awareness of the true nature of things (the laws of life), beauty and the Absolute. When touching upon this subject, we are in danger of abandoning the "down to earth" quality of Fundamental Painting, yet its mention in the artist's statements and its central role in the philosophy of aesthetics, calls for an investigation into this metaphysical topic.

In the texts accompanying the 1975 exhibition, the curators often emphasized the absence of a metaphysical component in Fundamental Painting. For example, in the text on Barnett Newman the exhibition brochure informed the viewer that the "painters in this show are far away from references to the metaphysical, the infinite, the abstract-sublime…" (3).[178] Likewise, the text on Yves Klein reads: "The mysticism that connects Yves Klein to his work, is totally absent in the painters in this exhibition" (4).[179] This polemic may well have been largely influenced by the critical trends of the era. For example, Boris Groys in his "The Suffering Picture" writes that "the entire contemporary critical discourse rests on the basic thesis … which says that the commercialized society of the 20th century destroys the art work's aura, its authenticity and identity" (108).

However, contemporary philosopher Groys is quick to add – based on a thesis by Benjamin Buchloch – that "[d]epriving original art of its aura causes its simulacrum to regain one," meaning that the sacrifice of the metaphysical is sacral sacrifice. Groys specifies: "In our day, the aura flees anyone holding on to it while haunting anyone who rejects it. This is why the post-modern picture is, in fact, not critical. It is not 'art about art' but simply traditionally auratic" (109). This is in line with the concept that Fundamental Painting keeps its traditional role of slowly revealing the mystery of life – of being. By focusing on the visual reality of painting, Fundamental Painting does neither reflect the world of objects nor any comprehensive world beyond itself. At the same time, its research on painting as a material fact, in which the viewer is the final element, automatically turns it into a research on the aesthetic experience of painting.

Fundamental artists, whose works are made to speak for themselves, in fact do not seem to shy away from the metaphysical. Not in the least. Robert Ryman (around whom the Fundamental Painting exhibition evolved) told Robert Storr in an interview on 17 October 1986 that he would like to communicate "an experience of enlightenment" to the viewer (Galerie Nächst St. Stephan 219). And American Fundamental painter Brice Marden, in his artist's statement for the *Fundamental Painting* show, mentioned the traditional role of an artist and function of art to lead the viewer to a glimpse of the Absolute of existence:

> For as long as man has wrestled with his Gods, there has been Painting.... Painting creates a space on a wall. That space is the expression of the vision of the painter. The painter strives to make his expression explicit because he wants to affect man. By so doing he works to keep man's spirit alive. (FP 42)

This painterly vision, in Marden's understanding, keeps the spirit alive by re-awakening it (or perhaps by reminding men of the divine dimension).

Likewise, Fundamental painter Robert Mangold is sympathetic to the notion of a slow revelation of beauty by means of an artwork. In a letter to David Carrier, dated 8 June 1995, he wrote: "when a painting is immediately beautiful or elegant, I question this," and he expressed the desire that, in his works, beauty be recognized "after a series of exchanges" in the process of "familiarization" (Schiff 283, note 64). In the case of painting, this means that beauty appears when the dialogue between the painting and its beholder surpasses the plain visual experience and enters the "seeing-viewing-experiencing" process. Thus, it can be assumed that it either follows on or is part of the sense of being, as explained previously.

Agnes Martin has always explained her paintings as a revelation, something given or sent to her from outside, which she as an artist merely executed. Briony Fer confirms this in her text *The Infinite Line: Re-Making Art after Modernism*, when she writes that Martin thought that an artwork could open onto an immaterial and meditative space, "that the simplest of means could invite the possibility of revelation," explaining more in detail:

> She used various worlds to describe the experience of boundlessness that art could give: "infinity," "joy," "bliss," "the sublime." To Martin there was nothing particularly feminine about her metaphysics, certainly nothing absurd. On the contrary, she identified with that most serious masculine tradition of metaphysics in Rothko and Newman (Rothko she knew, Newman she counted as a friend), ... But her particular form of interiority is also distinct from theirs, her metaphysical subject differently imagined. I concentrate on the word "infinity" because it opens onto this experience of boundlessness in the subject or spectator and yet it is also a term grounded within the discourses of the 1960s when "infinity" comes to substitute the word "sublime,"... For Agnes Martin ... it suggested the endless expansiveness of a transcendental subject. Martin always maintained something visionary, something that took vision beyond the merely literal. (47-48)

Thus, Martin did embrace the metaphysical component and insert herself into the history of aesthetics.

At the same time, this text by Fer confirms that in Martin's painting the traditional metaphysical elements take on a new form. The initially metaphysical experience of her work and its elements from looking at a painting that is flat on the plane avoids losing oneself in, for example, a color cloud as in Rothko's sublime. The eye wanders across the plane, similarly to wandering over a seemingly flat blue water and sky expanse with just the horizon shifting due to one's movement across the beach. At the same time, it opens an infinite vista in the viewer's mind – an awareness of being, based on the experience of painting. This confirms the need for this discourse on Fundamental Painting and the metaphysical factor at large. The metaphysical in Fundamental Painting has taken on a new form, it revolves around the notion of "surfaceness" and keeps the attention on the painting while at the same time informing of something beyond.

The European Fundamental painters show similar tendencies of more or less accepting the metaphysical in art – including their own art – as something undeniable. Tomas Rajlich's works (in early years untitled) since 2001 bear the names of gods and demons of various religions and the artist outright states that he is convinced of the metaphysical element in painting. Also Jerry Zeniuk is convinced that painting is about a quest for life – beauty is an inherent part of it, as he admitted in conversation with the author. Fundamental painter Edda Renouf even made a statement for the Fundamental Painting show from which one can sense very much the belief in the imbuement of all things with a kind of universal life spirit.

In explaining the working process, Renouf very clearly positioned Fundamental Painting in the tradition of the artist-creator and considered artworks as instruments of revelation, admitting the absolute metaphysical element and opposing it to the life-and-death cycle of human kind. She even stated that the artist retains his or her traditional role:

> Making an artwork is to partake in the indefinable process of creation. In working closely with the canvas, the paint, … I have more an inkling about the mystery – about the life, the death within these materials and myself. And although such a moment of working is in a sense only a minute part of total existence, it is time and again a very whole experience – one which reveals the eternal only if just for a second. And the magic of an artwork is that it can further convey this experience to others who are open to it, on the lookout for it. By working from within, opening the structure of the material, I seek to reveal the life, the energy already inherent in the linen canvas and the paint.

In a similar vein, Louis Cane in his statement wrote that with painting he wants to "hold on to [his] destiny, because, as we all know, painting is made of immortal masterpieces." More specifically:

> This is not saying anything out of the ordinary. Namely, at the end, the subject is faced with the law of mortality, a law that is written into the entire body as a mechanism, unchanging and final to that which makes it live: its language. See here, then, my language; it strongly resembles an attempt at seduction, yet it does not for that matter say less as one of the inherent particularities in painting and, I almost forgot…, [as] characteristic to the profession of painter. (Statement 3)[180]

Again, speaking of his work in the *Fundamental Painting* show, Cane here touched upon two fundamental concepts in aesthetics: For one, he points out beauty to be absolute, as opposed to the concept of beauty by way of "seductive enterprise," conforming to relatively recent philosophical considerations on the subjectivity of judgment in relation to beauty. Secondly, he mentions the mortality of mankind, which can be considered a reference to the element of immortality inherent in the act of painting, already touched upon by Marden.

Part of the creative activity of artists seems to have always been a quest to produce works that survive time, stemming from mankind's fascination with immortality. Namely, procreation – be it physical or artistic – is a way to partake in immortality, which is reserved for the divine. Contemporary philosopher Georges Steiner has summarized the importance of this fact for art: "The central conceit of the artist that the work shall outlast his own death, the existential truth that great literature, painting, architecture, music have survived their creators, are not accidental or self-regarding. It is the lucid intensity of its meeting with death that generates in aesthetic forms that statement of vitality, of life-presence, which distinguishes serious thought and feeling from the trivial and the opportunistic. (141)" The sense of being which is experienced in the presence of Fundamental Painting therefore solidly anchors it into the history of "good" art, as seen in relation to Minimalist painting in Chapter 3.2.3.

These works, then, necessarily relate to the metaphysical, the Absolute, and perhaps to the divine or to the trilogy of truth, goodness and beauty. Accordingly, despite the apparent denials by the critics, some of Fundamental Painting seems to be an outright quest for eternal existence and the divine mystery that imbues all in our universe through painting. All these convictions of Fundamental painters strongly point to both conforming to the history of aesthetics as voiced since Plato and believing in the metaphysical. They are a reference to the traditional role of painting and the painter.

Thus, like its predecessors, Fundamental Painting is "silent."[181] The spectator is not curious about the feelings of its maker. Its beauty is related more to the viewer's intellectual and spiritual faculties than to his emotions. Yet, to experience this "silent art," one needs to open up to the painting. If this does not happen, one can and should still work through the painting's recognizable formal norms and the artist's rules, as well as the comparison of these with those of other oeuvres, as a means to an end – Ariadne's thread connecting Fundamental Painting to earlier art. As Spector said, the contemporary (Fundamental) painter keeps his traditional role.

Therefore, the Fundamental concept of painting – its "seeing-viewing-experiencing" – does not deviate much from the Western norm of visual art. It just does not refer to a referent (the divine Other) anymore as much as it refers to the non-verbal experience of the context (the other actor, the viewer).[182] However, it is still the absolute concept of "being." According to the history of aesthetics, art has always been a recognition piece in search of that which is inexpressible, and if we examine Western Abstract Art in particular, it becomes clear that most art of compelling rank has a similar nature. For Fundamental painters (like Marden, Renouf, or Martin), it indeed refers to a metaphysical mystery. The essence of their process is this unique quality of art: the fact that it leads to higher consciousness.

Viewers in front of the painting, as they discover its elements, have at least the sensation of their senses and mind functioning more intensely. And, as the string of associations links up with their own personal history, they become conscious of their own being in relation to the world of painting. Thus, although Fundamental Painting does "not think philosophical thoughts," the "seeing-viewing-experiencing" process is a kind of initiation into spirituality – in terms of belonging to the immaterial (Gruen 133). The material world not being represented through even the most minimal means, Fundamental Painting is able to communicate an essence, which goes beyond the concrete elements from which a painting is composed. It also refers to the mind or rather innumerable sets of mental realms, which are as many as there are viewers.

The final dialogue manifests itself in a basic form that the viewer's limited senses can apprehend. Still, the visual discoveries that the viewer makes in this process of "seeing-viewing-experiencing" do not entirely explain the experience. The experience of a Fundamental painting is intimately linked to being, if only on a very personal level recalling similar experiences of this kind. Fundamental Paintings elicit a sudden awareness of existence – the viewer's own existence (and maybe also the existence of that which is incomprehensible to us, as other paintings throughout the history of art have done before). As Mangold puts it, the paintings offer up answers and "perhaps, this is the most profound emotion that a human being can experience" (66).[183] In Fundamental Painting, the "higher nature" of art has simply become the interiorizing of facts that once were exterior. The metaphysical element takes on a new form: its "surfaceness" opens up a world in the viewer's mind. A revelation of beauty is the result. It might not be immanent in the Western traditional sense, but it is still transcendent.

CONCLUSION

This study has brought to light and clarified a number of facts about Fundamental Painting, which includes both European and American works (the latter known as Minimalist painting, having already been the subject of extensive research). Namely, that it does exist, and that it stands for a unique current. The focus of this study has been to understand the nature of Fundamental Painting, which was first identified and presented in 1975 by the Stedelijk Museum Amsterdam following a rigorous international research. Independent curatorial endeavors and a number of shows in various other European countries confirmed the common perception of this new current in painting in the 1970s. In fact, the exhibition made its mark and embedded the event called Fundamental Painting into the history of art. The term's acceptance by a number of critics on both sides of the Atlantic, as well as its reappearance in Dutch art historical publications over the years bear witness to this.

And, as the show claimed, the phenomenon did indeed surge in the late 1960s in the United States and in the early 1970s in Europe. Both the critical press issuing from the *Fundamental Painting* show and the visitor survey to the same exhibition underlined the fact that this kind of painting had already been around and "in the air" for some time by the mid-1970s. These likewise confirmed the fact that Fundamental Painting was a logical continuation of earlier 20th century painting.

Its roots in, for the most part, 20th century painting and its relevance to its era have been traced and seem to have confirmed the curators' belief in 1975 that the characteristics of Fundamental Painting come from its formalist research and from the lessons of 20th century painting in Europe and in the USA. At the same time, the Stedelijk Museum in Amsterdam presented Fundamental Painting as a new beginning, The works of the various artists that this study was able to confirm as Fundamental painters in retrospect (only 11 of 18 included in the show and a couple of additions) corroborate the development of this current.

Today, the mentality of Fundamental Painting is still very much alive with painters of that generation, while at the same time the term remains largely unheard-of outside *connoisseur* circles and even now no one seems certain about how to define it. In other words, the Dutch endeavor to highlight a remarkable new mentality in art that surged in the early 1970s in Europe remains the only one to date. This study hopes to have clearly defined Fundamental Painting and demonstrated its right to exist, since it has proven its specificity and longevity through the works of the artists involved.

Fundamental Painting is painting strictly focused on the two-dimensional character of the medium with its typical tools and basic elements as well as on the creative process and the effects upon the viewer based on his viewing habits. As we could confirm by way of this detailed study, all this is indeed what gives the current's participants a common mentality and justifies its distinct identity in the history of art. Furthermore, the importance of Fundamental Painting was underlined by its position as not only a continuation of 20th century non-objective painting but also a continuation of painting throughout history which is consistent with the philosophy of aesthetics.

Notably, it appears that Fundamental Painting, in which the essence of both material and process are key, is possibly part of (but clearly more specific than) a larger body of painting from the 1970s which has been designated with names like "pittura pittura" (painting painting) and "astrazione analitica" (analytical abstraction), as discussed in chapters 1.2.2 and 1.2.3. The latter term has become a concept in Italy following German curator Klaus Honnef's show *Geplante Malerei*, whose artists were presented on the market in collaboration with Italian commercial galleries as those of Analytical painting. All these efforts to give a label, including the show *Fundamental Painting*, were the result of having detected a new kind of painting on the European artistic scene in the early 1970s (which a vast chronology of shows testifies to). Until today, the German-Italian curatorial world keeps on assimilating a vast range of European monochrome, non-objective painting of the 1970s generation under the abovementioned names.

This study can only congratulate Dippel's perspicacity in detecting at such an early stage the essential elements of a new mentality still in the making, separating this small groundbreaking group of Fundamental painters from the larger whole. The main difference between this Analytical abstraction and Fundamental Painting indicated by Dippel in her 1975 catalogue introduction to the show *Fundamental Painting* at the Stedelijk Museum in Amsterdam are mainly the poetic and atmospheric nature of works. Dippel also briefly listed the elements important to Fundamental Painting (format, size, scale, color, line, structure, texture, and their application). She followed the lead of American art critic Douglas Crimp (his text "Opaque Surfaces" concerning the American part of Fundamental Painting) and distinguished Fundamental Painting from similar tendencies to outline the framework. Considering each of the characteristics ascribed to Fundamental Painting by the curators of the in-depth, eponymous show, this study has retained their correctness and drawn the following conclusions on the reasons behind their enumeration:

Fundamental painters indeed have a preference for neutral formats or shaped canvases. The reason for this is that in first instance these are a recognizable and unified image, while the painting's elements and their interrelations slowly unfold. This is done by way of playing on the traditional ways of seeing. All-over composition or various forms of linear structures lead the viewer's gaze away from the center to allow for all the painterly elements to unfold in a harmonious manner – and back again to repeat the process. It makes the painting into a stable, self-centered entity.

We can confirm that for the same reason they have a preference for human scale. The size of the format and any modular elements are part of this. It's important to the Fundamental painter that these incite an intimate dialogue or read like an alter ego. Elements that indicate a potential expanse into the viewer's space emphasize the flatness and object-like quality of the artwork. The scale is no longer internal but external, meaning between the painting and its viewer.

This study has likewise shown that color in Fundamental Painting is indeed either a non-color or a sober, non-descriptive hue. The reason is that neutral color initially ensures visual unity. It plays a part in the slow discovery of the painting. We have discovered multiple layers of various colors underlie the topcoat in non-color or are often fused into a non-descript monochromatic painting. The non-color gray is favored for its quality of still being perceived as a color.

Besides, this study has pointed out that Fundamental painters use color not only as hue but also as material. The paint and its visual effects are very much part of the research into painting as painting per definition. Knowledge of the technical workings and effects of color as paint ensures that the Fundamental painting does not create an atmosphere. This confirms the fact that Fundamental Painting consciously avoids creating illusions, as Dippel claimed. And the fact that Fundamental painters only use line, which is more inherent to drawing than to painting, to counteract any description of a spatial figure and to insist on the flatness of the painted plane corroborates this.

Texture and facture are inherent elements of painting – as a material fact and a vestige of the artist's intervention. The structure that a painting has due to its support, or the texture that it acquires from the application of paint on this support, testifies to the painting's existence as an object in the viewer's reality. Just as with color and line, structure, texture and facture can be used to optically unify the picture plane. They underline the canvas's two-dimensional quality. Any and all variations can be exploited provided they achieve this goal, as this study has shown.

On the way, this study has confirmed Dippel's claim that the materials and tools used for Fundamental Painting are strictly painterly, and that their inherent qualities are respected. The new products on the market might be researched for their painterly qualities, but the way they will be used will always favor the proposition of painting that is fundamentally painting (a flat plane). At the same time, it has confirmed her statement that the creation of the painting is per definition the sole responsibility of the artist.

The process of painting a Fundamental Painting issues from the artist's knowledge of and skills in handling the inherent materials, tools, and other painterly elements. The proposition that defines a painting as a painting is well thought out beforehand. However, intuition plays an equally important role in understanding how the painterly elements behave during the painting process and then balancing them.

We have seen that Fundamental Painting is fundamentally painterly and tends to be modular: the artist researches the same elements over and over again within a set of chosen limits. The series, composed of intuitive rather than mathematical sequences, documents the artist's research and conclusions on painting in the form of painting. The creative process must be such as to allow the viewer to recreate it visually, in order to evoke a dialogue with and thereby an endless series of experiences in the beholder – again confirming Dippel's suspicion.

This study has allowed for drawing conclusions on the composition of Fundamental Painting. Namely, that there is not a composition in the sense of painting before the Fundamental era. It is non-objective and non-referential: a unified, structurally activated plane in visual symmetry. The painterly elements must all exist in a harmonious balance. The sought effect is indeed always flatness – as Dippel suspected.

Notably, the material elements are of equal importance as the visual elements inherent to painting. Only the most fundamental elements are used in their most fundamental way. The painter works strictly with that which is necessary – not less, not more – to arrive at the purest possible form of communication. The work stands in direct relation to the viewer, setting off an initial effect instantly upon viewing and then, finally there is revelation.

We have been able to conclude that the viewer is considered as an inherent element of Fundamental Painting and the viewing experience is an interactive one. Fundamental painting needs a viewer in order to exist. The artist integrates the painterly elements into the painting in such a way as to create a dynamic, concentric, self-absorbed viewing experience for the spectator. The painting solicits a dialogue.

It informs the viewer of these elements, their characteristics, how they were used, with which scope and so on, inciting him to question each aspect of painting. In order to keep the viewer focused on the painting and instill a rhythmical line of questioning, the composition is set up in a centric way to incite directional reading. It always leads the eye back to the painted surface, while encouraging a reading across the plane rather than into space (symmetrical painterly depth). The painting is what painting does.

All in all, it can be concluded that the quest of the Fundamental painter is one based on the constants, which are the typical painterly elements with the variants deriving simply from their range of application. All explorations concern painterly elements or considerations, inherent to the medium of painting. Knowledge of these elements and their potential effects comes from the formal scrutiny of painting at large, and especially painting from the Modernist era. Fundamental Painting is a modular kind of research into painting, where the painterly elements within the format are explored in plain, simple ways. Traditional painterly elements are used is their most basic form, they are balanced (so none dominates), or they are explored in detail one-by-one – throughout the artistic quest and in a new way.

All the painterly elements have been found to be applied to favor the "surfaceness" of the painted canvas, as per Dippel's American role model Douglas Crimp. What is unique here is that the Fundamental era (an inadequate categorical designation for the sake of history) takes painting on its quest for the Absolute one step further – or rather closer to the object. For a painting, which is by definition a two-dimensional object in our three-dimensional world, this means a most stimulating challenge. It means flattening the potential pictorial space onto the surface – making it unspatial – without losing the quality of a canvas as a three-dimensional thing in the viewer's reality. The composition now is external, the scale human (but not anthropomorphic), and the viewer scrutinizes the picture plane and in so doing activates their awareness, which in turn sets off an interactive experience between the viewer and the painting. An experience ensues, which is a visual, felt and cognitive interaction between these two entities. In this experience, Fundamental Painting consistently returns the focus on itself, on painting. It reflects on the history of painting and the viewer's painting history. A Fundamental painting is indeed painting about painting – yet ultimately about the viewer at the same time.

The conclusion of this is that the generation of convinced Fundamental painters has indeed stayed true to their chosen direction. This, in turn, testifies to Fundamental Painting's innately fundamental approach to painting and negates any idea that it could simply be a fad. Yet, the present study's in-depth analysis of the eighteen artists from the show has revealed a certain misidentification of Fundamental Painting at the time. Several artists were wrongly included in the *Fundamental Painting* show, while others would deviate from their base concept in subsequent years. Therefore, in retrospect, it can be confirmed that only nine (or at best eleven) painters from the show form the core of Fundamental Painting. These are its defining four American artists: Minimalist painters Agnes Martin, Robert Ryman, Robert Mangold, and Brice Marden. There are also the European painters Alan Charlton, Tomas Rajlich, Raimund Girke, Marthe Wéry, and Edda Renouf. Jerry Zeniuk and Stephen Rosenthal can be considered tangent figures. To be excluded from this current are the Americans Jake Berthot and Richard Jackson; the Dutchmen Jaap Berghuis, Rob van Koningsbruggen, and Kees Smits; Frenchman Louis Cane; and the German Gerhard Richter.

In fact, the conclusion we have arrived at in this study is not all too surprising. Jackson, Richter and Van Koningsburggen were already "miscast" at the time of the show. Museum director Edy de Wilde overruled the curators' choice against Jackson. In Richter's case, the convincing argumentation of his gallery representative Konrad Fischer assured his inclusion. And Van Koningsbruggen did not want to participate, because he did not feel an affinity with the concept of the exhibition. His works were included due to the influence of one of the lenders of works by other artists to the show.

Berghuis and Smits were relatively young at the time, which might explain their receptivity to a tendency that was "in the air" in those formative years but which they had not fully integrated as their works in the show testified to. Both would finally settle into a different direction. By contrast, the inclusion of Berthot and Cane seems to have been a simple misjudgment by the curators, which seems to have been based on the appearance of their works rather than on the artists' starting points.

Chief curator Rini Dippel stated that information channels were scarce and time was extremely limited, which did not allow for ample due diligence in preparing the exhibition. The curators' notes show a rather large selection skimmed down through process of elimination. But, obviously, it had slipped their attention that Berthot's work was poetical and Cane's came from an ideological point of view – both approaches specifically excluded in the exhibition catalogue.

After double-checking these same curators' considerations, in retrospect we discovered that also US artist Marcia Hafif slipped their attention. On the contrary, her work was able to be included but did not make it into the final show selection. European painter Vincenzo Cecchini, then again, did not even come to the curators' attention at the time. This said, the curators did make a point of stating that their selection was not to be considered as final.

With this study, I hope to have clarified the coherence and nature of Fundamental Painting and reinserted a couple more names into the category (omitted or wrongly eliminated from the 1975 show in favor of misjudged inclusions). Their coherent approach covering a range of visual results corresponds to the fact that – more than a defined group – Fundamental Painting is a mentality whose quest into the nature of painting was "in the air" in the 1970s. A quote from an interview by Robert Storr with Robert Ryman published in *Art Press* is appropriate here. Ryman explains:

> There are problems that you work on and there is an awareness of what has been done; what others have worked on and how they've approached painting and the solutions that they've come to. But it isn't a blanket kind of historical thing that everyone is involved with. I think everyone has to take little bites, little pieces of it and work on that,… Little things that you pick up here and there trigger insights. It's only afterward that you can look at a number of different painters from the same period and pick up the threads of what people were thinking at the time." (20)

This is in essence what this study has tried to do. In fact, the framework that the curators of *Fundamental Painting* tried to describe – stemming from a painterliness as personified by Martin, and ranging from the theoretical approach of Ryman all the way to the sensibility of Marden, while completed by concerns on form and shape as with Mangold – has been confirmed as the theoretical yet valid framework for all truly Fundamental works issuing from this mentality in Part 2.

In this context, this study has pointed out that the Fundamental painters' choice of the painting medium itself was rigorous in that it favored the continuity of formalist painting, at a time when most artists were turning away from traditions in art and in new directions. It was informed by the era of Conceptual Art that gained independence for ideas: thinking about art, traditions of perception, and the meaning of it all. Their research on painting through painting is situated within the continuation of modernist painting, which brought on new ideas about the uses of painterly elements. Such research does confirm some kind of continuity as well as position for Fundamental Painting in a way that proves its validity. This is why Dippel dismissed the term "reduced" (FP 12) for such kind of painting and made a point of listing its 20th century predecessors, both in the catalogue text as well as in the show's entrance hall. Part 3 of this study links the influences as named by the curators of the show to Fundamental Painting, explaining the similarities or differences and highlighting the formalist influences on the current. After scrutinizing the influences as presented in 1975, our conclusions are as follows:

This study challenged the concept of the curators of *Fundamental Painting* by taking one more step back to the very beginnings of 20th century non-objective painting. It pointed out how the Impressionist picture become a material item in itself and Post-Impressionism started the quest from a new kind of unified image, by putting flatness as an inherent characteristic of the medium into the spotlight. It traced the beginnings of key formalist elements in Fundamental Painting which were taking center stage, from here all the way to the early 20th century influences mentioned by the curators in the show. We believe that this study was able to show how gesture, application, and base were now material facts and how, soon, structural planes became expressive means.

We hope that this study has been able to specify how with Suprematism, facture entered the scene more as an element in painting, non-descriptive line started with Kandinsky, Cubism introduced the anchoring grid, and soon the *how* of painting became more important than the image. We have continued with pointing out how figure became interchangeable with ground, line became plane, and the plane approached the image and it became visually possible to recreate the creative act. The visual workings of formalist elements in early 20th century painting were researched, and the difference between the history of the monochrome vs. monochromatic propositions pointed out.

The reductiveness to reach the utter essence of the medium of painting would persist in the quest for the absolute all through the 20th century. It is here where we picked up the storyline as proposed by the curators of the *Fundamental Painting* show, but not before pointing out the importance of Piet Mondrian rather than Van Doesburg's Art Concret on Fundamental Painting. In this regard, the present study must clarify that there is disagreement with Rini Dippel in the sense that she stated in her notes "Gereduceerde Schilderkunst" that Fundamental Painting comes more from Malevich than from Mondrian (1) while, as this study has shown in chapter 3.2.1, Mondrian's late work was crucial in defining the concept of "surfaceness."

De Stijl and Van Doesburg's later Manifesto of Art Concret were very much at the base of Minimal Art, whose painters would become the core Fundamental painters. Yet, various painterly considerations and ways of interacting with the viewer make Mondrian's later works a step closer to Fundamental Painting. His modular geometric idiom modified by intuition, extending into the viewer's space and arriving at an entirely new space in painting, defines the approach and concept of space in Fundamental Painting. In fact, during the New York years, Mondrian's educative activities and his late works formed one of the crucial links between European early 20th century and the American postwar painting whose formalism created the basis for Fundamental Painting.

From here on, this study continued exploring the works of the predecessors to Fundamental Painting mentioned by the curators of the *Fundamental Painting* show. Some, more than others, indeed showed formalist elements of significance, while the Abstract Expressionists certainly appeared crucial to 1960s and 1970s Fundamental Painting. In this regard, we should mention that the curators' schematic overview was necessarily a European perspective, but – as noted in our introduction –, numerous (mainly American) studies on the influences leading up to Minimal Art and its painters are there to support the other perspective.

Abstract Expressionism was based on an American history of familiarity with European (non-objective) painting and the paramount search for a truly American style. Interest in painting from a formalist point of view had laid the grounds for the European influences like Josef Albers and Piet Mondrian. The elements of painting would be respected for their painterly qualities, especially by the Abstract Expressionists. Their painting was geared towards the unitary statement in one moment of reality, but it also counted on the emotional associations in interaction with the viewer. This "emotional" touch would come back in a good part of 1970s painting but would be abandoned by Fundamental Painting as a further step in "painting for painting's sake,"[184] following in Ad Reinhardt's footsteps, as we discovered. For Fundamental painters, the important thing was the interest in painting from a factual point of view as for something real in our world which creates an experience.

This study has explored how the Fundamental painting – like an Abstract Expressionist painting – is firmly anchored in the viewer's reality and thus considerations of placement matter. In both USA and Europe, in Fundamental Painting the viewer now was the final element to complete the painting in the "seeing-viewing-experiencing" of it (Mangold; Qtd. in Schiff 60). The artwork slowly unfolds its workings, coming into being visually. Visual impulses that pose the viewer the question what a painting is and does enter the scene. It implies a self-absorbedness of a painting. In this kind of work, although it is object-like, painting is the sole responsibility of the artist. In the 1970s, Fundamental Painting was the next logical step in the evolution of painting, by including the viewer but also putting the focus back onto the painting.

Following the other examples given by the curators, we discovered that postwar Europe worked through a rediscovery and reconsideration of painting which was similar to postwar US. Yet, such European painting seemed to come from a more complex background, including Eastern mystical traditions (like the concept of the fullness of the void). The few European Fundamental painters rather took their hints from the US postwar painters. Accordingly, this study has brought us to believe that Fundamental Painting is indeed more about a continuity of painting: its tradition, its formalist issues, its evolution.

Moreover, this study has revealed the significance of the influences on Fundamental Painting outlined by the 1975 eponymous show for a schematic summarization of the history of non-objective painting in Europe and this study's conclusion on its geographic roots. The curators asserted that Fundamental Painting appears only in the USA, the UK, and Benelux, while in Italy and – with a few exceptions – in France and Germany a different but similar kind of new painting appears (i.e. Analytical Abstraction). Likewise, they claimed that the opportunity for artists to acquaint themselves with Modernist and new American painting in exhibitions was an important factor in the rise of Fundamental Painting in Europe. This study demonstrated the latter to be true and found that these geographical locations and their differences are not coincidental.

This study has attempted to explain how the appearance of Fundamental Painting in the 1970s in certain geographies could indeed be traced back to the knowledge of pre-WWII geometric styles in combination with postwar opportunities for viewing important Modernist painting and American Abstract Expressionism. We traced how the knowledge of pre-war geometric currents was responsible for the heterogeneous revival emerging in many Western countries, including the former allies Germany and Italy (while Eastern and Central Europe remained isolated). Here, as this study explored in details, the impulse of a new kind of non-objective painting in the analytical vein transpired by the 1970s.

This study also traced how in the USA, the UK, and Benelux the postwar situation was different. The treatment of the history of painting in the US may seem somewhat oversimplified in this study but it is also clear that the US took up the thread in painting where it was cut short in Europe after WWII. It also briefly touched upon the fact why it was possible for the US to use all the formalist teachings of pre-WWII European painting without limitations. This allowed for both a new kind of impulse and freedom in evolving non-objective painting.

There was no rupture in the United States, and accordingly no need to resurrect a tradition in visual language following WWII, as was the case in Europe. This, in our opinion, brought post-war developments in the United States closer to the situation of the Netherlands and the UK. The United Kingdom was fertile ground for new impulses for the continuation of the painting tradition, aided by the influx of many

Modernist emigrant artists from the war-ridden Continent. It also benefited from a number of important exhibitions and collections.

The Netherlands had produced the cool non-objective vein in painting around WWI. And while had lost its tradition when De Stijl's main representatives emigrated and the neutral country was overrun by the Nazis, the Stedelijk Museum in Amsterdam tried to still preserve its knowledge by continuing their exhibitions program in avant-garde non-objective tendencies of the 20th century. Eventually this would lead to the definition and coining of the term Fundamental Painting in 1975. We can accordingly say that Fundamental Painting was not retrospective but innovative.

Thus, Part 3 of the study has given insights into the evolution of new painting mentalities in various countries in Europe in the 1970s. The Stedelijk Museum curators of the *Fundamental Painting* show in 1975 hinted at differing artistic developments. The present study has followed and sought to demonstrate their thesis. It pointed out the reasons for their disparate character: It seems that national considerations are an issue. The history of non-objective painting concerns certain geographical eras more than others, and it has been discovered that these saw the rise of analytical currents in the 1970s. Furthermore, this study could confirm that the nationalities in Fundamental Painting – a subcategory of the wider analytical current – correspond to the nations that had access to Modern and Abstract Expressionist painting. The personal history of the painters determines if their work tends more towards theoretical, sensible, or visual branches of the Fundamental Painting range.

Last but not least, in Part 4, this study explored the metaphysical component in Fundamental Painting. We wish to underline that in the texts accompanying the exhibition, the curators often emphasize the absence of a metaphysical component in Fundamental Painting. Yet, in retrospect and given findings in this study, we must disagree. We believe to have sufficiently proven that Fundamental Painting has not entirely lost its "aura" or metaphysical element:

As soon as the viewer enters into dialogue with a Fundamental painting, they are at eye level with the canvas. It is a very direct interaction on human scale. The viewer reacts to the painting based on the perception of themselves and this other entity in real space. The minute variations in the painting's surface document the painter's search; they are answers to questions in painting. The way in which the elements are applied gives the viewer the possibility to discover them one by one after a unitary first glance. This makes the experience of viewing both a recreation of the painting process and a personal associative history of the painting medium. In this very "down-to-earth" interaction the focus remains on painting, but the painting leads its viewer to a heightened awareness – communicating on something *beyond*.

Thus, this study can conclude that by way of the inherent dialogue between painting and viewer, Fundamental Painting speaks about being. The metaphysical element is now part and parcel of the reality of both painting and viewer. To achieve this, the Fundamental painting is the sole responsibility of its creator. It is this combination of the world of objects and the experience of painting as a recognition piece that makes this kind of painting unique. It is very down to earth, while preserving the traditional metaphysical component. Fundamental Painting respects its traditional role as a bridge, an instrument for revelation of being. It might not be immanent, but it still remains traditionally transcendent: it is a path to absolute beauty like any eternal art before its time.

This said, the intention of this study was not to go into a discourse on any philosophical theories; this might be an interesting perspective on Fundamental Painting for another study. We merely "listened" to the paintings and the words of their makers to come to this conclusion. The chief curator of *Fundamental Painting* Rini Dippel recently admitted in interview with the author on 26 August 2011 that she too fully agrees that Fundamental Painting is beautiful in the metaphysical sense of the word: meaning that Fundamental Painting indeed comprises a metaphysical element, which imbues it with its aesthetic quality and sets it apart from mere objects. In fact, both the works and the words of their creators confirm that their lifetime quest was not only for painting in the purely material sense together with its logical effects, but also for the more abstract realm of reactions that it solicits.

So, apparently, Greenberg was not totally wrong when stating that in the Fundamental era, painting was not anymore about the 1960s concern of its being an object or an artwork but about whether it was good art. Fundamental Painting not only questions what painting is but also what makes it good, what makes it art. This concept of good then again leads back to the concept of beautiful, more precisely: it leads back to the philosophy of aesthetics, to the concept of the good, truth, and beauty to signify the Absolute. In the end, it is this relation to both the history of painting from a formalist point of view as well as the philosophy of aesthetics throughout time that makes Fundamental Painting so significant. With this study, I hope to have reinserted Fundamental Painting into art history and corrected the evolutionary line in painting, for future generations of artists to take up the challenge and scholars to further explore this current more in depth.

Postscript

The technique of painting is easily determined, while the line, the color, the structure, and the shape bring to light their own language. The painting's expression and meaning are harder to define. When confronted with a Fundamental painting, it is obvious to the viewer that this experience is most powerful, but it is laborious or difficult to "translate." This is the task of art critics and historians, and I hope to have approached it as clearly as possible. This study was undertaken in search of a way to motivate viewers to actually look at art, which is the first step in the "seeing-viewing-experiencing" of artworks, in general, and Fundamental Painting, in particular. In the end, art is a complex and complicated spectacle, which speaks for itself better than any verbal language could ever do, and everything that the viewer has studied about art is merely a preparation for the experience.

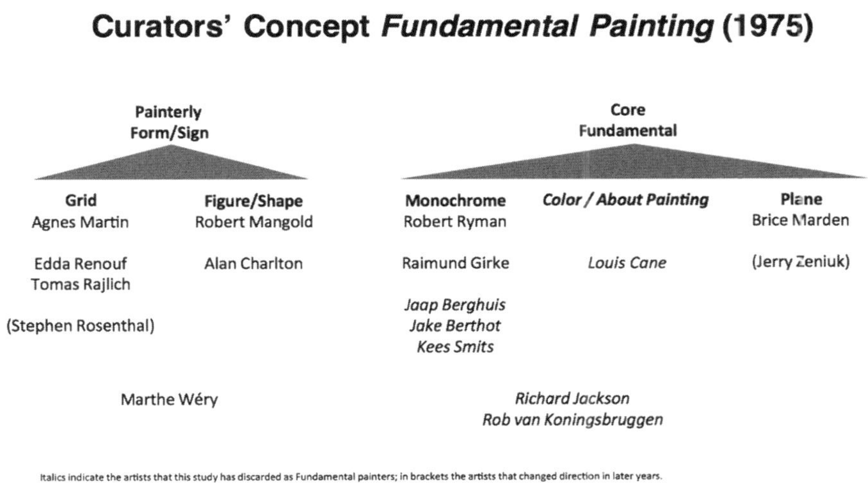
Curators' Concept *Fundamental Painting* (1975)
Painterly
Form/Sign
Core
Fundamental
Grid
Agnes Martin
Edda Renouf
Tomas Rajlich
(Stephen Rosenthal)
Figure/Shape
Robert Mangold
Alan Charlton
Marthe Wéry
Monochrome
Robert Ryman
Raimund Girke
Jaap Berghuis
Jake Berthot
Kees Smits
Color / About Painting
Louis Cane
Plane
Brice Marden
(Jerry Zeniuk)
Richard Jackson
Rob van Koningsbruggen
Italics indicate the artists that this study has discarded as Fundamental painters; in brackets the artists that changed direction in later years.

Fig. 1

PLATTEGROND FUNDAMENTELE SCHILDERKUNST: ZALEN 41-28

GROUND-PLAN FUNDAMENTAL PAINTING: ROOMS 41-28

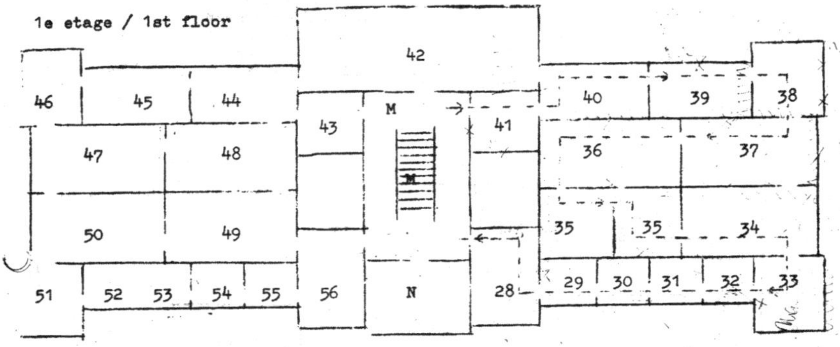

→	route
N	catalogus, reprodukties / catalogue, reproductions
M	hal boven / hall, first floor

Zalen/Rooms	
41	informatie/information
40	Ryman
39	Van Koningsbruggen/Richter
38	Marden
37	Girke/Zeniuk
36	Berthot/Berghuis/Smits
35	Jackson/Rajlich
34	Cane/Charlton
33	Mangold
32	diaprogramma/slide program
31	Rosenthal
30	Wéry
29	Renouf
28	Martin

Fig. 2

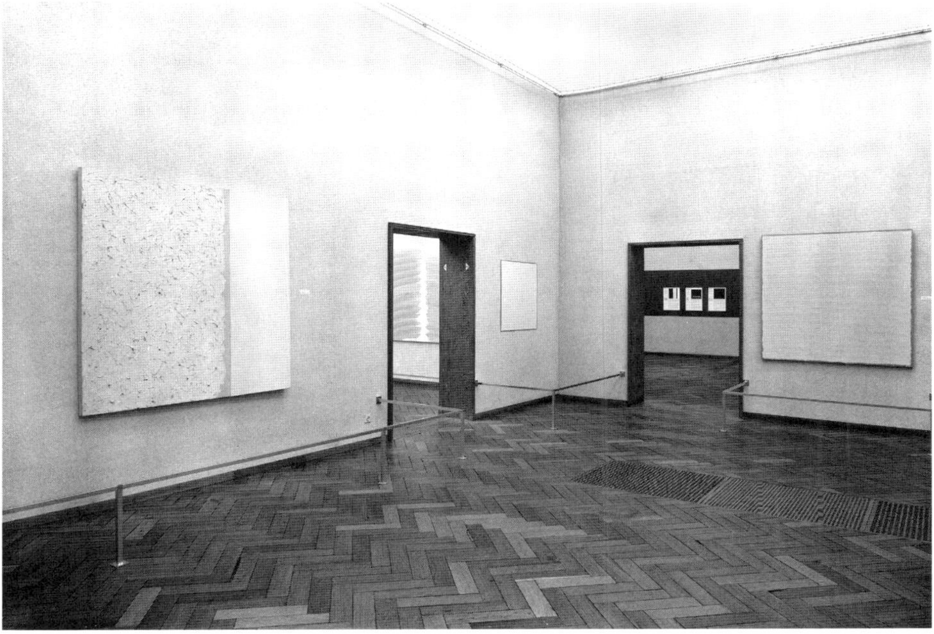

Fig. 3

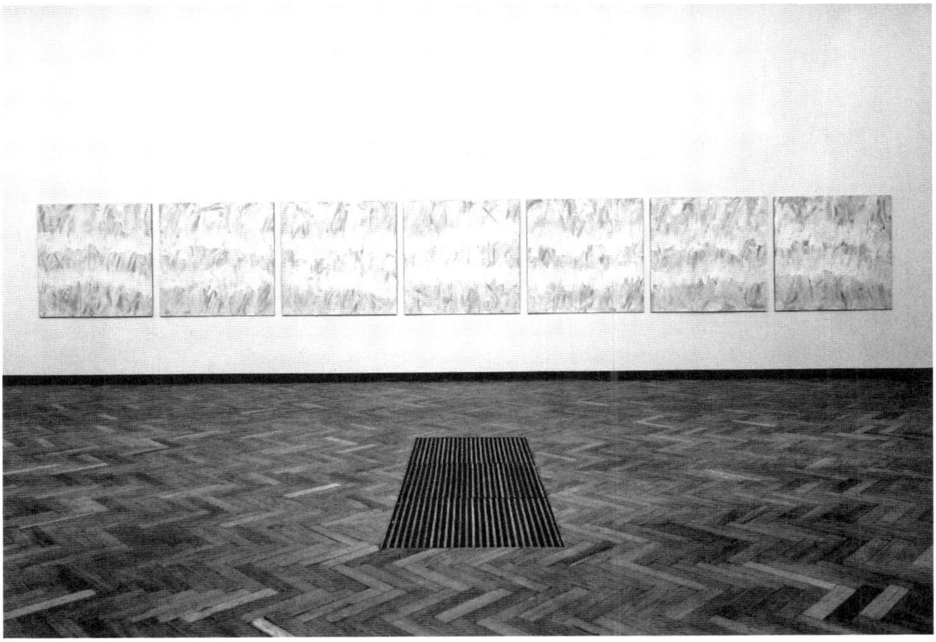

Fig. 4

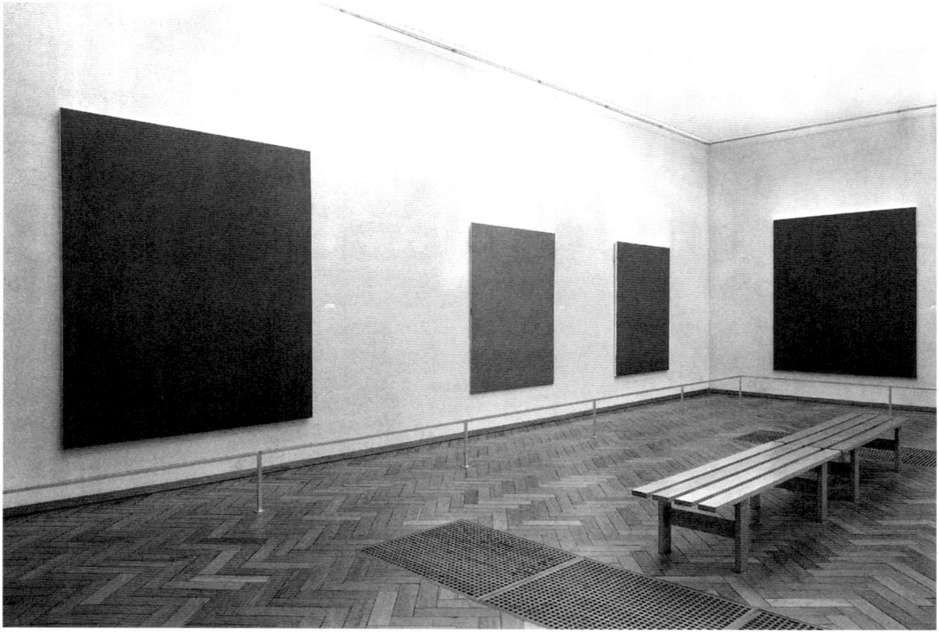

Fig. 5

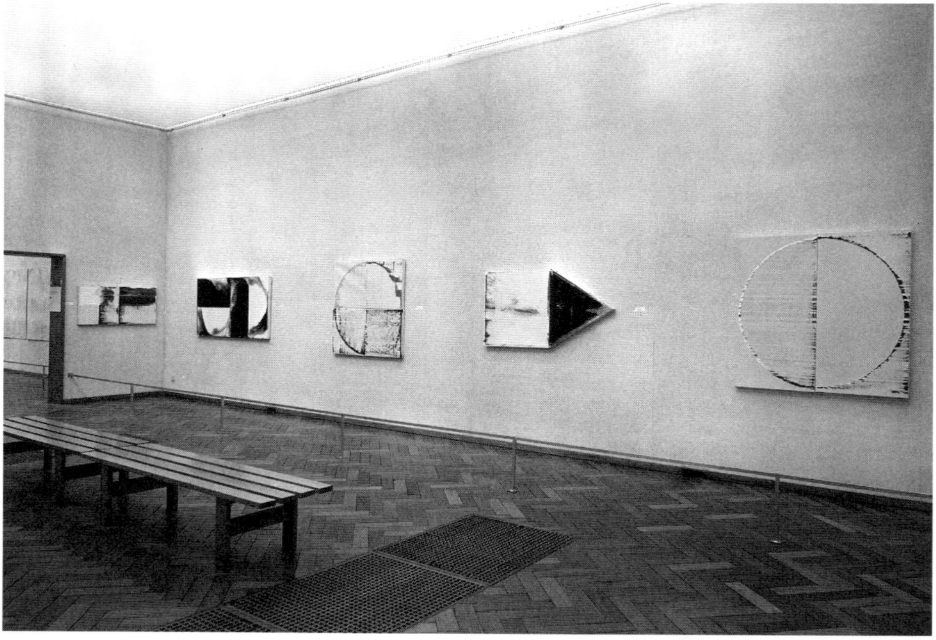

Fig. 6

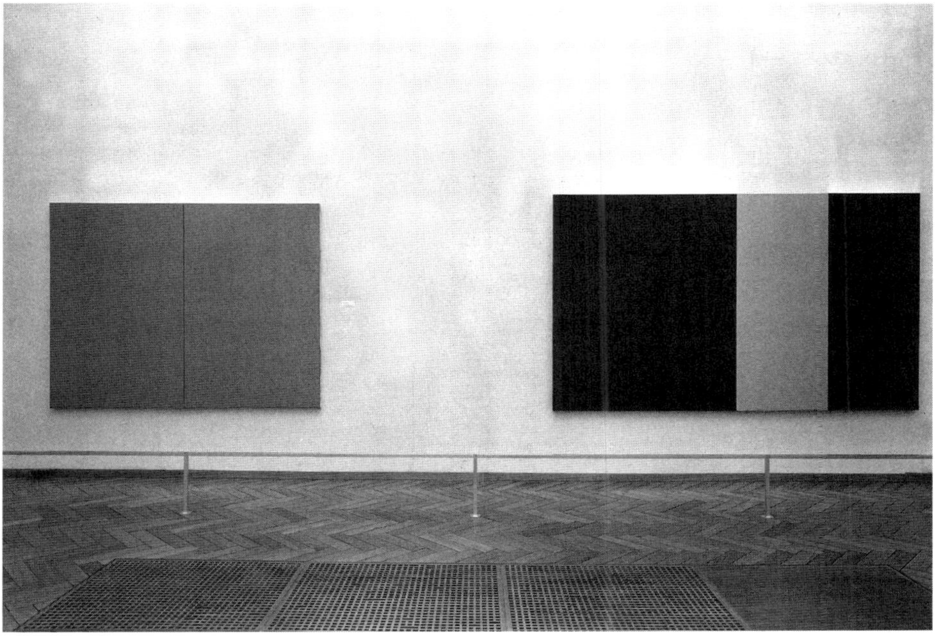

Fig. 7

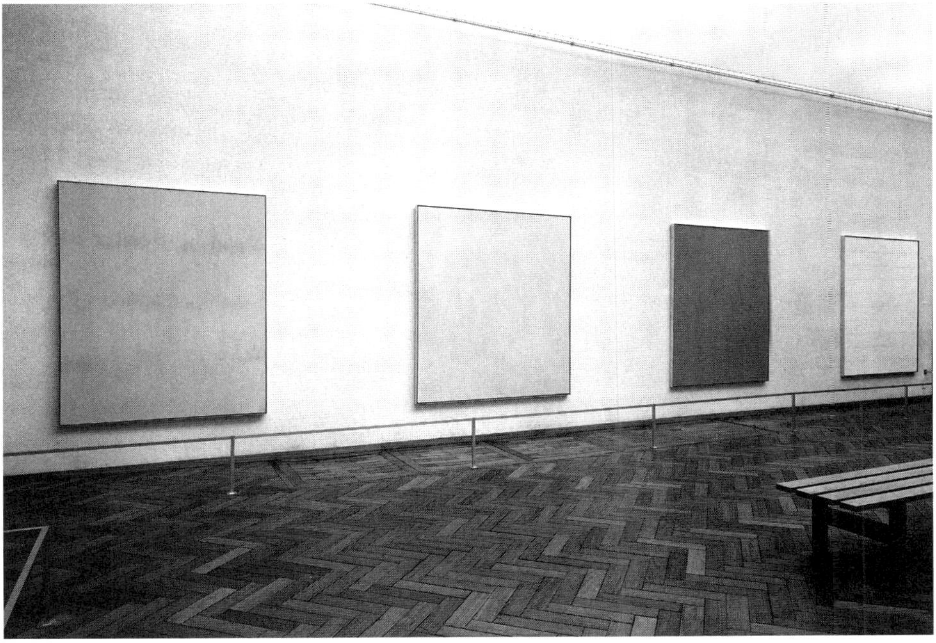

Fig. 8

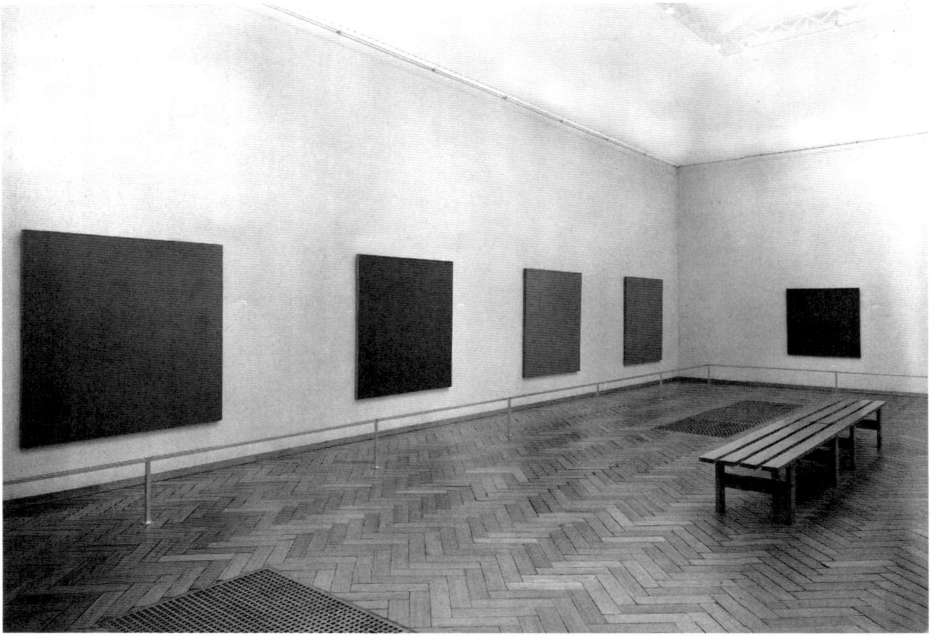

Fig. 9

© Jerry Zeniuk/OOA-S, 2021
Photo: © Stedelijk Museum Amsterdam

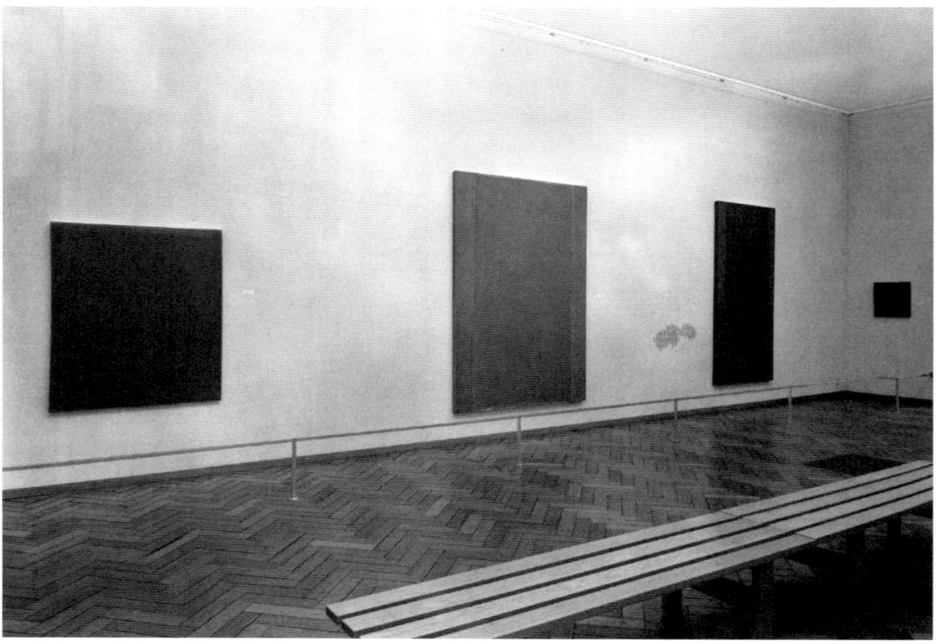

Fig. 10

© Jake Berthot/OOA-S, 2021
Photo: © Stedelijk Museum Amsterdam

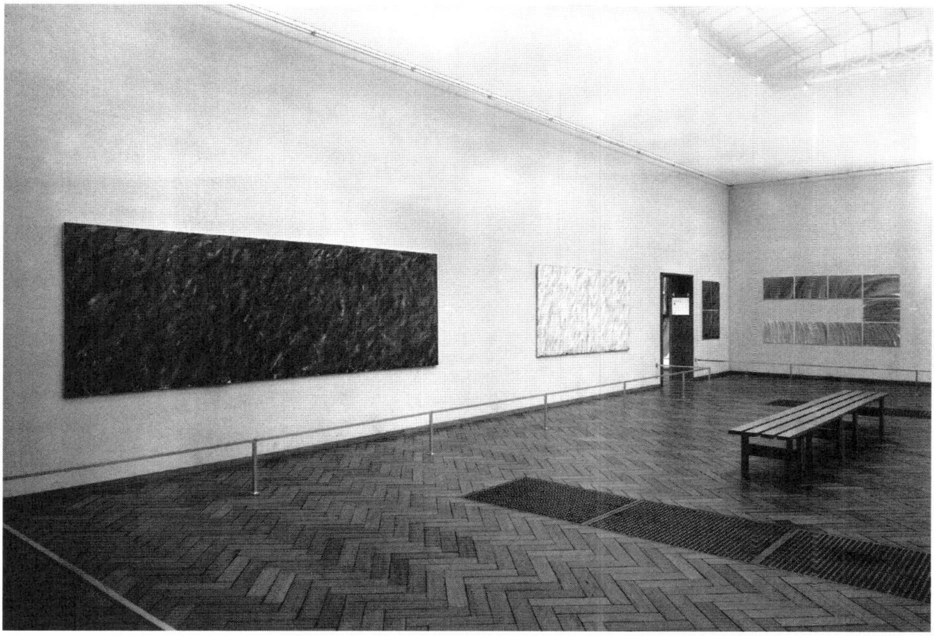

Fig. 11

© Jaap Berghuis/OOA-S, 2021, © Kees Smits/OOA-S, 2021
Photo: © Stedelijk Museum Amsterdam

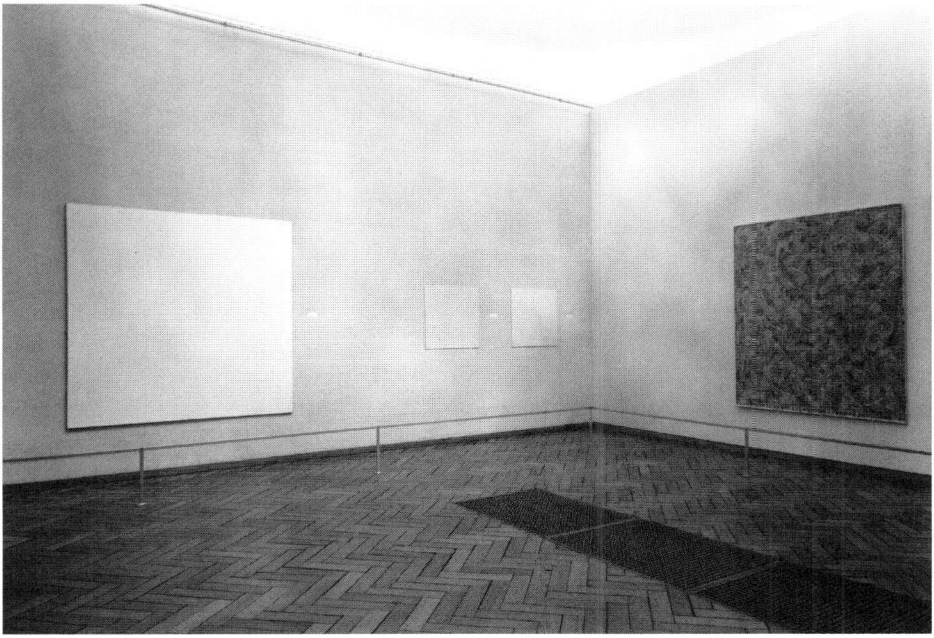

Fig. 12

© Tomas Rajlich/OOA-S, 2021
Photo: © Stedelijk Museum Amsterdam

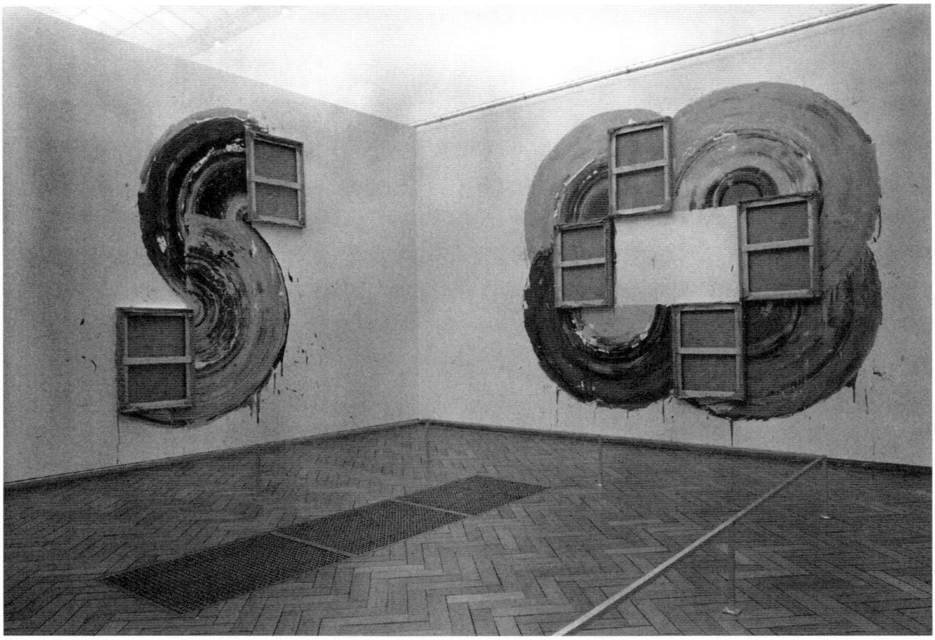

Fig. 13

© Richard Jackson/OOA-S, 2021
Photo: © Stedelijk Museum Amsterdam

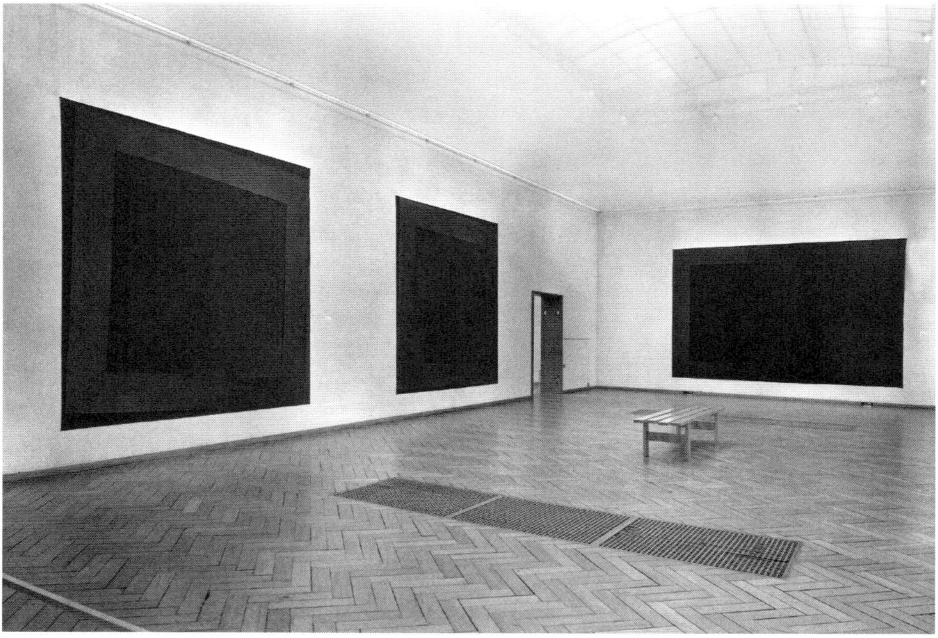

Fig. 14

© Louis Cane/OOA-S, 2021
Photo: © Stedelijk Museum Amsterdam

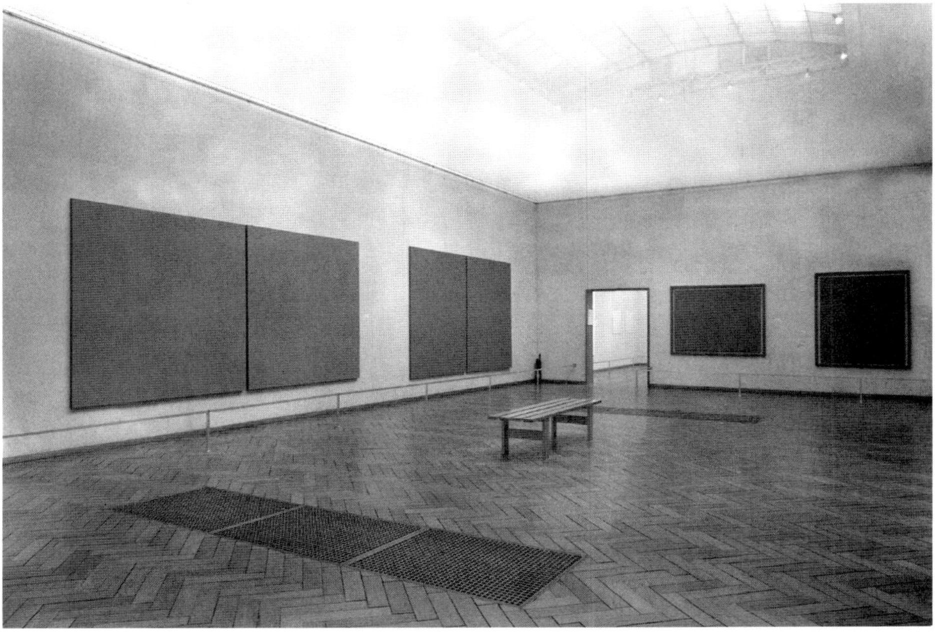

Fig. 15

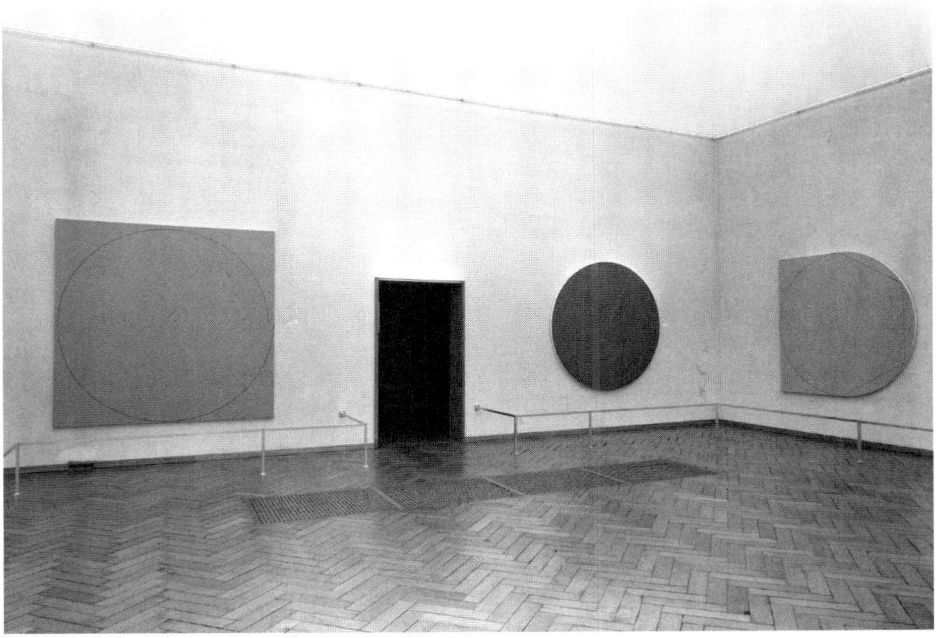

Fig. 16

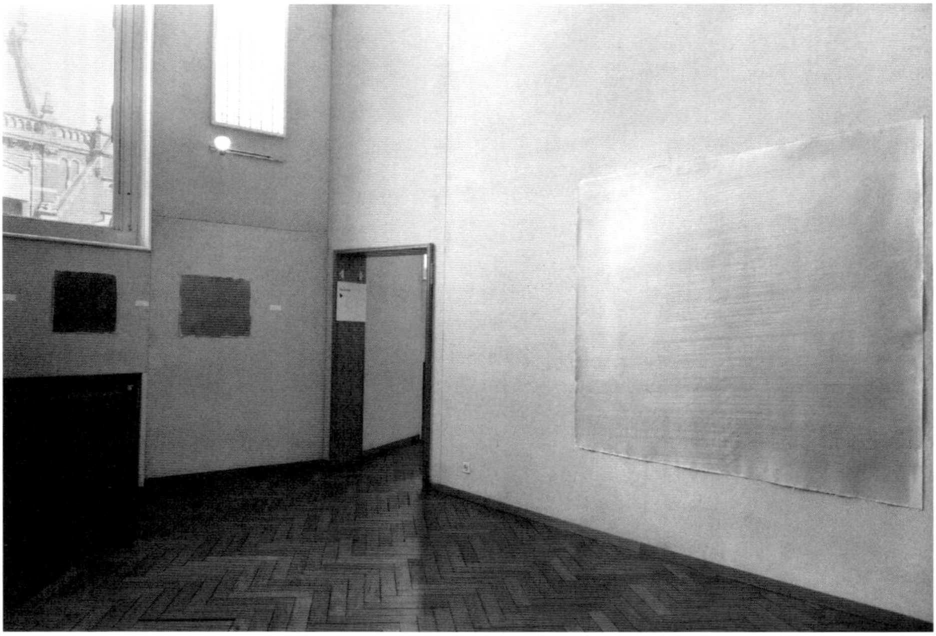

Fig. 17

© Stephen Rosenthal/OOA-S, 2021
Photo: © Stedelijk Museum Amsterdam

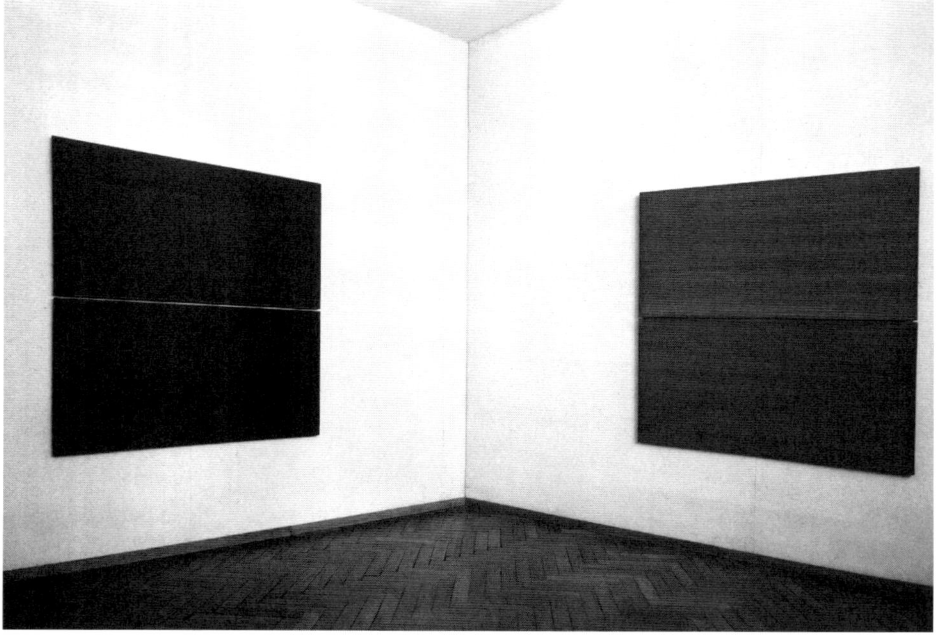

Fig. 18

© Marthe Wéry/OOA-S, 2021
Photo: © Stedelijk Museum Amsterdam

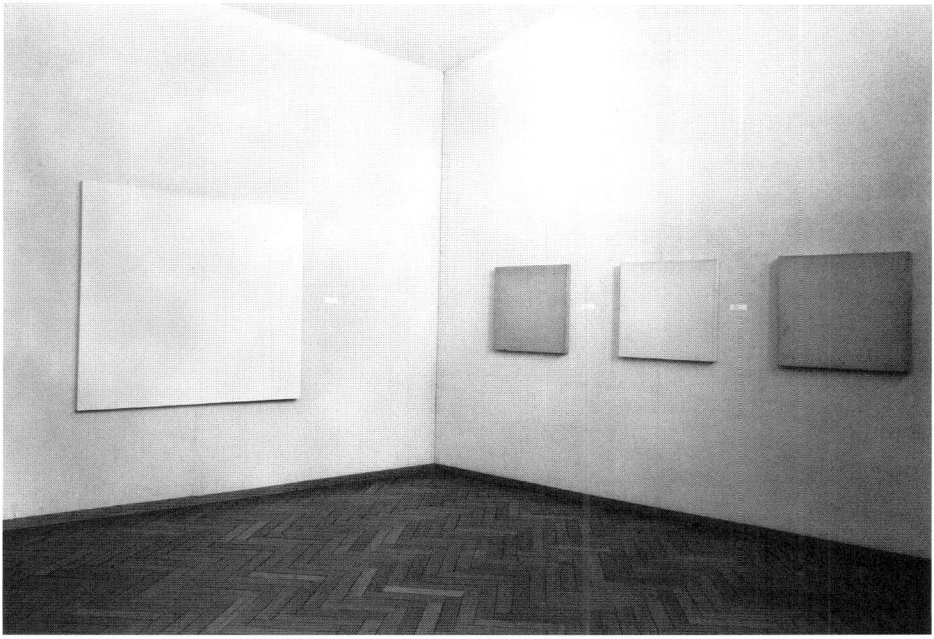

Fig. 19

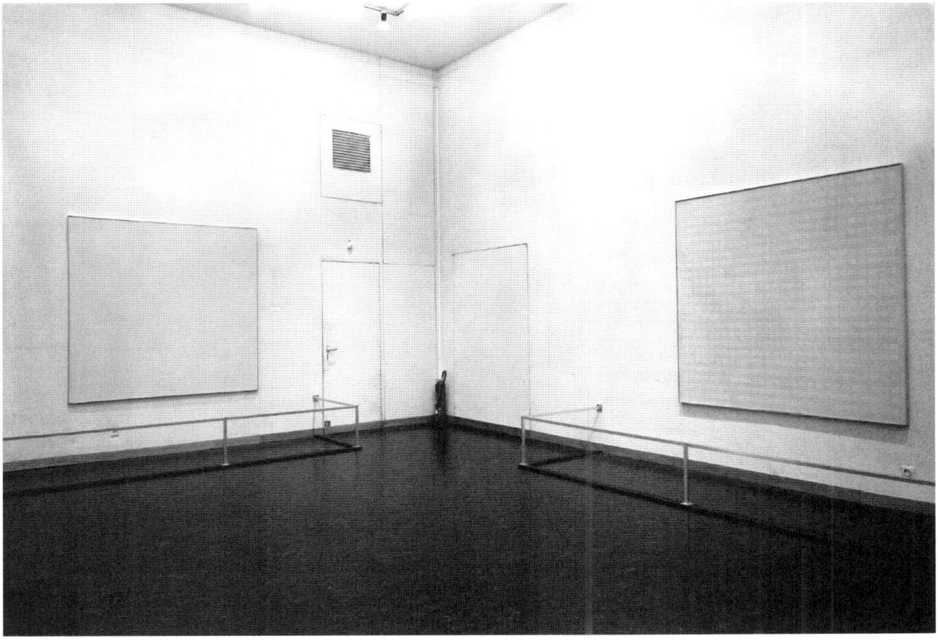

Fig. 20

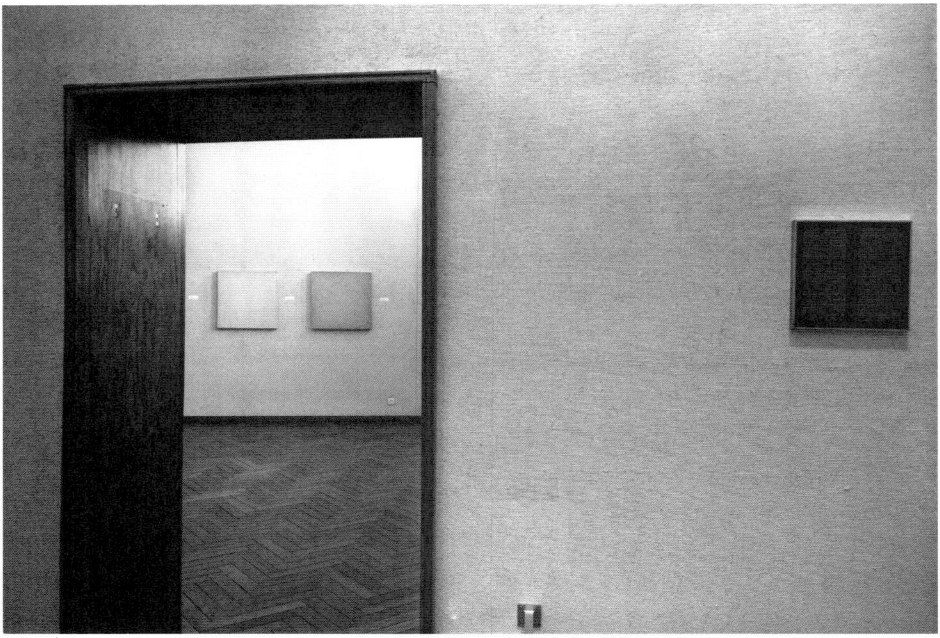

Fig. 21

De werken uit de collectie, waarnaar wordt verwezen in de informatiezaal, vindt men in:
The works from the permanent collection, referred to in the information room are exhibited in:

zaal/room	
12	Kelly
13	Reinhardt/Andre
42	Newman/Kelly/Stella
45	Klein/Manzoni
46	Johns
48	Malewitch/Van Doesburg

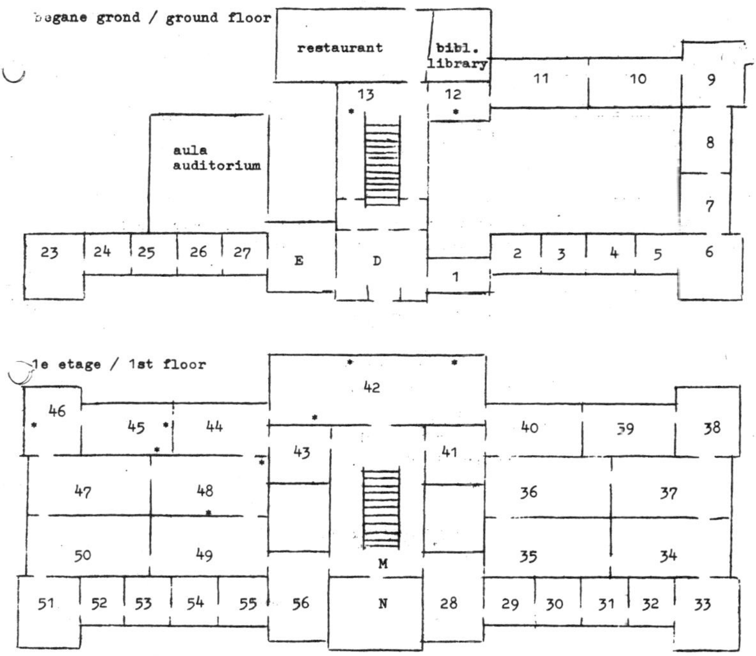

Stedelijk Museum, Amsterdam

Fig. 22

1 Curators Lothar Romain and Luca M. Venturi; Exhibiting artists Marco Gastini, Riccardo Guarneri, Tomas Rajlich, Piet Teraa, Dan van Severen, Enzo Cacciola, Riccardo Camoni, Vincenzo Cecchini, Raoul de Keyser, Joel Fischer, Ulrich Erben, Winfred Gaul, Giorgio Griffa, Carmengloria Morales, Gianfranco Zappettini, Noël Dolla, Vivien Isnard, Claude Viallat, Walter Darby Bannard, Jules Olitski, and Larry Poons.

2 Curator Uwe Obier; Exhibiting artists: Dan Freudenthal, Georg Frietzche, Raimund Girke, Gottfried Honegger, Thomas Kaminsky, Alfons Lachauer, Tomas Rajlich, James Reineking, Jan Schoonhoven, Alf Schuler, Phillip H. Sims, and Jerry Zeniuk.

3 Curator Italo Mussa; Exhibiting artists: Luciano Bartolini, Carlo Battaglia, Jaap Berghuis, Marcello Camorani, Louis Cane, Alan Charlton, Paolo Cotani, Robyn Denny, Marc Devade, Noël Dolla, Ulrich Erben, Marco Gastini, Raimund Girke, Alan Green, Giorgio Griffa, Riccardo Guarneri, Edgar Hofschen, Rob van Koningsbruggen, Vivien Isnard, David Leverett, Elio Marchegiani, Paolo Masi, Carmengloria Morales, Olivier Mosset, Claudio Olivieri, Antonio Passa, Jürgen Paatz, Pino Pinelli, Tomas Rajlich, André Valensi, Claudio Verna, Claude Viallat, Rudi van de Wint, Icke Winzer, Gianfranco Zappettini, and Jerry Zeniuk.

4 In the German show *Abstrakt*, organized by the Deutsche Künstlerbund, Fundamental painters Raimund Girke, Tomas Rajlich and Jerry Zeniuk, are grouped around predecessor Antonio Calderara (cf. Dippel); the group is designated as "Abstraktion im Anschauungs- und Sehraum. Das visuelle Feld: Die Farbe." Several "analytical" artists as per Italian definition are likewise included in this group.

5 "[D]e verf (verfbehandeling, streek, drager) moet centraal staan;" **From here on, all translations are by the author, unless otherwise indicated.**

6 "[D]eze groep schilders afgrenzen tegen de categorie 'vorm/teken'(Agnes Martin, Edda Renouf, Stephen Rosenthal, Tomas Rajlich, Bob Mangold, Alan Charlton etc.), de categorie 'over de schilderkunst' (Buren, Toroni, Mosset, de kunstenaars van de overleden groep Supports/Surfaces, etc.), evt. De categorie 'verf/licht/kleur' (Calderara, Olivieri, Graubner, Teraa, Verhoeven etc.).
De historische context dient duidelijk gemaakt.... Sommige werken van Gerhard Richter, etc.)"

7 "Bij onstentenis van het vorige voorstel is het onderwerp opnieuw kort besproken waarbij uiteraard dezelfde namen vielen (ongeveer). Er zijn echter een paar verschillen in de opzet:

1. De neiging bestaat om de vorige opzet (weinig mensen met relatief veel werk) toch te herzien in: wat meer mensen (zonder dat dit noodgedwongen minder werk hoeft te impliceren), en deze dan eventueel onderverdeeld in een soort kerngroep (Marden, Ryman, Van Koningsbruggen, Berghuis, Girke, Berthot) en een aantal randfiguren (Twombly, Hofschen, Jackson, Richter, Walker).
2. Al dan niet gedocumenteerd in fotos op de tentoonstelling, in een diaprogramma en/of in katalogus, deze groep afgrenzen tegen beeldende kategorieën:
a. Martin, Renouf, Rosenthal, Rajlich
b. Mangold, Charlton
c. Buren, Toroni, Mosset (etc.)
3. Historische context duidelijk maken? In het nabije verleden Rauschenberg, Johns – in iets minder nabije verleden Malewitsch.
Kees Smits."

8 "Na bezoek aan Art & Project ben ik positief over Rajlich.... Ik vind hem ... veel langer bezig. En vooral ook als figuur tussen kunstenaars als Martin en de echte schilders."

9 "1) Agnes Martin is naar leeftijd de oudste deelnemer van de tent. In haar schilderijen overweegt de lijn in horizontalen en verticalen. Niet met een raster, maar alleen met subtiele horizontale lijnen – en sinds kort met diagonale lijnen – werkt Stephan [sic] Rosenthal. Thomas [sic] Rajlich schildert weer over een min of meer regelmatig rasterpatroon, en staat tussen Ryman en Martin in. De frans-amerikaanse Edda Renouf werkt met het raster van het weefsel. Structuur en textuur ontstaat door de enkele draden die uit het weefsel van het doek worden verwijderd.
2) Robert Ryman heeft het meest van alle deelnemers de mogelijkheden van de verf, het oppervlak, de drager, technieken en media, onderzocht, zich daarbij hoofdzakelijk beperkend tot de witte verf. Veel minder structureel en vooral optisch werkt Raymund [sic] Girke, niet geheel terecht vaak met

Ryman vergeleken. Enige verwantschap toont het werk van Jaap Berghuis, in wiens werk kleur – zij het zeer ingehouden – een rol speelt. Brice Marden's schijnbaar koele reductie bestaat uit geschilderde panelen, met uiterst vlak oppervlak (met paletmes), samengevoegd tot 2 en 3-luiken. Eveneens met 'encaustic' (was en kleurstof) werkt Jerry Zeniuk: grijze en donkerbruine tot zwartachtige monochromen, die een opaque oppervlak vertonen (de structuur van het doek blijft zichtbaar na 25 lagen was). Verwant in de verte zijn ook de groenachtige monochromen van Jake Berthot, voor wie echter de rand van het schilderij – de afsluiting – vooral een uitdaging is.
3) Robert Mangold: geen verftoets, geen onderzoek van dragers, maar zuivere concentratie op de vorm van het doek en de vorm op het doek; meetkundige basisvormen – vierkant en cirkel en onderdelen daarvan – en de mogelijkheden daarvan binnen de gekozen beperking van het doekformaat, vaak in reeksen, zoals bij Ryman. Alan Charlton's schilderijen werken als reliëfs, waarbij de bepaling van de formaten en de verhoudingen ervan essentieel zijn. Grijze monochromen, geheel vlak geschilderd....
Alle genoemde kunstenaars maken wel gebruik van kleur, maar vaak op een 'verborgen' wijze. (Brice Marden is van plan om met helrood en geel te werken, Zeniuk gebruikt kleuren als rood en blauw, maar verwerkt ze tot grijzen, Ryman gebruikt onder zijn witten kleur, Mangolds kleuren zijn ongewoon, maar nadrukkelijk.)
5) Geen van allen maakt echter op zo'n uitbundige manier als Richard Jackson gebruik van kleur.... Het geschilderde schilderij – zorgvuldig gepland – maakt op zijn beurt weer een schilderij: kunst baart kunst. De enige kunstenaar in de tent. die een soort environment realiseert. Niet in kleur, maar in witten en zwarten (hoofdzakelijk) werkt Rob van Koningsbruggen. Ook bij hem bewuste bezinning op de essentie van het schilderij, grondvormen, textuur, maar bovendien onderzoek naar positieve en negatieve vorm, verschuivingen van het doek. Het schilderij drukt zichzelf af of maakt zijn contra-vorm."

10 A copy of each of the educative panels hung in the entrance room to the show was available in the documentation maps to the exhibition *Fundamental Painting* at the archives of the Stedelijk Museum Amsterdam. Current whereabouts at the Stadsarchief Amsterdam unknown.

11 "Het einde van de schilderkunst is deze eeuw vele malen aangekondigd. Herhaaldelijk werden 'grenzen' bereikt, die later weer overschreden werden. In de jaren 60 leek de schilderkunst overschaduwd door vele nieuwe uitingen van kunst, waaronder Minimal Art en Concept Art [sic]. Maar deze inspireerden haar ook opnieuw. De laatste jaren houden veel schilders zich bezig met nieuwe vormen van abstracte schilderkunst. Behalve van fundamentele schilderkunst spreekt men ook wel van stille, nieuwe, essentiële, geplande of analytische schilderkunst. De 18 schilders in deze thematentoonstelling vormen geen groep. Zij zijn bijeengebracht op grond van een gelijkgerichte belangstelling voor formele en fundamentele uitgangspunten van de abstracte schilderkunst. Het gaat hen om het schilderen als schilderen, om het schilderij als vlak en niet als 'gat in de muur'. Het schilderij is niet middel maar onderwerp geworden. De beeldende middelen worden opnieuw onderzocht: formaat – grootte – kleur – vorm – lijn – textuur – materialen (verschillende soorten verf, drager van de verf en verschillende middelen om de verf aan te brengen.). Deze middelen worden 'economisch' gebruikt. Er blijkt een voorkeur voor sobere kleuren als wit en grijs en voor het vierkante vlak. Compositie-elementen worden vaak achterwege gelaten. Verftoetsen en lijnen zijn gelijkwaardig over het doek aangebracht. De werkwijze is meestal een langdurig process, waarbij soms vele lagen verf over elkaar worden gestreken. Bij een aantal schilders ligt een sterk accent op het denkproces dat aan het schilderen voorafgaat, maar waarbij de intuïtie niet wordt uitgeschakeld. Er zijn veel raakvlakken èn verschillen met de abstracte schilders van vroeger en nu."

12 Italian exhibiting artists: Rodolfo Aricò, Carlo Battaglia, Paolo Cotani, Giorgio Griffa, Claudio Verna, and Carmengloria Morales (born in Chile); American exhibiting artists: Larry Bell, Marcia Hafif, Craig Kaufmann, Robert S. Zakanyck, and Minimalist painters Brice Marden and Robert Ryman.

13 Exhibiting artists were the Italians Rodolfo Aricò, Carlo Battaglia, Maurizio Bottarelli, Vincenzo Cecchini, Paolo Cotani, Franco Fumelli, Marco Gastini, Giorgio Griffa, Riccardo Guarneri, Vittorio Guarnieri, Elio Marechiani, Vittorio Mascalchi, Carmengloria Morales (born in Chile), Vincenzo Satta, Aldo Schmid, Claudio Verna, and Gianfranco Zappettini; Frenchman Robert Denys; the Germans Ulrich Erben, Winfred Gaul, Rupprecht Geiger, and Raimund Girke; and the Belgians Piet Teraa and Daan van Severen. The United States were represented by Bernard Cohen, John Hoyland, David Leverett, and Minimalist Robert Ryman.

14 Exhibiting artists were the Italians Carlo Battaglia, Paolo Cotani, Marco Gastini, Giorgio Griffa, Carmengloria Morales (born in Chile), Mario Nigro, Lucio Pozzi, Valentino Vago, and Claudio Verna. International guests were Louis Cane, Marc Devade, Blinky Palermo, Susanne Tanger, and Claude Viallat, Ulrich Erben and Lynn Umlauf, Diego Esposito, Bernard Cohen, David Leverett, Dorothea Rockburne, and Douglas Sanderson. Also works by Minimalist artists Brice Marden and Robert Ryman, and Abstract Expressionist Ad Reinhardt were shown.

15 Exhibiting artists in the section entitled "Analitica/Analytic:" Vincenzo Agnetti, Art & Language, Carl André, John Baldessari, Robert Barry, Bernd & Hilla Becher, Mel Bochner, Daniel Buren, Victor Burgin, Louis Cane, Enrico Castellani, Christo, Hanne Darboven, Jan Dibbets, Dan Flavin, Hamish Fulton, Giorgio Griffa, Hans Haacke, Michael Heizer, Douglas Huebler, On Kawara, Ellsworth Kelly, Yves Klein, Joseph Kosuth, Sol LeWitt, Richard Long, Francesco Lo Savio, Robert Mangold, Piero Manzoni, Brice Marden, Agnes Martin, Robert Morris, Barnett Newman, Kenneth Noland, Roman Opalka, Blinky Palermo, Emilio Prini, Ad Reinhardt, Dorothea Rockburne, Robert Ryman, Frank Stella, Richard Tuttle, Donald Judd, Lawrence Weiner, and Ian Wilson.

16 The following exhibitions comprised a number of artists considered by or proposed to the curators in view of the *Fundamental Painting* show: *Glossario, Qui Arte Contemporanea* (Griffa, Morales, Hafif), *Un Futuro Possibile - Nuova Pittura* (Twombly, Green, Griffa, Humphrey, Verheyen, Novros, Palermo, Baer, Diao, Erben, Graubner), and *La riflessione sulla pittura* (Devade, Erben, Esposito, Griffa, Morales, Palermo, Pozzi).

17 Further participants: Carlo Battaglia, Cy Twombly, Franz Gertsch, Alan Green, Jean-Olivier Hucleux, Ralph Humphrey, Jef Verheyen, Roy Lichtenstein, David Novros, Frank Owen, Blinky Palermo, A.R. Penck, Ben Schonzeit, Claudio Verna, Jo Baer, Georg Baselitz, David Diao, William Dutterer, Ulrich Erben, Ellsworth Kelly, Konrad Klapheck, Markus Lüpertz, Gotthard Graubner, Jules Olitski, Imi Knoebel, Sigmar Polke, Larry Poons, Norbert Tadeusz, and Joe Zucker.

18 Exhibiting artists: Jake Berthot, Antonio Calderara, Ulrich Erben, Marco Gastini, Winfred Gaul, Rupprecht Geiger, Raimund Girke, Kuno Gonschior, Gotthard Graubner, Giorgio Griffa, Riccardo Guarnieri, Edgar Hofschen, Brice Marden, Rune Mields, Carmengloria Morales, Mario Nigro, Claudio Olivieri, Edda Renouf, Dieter Ruden, Robert Ryman, Dan van Severen, Piet Teraa, Jorrit Tornquist, Icke Winzer, Gianfranco Zappettini and Jerry Zeniuk.

19 Exhibiting artists: Jake Berthot, Antonio Calderara, Ulrich Erben, Marco Gastini, Winfred Gaul, Rupprecht Geiger, Raimund Girke, Kuno Gonschior, Giorgio Griffa, Riccardo Guarneri, Edgar Hofschen, Rune Mields, Carmengloria Morales, Mario Nigro, Claudio Olivieri, Edda Renouf, Dan van Severen, Piet Teraa, Gianfranco Zappettini, and Jerry Zeniuk, as well as Minimalist painters Robert Mangold, Brice Marden, Agnes Martin, and Robert Ryman.

20 Exhibiting artists: Jaap Berghuis, Martin Barré, Enzo Cacciola, Carlo Battaglia, Noël Dolla, Paolo Cotani, Winfred Gaul, Marc Devade, Raimund Girke, Vivien Isnard, Giorgio Griffa, Jacques Martinez, Carmengloria Morales, John Seery, Rudi van de Wint, Claudio Verna, Gianfranco Zappettini, Claude Viallat, and Jerry Zeniuk.

21 See endnote 1

22 Exhibiting artists: Rodolfo Aricò, Carlo Battaglia, Enzo Cacciola, Bernard Cohen, Paolo Cotani, Noël Dolla, Ulrich Erben, Marco Gastini, Raimund Girke, Alan Green, Riccardo Guarnieri, Vivien Isnard, David Leverett, Gottardo Ortelli, Jürgen Paatz, Pino Pinelli, Claudio Verna, Claude Viallat, Icke Winzer, and Jerry Zeniuk.

23 American exhibiting artists: Josef Albers, Walter Darby Bannard, Larry Bell, Al Held Ellsworth Kelly, Morris Louis, Robert Mangold, Kenneth Noland, Jules Olitsky, Larry Poons, Ad Reinhardt, Robert Ry-

man, Mark Rothko, Frank Stella, and Cy Twombly; Exhibiting artists from Europe: Carl Battaglia, Jaap Berghuis, Enzo Cacciola, Louis Cane, Alan Charlton, Paolo Cotani, Marc Devade, Noël Dolla, Ulrich Erben, Marco Gastini, Raimund Girke, Alan Green, Giorgio Griffa, Edgar Hofschen, Vivien Isnard, Gottardo Ortelli, Jürgen Paatz, Paolo Patelli, Pino Pinelli, Gerhard Richter, Emilio Tadini, Rudi van de Wint, Claudio Verna, and Gianfranco Zappettini.

24 Exhibiting artists: Luciano Bartolini, Carlo Battaglia, Jaap Berghuis, Marcello Camorani, Louis Cane, Alan Charlton, Paolo Cotani, Robyn Denny, Marc Devade, Noël Dolla, Ulrich Erben, Marco Gastini, Raimund Girke, Alan Green, Giorgio Griffa, Riccardo Guarnieri, Edgar Hofschen, Rob van Koningsbruggen, Vivien Isnard, David Leverett, Elio Marchegiani, Paolo Masi, Carmengloria Morales, Olivier Mosset, Claudio Olivieri, Antonio Passa, Jürgen Paatz, Pino Pinelli, Tomas Rajlich, André Valensi, Claudio Verna, Claude Viallat, Rudi van de Wint, Icke Winzer, Gianfranco Zappettini, and Jerry Zeniuk.

25 Further participants: Enzo Cacciola, Ulrich Erben, Winfred Gaul, Kuno Gonschior, Gotthard Graubner, Alan Green, Edgar Hofschen, Carmengloria Morales, Claudio Olivieri, Blinky Palermo, Lucio Pozzi, Rudi van de Wint, and Gianfranco Zappettini, amongst others.

26 Further participants: Martin Barré, Luciano Bartolini, James Bishop, Vincenzo Cecchini, Marc Devade, Ulrich Erben, Winfred Gaul, Marco Gastini, Kuno Gonschior, Alan Green, Riccardo Guarneri, Giorgio Griffa, Carmengloria Morales, Claudio Olivieri, Jürgen Paatz, Lucio Pozzi, Martin Rous, Susanne Tanger, Oliver Thomé, Günther Umberg, Lynn Umlauf, Gianfranco Zappettini.

27 Further participants: Jean Degottex, Patrick Caillière, Pierre Joly, Carmengloria Morales, Olivier Mosset, Jürgen Paatz, Pino Pinelli, Gianfranco Zappettini, and Marc Devade.

28 Exhibiting artists: Martin Barré, Carlo Battaglia, Louis Cane, Marc Devade, Giorgio Griffa, Blinky Palermo, Claudio Verna, Claude Viallat and Rudi van de Wint.

29 As to commercial galleries, in 1973 Galleria Roberto Peccolo in Livorno organized *Tempi di percezione* (Times of perception) – followed by solo shows of artists Winfred Gaul, Carmengloria Morales, and Gianfranco Zappettini –, which travelled to the Dutch cities of Schiedam, Groningen, and Venlo in the autumn of 1975. Galleria La Bertesca in Düsseldorf organized *Grado Zero* (Zero degrees), which travelled to Bologna and Milan.
In the Netherlands, Galerie Swart in Amsterdam showed Rob Van Koningsbruggen, Howard Buchwald, Joan Mitchell, and John Walker. Art & Project, likewise in Amsterdam, showed Jaap Berghuis, Stephen Rosenthal, Alan Charlton, and Tomas Rajlich. Another Amsterdam gallery, Galerie Fagel, organized the show *Gewaarwording* (Perceptions), which included Antonio Calderara, Winfred Gaul, Riccardo Guarneri, Claudio Olivieri, Piet Teraa, and Gianfranco Zappettini, and gallery Seriaal, Amsterdam, showed Gerhard Richter. (FP 16; note 3).

30 "Bij de voorbereiding van de Fundamentele Schilderkunst was eigenlijk iedereen van mening, dat dit voor het grote publiek een moeilijke tentoonstelling zou worden. Begeleiding was daarom wenselijk. Na enig overleg werd gekozen voor twee vormen van begeleiding; een diaprogramma dat vooral over de tentoonstelling zelf zou gaan en een informatiezaal met tekstborden die enige raakvlakken en verschillen met andere abstracte schilders uit heden en verleden zou aanstippen."

31 "Mogelijk zullen vele bezoekers negatief reageren, omdat deze tentoonstelling niet voor een ieder begrijpelijk zal zijn. De gebruikelijke opmerkingen van: 'Wat moet het eigenlijk voorstellen'. Of 'Moet dit zonodig in een museum hangen', kunnen wel worden verwacht. Dat mag best, laat ieder zijn eigen vrije mening hebben, maar onze wetenschappelijke medewerkers willen U laten weten, dat naar hun mening de kunstenaars van deze tentoonstelling wel serieus hebben gewerkt. De werken op deze tentoonstelling zijn bijzonder kwetsbaar, de meesten hebben geen beschermende lijsten, de gebruikte verf is vaak met was vermengd, waardoor zelfs een lichte vingerafdruk zichtbaar blijft en niet meer is weg te werken. De grote vlakken en ook de ruitindelingen van vele schilderijen zullen bij sommige bezoekers de neiging opwekken om deze werken te bekrassen of te betekenen."

32 "Moeilijk te begrijpen lijkt de tentoongestelde eenvoud helemaal niet, omdat de schilderproblemen meestal al lang bekend zijn...."/"Besonders schwer fiel es nicht, die 'Einfachheit' dieser

Malerei verstehen und abschätzen zu können, denn in anderem Gewande sind einem die Probleme längt vertraut…."

33 "Het werk komt in één keer in zijn geheel over. Men kan zich heel goed in details verdiepen," and "De achttien kunstenaars op de tentoonstelling Fundamentele schilderkunst … zijn tot nu toe in Nederland buiten de kring van insiders bijna onbekend gebleven."

34 "Hadden voor velen de vorige thema-tentoonstellingen … weinig met de hun bekende kunst en zeker niets met schilderkunst te maken, dit keer is het anders."

35 "Om met zo weinig kunst te maken, moet men geniaal zijn."

36 "Dat is mijns inziens al teveel gezegd: zij beperken zich tot de grondslagen van het schilderij als materieel ding, aan een nadere differentiëring van de beeldende middelen komen ze nog niet toe."

37 "dat de meeste kunstenaars onderling zulke verschillende uitgangspunten en werkwijzen hanteren, dat zij nooit als groep beschouwd kunnen worden."

38 "Als beeld van een stroming is Fundamentele Schilderkunst uitstekende documentatie geworden."

39 "Het onderzoek naar methode en techniek waarop dit fundamentele schilderen neerkomt, is in de geschiedenis al zo dikwijls geleverd…."

40 "Het is een fascinerend en onvergetelijk doek."

41 "Einer dieser künstlich erzeugten Trends ist die 'fundamentele Malerei'…."

42 It is ironic that Dippel mentions that Italian institutions strongly supported a large number of Italian artists, in order for them to gain important positions in Fundamental Painting, while Bonomi in his text for the exhibition catalogue of *Pittura 70* complains three decades later that the Italian art scene did not do enough for this movement. See FP 11, and Bonomi 17.

43 Exhibiting artists: Vincenzo Cecchini, Winfred Gaul, Paolo Patelli, Pope [Galli], Tomas Rajlich, Claude Viallat. See Collovini.

44 Exhibiting artists: Dan Freudenthal, Georg Frietzsche, Raimund Girke, Gottfried Honegger, Thomas Kaminsky, Alfons Lachauer, Tomas Rajlich, James Reineking, Jan J. Schoonhoven, Alf Schuler, Phil Sims, and Jerry Zeniuk. See Obier.

45 Exhibiting artists: Marc Devade, Winfred Gaul, Raimund Girke, Alan Green, Carmengloria Morales, Tomas Rajlich, and Robert Ryman.

46 Fundamental painters included in the exhibition *Abstrakt* are Raimund Girke, Tomas Rajlich, Gerhard Richter and Jerry Zeniuk. Their works were contrasted to works of the previous generations, amongst others, Kazimir Malevich and Antonio Calderara.

47 See also the chapter 1.2.1. entitled "Definition of Fundamental Painting" for the coining of these terms.

48 Klaus Honnef coined the term "geplante Malerei" (planned painting), as the title of a museum show in 1974. It was accompanied by a commercial show under the title "analytische Malerei" (Analytical painting). In *Pittura Pittura*, Giorgio Bonomi explains that the term "pittura analitica" – the same term in Italian – was in fact coined by Filiberto Menna in 1973 in the catalogue to the exhibition *La riflessione sulla pittura* which took place at Acireale September through October 1973 (15 and 27; note 5). The term "nuova pittura" (new painting) was obviously used in the context of the exhibition *Un Futuro Possibile: Nuova Pittura* (A Possible Future: New Painting) at the Palazzo dei Diamanti in Ferrara – September through October 1973 – by curator Giorgio Cortenova, while Bonomi claims that a number of art critics had been using the term "nuova pittura" in their texts for some time. (Here it must be added that it is questionable if the combination of words *new painting* can be considered a term to designate a specific current in painting of the time.) The curator's notes refer to the show *Nouvelle peinture en France*, Musée d'art et d'industrie de Saint-Étienne, 1974; it showed the works of the 1970s French artists' group Supports/Surfaces, whose name is reminiscent of the mention "oppervlak – kleur - vorm" (surface - color – form). The term "fare pittura" (painting painting), then again was the title of an exhibition in 1973 by curators Bruno Passamani, Vittorio Fagone and Aldo Passoni, at the Museo Civico - Palazzo Sturm in Bassano del Grappa (VC), which showed only Italian artists. The term "pittura pittura" (peinture-peinture or painting as painting) was coined by Maurizio Fogiolo dell'Arco who in 1975 claimed to have considered it already as early as in 1968 (Bonomi, 27; note 6). The rest of the terms refer to

the writing or shows mentioned. In addition, it is to be noted that Italian critic Giovanni Maria Accame used the term "pittura riflessiva" (reflective painting) as from the mid-1960 for works by a number of Italian artists working in the analytical vein, while the term Analytical Abstraction was used as the title of the French show *Abstraction analytique: Fractures du monochrome aujourd'hui en Europe* by Bernard Lamarche-Vadel and Susanne Pagé in 1978. Artists Marcia Hafif, Jerry Zeniuk and Raimund Girke, amongst others, founded the group Radical Painting in New York in the 1970s to designate their work.

49 When he learned that the Stedelijk Museum Amsterdam was preparing the show Fundamental Painting, – without knowing the exhibiting artists – Klaus Honnef wrote a letter to Edy de Wilde, to bring to his attention the show that he had organized on "the same theme" in previous years. He enclosed the catalogue of *Geplante Malerei* from 1974 as well as a catalogue of works by Winfred Gaul and Gianfranco Zappettini. From De Wilde's answer, we learn that the curators of the Amsterdam show did consider the artists proposed by Honnef, but decided not to include them in the show.
Dippel wrote the following to De Wilde on this theme on 6 January 1975: "Wij ontvingen de heer Peccolo van de Galleria Peccolo uit Livorno. Werkt o.m. samen met Gaul, Galleria Del Milione in Milaan. Vertegenwoordigt vooral Zappettini en Carmen Morales.... Het heeft m.i. ook te veel een commercieel aspect."/"We received Mr. Peccolo of the Galleria Peccolo gallery in Livorno. He works with [Winfred] Gaul, Galleria del Milione in Milano, amongst others. He represents mainly Gianfranco Zappettini and Carmengloria Morales.... In my opinion, it also has a too commercial aspect."
Winfred Gaul apparently even received a personal letter expressing regret in not including him, while the Stedeljik Museum Amsterdam borrowed works by Jake Berthot from his collection. In a letter stamped 18 March 1975 by the museum reception, Gaul expressed irritation as he wrote: "Das ich dem Stedelijk Museum offenbar als Sammler bekannt bin, als Künstler aber offenbar nicht, überrascht mich eigentlich nicht mehr. Dennoch haben alle, die meine Arbeit seit 20 Jahren kennen, schätzen und kaufen, es als selbstverständlich angesehen, dass ich zu dieser Ausstellung eingeladen werde. Spätestens seit meiner Retrospektive vor 2 Jahren (die in 4 Museen gezeigt wurde) hat es sich herumgesprochen, dass ich bereits in den fünfziger Jahren vieles von dem vorgenommen habe, was dann Ende der sechziger Jahre in Amerika als 'Neue Sensibilität' propagiert wurde. Die Auswahl Ihrer Austellung beweist nur wieder aufs Neue, wie sich ein öffentliches Institut als Agent einiger potenzieller Händler manipulieren lässt."/"The fact that the Stedelijk Museum knows me as a collector, but not as an artist, does not surprise me anymore. Yet, to all who know, collect and value my work of the past 20 years, it seemed likely that I would be invited to participate in this show. Already since my retrospective show two years ago (which was shown by four museums), it is known that in the 1950s I did a lot of what later in the 1960s was propagated as 'new sensibility' in the USA. The selection in your exhibition once again shows how a public institution lets itself be manipulated as an agent for potential dealers." It is ironic that this aforementioned commercial aspect is exactly that which Dippel criticized in the proposition of gallery owner Roberto Peccolo. At the same time, Gaul himself unknowingly mentioned the reason why he was not included in the show, i.e. because his work relates to "new sensibility," which is exactly what the curators of Fundamental Painting excluded.

50 Contrary to the previous mention based on Dippel's catalogue text, it is important to note that the term Post-Minimal was already coined by Robert Pincus-Witten in 1971 (Chilvers 569). The term Concept Art was used by artist Henry Flynt as the title of an article, "Essay: Concept Art," in relation to Fluxus in 1961, while artist Joseph Kosuth and the British artist group Art & Language later started using it in a different context (Kosuth, Joseph. "Art after Philosophy, Part III." *Studio International*, Nov. 1969, pp. 212.). In 1970, the exhibition *Specific Object: Conceptual Art and Conceptual Aspects*, curated by Donald Karshan and shown at the New York Cultural Center, was the first to touch upon this movement as we understand it now.

51 Bonomi, it seems, even insinuates that Italian curators "invented" this new kind of European current in painting and coined the term before the Dutch. Bonomi cites a few possibilities for the beginnings of painting as exhibited in *Pittura 70: Pittura Pittura e Astrazione Analitica,* namely

the following shows: *Processi di pensiero visualizzati* (Lucerne, 1970) curated by Jean-Christophe Ammann and the Italian Germano Celant, *Per pura pittura* (Trieste, 1972) curated by Claudio Cerritelli, and *Iononrappresentonullaiodipingo* (Verona, 1973) curated by Italo Mussa (17). Marco Meneguzzo in the exhibition catalogue *Pittura analitica: Una ricognizione storica. Italia 1966-1978*, likewise mentioned the 1970 show as a curatorial beginning (Feierabend and Meneguzzo 216). We cannot deny the Italians' early attempts, at least, at developing or coining a similar style.

52 "De schilders die aan deze tentoonstelling deelnemen, zijn onderling uiterst verschillend. Dat ze toch samen gebracht worden, vindt zijn oorzaak in het feit dat zij allen in hun werk het schilderen zeer letterlijk nemen, als vak en als kunst, en zich bezinnen op de basis-gegevenheden van dat schilderen. Wat gewoonlijk als uitgangspunt geldt of als middel wordt bij hen tegelijkertijd doel. Vanuit een conventioneel denkpatroon een paradoxale toestand. Deze kunstenaars reduceren zeer bewust, beperken zich rationeel tot een aantal essentiële zaken van het schilderen. Dat betekent niet dat er geen intuïtie meer aan te pas komt of dat er als gevolg van een zuiver materiële benadering geen 'inhoud' meer zou zijn. Bij sommige kunstenaars zou men van een nieuwe koele romantiek kunnen spreken…."

53 Bonomi mentions the 1970 exhibition *Processi di pensiero visualizzati* to indicate the starting point of "pittura pittura" and Analytical Abstraction, as well as mentioning a number of exhibitions, which contained at least three artists also participating in the *Fundamental Painting* show to connect these various currents. Yet, a large part of these are small shows that were organized by commercial galleries (which most likely simply exhibited their gallery artists), and most of these artists were actually not included in the show *Fundamental Painting* nor in *Pittura 70*. On a museum level, only the section "Il nuovo astrattismo in Italia" (New abstraction in Italy) of the show *Rassegna della Giovane Pittura Italiana* (Genazzano [Rome], 8 through 30 September 1972, curated by Dario Micacchi and Cesare Vivaldi) mentioned by Bonomi included artist Vincenzo Cecchini, who could possibly qualify but was not included in the *Fundamental Painting* show; and only the exhibition *Tempi di percezione*, which was presented several times in both non-commercial and commercial contexts, included Girke, who also took part in *Fundamental Painting* in 1975. Thus, critically speaking, we should be skeptical of this enumeration

54 "'Rifondare' o, meglio 'rifare' o, meglio ancora, soltanto 'fare pittura con la pittura': questo è un assunto commune a tutti gli artisti che esaminiamo, i quali si trovano … a cercare di ripartire dal grado zero…."/"La pittura si identifica con il suo stesso fare, l'analisi su cui tutti si fondano … scaturisce nel momento stesso in cui si costruisce il quadro."/"Comunque, e in sintesi, tutti gli artist della pittura degli anni 70 lavorano sulle strutture, sugli elementi, fondanti e fondamentali della pittura: colore, luce, superficie, segno, quadro, cornice, corpo, gesto, pennellata, e cosi via."

55 This combination of terms could refer to their use by Immanuel Kant, as Klaus Honnef noted in *Analytishe Malerei*. Kant used the term "dialectical" for contradictions that issue from the knowledge of objects that we assume to have outside the limits of our experience. At the same time, Kant was convinced that a proposition is "analytical," when its validity is purely dependent on the definition of symbols that it contains. Such an interpretation would link Honnef's proposition to the words of Corà and correspond to the indefinable nature of Analytical Painting and its creation of a lyrical atmosphere.

56 In correspondence with the author, 4 May 2015, art historian Deborah Jenner pointed out that the square is not such a "neutral" shape as may seem, since it evokes the symbol of the mandala. Also Barbara Rose in her Editor's Note to *Art-as-Art* designates Ad Reinhardt's Black Paintings showing a Greek Cross as "mandalas" (185). In this context, the square makes reference to the human mind. In the 20th century, notably Carl Jung developed it as part of his individualization therapy, in which it stood for the "Self;" drawing a mandala was part of the Jungian therapy based on the notion of the collective unconscious (See Juan Edouardo Cirlot, *A Dictionary of Symbols*, Courier Cooperation, 1971, pp. 199-203). In fact, the mandala, said to be a "squaring of the circle;" symbolically unites all kinds of dualities and stands for the achievement of order, representing the longing for the non-spatial and non-temporal center (which is never visually represented but merely hinted at by the concentricity of the composition).

57 “Ich benutze [die Technik] in ihrer konventionellsten Form (Ölfarbe auf Leinwand über Keilrahmen) und akzeptiere damit die herkömmliche Determinierung des Bildträgers als einer rechteckigen Fläche, die an lotrechten Wänden, bequem übersehbar und gut beleuchtet, in künstlichen Räumen (Architektur) angebracht ist. Malerei bleibt davon so unberührt wie die Literatur von der üblichen Buchform....”

58 Alan Charlton's schilderijen werken als reliëfs, waarbij de bepaling van de formaten en de verhoudingen ervan essentieel zijn.

59 It is evident, as we will see, that Richard Jackson's lifetime work is in fact very far from being Fundamental painting and that his inclusion in the show was an accident. Rini Dippel, in conversation with the author on 26 August 2011, remembered that museum director Edy de Wilde insisted on Jackson's inclusion in the show based on a personal preference. The curators‘ notes from the preparation of the show confirm that they never did count Jackson amongst the confirmed participants.

60 “Robert Mangold: ... zuivere concentratie op de vorm van het doek en de vorm op het doek; meetkundige basisvormen – vierkant en cirkel en onderdelen daarvan – en de mogelijkheden daarvan binnen de gekozen beperking van het doekformaat....”

61 See also Colpitt, “Significance of Scale,” 73-79.

62 “Mangolds kleuren zijn ongewoon, maar nadrukkelijk.”

63 “Alle genoemde kunstenaars maken wel gebruik van kleur, maar vaak op een ‘verborgen’ wijze.... Zeniuk gebruikt kleuren als rood en blauw, maar verwerkt ze tot grijzen, Ryman gebruikt onder zijn witten kleur....”

64 “Als ich anfangs (vor ungefähr 8 Jahren) einige Leinwände grau zustrich, tat ich das, weil ich nicht wusste was ich malen sollte oder was zu malen wäre, und es war mir dabei klar, dass so ein erbärmlicher Anlass auch nur unsinnige Resultate zur Folge haben konnte. Mit der Zeit jedoch bemerkte ich Qualitätsunterschiede zwischen den Grauflächen und auch, dass diese nichts von der destruktiven Motivation zeigten. Die Bilder fingen an, mich zu belehren. Indem sie das persönliche Dilemma verallgemeinerten, hoben sie es auf; das Elend geriet zu konstruktiver Aussage, relativer Vollkommenheit und Schönheit, also zu Malerei. Grau. Es hat schlechthin keine Aussage, es lost weder Gefühle noch Assoziationen aus, es ist eigentlich weder sichtbar noch unsichtbar. Die Unscheinbarkeit acht es so geeignet zu vermitteln, zu veranschaulichen, und zwar in geradezu illusionistischer Weise gleich einem Foto. Und es ist wie keine andere Farbe geeignet, “nichts” zu veranschaulichen. Grau ist für mich die willkommene und einzig mögliche Entsprechung zu Indifferenz, Aussageverweigerung, Meinungslosigkeit, Gestaltlosigkeit. Weil aber Grau, genau wie Gestaltlosigkeit usf., nur als Idee wirklich sein kann, kann ich auch nur einen Farbton herstellen, der Grau meint aber nicht ist. Das Bild ist dann die Mischung von Grau als Fiktion und Grau als sichtbarer proportionierter Farbfläche.“

65 “Jerry Zeniuk: grijze en donkerbruine tot zwartachtige monochromen, die een opaque oppervlak vertonen (de structuur van het doek blijft zichtbaar na 25 lagen was).”

66 “Aufgabe der Buntheit, der Vielfarbigkeit, zugunsten der Einfarbigkeit bedeutet intensivere Bearbeitungsmöglichkeiten der Farbe, die Beschränkung der Quantität hat eine Steigerung der Qualität zur Folge. An die Stelle vieler Farben, die miteinander um das Vorrecht kämpfen, tritt eine einzige Farbe als Herrscherin, sie kommt zu ihrem Recht, sie wird frei und kann ihre volle intensität erlangen.
Zugunsten einer einzigen Farbe habe ich die Vielfarbigkeit verlassen, und ich habe – in logischer Folgerung – zu Schwarz-Weiss-Grau ist die in hohem Masse noch unerschlossene Farbigkeit, voller Geheimnisse und Abenteuer.
Erst dann wird Schwarz-Weiss-Grau Farbe (und bleibt nicht nur im graphischem Bereich), wenn ich das Schwarz in feinsten Abstufungen über unzählige viele Grauvarianten bis hin zum Weiss, der Farbe, die alles andere überstrahlt, treibe, wenn die Farbfläche durch ständigen Wechsel im Hell-Dunkel in Bewegung gerät.
Weiss, - Kälte und Hitze zugleich – Verkörperung des Reinen, des Lichten und Hellen.
Schwarz und Grau haben eine dienende Funktion, ihre Aufgabe ist es, das Weiss in feine Schwingung

zu versetzen, ihm mit Hilfe der Struktur über die ganze Bildfläche hin eine kontinuierliche Bewegung zu vermitteln, es sensibel betonen als Gegenspieler, das Weiss und steigern dessen Leuchten. Die Welt des Monochromen bietet innerhalb eng gesetzter Grenzen unausschöpfbare Möglichkeiten ganz neuen Charakters. Die Farbe wird, beschränkt aus sich allein, aller Fesseln ledig, erhält eigenes Leben und offenbart sich nun in ihrer vollen Kraft."

67 "Jaap Berghuis, in wiens werk kleur – zij het zeer ingehouden – een rol speelt."

68 "... die Verbindung aufeinander folgender, sich geringfügig unterscheidender Farbschichten ergeben eine fast homogene Farbigkeit und eine ausserordentliche Dichte und Intensität der Farbe. Der schichtwiese Aufbau betont neben dem Materialen der Farbe den Vorgang des Malens selbst und führt zu einer scheinbar ruhigen Farbigkeit, deren latente Energie erst mählich erfahrbar wird. Farbe wird wirksam im kaum Sichtbaren, im gerade noch Tastbaren."

69 "Robert Ryman heeft het meest van alle deelnemers de mogelijkheid van de verf, het oppervlak ..., technieken ..., onderzocht, zich daarbij hoofdzakelijk beperkend tot de witte verf."

70 "Op een gegeven moment terwijl ik aan het schilderen was met de kwast aan een schilderij met wit [sic] en zwarte verf, bemerkte ik dat op die kwast verf was blijven zitten. De verf op die kwast had een zelfde verloop, overeenkomst, als op het schilderij. De kwast werd een schilderij. Naderhand werd het rechter schilderij de kwast voor het linker schilderij. In feite interesseert het me niet hoe het idée (schilderij) is uitgevallen. Je schildert met verf dus er gebeuren onverwachte en onvoorziene dingen, gelukkig. Er ontstaat een vlek links boven of rechts onder. Dat heb ik niet in de hand en wil dat ook niet. Ik stel bijv.: Ik heb een zwart schilderij en een wit schilderij, even groot, en strijk die langs elkaar heen van links naar rechts. En loop mijn atelier uit."

71 "Le métier de peintre, une autre vue sur la couleur: Que dire en premier si ce n'est: 'regardez ma façon de traiter la couleur et vous verrez comment je 'traite' le reste ', ou: 'la couleur est la 'voie royale' que je prends pour modifier les règles et les constantes.' En fait le métier de peintre, ce pourrait être le métier de la couleur, et j'imagine très bien le sujet de ce métier, le sujet de cette pratique ; interpeller la couleur et lui dire : 'qu'est-ce que je fais avec toi que je ne connais pas' ; et elle de répondre : 'et bien 'démerde' toi comme tu pourras, après tout ce n'est pas mon problème ; Si tu me découvres langage....' Voilà au fond c'est cela la peinture : a-prendre la couleur pour re-connaître le langage que je lui fais tenir pour connaître de moi le pourquoi de cette envie de faire du langage avec 'elle'. Ce langage c'est celui d'un sujet peintre et quand il donne dans la couleur il m'indique tout d'abord la forme de désir que je vais entretenir et phantasmer avec ce que je nomme la malléabilité de la couleur. C'est-à-dire avec son absence apparente de sens, absence qui en faite une 'matière d'autant plus facile à travailler' qu'elle est sans pouvoir de résistance à l'emploi. Il ne faut même plus 'co-giter avant de s'en servir', du moins c'est ce que je croyais il y a quelques temps. Mais plus exactement et si je considère mon parcours, mon attitude, par rapport à cela, je suis forcé de revenir sur une précédente proposition ; Car en fait, en tant que peintre 'voir la couleur' demande non seulement de travailler les moyens 'techniques' dont elle relève, mais demande aussi de prendre connaissance de la transformation de ces moyens à travers précisément leur incessante augmentation due au 'pouvoir imaginatif' de la couleur.... En ce sens, c'est forcément dans la couleur qu'il a fallu 'mettre de l'ordre'. Le métier de peintre y a fait 'la part des choses'. Mais finalement n'est-ce pas là le 'propre' du travail du 'métier de peintre' ? N'est-ce pas quelque chose qui, par rapport à la couleur, rend compte d'une capacité de discernement à exercer dans l'infinité de la 'gamme' colorée. Le métier de peintre ? Ce qui témoigne qualitativement du rapport que j'entretiens avec une qualitativité abstraite : la couleur."

72 "Principieel ben ik met witte en lichtgrijze schilderijen begonnen. Met het beetje groen of grijsblauw dat gebruikt werd, was het resultaat toch een grijs-wit schilderij. Toch kan ik er niets aan doen – en dat is zo langzamerhand tijdens het werk ontstaan – dat ik schilderijen in kleur erg mooi vind.... Maar zelf kun je niet ineens overstappen, al zit de ontwikkeling er wel in, dat de schilderijen, met enkele jaren geleden vergeleken, meer gekleurd zijn.... – want ja, kleur hoort toch bij het schilderen."

73 "Dans l'ordre ... le dessin m'a toujours semblé être ce qui me décide, ce qui donc, subjectivement, me place et m'ajuste dans la contradiction dans la dualité forme/fond/couleur/blanc ou peint, pas

encore peint, etc.... Ce dessin, ce premier-jet, ce pro-jet est un premier pas qui décide la projection vers l'autre, vers sa possession.... Ainsi, je me souviens qu'un vieux professeur de peinture me conseillait : "Serrez les formes avec votre dessin et vous tiendrez la composition." A suivre ce 'conseil' ... j'y écoute encore le mot composition comme le mot compromis et le mot dessin comme le mot destin car c'est somme tout 'le dessin' qui décide du destin de la toile du peintre.... de ce par quoi il se sent vivre : son langage. Voilà donc mon langage ; il ressemble fort à une entreprise de séduction, il n'en dit pas moins pour autant une des spécificités propres à la peinture et j'allais oublier ... propre au métier de peintre."

74 "Année de rupture: abandon de la forme pour envahir entièrement la surface du support."

75 "[G]rafische lijn hoort niet by het schilderen" and "Een schilderij moet geschilderd worden, niet getekend."

76 "In de laatste schilderijen is het raster niet meer dan een constructie binnen het schilderij geworden. De vroegere, tot op een jaar geleden, gaven nog een ruimteljke indruk; optisch ontstond er ruimte op het oppervlak van het doek, wat ik zelf verkeerd vond. Alles moet op het oppervlak gebeuren, de illusie wil ik wegwerken: daarom is het raster gebleven. Alle lagen die er overheen geschilderd zijn, zijn gemaakt op het principe dat zij zoveel mogelijk in het vlak van het raster blijven.... Het raster is er als een element, dat helpt de schildering binnen het oppervlak te houden. Het is een element, net als verf en het linnen, gebruikt om het schilderij op te bouwen."

77 "De frans-amerikaanse Edda Renouf werkt met het raster van het weefsel. Structuur en textuur ontstaat door de enkele draden die uit het weefsel van het doek worden verwijder."

78 The word facture as used in art-historical texts (cf. Part II, chapter 1.5) most likely stems from the Russian word *faktura*, used in 1912 by David Burliuk as the title of an article on painting and in 1914 as the title of the influential book by Vladimir Markov. Facture is to be understood as the manner in which something – such as a painting – was made (by hand). See Summers, "Facture," Ch. 1.2.

79 "de mogelijkheden van de verf, het oppervlak...," "Grijze monochromen, geheel vlak geschilderd," and "Brice Marden's schijnbaar koele reductie bestaat uit geschilderde panelen, met uiterst vlak oppervlak (met paletmes)...."

80 "Als je tot aan de rand schildert zoals ik, met het schilderij staand op de vloer, dan kun je daar onderaan niet zo goed met je penseel bijkomen en ontstaat er een randje, dat niet helemaal uitgewerkt is. Maar dat randje hielp mij nou juist om het oppervlak van het schilderij echt vlak te houden; het schilderij, dat bedekt is met een laag verf, heeft daar beneden een uitloop, die optisch precies de plaats bepaalt, waar het vlak van schildering zit. Er is optisch niet meer diepte in het doek dan die onderste rand aangeeft."

81 "Eveneens met 'encaustic' (was en kleurstof) werkt Jerry Zeniuk: grijze en donkerbruine tot zwartachtige monochromen, die een opaque oppervlak vertonen (de struktuur van het doek blijft zichtbaar na 25 lagen was)."

82 "21 août 1974. Difficulté qu'il y a de scinder technique et esprit. Il importe avant tout d'activer "quelque chose" au niveau de la texture: cela implique d'abord une re-connaissance d'une matière de base, ou l'instauration d'une connivence. Par exemple, le papier; reconnaissance de sa trame; ensuite, inscription de mon intervention au niveau de la texture la plus fondamentale de la matière. Mon intervention ne se situe plus qu'à ce niveau. Elle est une opération d'effacement ou de modestie par opposition à la tendance qui viserait à s'imposer ou à imposer. La texture? C'est quelque chose de vivant, c'est à dire quelque chose qui se détruit. L'intervention est un prolongement de la vie, une tentative faite pour suspendre le processus de destruction."

83 "Je bent typisch iemand die op doek schildert, maar stel, dat je eens opdracht zou krijgen om een grote muur in een gebouw te beschilderen, hoe zou je dat dan doen?" and "Wat de technische kant betreft: ik ben gewend aan acrylverf op doek. En het klinkt misschien gek, maar bij zo'n opdracht zou ik toch niet direkt op de wand schilderen. Ik zou bijvoorbeeld de wand op de manier van behang met linnen laten beplakken en daarop schilderen, want ik vind voor mijn schilderijen de struktuur van het linnen belangrijk. Wat diepte-illusie betreft probeer ik de kleinst mogelijke dimensie te bereiken met het material, vandaar."

84 "Het principe van schilderen is naar mijn gevoel toch iets wat je met al je kracht, niet zozeer alle emoties, maar toch met alle wil in je moet kunnen doen."

85 "Bestimmte Elemente des Herstellungsprozesses sind die Materialien: sie fordern spezifische Verhaltensweisen, die ablesbar bleiben müssen. Der Dimension der Bildfläche angemessene, frei auslaufende Farbzüge bilden ein mehr oder weniger bewegtes Farbfeld, und die Überlagerung und die Verbindung aufeinander folgender, sich geringfügig unterscheidender Farbschichten ergeben eine fast homogene Farbigkeit ..... Der schichtwiese Aufbau betont neben dem Materialen der Farbe den Vorgang des Malens selbst ...."

86 "De methode van schilderen en de constructie van het schilderij bepaald ik vooraf. Het schilderij kan daarna non-stop gemaakt worden. Het schilderij moet die methode en die constructie bevestigen."

87 "Mon travail de peintre est toujours à la limite du mécanique et, de ce fait, porteur de contrainte. Mais il n'est qu'apparemment mécanique. Il est repris par cette tension corporelle du faire ou par le projet inscrit dans le faire. Ce projet: aller jusqu'au bout. Jusqu'au bout de la ligne; jusqu'au bout de la page, jusqu'au bout d'une succession de pages. Expériences elles-mêmes répétitives.....
Ce processus de remise en question de l'espace tableau s'est poursuivi progressivement. Il a été marqué par une première rupture au moment où il y eût refus d'inscrire une forme sur une surface, mais où il y eût en même temps reconnaissance d'une espace comme surface totale. Une deuxième rupture fut un éclatement ou un déploiement en une succession de surfaces en vue de pouvoir poursuivre une expérience en elle-même indéfinie parce que reposant sur un faire, une tension toujours revécue et toujours destinée à être revécue.
Si la série devient de ce fait indéfinie, c'est qu'elle s'inscrit au niveau de cette expérience et non pas – ou très accidentellement – à celui du résultat. S'il arrive qu'une série se termine, ce ne peut être que le signe d'un épuisement.... "

88 "La répétition. C'est la nature même de la trame des choses. La trame est toujours un phénomène de répétition. Ce fait, pour moi, justifie d'en rester à la trame ligne: elle est suffisamment diversifiée par la matière de base pour qu'elle ne paraisse pas épuisée....
A quoi correspond cette expérience? Il y a d'abord soumission à un fait.... Il y a ensuite une circonstance.... La trame et la recherché de la trame est une recherche de cohérence. Plus il y a soumission à la structure de base, plus il y a possibilité de maintenir la cohérence, ou de parvenir à une cohérence.
J'ai finalement l'impression que le fait de répéter ... me met dans les meilleurs conditions pour atteindre ce que je cherche. Il n'est pas possible de scinder la technique des dispositions mentales, ou la vie mentale, l'impression de vivre cérébralement. Il y a une sorte d'accord, qui se traduit par une activation au niveau des textures infimes de l'objet....
La série crée ce mouvement. C'est une lecture repetitive qui influence ou qui introduit la personne qui regarde."

89 On this definition of the terms rational and logical, see Wittgenstein, 165-167. By addressing issues in visual arts, Wittgenstein is known to have widely influenced the philosophy of aesthetics and many artists, including Minimal Art.

90 Dippel uses the words "anti-illusionist:" and "all compositional elements ... absent" and continues explaining her point by way of Theo Van Doesburg's Manifesto of Concrete Art.

91 "Komposition in herkömmlichen Sinne gibt es nicht mehr. Das ganze Bild ist ein einziges Strukturfeld, das wohl in Strukturbereiche gegliedert ist, in dem aber keine Formdominanten mehr auftreten. Die verschiedenen Strukturelementen, die der Farbfläche ein stilles, aber äusserst eindringliches Leben geben. Jedes noch so kleine Strukturelement hat als Teil des gesamten Strukturfeldes seine Funktion im Ganzen, ist aktiv und daher unentbehrlich." He continues: "Unterschiedliche Richtungswerte der einzelnen Strukturbereiche heben sich hervor und werden wieder in der gegenseitigen Durchdringung und transparenten Überlagerung verdeckt. Die Welt des Monochromen bietet innerhalb den gesetzter Grenzen unausschöpfbare Möglichkeiten ganz neuen Charakters."

92 "Elk schilderij is ... een afgedrukt parallelbeeld van mijn handelingen gedurende de tijd van maken."

93 Colpitt here follows the distinction as made by Monroe C. Beardsley in *Aesthetics: Problems in the*

Philosophy of Criticism (Harcourt, Brace & World, 1958), 31-34.

94 "C'est quelque chose qui se vit, qui se transforme en vivant.... C'est en tout cas quelque chose qui donne l'impression de participer à la pulsation profonde de la nature des choses, et par le fait même, sans doute, de soi-même. Une sorte d'accord qui se fait et qui se vit. Ou qui est provoqué. Ce qu'il en reste devrait, en principe, à son tour le provoquer, pour autant qu'il y ait disponibilité."

95 Painting as painting in the Abstract Expressionist sense will be discussed in the following chapter: it is mainly the awareness and acceptance of a metaphysical element and a viewer's more atmospheric aesthetic-experience of the painting that differentiates it from the next generation.

96 "Misschien nog het meest vergelijkbaar met de kleuren van Johns? Of een heel eigen ‚inbreng' van de westkust van de USA? ... kunst baart kunst."

97 "Die Anwesendheit eines Richter, der nicht die Materialien der Malerei analysiert, sondern Stilformen ironisiert, in einer solchen Ausstellung ist vollends unverständlich."

98 Barnett Newman's article "The Sublime Is Now" first appeared in *Tiger's Eye*, 6, December 1948, pp. 51-53. It contrasted his generation of US painters against the Europeans, calling the US image a "self-evident one of revelation, real and concrete" and posing the question "[I]f we refuse to live in the abstract, how can we be creating a sublime art?" He is also known to have used the word *sublime* in titles of his works, as for example *Vir Heroicus Sublimis* (1950-51) held at the MoMA, New York. In 1961, art historian Robert Rosenblum published his book *Modern Painting and the Northern Romantic Tradition: Friedrich to Rothko*, including a chapter entitled "The Abstract Sublime" covering Newman's generation of painters. Since, this term has been widely used in the context of Abstract Expressionism.

99 On the subject of Minimal Art and music, see Strickland, "Sound," pp. 119-256; or Potter, 120-121, for example. Dutch composer Roland Emile Kuit sees Ryman's paint strokes as improvisations, as an extemporization or free performance of a musical passage, within the square, which is at base a grid structure representing a timeline (Conversation with the author, 1 May 2006).

100 Information received from Jerry Zeniuk, who on 1 December 2012 recounted his conversation with Marcia Hafif, during the period they were both members of the group Radical Painting which they founded in New York in 1980, to the author in an phone interview. According to Zeniuk, this group was founded by artists Olivier Mosset, Marcia Hafif and himself. The term *radical* in this case refers to both their radical social stance and their radical return to the roots of painting.

101 "Aujourd'hui avec le temps, j'ai l'impression de commencer à faire la part de ces choses-là, ce qui veut dire tout simplement qu'un sujet artiste peintre prend possession de ses propres moyens à partir du moment où il est capable de ne pas oublier la biographie de sa propre pratique. SHI TAO dit dans ses propos sur la peinture (1641-1717) qu'en ce qui concerne la réceptivité et la connaissance, c'est la réceptivité qui précède et la connaissance qui suit. A considérer cela en tenant compte de ce que je viens de dire, je reconnais volontiers que SHI TAO a raison. Il a raison non seulement parce que sa phrase a la vérité de la pratique, mais aussi parce qu'il semble me proposer ainsi d'accorder une plus grande attention à ma propre réceptivité afin de ne pas avoir pour seule connaissance que la connaissance des autres. C'est comme cela que d'après moi, du temps passé à peindre peut devenir du temps passé à connaître."

102 "Schilderen, als puur visuele bezigheid heeft te maken met kijken, veel kijken. Kijken is belangrijker dan uitleggen."

103 "Bij sommige kunstenaars zou men van een nieuwe koele romantiek kunnen spreken, een houding die sterk afwijkt van de informele kunst, de lyrische abstractie en de actionpainting uit de jaren 50, al zijn er soms in de uiterlijke resultaten oppervlakkige overeenkomsten te zien. Deze essentiële schilderkunst (cf. Naomi Spector) had niet kunnen ontstaan zonder de minimal art en conceptual art (Men spreekt dan ook wel van post minimal painting). Zowel het reducerende aspect ervan als het planmatige – beter het bewust geplande – verbinden deze schilders met beide genoemde stromingen. Voor sommigen is ook het seriële en modulaire van belang.
Voor de verschilllende kunstenaars gelden uiteenlopende invloeden. Voor de meesten echter was Ad Reinhardt een grote voorganger, evenals Frank Stella en Jasper Johns, en verder terug in de historie vooral Malewitsch (meer dan Mondriaan)."

104 On a side note, it needs to be mentioned that 18th century color theories involving science (espoused by Cézanne and Seurat amongst others) were later explored by Synchronism, started by Morgan Russell and Stanton Macdonald-Wright in the United States around 1913-14. They believed that form is revealed by color. Their works often appear to represent a movement around a central vortex and have a prismatic radiance. About the same time, painters in France were independently working towards a kind of abstraction prone to a lyrical interpretation. These were Frank Kupka, Robert Delaunay, Fernand Léger, and Francis Picabia whose paintings were coined Orphist by Guillaume Apollinaire. This vein in abstraction is not relevant in the context of our discourse, however. It is more typical of Analytical Abstraction with its lyrical atmosphere, than of Fundamental Painting; therefore, we will only touch upon this fact briefly here for the sake of consistency.

105 "A tout dire je crois qu'une grande partie de la peinture, constituée ajourd'hui par ce qui s'expose dans les galeries, suit la politique de l'autruche. Plongée dans l'ignorance elle prétexte qu'il n'y a rien à savoir. Du moins possible elle met en scène le moins possible, la simplicité se révèle simplisme. Voilà un peu ce à quoi je pensais à peine sorti de l'exposition Cézanne à l'Orangerie (1974), Travail 'savant,' intelligent, pleine mesure de la couleur qui, en fait, renvoit à autre chose que les mots que j'utilise ici-même. Ainsi cette 'organisation' de la couleur et du dessin qui révèle chez Cézanne d'une multiplicité de moyens techniques, tout autant qu'elle en indique le détail, (au sens où l'on fait le détail de quelque chose) révèle aussi les contradications qui se jouent dans le sujet peintre à travers ce qui justement s'appelle le métier du peintre. Le 'métier de peintre', voilà bien en effet un terme qui, il n'y a pas si longtemps évoquait pour moi une inutile constante, quelque chose que j'entendais alors comme devant relever de 'l'ancienne peinture.' Or, sur ce point, je m'interroge car je me trouve aujourd'hui de plus en plus 'demandeur' de ce que j'ai pu, hier, acquérir sous ce terme. Comment se fait-il que j'ai le besoin de réactiver et de reproduire ce savoir pour 'faire avancer' ma peinture. Autrement dit, qu'est-ce qui vient par là si ce n'est une autre attitude du sujet qui détermine une autre vue sur la couleur, sur le dessin, sur les formes, et sur 'le temps de peindre'?"

106 Jerry Zeniuk claims that Stephen Rosenthal's painting comes from Matisse (as opposed to his own, which comes from Cézanne, resp. Mondrian); Zeniuk, telephone conversation with the author, 1 December 2012.

107 "Toen ik in 1913 in mijn vertwijfeld streven, de kunst van de ballast van het figuratieve te bevrijden, naar de vorm van het vierkant vluchtte en een beeld maakte, dat niets anders voorstelde dan een zwart vierkant op een wit veld, verzuchtte de kritiek en met haar de maatschappij: Alles waar wij van hielden is verloren gegaan. Wij zijn een woestijn…Voor ons staat een zwart vierkant op een wit veld." Quoted from *Kasimir Malewitsch: Die Gegenstandslose Welt.* Bauhausbücher 11. Munich, Albert Langen, 1927, p. 66.

108 The lack of clarity on the dates of creation of some of the "first" non-objective paintings is sometimes disputed: overall though, Kandinsky, Kupka, Malevich and Mondrian are considered the four pioneers of non-objective painting. For our discussion on Fundamental Painting it is not topical who really was the first or not.

109 The artists in Moscow knew the Western-European avant-garde thanks to exhibitions, publications and personal relations. What's more, Moscow had two large private collectors of Impressionist and more contemporary art forms – Schukin and Morosov – who maintained very close relationships with artists. See for example: https://www.guggenheim.org/arts-curriculum/topic/the-collections-of-shchukin-and-morozov.

110 As nanophysics were not yet known in Malevich's day and age, from a mathematical and particle physics perspective the perfect square was a shape that did not exist in nature. More importantly, as art historian Deborah Jenner pointed out in conversation with the author on 8 July 2015, Malevich was Russian Orthodox; the Orthodox Cross is a square and considered as an icon. Moreover, in Eastern mysticism (incl. Buddhism, Hinduism and Taoism) that Malevich took interest in, all creation starts with the Bindu point that can be represented by a black square, while Tao calls the infinite "a square without corners."

111 In fact, it elegantly reveals 'shunyata' or the Infinite as space itself, which is the 5th element in Hindu/Buddhism.

112 See for example, Sixten Ringbom, "Transcending the Visible: The Generation of Abstract Pioneers" in Maurice Tuchman, *The Spiritual in Art,* 131-153.

113 "Voor Robert Ryman in het bijzonder is dit werk van grote invloed geweest."

114 "Omstreeks 1918 schildert Malewitch niet alleen een wit vierkant tegen een witte achtergrond, maar ook andere witte vormen tegen een witte achtergrond, en stelt hiermee als eerste (samen met Rodchenko) het probleem van de monochromie centraal."

115 "Nach der Emanzipation der Farbe die Emanzipation der Fläche mit Hilfe der Faktur."

116 "Gemälde und Wand emanzipieren sich gegenseitig durch die Nullflächen-Malerei."

117 "Die Farbe wurde zum letzten Element einer historischen Malerei, die Faktur zum ersten Element einer neuen Malerei."

118 "In zijn manifest van de concrete kunst, april 1930 stelt [Theo] Van Doesburg een aantal punten op, die overeenkomsten tonen met de instelling van de schilders op deze tentoonstelling."

119 "Het kunstwerk moet geheel gedacht en gevormd zijn in de geest voor het uitgevoerd wordt.... Het schilderij moet geheel met zuiver beeldende elementen opgebouwd worden, dwz. met platte vlakken en kleuren. Een schilderkunstig element heeft geen andere betekenis dan 'zichzelf', bij gevolg heeft het schilderij geen andere betekenis dan 'zichzelf'. De constructie van het schilderij, evenals die van zijn elementen, moet simple en visueel controleerbaar zijn, exact, dwz. anti-impressionistisch."

120 "Van Doesburg benadrukt echter de rationele benadering van het schilderij veel sterker dan de kunstenaars in de tentoonstelling, voor wie ook de intuïtie van wezenlijk belang is."

121 Ironically, in the 1920s, De Stijl had started to fall apart over a dispute concerning the diagonal between Van Doesburg and Mondrian (who formed the core of the group, which was more a network of visual artists and architects linked by a common mentality [cf. Fundamental Painting] that communicated in writing). Mondrian accepted only verticals and horizontals, while Van Doesburg started basing his works on the diagonal. Mondrian would never paint a diagonal, yet the diagonal would obviously appeal to him in the 1930s. His latest canvases are hung at an angle, thereby visually creating diagonal lines.

122 "Der Begriff Factur taucht auf in einem Augenblick (1914), wo die Farbe als Material der Malerei schon obsolete erscheint. Der Begriff der Faktur sprengt also noch viel mehr als die Gegenstandslosigkeit und die Farbe (die Monochromie) das Staffelei-Bild. Gleichzeitig erlöst er die Malerei aus dem Gefängnis der Farbe und eröffnet ihr neue Möglichkeiten der Material- und Methoden-Wahl."

123 "Met formele middelen, zoals formaat, combinaties van kleuren, omvang van kleurvelden, die steeds vertical naast elkaar aangebracht zijn, wil Newman een metafysische betekenis aan zijn werk geven. Zijn titels geven een aanduiding voor de interpretatie van het werk. De schilders in deze tentoonstelling staan ver af van verwijzingen naat het metafysische, het oneindige, het abstract-sublieme..."

124 "Via de werkelijkheid tot het rijk der fantasie en abstractie komen, maar uit de niet-werkelijkheid, de chaos van de extase, komen tot iets dat een herinnering van het gevoel oproept dat bij het besef van totale werkelijkheid in een enkel moment ervaren wordt."

125 „die d.m.v. kleurvelden emoties op wil wekken, in tegenstelling tot de Action Paintings uit de 50er jaren, waarbij het gaat om de emotionele waarde van de actie van het schilderen."

126 "In kleuren die vaak niet zozeer contrasteren, maar dicht bij elkaar op de kleurencirkel liggen, schildert Rothko tegen een achtergrond rechthoeken, waarvan de omtrekslijnen parallel aan die van het doek lopen. De contouren van de rechthoeken zijn diffuus, de kleuren zijn nergens egaal aangebracht, maar steeds met een niet geheel dekkende wollige penseelstreek over elkaar heen geschilderd."

127 In June 1933, in a letter to Pierre Bonnard congratulating him on his show at Galerie Bernheim-Jeune, Paul Signac writes that "Everything seems easy," and the show makes him want to paint "Painting for painting's sake, nothing else." See Ferretti-Bocquillon, 322.

128 "Reinhardt verwerpt alles wat niet essentieel is in zijn kunst om tot het wezen ervan door te drin-

gen. Hij maakt eerst rode en blauwe monochrome schilderijen, van 1953 tot zijn dood schildert hij vierkante zwarte doeken waarin bij aandachtig kijken een Grieks kruis zichtbaar wordt. 'Ik ben bezig met het schilderen van de laatste schilderijen die iemand ooit ergens maken kan.' Ook uit Reinhardts kunsttheoretische publikaties blijkt dat het hem om de zuiverheid van de kunst gaat, om de kunst als kunst. 'Alles is in beweging, onderweg. De kunst moet stil zijn.' 'Het enige wat er over kunst te zeggen valt is dat zij één is. Kunst is niets dan kunst. Kunst is niet wat niet kunst is.' In deze tentoonstelling wordt de schilderkunst als schilderkunst aan de orde gesteld." Cit. from Reinhardt, Ad. "Twelve Rules for a New Academy," 1953.

129 In this regard, please note the term "minimal" is common to Zen Buddhism, but was newly applied to this kind of Modern art at this point.

130 Ad Reinhardt was close friends with fellow Columbia University alumnus Thomas Merton. For years, they corresponded with each other on art theory, abstract art, Zen and other religions, amongst other things. Merton apparently saw religious significance in Reinhardt's works, which later (by the time of his "Black Paintings") were influenced by Eastern philosophy, as their correspondence reveals. See Shannon et al., 384-385. An interesting concept in this regard is Merton's explanation on Zen, which he describes as "a concrete and loved ontology which explains itself not in theoretical propositions but in acts emerging out of a certain quality of consciousness and awareness. Only by these acts and by this quality of consciousness can Zen be judged.» What is meant is a certain kind of emptiness and the awareness of the fact that all existence is transcient. Part of this idea is that there is no such thing as a distinction between subject and object. See Merton, Preface, IX.

131 "In 1959 wilde Jasper Johns een schilderij maken met als onderwerp een cirkel. Met een vlakke, draaiende stok trok hij de cirkel. Hij vond dat het niet eerlijk zou zijn de stok weg te halen nu de cirkel voltooid was. De cirkel alleen zou een abstractie op linnen zijn. Met de passer ter plaatse vastgezet werd het schilderij weer een object: een werktekening voor het maken van een cirkel (Device Circle) Het onderwerp, de titel en de vorm van het schilderij vielen plotseling samen." Cit. from Steinberg, 21.

132 "Johns heeft zich in veel opzichten en al sedert meer dan 20 jaar bezig gehouden met problemen die door de schilders op deze tentoonstelling aan de orde worden gesteld. Met name met het hoe van het schilderen, de verfmenging, het opbrengen van de verf, het gebruik van was en ook met de vraag 'wat is een schilderij?' "

133 "De belangrijkste elementen van Kelly's werk zijn vorm en spanning. Een tijdlang maakte hij organische vormen die vaak door de rand van het schilderij worden afgesneden en zich voor het gevoel daarbuiten voortzetten. Hij werkt veel met de tegenstelling zwart-wit, maar ook met felle kleuren, rood, geel, groen, en blauw. Zijn vormen zijn de laatste jaren weer meer geometrisch, af en toe wijkt hij af van de gebruikelijke rechthoekige omtrekvormen en maakt hij schilderijen in de vorm van driehoeken en trapezia die samengesteld zijn uit verschillende doeken. Hiermee en door zijn kleurgebruik bereikt hij soms illusionistische effecten. Zo legt hij er nadruk op dat eens schilderij object en illusionisme tegelijk is."

134 "In de werken op de tentoonstelling worden vormen van illusionisme juist vermeden."

135 "Dit monochrome schilderij is opgebouwd uit banen die in een symmetrisch patroon op het doek gezet zijn, waarbij de omtreksvorm van het schilderij deze structuur volgt. Tussen de banen kan men het doek zien. De breedte van de banen is bepaald door de dikte van het spieraam. Door het gebruik van één kleur en symmetrie in de compositie, wil Stella bewust dieptewerking uitsluiten. Door de relatie van structuur en vorm, door de gelijke breedte van baan en spieraam, door de zichtbaar laten van het doek, door de afwezigheid van dieptewerking, benadrukt Stella het schilderij als object."

136 See Hudson, 152 ff.

137 "In de jaren 50 ontstonden ongeveer gelijktijdig in de USA en Europa vormen van abstracte schilderkunst, waarvoor kenmerkend is dat de verf spontaan, emotioneel en zonder plan op het doek wordt gebracht. In Amerika spreekt men van Abstract Expressionisme en Action Painting, in Europa van Lyrische Abstractie, Informele Kunst en Tachisme. Bij de Amerikaanse schilder Pollock is er geen sprake meer van compositie, de verflijnen en -vlekken vullen het hele doek op een gelij-

kwaardige wijze. De Europese Informelen schilderen vaak vrijwel monochroom, vormelementen ontbreken steeds meer en het schilderij heeft geen centrum meer. Van veel belang is de opperv-laktestructuur van het schilderij. Men herkent soms een uiterlijke overeenkomst in schilderwijze bij de schilders in de tentoonstelling, maar bij hen is meestal een overwogen planning aan het schilderen voorafgegaan."

138 "Sinds 1959 ziet Calderara af van weergave van de werkelijkheid. 'Ik kies horizontalen en verticalen, omdat deze niet in de natuur voorkomen.' Hij vereenvoudigt de vormen tot geometrische vlakken en beperkt zich tot enkele kleuren, die hij echter een grote intensiteit en lichtkracht weet te geven. De kleur lijkt het licht gevangen te houden. Calderara bereikt dit doordat vorm en kleur, maat en ordening onderling afhankelijk zijn in zijn werk. 'Ik zou het Niets willen schilderen, dat het Al is, het zwijgen, het licht. Maat, ordening, harmonie, het oneindige.' Calderara's schilderijen roepen een grote ruimtelijkheid op en zijn in die zin een vorm van abstract illusionisme."

139 "Of het nu wel of niet om de uitbeelding van een voorwerp, van een feit, van een idee of van een dynamisch verschijnsel gaat: de enige waarde van een schilderij ligt in het bestaan, in het totale zijn. Er hoeft niets gezegd te worden, alleen maar te zijn; twee harmoniërende kleuren of twee tonaliteiten van eenzelfde kleur vormen reeds voor de betekenis van een effen onbeperkt, absoluut dynamisch vlak een vreemd element; het oneindige is monochroom (éénkleurig), of beter nog, kleurloos - en is in feite een monochromie waar iedere kleurverhouding ophoudt, niet kleurloos?"

140 Klein signed the constitutive declaration of the New Realist group on 27 October 1960 with "Yves le Monochrome." See "Biography", *Yves Klein Archives*, www.yveskleinarchives.org/documents/bio_us.html.

141 Klein studied oriental languages, Zen philosophy and Judo. After over a year at the Kodokan Institute in Tokyo, he wrote a book entitled *Les fondements du Judo* (Grasset, 1954). Upon his return to France, he founded his own Judo school (1955-59). See for example De Bièvre, 277-281, or Tiampo, Ming. "Abdrücke des Immateriellen: Yves Klein in Japan." In: Morineau, 169.

142 "In 1957 exposeert Yves Klein 12 monochrome schilderijen in ultramarijnblauw, dat volgens hem de meest volkomen uitdrukking van de kleur blauw is. Hij wil er de oneindigheid en het immateriële mee weergeven en verwijst daarbij naar de blauwe wolkenloze hemel. Yves Klein 'de Monochrome' schilderde ook éénkleurige rozenrode en gouden werken. De kleuren hebben voor hem symbolische en mystieke waarden; door de zuivere kleur ondergaat hij de totale vrijheid. Voor Klein moet de kleur alleen zichzelf voorstellen, ontdaan van psychologische tradities. Als formaat kiest hij de rechthoek, die voor hem een kleurig vlak is en geen begrensde kleurige vorm. Om zo anoniem mogelijk te schilderen, verwerpt hij de kwast en gebruikt hij de roller; de persoonlijke distantie tot het schilderij is voor hem van groot belang. De mystiek die Yves Klein aan zijn werk verbindt, ontbreekt geheel bij de schilders in de tentoonstelling."

143 It is unclear who coined the term Minimalism with a capital "M." Judd used the term in an article on the artist Paul Feeley ("In the Galleries"). Philosopher of aesthetics Richard Wollheim used the term "Minimal Art" in an article for *Art Magazine* in January 1965. However, the article did not contain information on artists who are currently connected to this term. Wollheim used it to designate the works of Ad Reinhardt and Marcel Duchamp. The term "Minimal Art" reappeared in 1965 in Barbara Rose's article "ABC Art," which coined the term for the current as we know it today. After this, several art critics as for example Hilton Kramer and Corinne Robins used it in their reports on the show *Primary Structures* of 1966.

144 Lippard, Lucy, and John Chandler. "The Dematerialization of Art." *Art International*, Feb. 1968, pp. 31-36.

145 "Term voor een kunstrichting (2e helft 60er jaren) waarbij de werken een 'minieme kunstinhoud' hebben. Kenmerkend zijn de grote geometrische basisvormen, die associaties met de natuur uitsluiten. Het werk is vaak opgebouwd uit een reeks gelijke vormen, die meer gevoelsmatig dan rationeel zijn gekozen. (Een verschil met de Europese geometrische traditie.) De relatie met de omgeving is belangrijk; de werken worden bv. zonder voetstuk uitgevoerd. Bij het kleurgebruik is er een voorkeur voor wit, grijs en zwart, of de kleur van het materiaal (zie Carl André). De soberheid van vorm en kleur, die de concentratie op het werk als zodanig moet verhogen, herkend men ook

op de tentoonstelling. De 'minimal' kunstenaars stellen de vorm als vorm central, zoals de schilders in de tentoonstelling het schilderen als schilderen."

146 "Het is nooit een kwestie van wat, maar alleen hoe te schilderen. Het hoe ven schilderen is altijd het beeld, het eindproduct, geweest.... Het vierkante formaat is belangrijk. Het lijkt voor mij de meest perfecte vorm.... Witte verf is mijn medium. Die heeft wel met kleur te maken (namelijk de kleur van de ondergrond, de drager, die altijd ergens zichtbaar is)." Qtd. from Tuchmann.

147 "La pittura è un'attività (e una abilità) all'interno della nostra cultura. Il contenuto della pittura (come di tutte le altre cose) muta perciò continuamente. Tali cambiamenti costituiscono la nostra storia; e questo nessuno la può ignorare. Un contenuto si esprime attraverso una forma.... Sono quadri completamente dipinti a mano - in un momento in cui molti artisti si rivolgono ad altri mezzi espressivi (film, fotografia, linguaggio, il loro stesso corpo, luce). Questo contesto culturale da solo dà alla pittura a mano il suo contenuto specifico. Precedentemente (più che in Mondrian) vi è stata uns scelta molto cosciente e deliberata per la pittura - per la pittura in quanto osservazione lenta di qualcosa che appare sotto alle proprie mani."

148 "Abschliessend noch: mich fasziniert diese Art reduzierter Malerei ganz allgemein; weil ich glaube, dass sie voller Skrupel, und mit grosser Vorsicht eine Richtigkeit oder, besser, Verbindlichkeit von Malerei versucht, das sie eine Qualität anstrebt, die zum Gültigen und Allgemeinen tendiert. Das scheint mir wichtig, angesichts einer bedenkenlosen wuchernden Produktivität, die immer unverbindlicher wird."

149 Zeniuk, Conversation with the author, 1 December 2012.

150 "In de maatschappij is ook behoefte aan soberheid en eenvoud" and „In de hele maatschappij is een tendens aanwezig om alles opnieuw te bekijken, om naar de wortels terug te gaan."

151 Lynda Morris writes on this theme: "The combination of minimal sculpture and dematerialization overshadowed the development of minimalist painting in the mid-1960s. Europe became aware of minimal and conceptual work almost simultaneously. As a result painting appeared to be in a less crucial position than sculpture.... A position which left a natural space for painting to continue to question its own function.... The increase in exchanges between Europe and the USA has allowed a younger generation of European painters to develop an important distinction between the intention and the reality of their American models. When a revision occurs in the apparent order of art it also instigates a change in the understanding of existing artists and art objects." To believe Bruno Corà, in the 1970s, European non-objective painting took a new step in consideration on painting as well as towards a methodological definition: It tried to capture the essence of painting in relation to its inherent elements by analyzing the creative process. Corà believes that this focus on process is in fact the novelty (Bonomi 12). This should be considered in the light of the European multi-facetted non-objective, monochrome idiom - Pittura Analitica, Geplante Malerei, Nouvelle Peinture and so on – which is a wide range, yet only a few artists can be considered Fundamental painters. We can accept the opinion of this American critic specialized in the Minimal era, which produced the four American painters that form the core of the *Fundamental Painting* show, who considers it to be the next step after Abstract Expressionism and any painting forming an atmosphere and having a deliberate metaphysical meaning. It once again corresponds to the decisions taken by the curators of the *Fundamental Painting* show, from which the Italians were left out exactly because of these two reasons.

152 Note in this regard that Klaus Honnef confirms the theoretical approach of Italian and French postwar non-objective painters when he writes: "Doch während sich die französischen Künstler und Theoretiker – zahlreiche der ausübenden vertraten beide Positionen in der Personalunion – dem gestellten Problem [neue Malerei in den 70. Jahren] vornehmlich aus ideologischer oder psychoanalytischer Sicht widmeten, untersuchten es die italienischen mit der Sonde der Ästhetiktheorie und der strukturalistischen Linguistik" (*Kunstforum* 127).

153 "Conceptual art loopt vooruit op de doorbraak van een nieuwe mentaliteit, waarbij ook het traditionele kijken in het geding is. Zij zoekt vrijheid van waarnemen. Daniel Buren beschrijft Conceptual Art als een abstract-theoretisch onderzoek naar de essentie van het begrip kunst. Veel anderen beschouwen het als een kunstvorm, waarbij het materiële object door iets immaterieels, nl.

een idée, wordt vervangen. De ideeën betreffen vaak projecten die niet met zintuigen kunnen worden waargenomen; ze doen een beroep op het voorstellingsvermogen van de kijker. In diens geest wordt het kunstwerk als het ware pas voltooid. Veel schilders in deze tentoonstelling benadrukken het belang van het denkproces dat aan hun 'omgaan met verf' voorafgaat."

154 Cit. in WILLOUGHBY, Ian. Czechoslovak *Socialist Realist Art Exhibition opens at Rudolfinum* [online]. Press Release of the show Československý Socialistický Realismus 1948-1958. Praha, Galerie Rudolfinum, 2002. Český Rozhlas, January 2013. http://www.radio.cz/en/section/curraffrs/czechoslovak-socialist-realist-art-exhibition-opens-at-rudolfinum

155 As the Dutch art critic Kaspar Niehaus wrote on 11 August 1937 in the newspaper *De Telegraaf*, "the exhibition shows expressions of contemporary historical events, submarines and all kinds of planes; it likewise shows scenes of injured soldiers helping their peers, scenes of the daily reality of the working class, views of German villages, as well as portraits of peasants, landscapes, floral compositions, and ethnographical objects." (Translated by the author)

156 According to an article by Jan Engelsmann in the art magazine, *Kroniek van Kunst en Kultuur* the categories considered to be "entartete Kunst" by the Nazis were listed as the following: manifestations of the Jewish spirit and signs of cultural Bolshevism, a dismissive view of the Arian female, the mistreatment of heroes and peasants from a Jewish viewpoint, mental illness as well as any method and view of reality from the perspective of an ailing spirit.

157 The Scandinavian inability to arrive at Fundamental Painting might have been strongly influenced by the fact that Scandinavia managed to be excluded from WWII and therefore the effects and reactions on the artistic scene were not the same as in other countries in Western Europe. Rini Dippel mentioned in an interview with the author on 26 August 2011, that the curators did search also in Scandinavia but did not find anything that would come close to Fundamental Painting. The same could be said for Switzerland.

158 Note the word lyricism (cf. Analytic Abstraction). In 1953, Germany produced Group 53 (Informal painting), based on contacts with France. According to Klaus Honnef, the pivotal figure of this group was the painter Winfred Gaul. Also according to him, Gaul influenced Analytical Abstraction in Italy, where he partially lived (129). This might explain the German-Italian nature of "geplante Malerei" (Planned painting), coined by Honnef. In any case, once again it would underline its difference with Fundamental Painting. Remember Dippel's statement that Fundamental Painting is an attitude that strongly differs from informal art and also lyrical abstraction (FP 11).

159 "... untersuchten es [*neue Malerei* in den 70. Jahren] die italienischen [Künstler] mit der Sonde der Ästhetiktheorie un der strukturalistischen Linguistik."

160 The only "new" group of painters in France was most likely BMPT (1966-1967). It consisted of artists Daniel Buren, Olivier Mosset, Michel Parmentier and Niele Toroni. They were a group of conceptual painters. Each of the artists had a "trademark" way of painting, like a symbol on a monochromatic ground: verticals or horizontals, squares or circles. Their approach demanded that they decline communication of any kind of message and transmition of any kind of emotion through painting.

161 "Doch während sich die französischen Künstler und Theoretiker – zahlreiche der ausübenden vertraten beide Positionen in der Personalunion – dem gestellten Problem [*neue Malerei* in den 70. Jahren] vornehmlich aus ideologischer oder psychoanalytischer Sicht widmeten ...."

162 "la diffusion de l'art concret après 1950, en Europe, particulièrement en France, Suisse et Italie".

163 „Klub konkretistů byl tady [v Praze] v té době strašně radikální. Pak přijedu do Holandska a vidím, že ve srovnání s jejich skupinou Nul, která dělala opravdu radikální abstrakci, to byl takový trochu slaboduchý konstruktivismus."

164 It is interesting how painting in the Netherlands, the United Kingdom, and postwar New York shows Mondrian's influence. In the early 20th century he was a main representative of De Stijl. However, in Paris he and Van Doesburg embarked on separate paths. While Van Doesburg arrived at his Manifesto of Art Concret, Mondrian developed his intuitive geometric two-dimensional painting style. It is to be noted that Van Doesburg promoted the synthesis of the arts, while Mondrian always was a pure painter aiming at painting that unfolds on the two-dimensional surface

– as his lifetime work shows. Thus, although the curators of the *Fundamental Painting* show only mention Mondrian in relation to Malevich – who is indisputably influential in introducing paint as a material and non-objective painting as a new start (as seen in Part II) – and cite the Manifesto of Art Concret as the key text, it must be concluded that, based on historical fact, it is more likely Mondrian who was the "catalyst" for postwar American painting and, above all, Fundamental Painting.

165 Paraphrased from a conversation between Jerry Zeniuk and Marcia Hafif at the time that both were members of the Radical Painting group, quoted by Zeniuk in conversation with the author on 1 December 2012.

166 „[Fundamentální malba] je něco, co zde [v Československu] nikdy nebylo. Propásli situaci chtít něco takového tady. Nemají to tady, nechtějí to tady a nikdy ani chtít nebudou. U nás něco takového neakceptujeme. Tady chceme mít umění s příběhem."

167 "zmapovat tehdější specificky české směrování k abstrakci" and "Tzv. abstrakní umění se svými přednostně formálními aspekty nenašlo v Čechách ani tehdy, ani v budoucnu dostatečně živnou půdu. České umění vždy znovu zavazuje určité téma…."

168 "Než jsem odešel do zahraničí, zabýval jsem se lineárními strukturami, které měly pravděpodobně svůj původ v kresbách Kleeových, protože to byl jeden z umělců, o kterém jsme v tehdejší izolaci alespoň něco věděli." Tomas Rajlich in conversation with the author, 12 July 2012.

169 "Česká výtvarná scéna nebyla od těchto [západních] tendencí zcela odříznuta – v roce 1968 se v Praze například uskutečnila výstava Yvese Kleina –, zahraniční vývoj však sledovala jen z povzdálí a zprostředkovaně."

170 "Zásadní vliv na mě ale měla výstava Yvese Kleina v Národní galerii, která mi potvrdila, že je možno dělat úplně jiné věci, než se považovaly za uznané umění." Tomas Rajlich in conversation with the author, 12 July 2012.

171 "Klasická malba byla na konci šedesátých let prohlašována za mrtvou. V Americe slavili první úspěchy minimalisté, v Evropě pak umělci spjatí s mezinárodní skupinou ZERO (v té době již oficiálně rozpuštěnou), která také zkoumala možnosti výtvarného jazyka oproštěného na minimum. Současně se rozvíjelo konceptuální umění i neodadaistický Fluxus."

172 "[Holandsko] se na mě určitě také podepsalo. Je jiné než všechny ostatní země a holandské světlo je takové správné – vermeerovské."

173 "Praha nijak zvlášť' důležitá nebyla...", and „Na druhou stranu ale takový Ryman by zlatou barvu do ruky nikdy nevzal. Něco z českého baroka ve mně asi bude."

174 Participating artists: Hermann Bartels, Willi Baumeister, Claude Bellgarde, Enrico Borndoni, Enrico Castellani, Serge Charchoune, Piero Dorazio, Klaus Jürgen Fischer, Lucio Fontana, Johannes Geccelli, Ruprecht Geiger, Ernst Geitlinger, Raimund Girke, Raymon Grandjean, Oskar Holweck, Nicolas Ionesco, Yves Klein (Le Monochrome), Yayoi Kusama, Walter Leblanc, Rudolf Leuzinger, Francesco Lo Savio, Heinz Mack, Piero Manzoni, Georges Mathieu, Almir Mavignier, Christian Megert, Herbert Oehm, Otto Piene, Lothar Quinte, Arnulf Rainer, Mark Rothko, Ralph Rumney, Salvator Scarpitta, Günther Wolfram Sellung, Antonio Tapiès, Günther Uecker, Paul van Hoeydonck, Jeff Verheyen, Mark Verdstockt, and Hans-Peter Vorberg.

175 Citing KRAMER, Hilton. "The New Line: Minimalism is Americanism," *New York Times*, 26 March 1978, section D, p. 26; and referring to FOSTER, Hal. "The Crux of Minimalism." in: SINGERMAN, Howard, ed. *Individuals: A Selected History of Contemporary Art 1945-86.* Los Angeles: Museum of Contemporary Art, 1986, p. 173.

176 "La question de savoir si c'est de l'art ou pas importe peu. Je suis très hésitante lorsque j'emploie ce terme qui devient de moins en moins précis. C'est quelque chose qui se vit, qui se transforme en vivant. C'est en tout cas quelque chose qui donne l'impression de participer à la pulsation profonde de la nature des choses, et par le fait même, sans doute, de soi-même. Une sorte d'accord qui se fait et qui se vit. Ou qui est provoqué. Ce qu'il en reste devrait, en principe, à son tour le provoquer, pour autant qu'il y ait disponibilité."

177 "je me fais une certaine idée de la peinture mais … au fond 'peinture' n'est pas autre chose qu'une idée que je me fais de l'autre. Cet autre, c'est peut-être un souvenir."

178 "De schilders in deze tentoonstelling staan ver af van verwijzingen naar het metafysische, het oneindige, het abstract-sublieme…"

179 "De mystiek die Yves Klein aan zijn werk verbindt, ontbreekt geheel bij de schilders in de tentoonstelling."

180 "avec la peinture re-tenir mon destin puisque, comme chacun le sait, la peinture est faite 'd'immortel chef d'œuvre'. A entendre ici quelque chose, je postule qu'il n'est rien dit qui ne sorte de l'ordinaire, à savoir, en fin de compte au sujet face à la loi de la mort, loi qui s'inscrit dans tout corps comme mécanisme, comme immuabilité et comme finitude de ce par quoi il se sent vivre : son langage. Voilà donc mon langage ; il ressemble fort à une entreprise de séduction, il n'en dit pas moins pour autant une des spécificités propres à la peinture et j'allais oublier….propre au métier de peintre."

181 Lippard used the word *silent* for works by both the Abstract Expressionist and Minimalist painters, as well as Yves Klein. Weinmann used the word to refer to work across ages that lead to a slow revelation, as opposed to those who instantly touch us emotionally, throughout her teachings.

182 Cf. Hegel. See also Groys, 105-109.

183 Note that Mangold is "not trying to deny the role of emotion when planning the painting and then working on it, or when someone else is viewing it. However, [he does] not think of the final work as essentially emotional; [he sees] it also as logical and reasoned," as he explains in "Interview with Sylvia Plimack Mangold" (Schiff 66).

184 Term first used by Paul Signac when writing on an exhibition by Pierre Bonnard in 1933. Cited in *Paris-New York 1991-1992*, p. 303, note 198.

All references to online sources were correct at the time of writing.

BIBLIOGRAPHY

The following is a select bibliography, which does not purport to be complete, but includes all works cited in the study (including the page numbers, except for unpaginated and single-page works).
The abbreviation FP indicates the 1975 exhibition *Fundamentele Schilderkunst/Fundamental Painting* by Rini Dippel. Unpublished documents are held in the Stedelijk Museum Amsterdam archives, parts of which have been transferred to the Stadsarchief Amsterdam and digitalized (Access number 30041, Folders 4847-4852). These documents bear numbers starting with "STED." Furthermore, a number of newspaper clippings can be found archived in the Press Documentation department of the Rijksdienst Kunsthistorische Documentatie – Netherlands Institute or Art History in the folder *Fundamentele Schilderkunst*. These are indicated in the bibliography here below as "RKD."

Various uncited but valuable works are also listed here by way of recommendation to those interested in further exploring points addressed in this study. Equally valuable works dealing with related movements, philosophies, or later developments of specific artists are not included.

AGEE, WILLIAM C., and Susan C. Faxon. *Coming of Age: American Art 1850s to 1950s*. Yale UP, 2006.

ALLOWAY, Lawrence. *Systemic Painting*. Solomon R. Guggenheim Museum, 1966.

ANFAM, David. *Mark Rothko – The Works on Canvas: Catalogue Raisonné.* Yale UP, 1999.

ARNASON, H.H., ed. *A History of Modern Art.* Rev. and updated by Daniel Wheeler, 3rd ed., Thames & Hudson, 1988.

ASHTON, Dore. "The Avant-Garde: Subtle, Cerebral, Elusive." *Time*, 92/21, 22 Nov. 1968, pp. 70-77.

- - -. "Jake Berthot." *Arts Magazine*, 48, June 1974, pp. 33-34. *Jake Berthot*, Minneapolis (MN), Locksley Shea Gallery, 1974, n. pag.

Avenue. May 1975, p. 40.

BAKER, Kenneth. *Minimalism: Art of Circumstance*. Abbeville, 1988.

BATTCOCK, Gregory, ed. *Minimal Art: A Critical Anthology.* E.P. Dutton, 1968.

BEENKER, Erik. "Niks essentieels." *Nieuwsblad van het Noorden*, 25 June 1975, p. 15.

BERTHOT, Jake. Statement for *Fundamental Painting*, 1974. STED10087256518.

BERTLER, Matt, creator. *Jake Berthot. Youtube*, uploaded by Betty Cuningham Galllery, 12 Apr. 2012, www.youtube.com/watch?v=43rxLw_7B1A.

BILL, Max. Moderne Kunst aus der Sammlung Peggy Guggenheim. Poster. Kunsthaus Zürich, 1951. https://www.moma.org/collection/works/6093

BLESS, Frits. "Fundamentele schilderkunst – een nieuw begin? Terug naar de basis." *De Gelderlander*, 20 June 1975. RKD.

BLOK, Cor. "Hoe fundamenteel is fundamentale schilderkunst?" *De Groene Amsterdammer*, 4 June 1975, p. 17.

- - -. "Holland." *Studio International*, 190/976, July/Aug. 1975, pp. 74-75.

- - -, ed. *Nederlandse Kunst vanaf 1900*. Teleac, 1994.

BOCHNER, Mel. "Excerpts from Speculation [1967-1970]." *Artforum*, 8/9, May 1970, pp. 70-73.

- - -. "Serial Art, Systems, Solipsism." *Arts Magazine*, 41/8, Summer 1967, pp. 39-43. Battcock, pp. 92-102.

- - -. "The Serial Attitude." *Artforum*, 6/4, Dec. 1967, pp. 28-33.

BODE, Arnold. *Documenta, Kunst des XX. Jahrhunderts. Internationale Ausstellun*g. Reprint. Prestel, 1995.

BOIS, Yve-Alain. "Cézanne: Words and Deeds." Translated by Rosalind Krauss. *October*, 84, Spring 1998, pp. 31-43.

BONGARD, W. "Confidential information about the international Art Scene." *Art Aktuell*, 2/5, Jan. 1975, n. pag. STED10087256444-47.

BONITO OLIVA, Achille, et al. *Contemporanea*. Firenze, Centro Di, 1973.

BONOMI, Giorgio, et al. *Pittura70: Pittura Pittura e Astrazione Analitica.* Chiavari, Fondazione Zappettini, 2004.

BOUDAILLE, Georges, and Cathérine Millet. *Nouvelle peinture en France: pratiques, theories.* Saint-Étienne, Musée d'Art et d'Industrie, 1974.

BROOS, Kees. Interview with Tomas Rajlich, Spring 1975. Archives of the artist, Prague.

BUCHLOCH, Benjamin. "From faktura to factography." *October*, 30, Autumn 1984, pp. 82-119.

BUCHMANN, Sabeth. "The (Re)Animation of Medium Specificity in Contemporary Art." Dumbadze, Alexander, and Suzanne Hudson. *Contemporary Art: 1989 to present.* Wiley-Blackwell, 2013, pp. 107-116.

BUETTNER, Stewart. *American Art Theory: 1945-1970.* UMI Research P, 1981.

BUREN, Daniel. *The Ineffable - About Ryman's Work*. Jannink, 1999.

CANE, Louis. "Peinture fondamentale." *Art Press*, 10, July 1975, pp. 28-29.

- - -. "Le métier de peintre." Dec. 1974. STED10087256522-25. Statement.

CARRIER, David. "Robert Ryman on the Origins of His Art." *Burlington Magazine*, 139/1134, Sept. 1997, pp. 631-633.

CELANT, Germant, et al. *Arte come arte*. Milan, Centro Comunitario di Brera, 1973.

CENTRE GEORGES POMPIDOU. *Paris-New York 1908-1968*. Gallimard, 1991.

CHARLTON, Alan. *Alan Charlton: Immagine della Luce. Youtube*, uploaded by Villa Clerici, 12 May 2012, https://www.youtube.com/watch?v=rPrypXk2LuY.

- - -. *I am an artist who makes a grey painting*. Directed by Mark James, produced by Julian Harvey, London, M.J. Mood, 1990.

- - -. Letter to the author, 4 July 2012. Archives of the author, Zurich.

- - -. Letter to Edy de Wilde, 6 March 1975. STED10087255932. Statement.

- - -. "Es sind Bilder ganz entscheiden: ein Gespräch mit Doris von Drahten.» *Kunstforum International*, 108, June/July 1990, pp. 228-237.

CHILVERS, Ian, and John Glaves-Smith. *A Dictionary of Modern and Contemporary Art,* 2nd ed, Oxford UP, 2009.

CLAURA, Michel, and René Denizot. *Une exposition de peinture réunissant certains peintres qui mettraient la peinture en question*. Paris, 1973.

COLLOVINI, Diego. *Suoni della superficie*. Portogruaro, Galleria Comunale „Ai molini," 2001.

COLPITT, Frances. *Minimal Art: The Critical Perspective*. Washington UP, 1997.

CORTENOVA, Giorgio. *Empirica: l'arte tra addizione e sottrazione.* Ripalta, 1975.

- - -. "Grado Zero." Galleria La Bertesca, [circa 1974-75]. Archives of the Stedelijk Museum Amsterdam.

- - - . *Mostra Internazionale d'Arte. Un Futuro Possibile – Nuova Pittura.* Ferrara, Palazzo dei Diamanti, 1973.

CORTENOVA, Giorgio et al. *Cronaca: Percorso didattico attraverso la pittura americana degli anni 60 e la pittura europea degli anni 70.* Modena, Galleria Civica, 1976.

CRIMP, Douglas. "Opaque Surfaces." *Arte come arte*. Milan, Centro Comunitario di Brera, 1973. *Minimalism*, edited by James Meyer, Phaidon, 2007, pp. 257-260.

DE BIÈVRE, Guy. "A Full Void." *Voids.* JPG-Ringier, 2009.

DE BOER, Cees, and Uwe Rüth. *Aspekte Niederländischer Kunst heute*. Marl, Skulpturenmuseum Glaskasten 1996.

DE CARPENTER, Jan. "Kijk eens Kunst" *Dagblad voor de Zaanstreek*, 7 May 1975, n. pag.

DEUTSCHE KÜNSTLERBUND. *Abstrakt.* Cantz, 1993.

DEWEY, John. *Art as Experience*. Perigee, 1980.

DE WILDE, Edy. Introductory speech to *Fundamental Painting* [1975]. STED10087256436-37.

- - -. Letter to Count Panza di Biumo, 3 Dec. 1974. STED10087256420.

- - -. Letter to Count Panza di Biumo, 1 July 1975. STED10087256371.

- - -. Letter to Klaus Honnef, 7 Feb. 1975. STED10087256229.

- - -. Letter to Richard Jackson, 30 June 1975. STED10087256150.

DIAMONSTEIN-SPIELVOGEL, Barbaralee. "Inside New York's Art World: Robert Ryman." *Youtube*, uploaded by DukeLibDigitalColl, 15 Dec. 2008, https://www.youtube.com/watch?v=g-P3LwTFj488.

DIPPEL, Rini. "Fundamental Painting." *Peinture, cahiers théoriques*, 10 Nov. 1975, pp. 192-200.

- - -. *Fundamentele Schilderkunst = Fundamental Painting*. Translated by Ina Rike. Preface by Edy de Wilde, Stedelijk Museum Amsterdam, 1975, pp. 10-16.

- - -. *Fundamental Painting*, 1979. Archives of the Stedelijk Museum Amsterdam, *Fundamental Painting.* CD839.

- - -. "Gereduceerde Schilderkunst." STED10087256452-53.

- - -. Letter to Douglas Crimp, 2 July 1975. STED10087255933.

- - -. Letter to Edy de Wilde, 10 Jan. 1975. STED10087256458.

- - -. Letter to Naomi Spector, 4 Dec. 1974. STED10087256036.

- - -. Note to Edy de Wilde. 6 Feb. [1975]. STED10087256538.

- - -. Note to Edy de Wilde [circa 1975]. STED10087256531.

- - - ."Schilderkunst als schilderkunst. Naar aanleiding van de tentoonstelling 'Fundamentele schilderkunst' 1975." Imanse, pp. 174-198.

- - -. "Verslag: New York, New York, 10-19 december 1974." 3 Jan. 1975. STED10087256508-11.

D'ORGEVAL Domitille. "Le Salon des Réalités Nouvelles: Pour et contre l'art concret. "Lemoine, et al., pp. 24-39.

EIJKELBOOM, Jan. "Stille schilderijen in Amsterdams Stedelijk." *Het Vrije Volk*, 22 May 1975, p. 17.

ENGELHARD, Günter. "Calvinisten der Leinwand: Fundamentale Malerei in Amsterdam." *Deutsche Zeitung*, 9 May 1975, p. 10.

- - -. "Malerei heute." *Die Weltwoche*, 1975. RKD.

ENGELMAN, Jan. *Kroniek van Kunst en Kultuur.* 1975. RKD.

FEIERABEND, Volker, and Marco Meneguzzo, eds. *Pittura analitica: Una ricognizione storica. Italia 1966-1978.* Galleria Fumagalli, 2008.

FER, Briony. *The Infinite Line: Re-Making Art after Modernism*. Yale UP, 2004.

FERRETTI-BOCQUILLON, Marina et al. *Signac, 1863-1935*. Yale UP, 2001.

FORMA 1. "Il Manifesto Forma 1 (marzo 1947)". *Slideshare*, uploaded by Carla Accardi, 24 Feb. 2016, www.slideshare.net/siciliambiente/attpt-carla-accardi.

FRENKEN, Ton. "Het Stedelijk signaleert een recente stroming. Grondlagen van het schilderij." *Eindhovensch Dagblad*, 17 May 1975, RKD.

FRIED, Michael. "Art and Objecthood." *Artforum*, 5/10, June 1967, pp. 12-23.

- - -. "Shape as Form." *Artforum*, 5/3, Nov. 1966, pp. 18-27.

FRITZ-JOBSE, Jonneke. *De Stijl Continued*. 010 Publishers, 2005.

FUCHS, Rudi, et al. *Donald Judd*. Distributed Art Publishers, 2004.

"Fundamenteel op Komst." *Uitkrant*, 9/8, Apr. 1975, p. 8.

GACHNANG, Johannes. Letter to Edy de Wilde, 6 Feb. 1975. STED10087256170.

GALERIE NÄCHST ST. STEPHAN. *Abstract Painting of America and Europe*. Ritter, 1988.

GARRELS, Gary. *Robert Ryman*. Dia Art Foundation, 1989.

GAUL, Winfred. Letter to Edy de Wilde, 18 Mar. 1975. Archives of the Stedelijk Museum Amsterdam, *Fundamental Painting*.

GIRKE, Raimund. Statement for *Fundamental Painting*, 9 Mar. 1975. STED10087255947.

GLASER, Bruce. "Questions to Stella and Judd." *Art News*, 65/5, Sept. 1966, pp. 55-61. Battcock, pp. 148-164.

GLIMCHER, Arne. *Agnes Martin: Paintings, Writings, Remembrances*. Phaidon, 2012.

GRANT, Simon. "Artist Piet Mondrian in London: The Forgotten Years." *The Guardian*, 25 June 2010, www.guardian.co.uk/artanddesign/2010/jun/25/artist-piet-mondrian-london-years.

GREENBERG, Clement. "After Abstract Expressionism." *Art International,* 6/8, 25 Oct. 1962, pp. 24-32. *Clement Greenberg: The Collected Essays and Criticism*, edited by John O'Brian, Vol. 4, U of Chicago P, 1993, pp. 121-133.

- - -. "Modernist Painting." *Clement Greenberg: The Collected Essays and Criticism. e*dited by John O'Brian, Vol. 4, U of Chicago P, 1993, pp. 85-93.

GROYS, Boris. "The Suffering Picture." *Das Bild nach dem letzten Bild*, edited by Peter Weibel, Walther König, 1991, pp. 99-111.

GRUEN, John. "Robert Mangold: 'A Maker of Images – Nothing More and Nothing Less'." *Artnews*, 86/6, Summer 1987, pp. 132-136.

HAASE, Amine. "'Fundamentale Malerei' im Amsterdamer Stedelijk-Museum; Ein Kunsttrend aus der Retorte?" *Rheinische Post*, 9 June 1975, RKD.

HAFIF, Marcia. "True Colors." *Art in America*, 77/6, June 1989, pp. 128-139.

- - -. "On Composition." *Malerei Pur*, Kiel, Gesellschaft fur akustische Lebenshilfe, 1991, n. pag.

- - -. "Why Paint, 1989." *Marcia Hafif,* Neuss, Galerie Conrads, 1990, n. pag.

- - -. "Robert Ryman: Another View." *Art in America*, 67/5, Sept. 1979, pp. 88-89.

HARRISON, Charles, and Paul Wood, eds. *Art in Theory, 1900–2000: An Anthology of Changing Ideas*. Blackwell, 1996.

HASKELL, Barbara. *Agnes Martin*. Harry N. Abrams, 1992.

HERMERÉN, Göran. *Representation and meaning in the visual arts.* Lund UP, 1969.

HONNEF, Klaus. "Die geplante und analytische, fundamentale und elementare Malerei – bevor sie radikal wurde: die siebziger Jahre." *Kunstforum International,* 88, Mar.-Apr. 1987, pp. 127-133.

- - -. "Analytische Malerei." *Geplante Malerei*. Galleria del Millione, 1974.

- - -. *Geplante Malerei*. Westfälischer Kunstverein, 1974.

- - -. Letter to Edy de Wilde, 4 Feb. 1975. STED10087256230.

HONNEF, Klaus, and Cathérine Millet. *Analytische Malerei/Analytic Painting/Peinture analytique/Pittura Analitica*. Masnata, 1975.

HUDSON, Suzanne P. *Robert Ryman: Used Paint*. MIT Press, 2009.

IMANSE, Geurt, ed. *De Nederlandse Identiteit in de Kunst na 1945*. Meulenhoff/Landshoff, 1984.

JACKSON, Richard. "Interview Richard Jackson at Art Cologne 2016." *Youtube*, uploaded by VernissageTV, 14 Apr. 2016, https://www.youtube.com/watch?v=yMhqrriNA2o.

JOBSE, Jonneke. "Schilderen met de borstel." *NRC Handelsblad*, 12 Dec. 1975, p. CS.

JUDD, Donald. *Complete Writings 1959-75.* New York UP, 1975.

- - -. "In the Galleries: Paul Feeley." *Arts Magazine,* 34/8, May 1960, pp. 60-61.

- - -. "Specific Objects." *Arts Yearbook* 8, Art Digest, 1965, pp. 74-82. www.juddfoundation.org/ _literature_108163 /Specific_Objects.

JUFFERMANS, Jan. "Schilderen om het schilderen." *Algemeen Dagblad*, 3 May 1975, p. 23.

- - -. "Schilderijen zonder poespas." *De nieuwe linie*, 21 May 1975, p. 9.

KAAL, Ron. "Oude koek in een nieuw trommeltje." *Haagsche Courant*, 1975, pp. 44-45.

KANDINSKY, Wassily. *Concerning the Spiritual in Art.* 1911. Dover Publications, 1977.

- - -. Papers 1911-44. 1913. Getty Research Institute, inv. 850910. KANDINSKY, Wassily. *Kandinsky: Complete Writings on Art*, edited by Kenneth C. Lindsey and Peter Vergo, Da Capo, 1994.

- - -. *Point and Line to Plane*. 1926. Dover Publications, 1979.

KARSHAN, Donald. *Specific Object: Conceptual Art and Conceptual Aspects.* New York Cultural Center, 1970.

KAY, Reed. *The Painter's Companion.* Webb Books, 1961.

KEERS, Frits, and Geert van Beijeren. "Grenzen van de schilderkunst (1e opzet)." [1974]. STED10087256451.

KELK, Fanny. "Saaie tentoonstelling." *Het Parool*, 22 May 1975, RKD.

KINLEY, Catherine. Interview with Robert Ryman, 11 April 1992; and Zelevansky, Lynn. Interview with Robert Ryman, 1 to 7 July 1992. Qtd. in: Kinley, Catherine, and Lynn Zelevansky, "Catalogue Notes". Storr, p. 44.

KLEE, Paul. *Beiträge zur bildnerischen Formlehre.* Schwabe Verlag, 1979.

KRAMER, Hilton. "An Art of Boredom?" *New York Times,* 5 June 1966, section 2, pp. 145.

KRAMPEN, Martin, ed. Observation and Formulation: Foundation course with exercises, based on a film script by Josef Albers. DVD and booklet. Hatje Cantz, 2009.

KRAUS, Živa, et al. *La Biennale di Venezia 1978: from nature to art, from art to nature*. Electa, 1978.

KRAUSS, Rosalind. *Bachelors.* MIT Press, 1999.

- - -. "Grids." *The Originality of the Avant-Garde and other Modernist Myths*, MIT Press, 1985, pp. 9-22.

KUBLER, George. *The shape of time: remarks on the history of things*. Yale UP, 1962.

KÜCKELS, Barbara. *Bilder ohne Bilder*. Rheinland-Verlag, [1977].

KULTERMANN, Udo. *Monochrome Malerei.* Städtisches Museum Morsbroich, 1960.

Kunst & Cultuur. 8/10, 16 May 1975, RKD.

Kunst Echo's, 4/5, 15 May 1975, RKD.

KUNSTVEREIN ARNSBERG. *Fundamentale Malerei*, 1988. Poster.

KURTZ, Bruce. "Documenta 5: A Critical Preview. Interview with Robert Ryman." *Arts Magazine*, 46/8, Summer 1972, pp. 30-43.

KUSPIT, Donald. "Robert Ryman: Reductionism – Entropy." *Art in America*, 67/4, July/Aug. 1979, pp. 88-89.

LAMARCHE-VADEL, Bernard, and Susanne Pagé. *Abstraction Analytique: Fractures du monochrome aujourd'hui*. ARC - Musée d'art moderne de la Ville de Paris, 1978.

LAMBERTINI, Luigi, and Lara-Vinca Masini. *Tempi di percezione.* Livorno, Casa della Cultura, 1973.

LANCE, Mary. *Agnes Martin: With My Back to the World*. New Deal Films, 2003.

LA ROCCO, Ben. "Stephen Rosenthal 06-08." *The Brooklyn Rail: Critical Perspectives on Arts, Politics, and Culture*, May 2008, www.brooklynrail.org/2008/05/artseen/stephen-rosenthal-0608-paintings.

LEMOINE, Serge, et al. *Art Concret.* Réunion des musées nationaux, 2000.

LEMOINE, Serge. "Un siècle d'art concret." Lemoine, et al. pp. 11-14.

LIPPARD, Lucy R. "After a Fashion: The Group Show." *Hudson Review,* 19/4, Winter 1966-67, pp. 620-626.

- - -. "New York Letter: Recent Sculpture as Escape." *Art International, 10/2,* Feb. 1966, pp. 48+.

- - -. "The Silent Art." *Art in America*, 55/1, Jan.-Feb. 1967, pp. 58-63.

- - -. "As Painting is to Sculpture: A Changing Ratio." *American Sculpture of the Sixties* by Maurice Tuchman, Los Angeles County Museum of Art, 1967, pp. 31-36.

LIPPARD, Lucy, and John Chandler. "The Dematerialization of Art." *Art International*, Feb. 1968, pp. 31-36.

MALEVICH, Kazimir. "From Cubism and Futurism to Suprematism: The New Realism in Painting." 1916. *Art in Theory, 1900–2000: An Anthology of Changing Ideas*, edited by Charles Harrison and Paul Wood, Blackwell, 1996, pp. 166–176.

- - -. *The Non-Objective World: The Manifesto of Suprematism.* 1927. Dover Publications, 2003.

MANCUSI-UNGARO, Carol. Interview with Brice Marden, 1 Sept.1992. Menil Collection Archives, Houston, adp.menil.org/?page_id=60.

- - -. "Marden's Materiality: The Monochromes." *Plane Image: A Brice Marden Retrospective*, edited by Garry Garrels, Museum of Modern Art, 2006, pp. 110-119.

MANGOLD, Robert. "Interview by Robin White." *View*, 1/7. Dec. 1978, pp. 1-24.

- - -. "Interview with Sylvia Plimack Mangold." *Robert Mangold*, texts by Richard Schiff et al. Phaidon, 2000, pp. 59-69.

- - -. "Thoughts on my Work." 1975. STED10087256519. Statement.

MARDEN, Brice. *Brice Marden*. Solomon R. Guggenheim Foundation, 1975.

- - -. *On Blocks*. 1976. Youtube, uploaded by svsugcarter, 25 Feb. 2008, www.youtube.com/watch?v=W0WT-QAU_ik.

- - -. Statement for *Fundamental Painting*. STED10087256215.

- - -. "Brice Marden on Newman and Rothko." *Youtube*, uploaded by FLYPMedia, 1 May 2009, www.youtube.com/watch?v=l2I4oxEC3vU.

MARKOV, Vladimír. *Faktura.* St. Petersburg, Soyuz Molodezni, 1914.

MARTIN, Agnes. *Gabriel.* 1976. 28 Oct. 2011, Theater 2, MoMA, New York. Screening.

MATHIEU, Georges. *De la révolte à la renaissance: au-delà du Tachisme*. Gallimard, 1973.

McEVILLEY, Thomas. "Absence Made Visible." *Artforum*, 30/10, Summer 1992, pp. 92-96.

MENEGUZZO, Marco. *Analytica.* Annotazione d'Arte, 2008.

- - -. *Pittura Analytica.* Galliate, Castello Visconteo-Sforzesco, 2003.

MENNA, Filiberto, et al. *La riflessione sulla pittura.* Acireale, Palazzo Comunale, 1973.
MERTON, Thomas. *Mystics and Zen Masters*. Farrar, Straus and Giroux, 1967.
MIGNOT, Dorine. "Werkbespreking *Grenzen.*" 16 Jan. 1975. STED10087256505.
MILLER, Dorothy. *The New American Painting as Shown in Eight European Countries 1958-1959.* MoMA, 1959, www.moma.org/documents/moma_catalogue_1990_300190211.pdf
MILLET, Catherine. *La grande histoire de la peinture moderne. Tendances d'aujourd'hui : 1960-1980.* Vol. 6. Skira, 1982.
Minimalism Germany 1960s. Press release. Berlin, Daimler Contemporary, 2010. http://art.daimler.com/en/minimalism-germany-1960s-2/
MININI, Massimo. "Girando per l'Europa" *Brescia Oggi*, 24 May 1975, RKD.
MORINEAU, Camille, ed. *Yves Klein*. Centre Georges Pompidou, 2006.
MORRIS, Lynda. "Strata: Paintings, Drawings, and Prints." *Studio International*, 187/963, Feb. 1974, pp. Review 12-13.
MORRIS, Robert. "Notes on Sculpture [Part 1]." *Artforum*, 4/6, Jan. 1966, pp. 42-44.
- - -. "Notes on Sculpture [Part 2]." *Artforum*, 5/2, Oct. 1966, pp. 20-23.
- - -. "Notes on Sculpture [Part 3]." *Artforum*, 5/10, June 1967, pp. 24-29.
- - -. "Notes on Sculpture [Part 4]." *Artforum*, 7/8, Apr. 1969, pp. 50-54.
MUSSA, Italo. *I colori della pittura: Una situazione europea = Colours in Painting: A European Situation.* Rome, Istituto Italo-Latino Americano, 1976.
MYERS, Bernard. "Postwar Art in Germany." *College Art Journal*, 10/3, Spring 1951 pp. 251+.
NAMUTH, Hans. *Pollock Painting in Action. Making Sense of Modern Art.* San Francisco Museum of Modern Art, 2000.
- - -. "Hans Namuth – Pollock Painting (1951)." *Youtube*, uploaded by Avant Garde, 24 April 2013, www.youtube.com/watch?v=KNwvUco146c.
NEWMAN, Barnett. "Barnett Newman Interview." *Youtube*, uploaded by ChromaticHouse, 26 May 2010, https://www.youtube.com/watch?v=N6sU6ft9Xjg
- - -. *Barnett Newman: Selected Writings and Interviews.* Edited by John P. O'Neill, U of California P, 1992.
- - -. "Newman speaks about his art." *Youtube*, uploaded by Kunstspektrum, 5 March 2014, www.youtube.com/watch?v=e2c0h1wnxf0.
- - -. "The Sublime Is Now." *Tiger's Eye*, 1/6, Dec. 1948, pp. 51-53. *Art in Theory 1900-1990*, edited by Charles Harrison and Paul Wood, Blackwell, 1996, pp. 572-574.
NIEHAUS, Kaspar. "Kunstmanifestatie van het Derde Rijk." *De Telegraaf*, 11 Aug. 1937 (Evening ed.), p. 37.
NODELMAN, Sheldon. "Sixties Art: Some Philosophical Perspectives." *Perspecta: Yale Architectural Journal*, 11, 1967, pp. 72-89.
OBIER, Uwe. *Von der Ungleichheit des Ähnlichen in der Kunst.* Lüdenscheid, Städtische Galerie, 1983.
OSTROW, Saul. "Brice Marden by Saul Ostrow." *Bomb – Artists in Conversation*, 22, Winter 1988, bombsite.com/issues/22/articles/985.
OUT, Nico, et al. *Zesmaal schilderen.* Vlissingen, Culturele Raad, 1987.
PANOFSKY, Erwin. "Three Decades of Art History in the United States: Impressions of a Transplanted European." 1955. *Meaning in the Visual Arts,* edited by Irving Lavin, Princeton, Institute for Advanced Study, 1995, pp. 321-346.

PETERS, Philip. "The Metaphysical Monochrome or the perfect painting?" *Tomas Rajlich 1969-1993,* Brescia, Palazzo Martinengo, 1993, n. pag.
PINCUS-WITTEN, Robert. "Robert. Ryman, Marden, Manzoni: Theory, Sensibility, Mediation." *Artforum*, 10/10, June 1972, pp. 50-53.
- - -. "'Systemic' Painting." *Artforum*, 5/3, Nov. 1966, pp. 42-45.
POTTER, Keith. *Four Musical Minimalists: La Monte Young, Terry Riley, Steve Reich, Philip Glass.* Cambridge UP, 2002.
RAJLICH, Claudia. "La Série des Looped Line Zone Paintings de Robert Mangold: leurs éléments et antécédents, leurs influences et signification." DEA d'histoire de l'art, directed by Serge Lemoine, Université Paris IV – Sorbonne, 2001.
RAUSSMÜLLER, Urs, ed. *Robert Mangold.* Hallen für Neue Kunst, 1993.
REBAY, Hilla, ed. *Wassily Kandinsky on the Spiritual in Art.* First complete English translation. Solomon R. Guggenheim Foundation, 1946.
REINHARDT, Ad. "Art-as-Art." *Art International*, VI/10, Dec. 1962, pp. 36-37.
REISE, Barbara R. "Robert Ryman: 'Unfinished III (Position).'" *Data,* 4/II, Spring 1974, pp. 32-39.
RENOUF, Edda. Statement for *Fundamental Painting*, 1975. STED10087256530.
RICHTER, Gerhard. Letter to Edy de Wilde, 23 Feb 1973. STED10087256355-56. Statement.
ROBINS, Corinne. "Object, Structure or Sculpture: Where Are We?" *Arts Magazine*, 40/9, Sept.-Oct. 1966, pp. 33-37.
ROMAIN, Lothar, and Luca Venturini. *A proposito della pittura... = Betreffende het schilderen... = Concerning Painting...* Museum Van Bommel-Van Dam, 1975.
ROQUE, Georges. "Nihilisme et affirmation de la peinture." CLÉS, 7/6, June 1975, p. 202+.
ROSE, Barbara. "ABC Art." *Art in America, 53/5,* Oct.-Nov. 1965, pp. 57-69.
- - -. *American Painting: The Eighties.* Urizen Books, 1979.
- - -. "Looking at American Sculpture." *Artforum*, 3/5, Feb. 1965, pp. 29-36.
- - -. "New York Letter." *Art International*, 7/9, Dec. 1963, pp. 62-64.
ROSENBLUM, Robert. "The Abstract Sublime." *ArtNews*, 59/10, Feb. 1961, pp. 38+.
- - -. *Modern Painting and the Northern Romantic Tradition: Friedrich to Rothko*. Icon, 1975.
ROSENTHAL, Stephen. Statement for *Fundamental Painting*, 1975. STED10087256495.
ROUSOVÁ, Hana. *Linie, barva, tvar.* Východočeská galerie Pardubice, 1989.
RUBIN, William. *Frank Stella.* New York, Museum of Modern Art, 1970.
RUDIKOFF, Sonya. "Language and Actuality: A Letter to Irving Sandler." *Arts,* 34/6, Mar. 1960, pp. 23-25.
RYMAN, Robert. "Art in the Twenty-First Century: Paradox." *Art:21.* Season 4. *Youtube*, uploaded by Art21.org, 4 April 2008, www.youtube.com/watch?v=Synu1N4Ajl4&playnext=1&list=PL5160F9B93CFC6716&feature=results_video.
- - -. Artist's statement for *Fundamental Painting*, 1975. STED10087256521.
- - -. *Variations+Improvisations.* Phillips Collection, Washington D.C., 2010. Wall texts.
SBORGI, Franco. "Traces for analytical painting." SBORGI, Franco, and Sandra Solimano, eds. *Pensare Pittura: Una linea internazionale di ricerca negli anni settanta.* Genova, Museo d'Arte Contemporanea di Villa Croce, 2009, pp. 160-163.
SCHIFF, Richard, et al. *Robert Mangold.* Phaidon, 2000.
SEITZ, William. "Contemporary Sculpture." *Arts Yearbook*, 8. Art Digest, 1965.

SHANNON, William, et al., eds. *The Thomas Merton Encyclopedia*. Orbis Books, 2002.

SKŘIVÁNEK, Jan. "Na obrazy se musí koukat." *Art+Antiques*, 12/15, Dec. 2008, pp. 12-18.

SMITH, Owen. *Fluxus: The History of an Attitude*. San Diego State UP, 1998.

SMITH, Roberta. "Robert Ryman derives poetry from white on white." *New York Times*, Sept. 24, 1993, p. C28.

SMITS, Kees. Statement for *Fundamental Painting*. [circa 1974-1975] STED10087256520.

SPECTOR, Naomi. "Essential Painting." *Robert Mangold*. La Jolla Museum of Contemporary Art, 1974.

- - -. *Robert Ryman*. Whitechapel Art Gallery, 1977.

- - -. "Robert Ryman at the Whitechapel." *Robert Ryman*. Whitechapel Art Gallery, 1977, pp. 9-15.

SPÖTER, Walter, ed. *Documenta 6*. Vol. 1. P. Dierichs, 1977.

STEDELIJK MUSEUM AMSTERDAM. "Algemene informatie voor het bewakingspersoneel over de tent. Fundamentele Schilderkunst." Created by Hoofd Afdeling B.V.D.. 25 April 1975. STED10087256517.

- - -. Floor Plan, [1975]. *Fundamental Painting*. STED10087256526-27.

- - -. "Over de opzet tent. 'grenzen van de schilderkunst'." [circa 1974-1975]. STED10087256503.

- - -. Press Release [1975]. *Fundamental Painting*. STED10087256528.

- - -. Questionnaire [1975]. *Fundamental Painting*. STED10087256551-54.

- - -. "Schilderkunst. Noemers tot nu toe gebruikt." [circa 1974-1975]. STED10087256440.

- - -. Table, [1974-1975]. *Fundamental Painting*. STED10087256441.

- - -. "Teksten van en over abstracte schilders van vroeger en nu, met betrekking tot de tentoonstelling *Fundamentele Schilderkunst*." [1975]. STED10087256543-49. Brochure.

STEEN, [?]. "Verslag van de enquête bij de tentoonstelling Fundamentele Schilderkunst." Pedagogisch-didaktisch Instituut, Universiteit van Amsterdam, [1975]. STED10087256555-60 and STED10087256562-63.

STILES, Kristine, and Peter Selz, eds. "Geometric Art: Introduction." *Theories and Documents of Contemporary Art: A Sourcebook of Artists' Writings*. U of California P, 1996, 63-73.

STEINER Georges. *Real Presences*. U of Chicago P, 1989.

STORR, Robert. "Robert Ryman: Une approche réaliste de la peinture." *Art Press*, 112, March 1987, pp. 19-23.

STORR, Robert. *Robert Ryman*. Tate Gallery, 1993.

STORR, Robert, et al., eds. *Robert Ryman*. Museo Nacional Centro de Arte Reina Sofia, 1993.

STRICKLAND, Edward. *Minimalism: Origins*. Indiana UP, 2000.

SUMMERS, David. *Real Spaces: World Art History and the Rise of Western Modernism*. Phaidon, 2003.

ŠVÁCHA, Rostislav, and Marie Platovská. *Dějiny Českého Výtvarného Umění 1939/1958*, Vol. V. Academia, 2005.

TATE MODERN. *Rodchenko & Popova: Defining Constructivism*. London, 12 February – 17 May 2009. Exhibition.

TAVRIS, Carol, and Carole Wade. *Psychology*. HarperCollins, 1996.

TAYLOR, John F.A. *Design and Expression in the Visual Arts*. Dover Publications, 1964.

TEGENBOSCH, Lambert. "Kunst als ambacht: Fundamentele schilders in het Stedelijk Museum." *Volkskrant*, 3 May 1975, p. 9.

TELLER, Davida. "Perception of lightness and color." *Vision and the Visual System*, edited by John

Palmer, Ch. 22, pp. 559-578. faculty.washington.edu/jpalmer/files/Teller/ByChapter/teller-Chapter22.pdf.
TOMKINS, Calvin. *Off the Wall: Robert Rauschenberg and the Art World of Our Time.* Penguin, 1981.
TUCHMAN, Maurice, ed. *The Spiritual in Art: Abstract Painting 1890-1985.* Abbeville Press, 1986.
TUCHMANN, Phyllis. "An Interview with Robert Ryman." *Artforum*, 9/9, 1971, pp. 46-53.
VAN DER BLOM, Ad, et al. *Nederlandse Schilderkunst: Tussen Detail en Grandeur.* ICOB, 1997.
VAN DER WAALS, J.C. "Kunstkroniek." *Het financiële dagblad*, 10-12 May 1975, p. 12.
VAN DOESBURG, Theo. "Base de la peinture concrete." *Art Concret*, 1/1, April 1930.
- - -. Introduction. *De Stijl*, Fall 1917, n. pag.
VLČEK, Tomáš et al. *Tomas Rajlich: 27 Paintings from 1969 to 2008*. Prague, National Gallery, 2008.
VAN GARREL, Betty. "Nulkunst in de nadagen." *NRC Handelsblad*, 6 June 1975, p. CS.
VAN GÖSSELN, Hannes. Letter to Geert van Beijeren, 5 March 1975. STED10087256052. Statement by Jerry Zeniuk.
VAN KONINGSBRUGGEN, Robert. Statement for *Fundamental Painting*. STED10087256502.
VAN TUYL, Gijs, ed. *Elementary Forms of Contemporary Painting and Drawing in the Netherlands.* Amsterdam, Visual Arts Office for Abroad, 1975.
VIALLAT, Claude. "Dossier Support(s)/Surface(s): La Dernière des avant-gardes?" *Art Press*, 154, Jan. 1991, pp. 14-21.
VON GRAEVENITZ, Antje. "Brief aus Amsterdam: Malerei als Faktum oder: 'das Einfache ist kein Pappenstiel'." *Kunstforum International*, 14, 1975, pp. 192-196.
- - -. "Neuer Trend im Kunstinteresse?" *Süddeutsche Zeitung*, 2 June 1975, p. 123.
- - -. "Verf is verf." *Vrij Nederland*, 31 May 1975, p. 31.
VOLPI ORLANDINI, Marisa. *Glossario, Qui arte contemporanea*. Editalia, 1973.
WATT, Alexander. "Paris Letter: Nouveaux Réalistes." *Art in America*, 2, 1961, pp. 106-112.
WEIBEL, Peter. "Das Bild nach dem letzten Bild." *Das Bild nach dem letzten Bild*, by Jean-Christophe Ammann et al., Walther König, 1991, pp. 183-213.
WEINMANN, Francesca. *The Path Toward Beauty: Through Texts and Works of Art.* Aperion Books, 2012.
WEISS, Evelyn, et al. *Prospect '73: Maler, Painters, Peintres.* Düsseldorf, Städtische Kunsthalle, 1973.
WÉRY, Marthe. Letter to Rini Dippel, 6 March 1975. STED10087256492. Statement.
- - -. *Marthe Wéry*. Gemeentemuseum Den Haag, 2011. Wall texts.
WILSON, Anne. "Linear Webs." *Art & Artists*, 1, Oct. 1966, p. 46-49.
WHITFORD, Frank, ed. *The Prestel Dictionary of Art and Artists in the 20th Century.* Prestel Verlag, 2000.
WITTGENSTEIN, Ludwig. *Tractatus Logico-Philosophicus.* 1921. Dover, 1999.
WOLLHEIM, Richard. "Minimal Art." *Arts Magazine*, 39/4, Jan. 1965, pp. 26-32.
WYLIE, Charles. *Robert Ryman.* Yale UP, 2006.
ZENIUK, Jerry. Telephone conversation with the author, 1 Dec. 2012. Archives of the author, Zurich. Transcript.

COLOPHON

Publisher: KANT Publishers, Prague
Orders: info@kant-books.com

Revised version of the original Ph.D. dissertation *Fundamentální malba: Vznik, charakteristika, kořeny a význam*, Charles University Prague,
© 2013 Claudia Rajlich

Cover Design: Karel Kerlický and Claudia Rajlich
Editor: Roy Bicknell, Amsterdam
Printed by: Tiskárna Protisk, s.r.o., České Budějovice

ISBN: 978-80-7437- 336-7